Teresa of Ávila

God Alone Suffices

Jean-Jacques Antier

Translated by Claire Quintal

auline
BOOKS & MEDIA
Boston

Library of Congress Cataloging-in-Publication Data

Antier, Jean Jacques, 1928–
   [Thérèse d'Avila. English]
   Teresa of Avila : God alone suffices / Jean-Jacques Antier ; translated by Claire Quintal. — 1st English ed.
      p. cm.
   Includes bibliographical references and index.
   ISBN 0-8198-7423-X (pbk.)
   1. Teresa, of Avila, Saint, 1515-1582. 2. Christian saints—Spain—Biography. I. Title.
BX4700.T4 A6313
282.092—dc22
[B]
                                      2006031319

The Scripture quotations contained herein are from the *New Revised Standard Version Bible: Catholic Edition,* copyright © 1989, 1993, Division of Christian Education of the National Council of the Churches of Christ in the United States of America. Used by permission. All rights reserved.

Auclair, Marcelle. *Saint Teresa of Avila,* translated by Kathleen Pond. Copyright © 1988 by St. Bede's Publications. Used with permission.

Excerpts used in this work are taken from the following books published by ICS Publications, 2131 Lincoln Road, N.E., Washington, DC 20002-1199 U.S.A. www.icspublications.org. Used with permission.

The Collected Works of St. Teresa of Ávila, Volume One, translated by Kieran Kavanaugh and Otilio Rodriguez. Copyright © 1976 by Washington Province of Discalced Carmelites.

The Collected Works of St. Teresa of Ávila, Volume Two, translated by Kieran Kavanaugh and Otilio Rodriguez. Copyright © 1980 by Washington Province of Discalced Carmelites.

The Collected Works of St. Teresa of Ávila, Volume Three, translated by Kieran Kavanaugh and Otilio Rodriguez. Copyright © 1980 by Washington Province of Discalced Carmelites.

The Collected Letters of St. Teresa of Ávila, Volume One, translated by Kieran Kavanaugh. Copyright © 2001 by Washington Province of Discalced Carmelites.

The Collected Works of St. John of the Cross, translated by Kieran Kavanaugh and Otilio Rodriguez. Copyright © 1964, 1979, 1991 by Washington Province of Discalced Carmelites.

Since only the first volume of Teresa's correspondence is currently available in English, some excerpts from her letters written after 1577 are from Kieran Kavanaugh's yet unpublished second volume of letters (where noted), while others have been translated from the original edition of this book.

Cover design by Rosana Usselmann

Cover art: Francois Gerard (1770–1837). *Saint Theresa,* 1827, oil canvas. Photo: Erich Lessing / Art Resource, NY. Maison Marie-Therese, Paris, France.

Original edition published in French under the title: *Therese d'Avila la crainte à l'amour*

Copyright © Perrin 2003

First English edition, 2007

Published by Pauline Books & Media, 50 Saint Paul's Avenue, Boston, MA 02130-3491. www.pauline.org.

Printed in the U.S.A.

Pauline Books & Media is the publishing house of the Daughters of St. Paul, an international congregation of women religious serving the Church with the communications media.

1 2 3 4 5 6 7 8 9   11 10 09 08 07

GENEOLOGY OF TERESA OF ÁVILA

ALONSO SÁNCHEZ
Middle-class, Jewish commoner who lived in Toledo
Cloth and silk merchant
Married to **Teresa** (Jewish)

JUAN SÁNCHEZ
Called Juan de Toledo († 1507)
A merchant of precious cloth in Toledo then Ávila
Converted to Christianity (1485), accused of apostasy, then reconciled
Collector of royal and ecclesiastical taxes in Ávila
Married to **Inés de Cepeda**, daughter of a noble Catholic family in Ávila

ALONSO SÁNCHEZ Y CEPEDA
First marriage (1505): **Catalina del Peso y Henao**
(† 1508). Two children: **Juan** (1507)
and **Maria** (1508).
Second marriage (1509): **Beatriz de Ahumada**
(born 1494 in Olmedo, noble Castilian, † 1528)

(CEPEDA Y AHUMADA)

RUY SÁNCHEZ Y CEPEDA

PEDRO SÁNCHEZ Y CEPEDA

FRANCISCO SÁNCHEZ Y CEPEDA
Eight children, Teresa's cousins

| **HERNANDO** | **RODRIGO** | **TERESA** | **LORENZO** | **ANTONIO** | **PEDRO** | **JERONIMO** | **AGOSTINO** | **JUAN** | **JUANA** |
| 1510–1565 | 1513–1554 | 1515–1582 | 1519–1580 | 1520–1546 | 1521–? | 1522–1577 | 1527–1582 | ? | 1528–? |

In memory of my grandmother,
Louise Sarlat-Antier,
a Carmelite tertiary at the Carmel of Puy-en-Velay,
who initiated me into the spirituality of St. Teresa de Jesús

Contents

PART TWO

Teresa's Achievements

Foreword

"He is living, the God before whom I stand!" exclaimed Elijah, the prophet who inspired the foundation of Carmel. St. Teresa, reformer of the Order, also pronounced these words. Because they seem to me, even today, a burning question of the hour, I have, in turn, dared to embark upon a biography of this extraordinary woman of sixteenth-century Spain, marked from childhood by the call of Transcendence. St. Teresa answers my expectations, which are also those of our modern world, searching for sound values capable of serving as a foundation for life. In his youth, Henri Bergson, the French philosopher (1859–1941), would say that if he were certain of God's existence and that God loves us, he would dance for joy.

Teresa furnishes this proof: an experience of the divine presence within her, founded upon a personal encounter with Christ as intense as the one that some of today's Carmelites can come to know. One of them has described this experience to me thus, evoking "the very source of her being and her life":

> One night, Grace passed by, powerful, lightning-like, penetrating my entire being. My mind opened up then and I knew God, God [who is] Love. Immense Love, surging [within me], lifting me up, overflowing on all sides; and from that instant on, everything was different, my entire life was toppling over and I wanted to give back love for love.

This is an experience that people living in the world can also have. Yes, he is living, the God before whom I stand!

The life of Teresa of Ávila is, first of all, the deeply moving proof of a call from God, the necessary Existing One, the refutation of the philosophy of the absurd and the nothingness that shrouds in gloom our so-called civilized societies. But her life is not only a theophany, a visible manifestation of God through the evidence of Transcendence alive within us; it is also an invitation to a more perfect, more loving life proceeding from the gift of self. It is a challenge to a world in which the majority of people are perhaps not egotistical, cynical, violent, depraved, and intolerant, but rather unconscious of the prodigious adventure that they are invited to live: a fulfilling experience of the Absolute.

Entering into the life of Teresa de Jesús, I went from surprise to surprise. On many occasions in her youth, she was being called, as if a force were trying to pull her away from the mediocrity that bogged her down. It was in seeking herself—a humanistic process—that she found herself. In trying to find herself, she also found her God—a spiritual process. As she describes in her books, this is none other than a search for the God who invites us to love him. Christ, whom she discovered little by little, invaded her life, delivered her from her anguish, and filled her to overflowing with his love. Experiencing that famous *itching of the wings* of which Socrates spoke, Teresa felt invited to give all to this Love that called out to her. "To risk one's life, everything is there," she finally said. And she threw herself into the spiritual adventure. She had gone from doubt to certainty, *from fear to love*.

Parallel to this, her psychological growth would bring her, three centuries before Freud, to discover her interior space: the unconscious, the source of our repressed memories and hidden energies. It is here that Teresa's contribution is revealed in the lineage of the Fathers of the Church. St. Augustine and St. Thomas Aquinas had already emphasized the human faculty to know one's profound self and God's action at this intimate level. In a crystal-clear manner, Teresa illustrates an unsettling mystery: the human spirit is designed to receive God's imprint. It is up to us not to remain on the outside, patrolling the ramparts of the *interior* castle.

This is when the dialogue of love between the Inviter and the invited gets under way. No one has spoken of mental prayer, that intimate devotion, more eloquently than Teresa has. And that is how this woman, ignorant—as she called herself—of an avant-garde rationalism, in conjunction with a faith working to establish itself (even as she grew interiorly), committed herself to the way of perfection, following the Christ who was slowly revealing himself to her.

We shall see how beyond the ecstasies and through the visions, locutions, and revelations, her personal relationship with God gave rise to a light and a force of action, an energy surpassing human powers, giving her the ability to accomplish, with God, the mission to which he destined her.

That is why, instead of locking herself in her cell, Teresa went forth into the world the way a butterfly, emerging from its chrysalis, flies out into space. A seeming paradox, this cloistered Carmelite was called to action to accomplish God's will. She presented herself to the world through prayer and the offering of her entire life. The foundation of her action is hidden in her contemplation, and that is why the Church has declared her "the mother of spiritual persons."

From the moment God called to her, Teresa returned love for love. She reformed Carmel by creating small, fervent communities founded with the support of St. John of the Cross, that other adventurer of the spiritual life. We shall attempt to understand the secret of these Carmels, brought back to the purity of their saintly founders. It begins with desire, fraternity, and fervor, unfolding toward that love of God that reconciles us with creation and allows us to enter into the Creator's plan.

From the start, Teresa, whose "feminist" audacities made the Fathers of the Inquisition bristle, knew herself to be an ignorant woman whose body let her down. Her weakness became her strength when she allowed God to act within her. Her physical weakness offers a startling contrast to the supernatural strength that revealed itself in her and carried her along—sometimes to the breaking point. We shall not conceal the obscure side hidden within her, consubstantial with human nature, composed of shadow and light. Nor will we conceal the body's breakdowns or the unusual manifestations, such as the levitations, which she related in her books while deploring them and which are like the dross of the mystical adventure—though perhaps also signs.

Yes, what is striking in this surprising life is not the strength of the great Teresa but her weakness, which was just as fruitful as that of her spiritual daughter, little Thérèse of the Carmel at Lisieux—who became the patron of missions without leaving her Carmel—the most beautiful fruit that Teresa has given us.

With her books, that immense body of work that goes from pungent autobiography to the highest-level description of mystical states, Teresa established herself as one of the greatest witnesses of the interior journey. Fr. Abiven wrote:

> She has nothing to tell us except what happened to her...she does this with a subtlety of analysis and a felicitous style of incomparable expressions, testimony of what divine grace can effect in a human being. With her, the mystical fact imposes itself as one of the inescapable dimensions of the human adventure.[1]

Through their richness, Teresa's writings are a message of hope for everyone: interested theologians, other religious, and even atheists, philosophers, psychologists, doctors... Through her knowledge of the human heart, she addresses herself to every person of good will in search of truth.

The influence and significance of the one who called herself "the little nothing" thus crosses the centuries from Ávila, the city of Old Castile surrounded by ramparts that her genius and her patience would one day shatter. With her, let us enter into this incomparable city where she first saw the light of day.[2]

Acknowledgments

I wish here to thank the persons who were willing to assist me on more than one account, notably:

Father Jean Abiven, O.C.D., a Carmelite of the Avignon-Aquitaine Province (Carmel of Broussey), author of works of reference and articles on St. Teresa. His patience was equaled only by his erudition.

The French Carmels of Angers, Avon, Carros, Clamart, Laval, Montmartre, and Toulouse; the Swiss Carmel of Develier.

The Carmels of St. Joseph at Ávila and the Incarnation.

Carmelite Publications, and especially Father Jean-Gabriel Rueg of the Toulouse Carmel. The periodicals *Carmel*, *Études carmélitaines*, so faithful in perpetuating the memory and the works of Teresa of Ávila.

The Cistercian Sisters of Laval.

Pascal Grousset, a Bergson scholar.

The bookstores of *La Procure* in Paris and Nice, the Siloé bookstore in Laval.

My editors, Xavier de Bartillat and François-Xavier de Vivie, and their collaborators.

Finally, I wish to thank my wife, Yvette, for her constant and attentive assistance.

PART ONE

Teresa's Life

*"There is never an end to our making
the absolute gift of ourself to God."*

— TERESA OF ÁVILA

CHAPTER 1

Ávila in Castile

On the high plateaus of Old Castile, in the heart of the central Cordillera, the city of Ávila rises to an altitude of more than 3,500 feet, the highest city in Spain.

This fortress-city, built upon granite, was entirely encircled by an enormous rampart, a wall 8,290 feet long, thirty feet high, and flanked by eighty-eight identical round watchtowers from which garrisons of harquebusiers kept watch. Constructed at the end of the eleventh century, at the time of reconquest over the Moors who had occupied Spain, the rampart was never breached.

The city was accessed through nine gates, each one protected by a steel portcullis and outer chapels, recalling that strength is as much spiritual as material in nature. For Ávila, city of knights, was also the city of saints, churches, and monasteries. Even the cathedral was fortress-like, as were the city's granite palaces, havens of its knights when they were not fighting somewhere in the world.

The city was entirely paved in stone. On its sloping streets, the lower classes, packed into houses made of mud walls daubed with clay, rubbed shoulders with the more or less penniless noble families.

Here and there, set among the gloomy districts of narrow lanes, one might be suddenly surprised to come upon vast squares flooded with sunlight. During the invasions, they served as places of refuge for the peasants seeking shelter while the siege lasted.

A hubbub continually rose from the old city. The hammers of the workmen forging swords and armor drowned out the rumble of carts, the cries of children, and the neighing of soldiers' horses as they passed through the city. And the bells tolled—the deep sounds coming from the great church bells and the more discreet chimes from the convent bells—calling followers to religious services. The entire city lived according to the rhythm of religious services. With fourteen churches and twelve convents, this city built of stone lived its faith as it lived the reconquest of its lands. It reached out its arms toward the blue sky, sparkling with light during the day and riddled with stars at night. From the churches, where everything served as a pretext for celebration, rose the swelling tide of hymns after the chiming of the bells.

Contrary to the imperial capital city of Valladolid[1] and others, which had grown soft by the influx of gold from the conquistadors, Ávila, city of saints and knights, remained austere in its lifestyle. According to the old, oft-repeated proverb, in Ávila there were only stones and saints—and men at arms. It was a city of faith but also of war, strengthened by its troops of mounted harquebusiers, those warriors of Ávila feared throughout Europe. Ávila was the city of the loyal ones and of the knights who went off to Seville to embark for the New World now that there were no longer any Moors to combat at home.

There were no fanciful Italianate architectural details in the beautiful residences of pink or gray stone that housed its eminent citizens. One senses that the major fear of the people of Ávila—after hell, famine, and the plague—was invasion. To be sure, the Muslims who had come from Africa had been chased from Spain after eight centuries of occupation. But they could return. And the memory of the last Spanish emirate, that of Granada, was so near! The Moors had been driven out only in 1492, a mere twenty-three years before Teresa's birth. In Ávila, each tower, each crenel seemed to cry out the city's motto: *Antes romper que quebar*—"Break rather than submit." Teresa would later adapt this slogan to her own use: "One may well die; to be defeated, never."

From the top of the bell tower of Santiago, the view looks out over the countryside—some sparse fields of barley, but mostly uncultivated land: arid, dry, and bare, strewn with rocks and stones, scorched by the sun in the summer and frozen in the wintertime by the wind that bends the cypress trees and the *encinas*, the cork oaks. In the distance rise the peaks of the Sierra de Gredos; farther south the Albles Mountain is covered with snow during the winter. If the city was secure, the same could not be said of the countryside. Travelers avoided being out at night for fear of coming upon those wandering and voracious gangs, the dregs of the demobilized mercenaries, or of running into *bandoleros*: black-sheep peasants armed with flintlocks, out-of-work foreigners, or Moriscos (Moors who had been left behind). And so at night the granite parapet was closed, the portcullises were lowered, the sentinels mounted their ramparts, and the cry of the lookouts could be heard: "Keep your eyes open!"

Formerly, in times of siege, to doze off was tantamount to dying! Teresa would remember this for other reasons.

Very near the noble residence of her parents, the Ahumada y Cepedas, stands Ávila's imposing cathedral. The originality of its apse draws one's attention because it protrudes beyond the parapet, and thus it had to be fitted out as a fortified tower in order to be included in the ramparts. As a child, Teresa, holding her oldest brother Hernando's hand, would have walked the street running alongside the massive edifice. For a long time, she must have pondered the street's name, the Street of Life and Death. Inside the cathedral, in the shadow of its gray stone walls speckled with crimson, Teresa would have listened with fascination to the fulminating preaching of the Dominicans, who might be denouncing heresies or keeping count of the thousands of newly-baptized Native American souls saved from hell by the flood tide of the conquistadors. Closing her ears to these waves of oratory, she contemplated, with tears in her eyes, "the very wounded Christ" venerated during Holy Week.

What did she retain of the torrent of history that flowed through her veins? At her birth in 1515, Isabella of Castile and Ferdinand of Aragon, those mythic Catholic sovereigns, still reigned. Their love marriage had founded the power of Spain and carried within it the seed of her unification. In 1516, they were succeeded by the future Charles V, King Ferdinand's grandson.[2] Spain would eventually forget eight centuries of Muslim occupation: the invasion of the peninsula through the Strait of Gibraltar in 711 by the hordes of the Arab chieftain Tarik Ibn Ziyad, a Moroccan Berber, and the *jihad*, or holy war, sweeping across what would later become Spain; the occupation within ten years' time of four-fifths of the Iberian peninsula; the last resisting Christians being driven back to the foot of the Pyrenees; the establishment of the caliphate at Cordoba, the center of the Almoravid Empire, which would reign over the country. But in the far north with the Pyrenees at their back, the small states of Navarre, Aragon, Catalonia, and Castile had resisted. United, they had become focal points for the resistance to *jihad*. The backward tide of the Moors had begun. Toledo and Ávila were retaken in 1085. Ávila hastened to erect its formidable rampart. In 1212, the battle of Las Navas de Tolosa brought the Muslim hegemony to an end. At the end of the thirteenth century, Islam, which had lost Gibraltar, was in possession only of the Emirate of Granada, which fell in 1492, swept away by the soldiers of Isabella of Castile.

These savage wars had allowed Spain to form its unity around the Catholic sovereigns of Castile and Aragon. Centuries of conflict against the Muslim occupiers had forged a hardy and intrepid race of Spaniards. Thus, when Charles V, the new Holy Roman Emperor of the West, heir of Charlemagne, installed himself with his court in the royal palace at Valladolid, the historic capital of Castile, he could presume to symbolize the new strength that was about to conquer the world: Cortez in Mexico, Pizarro in Peru, Magellan at Rio de la Plata and in the Philippines.

At the time, Spain was sagging under the weight of gold from the old indigenous civilizations. In Europe, this was also a century of enlightenment and art, the Renaissance in which many shone: El Greco, the Cretan-born artist of Toledo, painter of mystical faces; the Castilian Cervantes, minstrel of the picaresque novel; the Dutch philosopher, Erasmus, the greatest humanist of the time; Titian, Veronese, and Michelangelo of Italy. Soon there would be Shakespeare in England. In France, the châteaus of the Loire, put into verse by Ronsard and du Bellay, were being built.

At the political and religious levels, two men dominated the world, but not without committing excesses: the Hispano-German emperor and the Roman pope. There were shadows blackening the scene. In Spain, only the tiny minority in power profited from Native American gold. The Inquisition was attempting to stifle the minds of those whom the Church perceived as too innovative. The conquest of America was being carried out to the detriment of millions of indigenous peoples who were being massacred in the name of the faith. In Spain, the Jews and the integrated Muslims who refused to convert were being hunted down.

Even in Europe, in spite of the Turkish menace weighing upon it from the Mediterranean, Catholics were tearing each other apart. In 1521, when Teresita was only six years old, Emperor Charles V entered into a savage struggle against Francis I, king of France, who was contesting his imperial crown and his Italian territories.

But Charles henceforth reigned over an empire where the sun never set. Head of the Church of Spain, in agreement with the pope, he saw to it that his subjects lived under the law of the Church of Rome, of which he was the secular arm. He helped the Church in attempting to extinguish the conflagration lit by heretics in Germany and France, and he filled ecclesiastical offices and attempted to reform decadent religious orders. He imposed the Catholic religion—helped by the Inquisition, which was composed of learned Dominican monks—not only upon his own subjects, but upon all the peoples he had the opportunity to confront.

Under his reign, the faith in Spain, which was profound and serious, would produce a plethora of saints. Thanks to Cardinal Cisneros, minister of King Ferdinand, Spain had avoided the religious upheavals convulsing the rest of Europe. It was because of this spiritual unity that Spain, by concentrating its vital energies, was able to become the premier world power, utilizing the gold from Peru and the silver of Rio de la Plata. It arrived in Seville by entire galleon convoys, where it was being counted by the *Casa de Contratación* for the royal treasury, which redistributed it to the soldiers, sailors, government officials, and lords.

In the midst of these revolutions that were founding Spain and reconstituting the face of Europe by annexing the world, what place did Teresa's family occupy?

Chapter 2

Ahumada y Cepeda

Teresa came into the world on March 28, 1515, in Ávila, the daughter of Alonso Sánchez y Cepeda, a newly minted nobleman born in Toledo. Her mother, Beatriz de Ahumada, was a member of the noble Castilian Olmedo family. Teresa was baptized on Wednesday of Holy Week, April 4, in the parish church of San Juan. On the same day, by a strange coincidence, a fervent throng was attending the dedication of a new monastery, Our Lady of the Incarnation, where, twenty years later, Teresa would come asking for the habit of Our Lady of Mount Carmel.

In this city of Ávila, peopled by about ten thousand inhabitants, Teresa's parents belonged to the local nobility, although their palace was a relatively modest one and their family fortune already somewhat eroded. No one in the family was engaged in any remunerative activity, and the revenues from the lands were meager.

Teresa's father, Alonso de Cepeda, was a disconcerting man with an average appearance. This refined nobleman maintained a staff of servants and an equipage in keeping with his rank, but his life remained rather austere. A fervent Catholic, he was half Jewish. Socially privileged and proud to be so, he saw himself as humane, refused to own slaves, and treated the little Moorish slave-girl that his brother had entrusted to him as the equal of his own twelve children. He sometimes visited the poor districts of Ávila, distributing food and clothing and caring for the sick. He wore a sword without conviction, but in 1515 he had fought in Navarre in answer to the call of his king, Ferdinand the Catholic, to defend Pamplona, menaced by the French.

However, contrary to what his sons would become, he was not an outstanding war leader. This peaceable man loved family life and nurtured his soul with spiritual reading. And if, from time to time, he leafed through *Overseas Conquest*, which described the exploits of the conquistadors in America, he quickly returned to the theological and even mystical writings that brought peace to his anxious soul.

Yes, everything was paradoxical about this distinguished gentleman, both solemn and regal, who kept his sensitivity hidden. Authoritarian and paternalistic like Spanish men of his time, he nevertheless saw himself as a forward-looking person; he taught his children himself, both boys and girls, expecting them to be able to read fluently before the age of seven.

As the eldest son, having inherited large estates—agricultural land, farms, flocks, a residence in the city worthy of a nobleman, as well as a dwelling in the country—Alonso de Cepeda appreciated the security that a fortune bestows, all the while sincerely adoring the poor Christ. He also knew how to dress according to his rank so as to bring honor to his own.

As administrator of the fortune inherited from his father, or as manager of the estates of his spouses, he could have been perceived as a capable businessman. In reality, he was not gifted in this sphere; he was, little by little, ruining himself.

In 1508, having lost his first wife, Doña Catalina del Peso y Henao, with whom he had two children, he had married the following year, at the age of thirty, the beautiful Beatriz de Ahumada, who was fifteen at the time. Descended from a noble Castilian family, she would bear him ten children before dying in 1528 at the age of thirty-three, shortly after the birth of Juana. Teresa was then thirteen. The poor man found himself feeling desperate and quite amazed at being surrounded by this noisy brood that would soon gain an idol and fairy godmother in Teresa. By then, Alonso's character had changed. His natural moral rectitude had begun, bit by bit, to border on scrupulosity.

If his mother's noble lineage—the *hidalguia*—presented no problem, it was otherwise on his father's side. The municipal authorities of Hortigosa, near Ávila, where the family owned lands, questioned the family's nobility. They dared to claim a very modest tax of one hundred *maravedis* from Don Alonso and his three brothers, the Sánchez y Cepedas! This matter seemed intolerable to the family in principle because it cast doubt on their status as *hidalgos*, exempt from taxes as "noblemen descended from a noble father and grandfather."

Which they were not. Their grandfather, Alonso Sánchez, a middle-class commoner who was a cloth and silk merchant, did not hide his Jewish origins, and neither did his wife, Teresa. Their son, Juan Sánchez (Teresa's grandfather), known as Juan de Toledo, had also lived in Toledo, the capital of New Castile, an opulent and historic city in which Charles V would sometimes reside. The city was proud of its bishop, primate of Spain; its wealth from its commerce in silk, arms, and works of art; and its university that trained the elite of Spain. It was an unrivaled city of which Isabella, the Catholic queen, was wont to say: "Nowhere do I feel stupid except in Toledo."

Juan de Toledo's ambition was as strong as his genius. In order to marry Inés de Cepeda, daughter of a noble Catholic family, Juan had converted to Catholicism in 1485. He had crossed the Rubicon and had become integrated, as had so many other Jews whose commercial interests were greater than their religious convictions. These Jews could be found in Catholic families, including among the royalty and those who could count illustrious prelates among their members. This posed no problem in the fifteenth century, provided that the tiny minority of Jews, and often Muslims as well, allowed themselves to become *assimilated.*

This *converso* (Christianized Jew), Juan Sánchez, was a remarkable person. A merchant of precious cloth in Toledo, he was, like his father, a dynamic and tenacious businessman. He had not only made a brilliant marriage that integrated him into the dominant class, he had also amassed a considerable fortune.

Why did the Sánchez y Cepeda family leave splendid Toledo to settle in austere Ávila? Was it to escape Juan's Jewish origins? No. The reason, instead, was because of a scandal that arose when jealous persons accused Juan of practicing his Jewish faith in secret—a crime of apostasy in the eyes of intolerant Catholics.

Juan admitted to having done so. The archives of the Holy Office of Toledo, that redoubtable ecclesiastical tribunal, attest that "on June 22, 1485, Juan de Toledo, a merchant, son of Alonso Sánchez, confessed to the priest inquisitors of having committed numerous and serious offenses of heresy and apostasy against the holy Catholic faith."[1]

Juan made amends, publicly carrying from church to church for seven consecutive Fridays the small *sanbenito,* the scapular of the repented, and the cross in procession with other "reconciled" persons.

This punitive sanction was cruel in nature. The humiliation seemed intolerable to Juan and his family. They left Toledo along with a caravan of wagons loaded with their belongings and settled seventy-five miles to the north in Ávila, the native city of Inéz de Cepeda. Juan started his business once again as a merchant of luxury cloth in *Calle des Andrinos*.

Juan Sánchez prospered in Ávila, where his talents worked marvels in that epoch of ostentatious display. When the king forbade the use of silk in order to restrict clothing expenses, Juan lived by renting his lands to tenant farmers, and then he became a government employee, a collector of royal and ecclesiastical taxes. Quite possibly, he even may have been among the secretaries of King Henry IV of Castile.

However, his trial in Toledo had burned him. Juan discreetly purchased a false certificate of nobility, as all rich *conversos* were now doing. And he strengthened this newly acquired nobility by having his sons marry into the Catholic aristocracy.

Teresa knew all of this; it was an open family secret despite the care taken by her brothers and cousins to hide the fact in order to preserve the privileges attached to the *hidalguia* (the nobility). Referring to this sleight of hand, Teresa spoke in private "of the vile and sordidly low villains and converted." And if she did not refer to this in her autobiography, it was so as not to mortify and thus provoke a scandal in the families so sensitive on this point of honor. Evidently for her, who called herself a "little nothing," shame did not mean having Jewish blood but having bought a false certificate to obtain access to the nobility and "purity of blood."

The four sons of Juan Sánchez, Alonso (Teresa's father), Ruy, Pedro, and Francisco, made brilliant matches, but their *hidalguia* could be challenged. In 1509, to obtain the hand of the noblewoman Beatriz de Ahumada, Alonso asked the royal chancery of Valladolid, capital of the kingdom of Old Castile, for a certificate "of purity of blood." Even though his father was a converted Jew, he obtained it. Had the judges allowed themselves to be misled by the father's false certificate? It is more likely that they had taken into account both the fact that Juan's Catholicism was not faked and that he was known for his philanthropy. The four sons of the Jewish commoner Juan Sánchez were duly qualified by the ecclesiastical tribunal as "very proper men, honest and rich, their horses of good quality and their persons well-dressed, of excellent conversation, behaving as men of gentle birth and frequenting the sons of noble families related to the aristocrats of Ávila." In a word, their "integration" had been successful.

Two interesting facts stand out from these complicated family questions. In the first place, Teresa had one-quarter of Spanish-Jewish blood coursing through her veins. And secondly, as many signs would demonstrate, she took after her grandfather, Juan Sánchez de Toledo, a man of exceptional qualities who had overcome immense difficulties stemming from his Jewish origins.

Juan's eldest son, Alonso Sánchez y Cepeda, married Catalina del Peso y Henao in 1505 and received as a wedding gift the *Casa de la Moneda* in Ávila. After giving birth to two children, Juan and María, Catalina died in 1508, no doubt of the same plague that killed Juan Sánchez de Toledo. In 1509, Don Alonso remarried, choosing a young beauty from Olmedo, Beatriz de Ahumada. As her dowry, she brought the estate of Gotarrendura near Ávila.

Juan Sánchez de Toledo had been a tireless worker and a circumspect merchant, but as much could not be said of his son Alonso. His conduct was, in all ways, irreproachable if one overlooks the false certificate; it was not out of laziness that he was content to live from his private means. Having chosen the social status of *hidalgo*, Juan de Toledo and his four sons could not work without falling from honor and thus immediately revealing their origins as Jews and commoners. Teresa's father, a man of principle, pious and peaceful, contented himself with taking advantage of the abundance of wealth inherited from his father and acquired from his two wives. With scrupulous care he raised his many children: three daughters and nine sons.

The Ahumada y Cepeda residence consisted of two main buildings adorned with patios and gardens from which rose the cry of a peacock, the cackling of fowl, and the neighing of horses in the stable. This beautiful family mansion with its square tower opened out onto well-irrigated lawns and gardens where fruit and vegetables grew as well as flowers.[2]

The great common room, filled with small windows that were closed at night by iron shutters, was comfortably furnished but not without a certain Castilian austerity far removed from the Italian luxury fashionable at the time. In one corner was a clavichord, which allowed the girls to learn music while the boys trained in swordsmanship on the patios. Rugs from Flanders covered the marble floors, enlivened by brightly-colored silk cushions.

In the winter, harsh in Ávila because of the altitude, fireplaces and braziers, tended to by the servants, warmed the air. On one wall, a reredos by the painter Juan de Padilla depicted scenes from the life of Christ. The facing wall displayed weapons of war: lances and crossbows, swords and sabers, with each knight's shield. Among Teresa's nine brothers, seven would embrace a military career.

A silent and meditative woman, Doña Beatriz would turn her spinning wheel to spin her wool or weave an exquisite silk shirt for her master and lord. Closeted in his nearby study, Don Alonso would remain engrossed in one or another scholarly work of theology, such as Ludolph of Saxony's *Life of Christ*—a work that had deeply moved Ignatius of Loyola.

Doña Beatriz, delicate of health, was only twenty-one when Teresa was born. Both tender and distant, she was devoted to her many children and was a passionate reader of novels of chivalry. But as soon as night fell, she would retreat to her private chapel, where she would give herself over to her real nature, both religious and anguished.

What caused her anguish? Teresa would later write in her autobiography, *The Book of Her Life*,[3] "She spent her entire life in the midst of great infirmities." With her ear glued to the door, Teresita could hear her mother praying and moaning. It troubled the child to the depths of her being and confirmed her precocious intuition that, in spite of its wealth, the family was not immune to misfortune.

Beatriz de Ahumada was a woman of contradictions. At Teresa's birth, she was reputed to be one of the most beautiful women in Castile, but she paid no attention to this. Gracious while remaining austere, she fled all coquetry and dressed in black—just as the old noble Spanish *duennas*. Outwardly, she seemed to be even tempered, but this was only a façade. Teresa quickly realized that the thought of death and eternal salvation tormented her tender mother. This atmosphere of anxious piety in which Teresa could see her mother prostrating herself gradually acted upon her own character. The innocent child was impelled to abandon herself also to prayer and to that crucified God whose tragic mystery haunted her.

Very early on, Teresa had learned to read and even to write, at that time a rare achievement for girls. While her father insisted she read books of piety, she, like her brothers, devoured the novels of chivalry their mother gave them in secret despite paternal reproval. Very close in age to her brother Rodrigo, Teresa also read with him the lives of holy martyrs. Together they dreamed of imitating them "in the land of the Moors," although they were not too sure where that was, no one being certain that the last of the Spanish Moors had gone back over the Strait of Gibraltar. During the evenings, the exploits of hotheaded Catholics during the time of the Muslim occupation would be retold, stories of men who did not hesitate to provoke the established authority in order to merit martyrdom.

Teresa was seven and Rodrigo nine when the two children, escaping their house, set out one day without any baggage "to the land of the Moors [to] beg them, out of love of God, to cut off our heads there" in order "to enjoy very quickly the wonderful things I read there were in heaven."[4] They had managed to get past the enormous walls of Ávila and were on their way south on the road to Toledo. "We were terrified of what we read about the suffering and the glory that was to last forever!" In *The Lives of Saints*, the *Flos Sanctorum*, which Teresa was already reading with Rodrigo in Castilian, it was written that martyrdom allowed a person to obtain the immediate enjoyment of paradise, "forever and ever and ever!" *Para siempre!*

All the same, neither Teresa nor Rodrigo was unhappy in the large house of Don Alonso. But Teresa, who had convinced her brother to run away, sensed the fragility of their earthly happiness. Their heroic adventure was an early sign of "her very determined determination" to go through with her decisions to the very end, as well as of her gift for persuasion, her communicative faith that convinced her brother to go along with her. War was raging everywhere: in Flanders, Italy, Africa, America. Premature death was mowing down the rich as well as the poor, children as well as the elderly. Everyone and everything was thus vulnerable and menaced here below. Even behind the enormous and protective walls of Ávila hovered muted menaces. Not only was plague endemic but famine also, along with invasions. Otherwise, why would the city maintain such high walls reinforced with towers? Why have armed men patrolling the ramparts, and why would *hidalgos* leave the city, many of them never to return?

Charles V, son of Joan of Castile and Philip, archduke of Austria, had become king of Spain in 1516 and had completed the unification of the country. Emperor of the West in 1520, he would fight against Francis I, king of France, while pursuing the politics of the conquest of America undertaken by the sovereigns of Castile and Portugal. Religion merged with politics.

In 1517, supported by the Germanic princes, the theologian monk Martin Luther had launched the Protestant Reformation, a reform bred by the decadence and centralizing excesses of the Roman Catholic Church. The pope had excommunicated Luther in 1520, putting the seal on the schism that reached the Netherlands, England, and then France only partially.

Each Sunday at church, Teresa listened to the Dominican preachers thunder against the German and French heretics, condemning them to the eternal damnation that would also doom those Spanish Catholics too lukewarm in their eyes. Thus there existed "the eternal flames" as opposed to the delights of paradise. A person had to choose.

In the young Teresa, two apparently contradictory emotions were at war. A strong vitality attracted her to pleasure of an immediate and palpable sort, which could be concretized in that fascinating gold her father sometimes took out of a leather pouch or a chest of precious wood: Spanish doubloons,

Castilian ducats, American pesos, French *pistoles*, and those florins brought by the emperor's Flemish subjects. Her interest was held by golden jewels, family heirlooms set with precious stones that had come from faraway civilizations or from some Italian jeweler established in the old city.

However, "there existed another different world: eternal, while the other is a dream." Teresa would write those words at the age of forty-seven in *The Way of Perfection*, but they were already inscribed in her childhood mind. They posit a faith in that other world where mothers would not die at the age of thirty, where fathers would not massacre each other at war, where brothers would not go off in search of illusory conquests—a world dominated by love! And Teresa would add the words that may serve as the key to understanding her childhood flight: "One has to experience it, for it is quite another thing to think about it as to believe it."

The heroic flight of the two children was brought to an end three miles from Ávila. Their uncle, Francisco de Cepeda, recognized them as he rode his horse along the route. He snatched them up and brought them back home. Rude return to reality! The young Teresa stuck to her guns even though her father explained that the Moors were now far away, beyond the Mediterranean, Boabdil, the last emir of Granada, having gone back over the Strait of Gibraltar in 1492. Only the murderous, short-lived raids of the African Saracens, disembarking from their boats (called *Xebecs* or *chebecs*) on the coasts of Andalusia, were still feared.

Deprived of martyrdom, little Teresa took refuge in piety. What does such a word signify to a child of seven? Perhaps a mysterious relationship of love. Was she already affected by the desire to "see God"? No. She was just assiduous in prayer, which makes it possible to approach the mystery. She attempted to build a hermitage in the garden just as she was trying to build herself. She played at being a nun with her girlfriends, and she was unremitting also in giving alms, for her motives were not egotistical. In imitation of her father, a surge of pity pushed her toward the poor, and to this pity was added her tenderness, for everything in her was already love.

While Hernando and Rodrigo, two of her older brothers, were preparing themselves through study and the handling of arms to become perfect knights, dreaming of glorious exploits in the New World, Teresa was living her everyday life intensely within the well-guarded family perimeter. Quick-witted, she rapidly learned how to read, write, and count, and she pursued the instruction common for young noblewomen of her day. Not much was required—and Latin, Greek, and mathematics were not included. What a pity, given her brilliant natural abilities!

Teresa also loved to play with her older brothers, who were amused by her vivacity of spirit and her humor. They told her about the conquistadors' exploits, the Atlantic crossings of galleons and caravels, infinite horizons, terrifying storms, horrible marine monsters, and the discoveries of thousands of unknown marvels in the countries of gold, silver, and precious stones.

These discoveries were allowing Spain to enrich itself enormously. Hernando and Rodrigo, who would soon take part in the conquest, were ignorant of its motivating forces. The great pillage of the New World opened the golden age of Spain as well as a century of barbarism under the pretext of bringing civilization and the Gospel. The Romans, then the Arabs, had generalized slavery. With the Spaniards and the Portuguese, state-sponsored genocide would now be instituted despite the efforts of Charles V, alerted by the missionaries, to oppose it.

At the economic level, the gold pouring into Spain was not having only positive effects. If Spain was becoming the premier world power, gold was corrupting the aristocracy and giving rise to inflation through an excess of currency that reduced entire sections of the working class to poverty.

When night came, the children, lingering in the perfumed patios, lifted their eyes toward the sky gleaming with stars. Solemnly, Hernando would explain to the dumbfounded Teresa that, according to a certain Polish astronomer by the name of Copernicus, the sun did not turn around the earth and, because of this, the earth was no longer at the center of the universe as the Bible maintained. Alarming revelation!

But the children quickly returned to their games. Together, they sang and danced—even Lorenzo, Antonio, and Pedro, the youngest. Teresita played the castanets with the passion of an Andalusian, carrying her brothers along in her wake. She was their queen, their little fairy!

Suddenly, her resounding laughter would die out. Becoming serious once again, she would go to the orchard or to her father's garden to smell the flowers and gather her thoughts. What did Hernando mean when he spoke of embarking at Seville for the Rio de la Plata in Argentina? Of course she knew the name of this immense estuary discovered in 1520 by the Portuguese Magellan, who had undertaken for Spain the first voyage around the world, thus challenging the notion of space and humanity. She also knew that a Genoese sailor, Christopher Columbus, in the service of Isabella of Castile, had discovered the fabled continent of America in 1492. Twenty years later, the very year of Rodrigo's birth, Cortez had conquered Mexico, opening the way to other conquests in Peru and in Chile when he found that entire populations did not know Christ!

Troubled, Teresa would reassure herself by visiting her father's stables, caressing the horses and the dogs, which gave her a warm welcome. Then, having smelled the aromas floating in the air, she, a lover of food, would go to the large kitchen to find out what was being prepared. She would recognize the smells coming from the cooking pots and watch the preparation of pastries and jams, able to isolate each warm, sweet fragrance—vanilla, cinnamon—as she awaited the moment when she would be allowed to taste.

Already fashion conscious, Teresita loved beautiful clothes: braided, embroidered, colorful. She regretted that her mother no longer wore the brightly colored, sumptuous dresses worthy of her rank. Sometimes in the evening, complying with her daughter's wish, Doña Beatriz would take them out of their chests where they lay as in reliquaries and spread them out on her bed. Fascinated, *la niña* admired the beauty of the velvets, the taffetas, and the satins, the harmony or contrast of colors, the silk, gold, and silver embroideries.

Making the most of this penchant, Teresa's mother taught her how to embroider and how to choose motifs. Teresita was becoming an expert seamstress, a talent at which she would excel all her life, later cutting and sewing the homespun robes and the toques and veils of her nuns.

Aware of and somewhat worried about her daughter's personality, Doña Beatriz tried to channel Teresa's bubbling vitality and her sometimes excessive actions by bringing her back toward the great desire for God that was already calling out to her. Both headstrong and tenderhearted, curious and generous, Teresita revealed the wealth of her personality during her childhood.

The death of Doña Beatriz a few days after the birth of her tenth child came as a terrible shock to Teresa. She was thirteen years old. Then, emerging from the fog in which her spirit was losing itself, she knelt "before an image of our Lady and besought her with many tears to be my mother." And it seemed to her that she heard an affirmative answer. Above this *Virgen de la Caridad* (Virgin of Charity) with her gentle, sad look, dressed and crowned like a queen, she saw a naked Christ on the cross, a deeply moving contrast.

CHAPTER 3

Maddeningly Beautiful

(1528-1530)

or a girl, age thirteen signaled a great change: the passage from childhood to adolescence. Teresa had now become a young lady. Her attributes of mind and heart added to her natural charm. She was noticed. Now more aware of her body, she knew that she was beautiful and was discovering the joy of being appealing to others, to love and to be loved.

Marcelle Auclair has painted the following picture of her at fifteen:

[She was] maddeningly beautiful, endowed with an "extraordinary" loveliness of feature.... A wealth of chestnut hair, naturally curly, set off her high forehead and fluffed around her laughing face which altered so much with her lively and continually changing expression that it was difficult to say if it was round or oval.... It was the full red mouth closing over dazzlingly white teeth which most revealed her personality and the black, rather prominent eyes, round, well-set, as they lit up with enthusiasm or glowed softly with tenderness as occasion demanded, or again sparkled with mischief or coquettishness.... People spoke of the gracefulness of her carriage and of her lovely hands.[1]

"Perfect in everything, she also had an indefinable appeal," added María de San José, who would become her friend.

Another contemporary, Fray Luis de León, confirmed this in his *Vida de la santa Madre Teresa de Jesús*:

She charmed and captivated everyone's heart. Her beauty and the care she took of her person, the refinement of her conversation, the softness and civility of her manner, embellished her still further, with the result that the layman and the saint, the worldly person as well as the ascetic, from the oldest to the youngest, became her prisoners, beguiled by her. As a child

and as a young woman in the world, and as a religious, she was for everyone who saw her what the magnet is to iron.

Reading novels of chivalry fired her imagination. "I was so completely
taken up with this reading that I didn't think I could be happy if I didn't
have a new book."[2] And she dreamed of the virile knight who would steal
her away.

Not only was she reading voraciously, she was also already writing! It was
a novel that revealed her tastes, *The Knight of Ávila*. Her brother Rodrigo,
who was fifteen at the time, helped her a little; everyone, relatives and
friends, were in agreement as they praised her novel's style, composition,
inventiveness, and character study. But they never imagined that the budding author would one day bestow its letters patent of nobility on the
Spanish national language.

After her mother's death, Teresa grew closer to her father, who adored
her. With her nine brothers, Teresa lived almost exclusively in a masculine
world. Her half-sister María was too much older to be close to her; and
Juana, the youngest child, was still just a nursling. So Teresa found herself
surrounded by the boys, who worshiped her. Each one, more boisterous
than the other, was eager for a military career that would seal his assimila-
tion into the Castilian nobility. And thanks to the colonial expeditions, it
was now possible to become rich through means other than trade!

The family also entertained at San Domingo Place. Although naturally
distrustful, Don Alonso could not close his doors to the cousins of the
Ahumada y Cepeda family, all the more so because his residence was separated from the home of his brother, Francisco Álvarez de Cepeda, by only
an alleyway, *la calle de la Dama*, the Lady's Lane!

One of these cousins, who was fifteen or sixteen, fell in love with Teresa.
Being very flirtatious, she did whatever necessary to make this happen! "I
began to dress in finery and to desire to please and look pretty, taking great
care of my hands and hair and about perfumes and all the empty things in
which one can indulge, and which were many, for I was very vain." Beauty oils,
rouge, perfumes derived from musk, amber and coral necklaces...what could
be more natural for a young girl of a noble family destined for marriage?

But it went even further: "When I began to know that certain persons
liked me, and I found them attractive, I became so attached that my memory was bound strongly by the thought of them."[3]

Although he had married a girl of fifteen, Don Alonso had no intention
of allowing his own daughter to marry so young. Since he had just lost his
wife and was about to marry off his oldest daughter, María, he wanted to

keep Teresa with him as long as he possibly could. She would soon become
indispensable to him in matters for which he had so little talent: managing
the household, looking after the younger children, supervising the female
staff, and even taking care of his books. Not a single one of his grown sons
showed any interest in managing their patrimony; they thought only of rid-
ing, hunting, soldiering, and girls. With good reason, this jealous father
closed his doors to potential suitors, who were becoming more and more
numerous. But he could not close the doors against his brother, Francisco,
and Francisco's four daughters and four sons, many of whom were Teresa's
age. One is obligated to one's family.

As soon as Don Alonso left Ávila to visit his property of Gotarrendura,
the young people would get together to talk, eat, play music, dance, and woo
one another—sometimes very closely. Teresa was the center of attention. She
had everything: youth, beauty, wealth, nobility, intelligence, and even the
gift of writing. She was admired. A natural seductress, she took pleasure in
it all, and she did it with help from the female domestic staff! "In them I
found a helping hand for every kind of wrong," she later admits.

Knowing the rectitude of her character, it is not astonishing that Teresa
gave such importance to this entangled part of her life in her autobiography.

> I had some first cousins who often came to our house, though my father
> was very cautious and would not allow others to do so; please God he had
> been inspired to do likewise with my cousins...we always went about togeth-
> er. They liked me very much, and I engaged in conversations with them
> about all the things that pleased them. I listened to accounts of their affec-
> tions and of childish things not the least bit edifying; and, what was worse,
> I exposed my soul to that which caused all its harm.

Teresa slid from what can be called "the temptation of the flesh" toward
another, more subtle one that concerned the spirit. She accuses herself of
having become the intimate friend and confidante of one person, no doubt
one of her female cousins. Later, she judges this person's influence as
appalling from all points of view. The friendship "so changed me that hardly any virtue remained to my naturally virtuous soul."

It is because of the influence of this person ("and another girlfriend of
the same type") that she had not "remained whole in virtue."

First of all, she had lost, at least in part, the intense faith of her childhood. From this loss came all harm and dubious companionship:
"Afterward, having lost this fear of God completely, I only had the fear of
losing my reputation." For a Spanish woman at that time to say that she disregarded her reputation would mean that she had conceived an illegitimate

child. Naturally, Teresa would never have accepted to fall that far. The point of honor, her last remaining rampart, held her back.

Just how far did she go with her seductive cousin? The daughter of the pious Alonso does not tell us. "The fear of losing my reputation...brought me torment in everything I did. With the thought that my deeds would not be known, I dared to do many things truly against my honor and against God."

We know no more than this, except that these facts, which today might appear to be insignificant, had a destructive effect upon Teresa.

She, who at age fifteen reigned over the great house of the Ahumada y Cepedas, had discovered her power of seduction without recognizing its dangers for herself and for the young men crowding around to court her. Whichever way she turned, she would get all worked up. The stories of chivalry she was now reading without constraint affected her, and after reading these exploits of warrior heroes, she would revel in the stories of those martyred for their faith that she heard in the homilies of the religious. She would then experience the painful impression of betraying Christ from whom, as a child, she had received an invitation.

This whirlwind of contradictory desires troubled her deeply. She also reproached herself for deceiving her father's trust by having an amorous relationship with a cousin, which seemed to her quite banal in her lucid moments. She was too wise, straightforward, and perspicacious to think that it could be a love that would last forever. In any case, it would have reduced her to living like her mother had, sacrificed to the births and to the all-absorbing cares of too numerous a brood.

In this complex affair in which Teresa felt carried along where she did not want to go, it is evident that her destiny very nearly took another turn. All it would have taken was for the flirtation to go too far, driven by giddiness on her part, a momentary madness resulting in an unwished-for pregnancy and culminating in the hasty marriage that was the mediocre fate of so many couples.

At Ávila, in that year 1531, the most brilliant festivities were taking place in quick succession. Already, the marriage of her older half-sister María with Martín de Guzmán had been the occasion for many days of joyous reunions among cousins, relatives, and friends. During these days, Teresa had had the opportunity to shine and to practice her seductive powers. For the first time, she had also experienced jealousy upon seeing her appointed suitor lavish his attentions upon other beauties. Faced with the impermanence of the human feelings that she was experiencing in her flesh and spirit, she felt herself growing dizzy, but she did not understand the folly of her life, which she was in the process of destroying. Events were beyond her control.

Her half-sister's marriage was only a beginning. Ávila was preparing to receive the imperial cortège, which was coming from Toledo with great fanfare. Empress Isabella herself was bringing the heir apparent, the *Infante* Philipe, the future King Philip II, who was four years old. In Ávila, he would be receiving his court outfit, leaving behind his childhood dress for the masculine garb suitable to his future role in life. All of this was more than enough to make heads spin among the youth of Ávila.

And Teresa's also! Intoxicated by her successes, wildly exhilarated by her power of seduction, she moved along as though beside herself, forgetting the deep part of her being, putting aside all prudence, numb to the fear of God that had been instilled in her.

The festivities had begun twenty days before the arrival of the imperial retinue. In an Ávila decked out with flags, the tournaments, jousts, and receptions followed one after another in a general atmosphere of frenzy punctuated by the peal of bells and the salvos of arquebuses. As a daughter of the regional nobility, Teresa was expected to assist at all of the festivities with her older brothers and her cousins in their finest attire: doublets bedecked with gold, silken breeches, the velvet toque, and the famous cape *à la française*, thrown over a single shoulder and turned up by a small sword studded with precious stones.

Attired in her mother's most beautiful gowns, surrounded by her richly dressed and dashing admirers, Teresa was positively losing her head, intoxicated by her surroundings and by the pleasure of finding her favorite escort on every occasion.

At last, Don Alonso became aware that his beloved daughter risked turning out badly, or, at the very least, damaging her reputation. On July 13, at the height of summer and only two weeks before the anticipated great imperial event, he abruptly decided to place her in a boarding school, that is, in a safe place, as a secular boarder in the strict convent of the Augustinian Sisters of Our Lady of Grace. When she cried out in protest, he used the pretext that her newly married half-sister, María, was no longer available to chaperone her.

Had one of the servants exposed Teresa's amorous relationship with her cousin? And what exactly had been revealed?

> So excessive was the love my father bore me and so great my dissimulation that he was unable to believe there was much wrong with me, and so he was not angered with me. Since this period of time had been brief, and

though he knew something, nothing could be said with certainty. For since I feared so much for my honor, I used every effort to keep my actions secret....

Nonetheless, Don Alonso was separating himself from his favorite daughter—not by marrying her off, the most natural solution, but by placing her as a boarder among austere religious women. He hoped that by doing so, he was preserving her from the pitfalls of the devil and the premature attentions of young men, giving her the time to regain her self-control. He envisioned reintegrating her into the family home with a strong soul and an informed mind, where she would reign without peril while awaiting a brilliant marriage carefully arranged by him. So thought this belatedly worried father, who did not realize that he was tearing Teresa away from loving the world and a trivial youthful attachment. His decision pushed her headlong into an infinite love—one that she was already carrying within her without having yet become aware of it.

CHAPTER 4

The Damsel Above

(1531–1535)

O̶ur Lady of Grace convent, built outside the city on the site of a
mosque (the great bell in its steeple had been cast from the bronze
of a cannon taken from the Moors) was not a boarding facility for young,
wellborn women. The forty women religious of the Order of St. Augustine
were dedicated to prayer in a strict enclosure and took in only ten or so
young women of the Castilian aristocracy to complete their education and
their spiritual formation. The program consisted of reading, writing, music,
and included embroidery and lace-making, but not Latin and Greek, which
were subjects reserved for men in the universities. These subjects remained
forbidden to women, effectively excluding them from any medical or philo-
sophical formation and even from reading the Bible.

The convent's reputation was based upon the sanctity of its religious,
who were "very modest, religious, and circumspect," wrote Teresa.[1]

The *doncellas* (young ladies) were entrusted to an exceptional woman,
Mother María de Briceño, thirty-four years old, who taught the boarders.
This mystic, a fervent devotee of the Eucharist, had been favored with a miracle: at Mass one day, when she had believed herself to be unworthy of
receiving Communion, a luminous host had left the ciborium and flown to
her lips.[2]

The first days were difficult. Teresa, the spoiled child of the Cepedas,
had never been shut in like this, and after the whirlwind of festivities and
freedom, she suffered cruelly from the situation. She felt that she was being
humiliated and "more than that because of my suspicion that they knew
about my vanity." She was, as she wrote, "strongly against my becoming a

nun"[3] and declared that she was "extremely outraged" by the penances they imposed upon themselves.

No more finery, jewels, perfumes, nor servants for her. She also suffered because of her separation from the band of joyous cousins whose queen she had been. As for her handsome cavalier, she admits that she received some clandestine "messages," no doubt brought to her by the girl cousin who had exerted a noxious influence over her. Then he forgot about her.

This dangerous transition, during which she could have revolted, did not last thanks to Mother María de Briceño, whose spirituality, joined to a natural goodness, moved Teresa deeply. The mystical personality that had revealed itself in Teresa's early childhood and then had been forgotten, suppressed to the very depths of her soul, was awaking in contact with this luminous woman. "I was glad to hear how well she spoke about God," writes Teresa. And not only "about the reward the Lord grants those who give up all for Him," paradise no doubt for tomorrow, but love for today!

She was learning to be astonished. For Teresa, religion was still only the surest means of escaping hell and acquiring "eternal happiness." A singularly self-interested approach! Mother María radiated otherwise, as did many of the young students under her guidance. "And if I saw someone with the gift of tears when she prayed, or other virtues, I greatly envied her. For so hard was my heart that I could read the entire *Passion* without shedding a tear. This pained me." Little by little, Teresa felt herself being liberated, purified of that time she had spent lost in the world, preoccupied only with herself and the sole vanity of appearing to good effect.

Shaken to the very depths of her being, Teresa discovered the love of the crucified God and recognized that he was living within her. Although she did not realize it, the day of that realization was the first day of her religious vocation. She was laying the first stone of that "interior castle" with its "seven dwellings" that she would later describe after having "walked through them often" and tasted their delights.

Teresa was essentially a woman of desire. In her, the desire for God had its origin in childhood when she devoured the lives of martyrs and saints, "the suffering and the glory that was to last forever." "As I said this over and over, the Lord was pleased to impress upon me in childhood the way of truth."[4]

"Desire raised her beyond the limit where it is born," writes Reverend Denis Vasse, a psychoanalyst.[5] This desire, dormant in the most intimate part of herself, was awakened by two extraordinary circumstances: the break with her family environment that was orienting her toward becoming a wife and mother, and the meeting with María de Briceño, inspired bearer of the Spirit.

The gratuitousness of the divine gift and ineffable love are the foundations of mystical desire. But the liberty to refuse them remains inalienable. In Teresa, human temperament resisted; there were all of those attachments to this world of pleasure and well-being, of appearance, sensuality, and what she calls "good pleasure," which she had just left behind.

Liberty! Mother María invited her to ask God to show her the state in which she would best serve him with all her heart. As a religious? Her flesh bristled at this idea: "But still I had no desire to be a nun, and I asked God not to give me this vocation; although I also feared marriage."

Knowing her mother's fate, dead of exhaustion at the age of thirty-three after having given birth to her tenth child, one can understand Teresa's fear. And whatever love Don Alonso may have felt for his wife, Teresa the rebel was revolting against the destiny of married women of her time: submissive to spouse, family, and clan. Already, just after the beginnings of Teresa as the mystic spouse of God, appears Teresa the feminist, who would later discuss, regarding the Carmelites, "the great favor God has granted them in choosing them for Himself and freeing them from being subject to a man who is often the death of them and who could also be, God forbid, the death of their souls."[6]

Finally, given the impossibility of a woman carrying a sword and becoming a conquistador, the religious state seemed to her to be the better of her two choices. And this awakening of the interiority within her allowed her to perceive, even here below, countries to conquer quite the equal of Mexico and Peru!

But not at Our Lady of Grace. Teresa found these Augustinians too austere, too devoted to excessive penance! It was enough for her to see certain novices hesitate on the threshold of their engagement.

Teresa knew of a certain monastery of Carmelites, Our Lady of the Incarnation, in Ávila at the foot of the northern ramparts. Her close friend, Juana Suárez, had recently made her profession there. Pushing penance too far was carefully avoided at Our Lady of the Incarnation, and the religious were not totally cut off from the outside world thanks to the parlor visits, which the best society of Ávila attended. As with the Augustinians, the presence of young lay boarders leavened the monastic solitude.

Teresa hesitated nonetheless. To shut herself away for life behind those walls and grilles! Renounce her liberty to obey a rule! But what liberty was there for a Spanish woman of the sixteenth century?

Fray Luis de León, one of the first biographer-witnesses of Teresa, adeptly summarized the turmoil that had taken hold of "the girl upstairs," a term used to designate the young lay boarders, and which I like to translate as "the damsel above." "The spirit attracted her to the convent, the senses distanced her from it; they both waged battle within her and made of her soul a combat area."

The struggle grew to such an extent that, eighteen months after her entrance at Our Lady of Grace, Teresa was losing sleep and her appetite over it. Then she fell ill. In her head, crushed by migraines, these words of the Gospel that María de Briceño had whispered to her jangled in her ears: "Many are the called and few, the chosen."

Of this sickness we know nothing. Teresa remained discreet. But for her it could not have seemed a whim of fate, even less a curse: "[The Lord] sent me a serious illness so that I had to return to my father's house. When I got better, they brought me to visit my sister, who lived in a nearby hamlet.... There lived along the way one of my father's brothers...."

Since becoming a widower, her uncle Pedro Sánchez de Cepeda was living in seclusion in a modest manor house of blue granite in the village of Hortigosa, which was surrounded by barren mountains deep in the Castilian countryside about twelve miles from Ávila. It was a poor village with a river running through it that dried up in the summertime. In the arid Castilian plateau, stripped bare, fields of rye and some livestock enclosures were its only resources. But the air was dry and pure and, on the rocky road, that peasant on his donkey did not seem to be unhappy.

Christ and books of piety were Don Pedro's all-encompassing passions. He was waiting only to complete his son's education before relinquishing all of his earthly possessions and becoming a monk at Guisando. In his single-story long house, he received very few people and only those persons who comforted him in his vision of the world: here below, all is nothingness; our hope is elsewhere, and we must prepare for it.

Teresa was not the type of visitor he usually received, but she was his niece and, from the very first day, he gave in to her charm. She enjoyed Hortigosa, listening to the wind that bent the poplars. She prepared their modest meal: garlic soup and goat cheese on brown bread.

They observed one another. With a sure instinct, the uncle was quick to detect the desire for God in his niece. For her part, Teresa could not help but compare her uncle's *fervor* with the *piety* of Don Alonso, her father. Her father's piety was sincere but somewhat conventional and stilted. Don Pedro's was fiery and communicative. He lived his faith.

Having placed his trust in her, he opened to her what he considered to be his most precious possession: his library, which she plunged into with delight despite the seriousness of the titles. Don Pedro's eyesight was declining, and he benefited from his niece's visit and her taste for books by asking her to read aloud to him. When he took down the *Letters* of St. Jerome from its shelf, she was startled. "Although I did not like them [his good books], I pretended to. For, in this matter of pleasing others, I went to extremes, even when it was a burden to me...."

When she left him, she said that she had been deeply changed. Her reading of the learned hermit who had dared to translate the Bible into Latin—the Vulgate—had implanted the following doubt in her: in the world here below, all is nothingness, everything is brief. And from this obvious fact the question ensued: "What are you doing in this world, you who are greater than the world?"

Which brought her back to the life choice of Mother María de Briceño: shut yourself away in a convent to look for God. Religious life is austere, but it is both the best and the surest way. There one is protected from the world, its temptations, and the conjugal and maternal slavery imposed upon women. But one has to endure its weighty counterpart: confinement, asceticism, religious services, silence, the companionship of sisters one has not chosen.... However, "the trials and hardships of being a nun could not be greater than those of purgatory," and "I really merited hell...it would not be so great a thing while alive to live as though in purgatory."

Ah, but to allow her beautiful body to dry up from fasting and ascetic practices? But "afterward I would go directly to heaven, for that was my desire." Egotism? Realism? St. Jerome had an answer for everything: "To prefer virginity to marriage is not to denigrate it." As for asceticism: "Nothing is hard for someone who loves."

Love? Love truly from behind the grilles of a cloister? Was this possible? St. Jerome affirmed it to be so: "May the secret of your chamber keep you always, that always inside it the Spouse will play there with you. You pray, that is to speak to the Spouse. You read, it is he who is talking to you."

When she left Hortigosa to return to her father after a stay with her half-sister, Teresa remained torn and perplexed. She contemplated her sister María's difficult life, the life of a woman caught between an authoritarian, demanding husband and the prospect of many pregnancies. Although Teresa was not yet fully aware of the real difficulties that religious faced, her experiences had certainly not convinced her of the superiority of conjugal life over religious life.

At home, however, everything was happiness for her. She was adulated. She allowed herself to be recaptured by the world. And the little ones— Agostino, Juan, and Juana—needed her so very much since María's departure! Perspicacious, she knew how to draw out their personalities, understand them, and guide them according to their characters while surrounding them with tenderness. Her skill at organization, her sense of order, and her intuition at guessing the needs and concerns of each one made her a remarkable household manager, to the great joy of her father and the entire family.

In the spring of 1534, Ávila organized a great celebration for the visit of Emperor Charles V. Teresa took part, more dazzling than ever in her mother's costly dresses.

For her, all of this was only a diversion. She knew that one day or another she would have to choose between marriage or the convent. She had just turned nineteen. Don Alonso had lost count of the number of candidates for her hand. Teresa rejected them all with a slight smile, but she would find herself falling back on her dilemma: marriage or the convent. She would ask herself which was "the best and safest state"? Life here below, the life of the world, was so beautiful for someone of her class! No. Not for a woman, even one belonging to the privileged classes, even one married with a dowry of three thousand gold ducats that would ensure her a certain independence. Paradoxically, the only happy women she knew were the rich widows! That's what it amounted to!

For three months she hesitated. Once again, she became ill. Her fever and her faintings unnerved the people around her. The persuasive voice of María de Briceño reverberated within her: "Many are the called and few, the chosen."

Teresa would later write about

> the nothingness of all things, the vanity of the world...and to fear that if I were to die I would go to hell. And although my will did not completely incline [me] to being a nun, I saw that the religious life was the best and safest state, and so little by little I decided to force myself to accept it.

She dared to confide in her father about the matter. As she later wrote, she saw herself once again in his office. Don Alonso sat rigid before an open book behind his ebony table inlaid with ivory. His hand, which trembled slightly, fingered a rosary with boxwood beads. Where did she find the heroic courage to leave this adored father, to shatter him? She, so tender, forced herself to assume an almost harsh tone of voice that he did not recognize: "I am going to leave you, to enter the Carmel. I have understood that there is no other way but the convent for me. From now on, I belong only to Christ. I must die to everything...."

Don Alonso remained dumbfounded, as if thunderstruck. That she would one day leave to be married was in the nature of things, but he could not bring himself to understand how she could abandon him selfishly at a time when the household could not do without her. She was the house's angel, looking after the children and their father, enveloping them with her attentive love. If at least she had been fired up by an irresistible love of Christ.... But there was nothing of this, he rightly sensed. The discreet touch that had lightly brushed her at Hortigosa was now but a memory. There remained only the fear of losing herself, the fear of hell, the selfish desire to "ensure her salvation."

As a result, nothing went as Teresa had foreseen: her father's tears, his entreaties, and then the inevitable capitulation. Had he not always bowed to the wishes of his *niña*? And would he not be flattered knowing that she would soon be the "spouse of Christ"?

No. He immured himself in his indignant despair. He gave way on nothing. Conscious of his right and his duties as the father of the family, he cried out: "No! It is no, Teresa!"

For the first time he was refusing her something. She remained stunned at his distressed, tragic, distraught look. He added with a desperation that devastated her: "You will do whatever you wish after my death!"

At that time, a person did not argue against a father's orders. But instead of giving up, she dug in her heels. "I was so persistent in points of honor that I don't think I would have turned back for anything once I told him."

Why would she not wait a little to give her father time to get used to her decision, which she had presented to him too harshly? She knew so well how to bring him around to her way of thinking. But, "I was afraid of myself and my frailty and of backing down...." She was afraid of changing her mind, of finally opting for the world and its dangers, for she still remained tempted by this world that contained so much beauty, so many riches, tempted by a great human love and children whom she adored. On the other hand, religious life was not without risks. A person could also lose herself there! Is it not said that the devil often hides under the straw mattress of religious women? No enclosure stops him, *this villain deprived of love!*

Her uncertainty lasted for several months. In August 1535, her brother Rodrigo, the favorite companion of her games and the follies of her youth, boarded a ship in Seville. He was bound for South America in Mendoza's expedition to the Rio de la Plata, the river of silver, following the dangerous road adopted by Hernando, her oldest brother, who was already fighting there. All her other brothers were also waiting only to reach the required age before leaving to make their fortune as conquerors in Peru, "the land of gold" (*Eldorado*), accompanied by missionaries to convert souls to Christ!

Before leaving, Rodrigo, who had not yet married and had foreseen for himself a brutal death, had ceded his share of inheritance to Teresa so that she could make a brilliant marriage.

But what of Teresa? She would leave also. For another *Eldorado*. As for her father...she trembled as she remembered the fearsome exhortations of St. Jerome in his *Letter to Heliodorus*: "What are you doing under your father's roof? Even if your father stretches out over the threshold to bar the way, step over the body of your father!"[7] No, it was not yet the love of God crucified that called her to give everything up. There was only one reason: to ensure her salvation by the surest of means.

But was it only that? *The desire* to love God also burned within her, a tiny, discreet flame. The divine touch, which she had already experienced, gave her a premonition of the great love, one that she would never find in the world. For this, it was necessary to leave everything behind, give every-thing away, risk everything!

THE DAY HAD NOT YET RISEN over Ávila on that November 2, 1535. In the western section of the old medieval city on *Plazuela* San Domingo, the mon-umental portal ornamented with wrought iron opened slightly and silently. A boy of fifteen furtively slipped through the opening. Already people were going about in the square, women on their way to an early Mass and a crowd of peasants with loaded carts hurrying to find a good spot at the market.

The boy signaled to the woman wrapped in a large brown cape who was following him. Under the veil that half hid her youthful, apprehensive face shone two admirable and resolute dark eyes.

The adolescent closed the heavy door of the paternal residence, taking care not to make any noise. The heart of young Antonio de Cepeda was beat-ing wildly. After accompanying his sister to the door of the Carmel, he would go to the Dominican Fathers and ask them to accept him into their monastery. Teresa had convinced Antonio in the same way that, as a child, she had persuaded Rodrigo to follow her to the land of the Moors to be decapitated and thus obtain eternal salvation through martyrdom.

He looked his older sister in the eye to find the courage that he lacked. But all he saw there was the reflection of his own distress. He glanced up at the façade of the austere and noble stone dwelling of the Ahumadas and at the family coat of arms of the maternal branch: the leaping lion, the three crowns of Sancho, king of Castile and León. Engraved in the stone, a burned-out tower recalled that ancestor who had set fire to his own château rather than surrender to the Moors. In Castilian, *Ahumada* means "fire."

Teresa followed her brother's look. She was in the process of setting fire to her childhood memories, to life as a spoiled child, to an adolescence lived in a superficial manner, in order to preclude looking back. But what heart-break!

> I remember, clearly and truly, that when I left my father's house I felt that separation so keenly that the feeling will not be greater, I think, when I die. For it seemed that every bone in my body was being sundered. Since there was no love of God to take away my love for my father and relatives, every-thing so constrained me that if the Lord hadn't helped me, my reflections would not have been enough to continue on. In this situation He gave me such courage against myself that I carried out the task.[8]

"Come on, Antonio!"

They were swept along the streets by a glacial autumn wind from the north. Some women were hurrying toward the San Vicente Basilica. From all sides came the sound of the tolling bells, for it was November 2, the Day of the Dead! The brother and sister, running more than walking through the old streets, passed through the enormous wall at one of the nine gates of the rampart whose portcullis had just been opened. Then they were out-side the city, their hearts still beating for fear of being pursued.

They walked on the mule path that ran along the northern embank-ment of Ávila's ramparts. They were already in the arid countryside—there was very little greenery and many stones. Then they descended the slope leading to the valley where the Adaja River flows, a torrent of clear water over whose old bridge they crossed.

At last, the Carmel, with its high walls almost without exterior windows, rose before them. Kitchen gardens and orchards surrounded this large monastery. The two young people stopped at the door to catch their breath. Teresa had arrived. She would not go back. She turned toward her brother. In an impassioned embrace that signaled her goodbye to the family and to all that she had loved, she tearfully clasped him in her arms. And then there he was, already running down the road toward the Dominican monastery.

Teresa's hand reached for the small chain of the bell, whose shrill sound resonated behind the high walls. Long wait. Finally, the small grilled win-dow, the spy-hole, opened, and the questioning glance of the convent's turn sister shone in the shadow. She recognized the visitor, smiled at her, and half opened the great door. Teresa rushed in. She breathed. Yes, she had arrived! Had she really arrived?

But now a young religious was rushing toward her, Juana Suárez, the friend and confidante long attached to her father's house. We can guess that she had been party to the plot, as her complicit look would have indicated.

"Come in, Teresa! I'll take you to mother prioress."

Corridors, the cloister's ambulatory, a monumental stairway, while Teresa's heart began to race again. She became frightened. She would have liked to flee, to turn back. Too late!

The office-oratory of the Reverend Doña Francisca del Águila, prioress of Our Lady of the Incarnation, was austerely furnished: an oak desk, a bookcase, some chairs, a prie-dieu upholstered in red leather. On the white-washed wall was a large crucified Christ.

Sister Juana Suárez slipped away discreetly. Mother prioress was astonished to see Teresa arriving so early in the morning without warning. But as a relative of her father, Don Alonso, she knew Teresa well as a regular visitor to the parlor of the Incarnation, where she visited her friend Juana weekly.

Teresa was still trembling. She knelt at the feet of mother prioress.

"Very Reverend Mother, I humbly solicit the habit of Our Lady of Mount Carmel."

The religious was startled. Teresa de Ahumada y Cepeda, the queen of Ávila's gilded youth, Don Alonso's daughter! After a long silence, she uttered: "The community will decide that, daughter. But I am surprised that you are not accompanied by your father, the Don."

"My father does not accept my vocation. He remains inflexible."

The nun's face closed in upon itself.

"Our Rule is also. We need to have his agreement."

Teresa was panic-stricken. All was lost! She would never convince her father. Had she really hoped that mother prioress would disregard this? In a flash, she understood the folly of her flight with Antonio, so like the one she had undertaken as a child long ago with her little brother Rodrigo, which had ended with their humiliating return home.

She rebelled. She was twenty years old. She was no longer a *niña*, Don Alonso's little girl. She felt her heart tighten. The "point of honor" compelled her not to give in on anything. But she was in the process of botching her life. Was this how a person gave herself over to Love—by crushing love? In wanting to place before her father a *fait accompli*, she had betrayed him, who had always placed his trust in her. And betrayed her brothers and sisters also, this family that she cherished and that had reconstituted itself around her after their mother's death. Tears flowed from her eyes.

Reverend mother prioress remained puzzled. She was flattered by this new postulant, but she did not want to rush anything. She continued slowly: "First of all, your father must be reassured; for I suppose that you left without telling him, hoping to make him yield by placing before him an accomplished fact?"

"Yes, very Reverend Mother."

"I shall beseech him to come. Perhaps, if God wills it, he will let himself be moved? While waiting, go and pull yourself together. How pale you are, Teresa! Sister Juana will take you to a postulant's cell."

THE SMALL ROOM—barely ten feet by ten feet—overlooked a peaceful garden. Some lay sisters in brown robes and white veils were working there in silence. The sun had not yet risen, but tiny chirps from the birds in the trees could already be heard. Here everything exuded peace. It was not happiness, rather a waiting for God in liberty and trust. Before closing the door, Juana had lit a candle, which illuminated the white walls in a subdued manner. She had placed a bowl of warm milk on a small table. A cross affixed to the wall was an invitation to prayer. A straw mattress with its brown wool blanket was placed directly on the tile floor. Teresa felt a pang of anguish as she thought of her father's house with its carpets from Flanders, its cushions of bright silk, its great wood fires warming the air. The humidity of this cell, which was never heated, permeated her being, she who only yesterday had huddled close to the braziers in her father's house.

On the wall facing the prie-dieu, the crucified Christ looked down upon her. Teresa knelt, closing her eyes. Immediately, her mind was engulfed by her past, the smiling faces of all those who loved her and whom she cherished: her parents, her brothers, her sisters, her cousins, her numerous relatives, her friends. By abruptly leaving her father's house without any thought of returning, she had believed that she was detaching herself from them. But they were all there before her, more present than ever. She felt again the pain of her flight as if she had been stabbed. Ungrateful and insensitive daughter, she had duped this beloved father. She felt pulled apart for having cut to the quick the ties of affection uniting her to her near and dear ones, who had become so important to her after the death of their mother.

And now she found herself at the Carmel in this small postulant's cell. Facing the Crucified One, she trembled, not hesitant but overwhelmed as she awaited the final test—her father's arrival. The light of the almost-white rising sun penetrated through the window's oval opening, illuminating the naked walls. She looked fixedly at the Christ as if to defy him: "If you want me here, make a miracle happen!"

Teresa, so alive and so human at the same time, was still far from the love of God and so close to the tenderness of her own family! She now had to sever these ties by risking her whole life. How could she not feel split apart and torn asunder? Lucid and distressed yet determined, she also knew that she had to choose what she wanted to become. This inner battle conducted alone in the secret of her heart had passed unnoticed by her father.

Her father! Time seemed to stand still when the door opened in silence. The tiny, frightened face of Juana Suárez appeared, pale under her black veil.

"He is here, Teresa. Don Alonso is waiting for you with mother prioress. May God protect you!"

Teresa stood up. All fear and remorse had left her. She was like her brother Rodrigo embarking at Seville for the Rio de la Plata; she was like a conquistador, for better or worse. What was essential was to risk one's life!

The details of this interview in the office of mother prioress are not known to us. Did Teresa's firmness succeed in convincing this indignant father, torn to pieces, who could have exerted over her a kind of blackmail by refusing to pay the dowry required to enter this Carmel devoid of resources? Was he moved by an injunction of the Christ who wanted all of her for himself? Was he also struck by his daughter's calm determination, her will to conquer that inner kingdom, that silent empire that does not change and would not know how to deceive, a stark contrast to the pleasures and perishable riches of the earth? To achieve something other than the respectable and normal conjugal destiny of a noble Castilian woman? We have but one life to live. Teresa legitimately aspired to love. She now knew that only Christ's love would not deceive her. And if she, the rebel, finally agreed to submit, it would not be to this adored father, nor to a husband, tender and attractive though he might be, but to this mysterious God who was calling her.

The following day, November 3, 1535, Don Alonso Cepeda contracted before a lawyer to give each year to the Monastery of the Incarnation twenty-five *fanegas*[9] of grain, half wheat, half barley, or in lieu of this, two hundred gold ducats.[10] In return, the Carmelite postulant renounced her rights to the family inheritance and transferred her eventual share from Rodrigo's estate to her sister Juana. Don Alonso also gave his favorite daughter

> a bed, blankets and some quilts, six linen sheets, six pillows, two mattresses, two cushions, a carpet, and all necessary holy habits, one of

black broadcloth and the other of a thicker cloth; three underskirts, one of gray wool, a white one, and one of coarse muslim; a warm sheepskin garment, coifs, shirts, shoes; finally, the books that it is customary to give to cloistered nuns.[11]

After a year of novitiate, Teresa de Ahumada received the brown Carmelite habit from the hands of Mother Francisca de Águila. As a young temporary professed, Teresa continued to wear the white veil of the novices.

As soon as I took the habit, the Lord gave me an understanding of how He favors those who use force with themselves to serve Him. No one noticed this struggle, but rather they noted that I was very pleased. Within an hour, He gave me such great happiness at being in the religious state of life that it never left me up to this day, and God changed the dryness my soul experienced into the greatest tenderness.[12]

CHAPTER 5

Our Lady of the Incarnation

(1536-1537)

The Carmel of Our Lady of the Incarnation,[1] built outside the walls in 1513 on a small hill north of Ávila, is an architectural success. Very large for a Carmel, it had been foreseen that it would accommodate more than one hundred and fifty choir nuns, lay sisters, boarders, and domestic staff. It consisted of two cloisters with walkways—some one hundred thirty feet long—one at ground level and another on the floor above that overlooked verdant patios. The cells of the Carmelites opened onto the cloisters. Some of them had been joined together to constitute small, more agreeable lodgings reserved for the cloistered nuns of the aristocracy, richly endowed as Teresa. A large central stairway gave access to the upper story from which could be seen the massive ramparts of Ávila and the bleak countryside of Castile, a desert of stones and sand out of which rose some cypress trees. The community cultivated a large kitchen garden and an orchard that were irrigated by running water.

On Sundays the people of Ávila crowded into the large monastery chapel, where the bishop of Ávila often celebrated Mass. The faithful could not see the Carmelites, who sat close together in the chancel to the right of the altar behind a wrought-iron grille. All of the Carmelites waited patiently, however, for families and friends would meet them after Mass in the patios and numerous visiting rooms that then came to life. Food prepared by the families would be shared, and it was not forbidden to taste the sweet fruity wines that accompanied the pastries and other delicacies. Such was the Carmel of Spain's Golden Century.

The Incarnation occupied a vast area offered by Doña Elvira de Medina, a noble lady who was a votary of the Virgin and who had also financed the construction of the buildings. Separated from the city by the valley where the Adaja flowed, the site, isolated and secluded, had an austere Castilian beauty; it was an ideal place to pray and contemplate. Teresa would write of it in her *Life:* "It helped me also to look at fields, or water, or flowers. In these things I found a remembrance of the Creator. I mean that they awakened and recollected me and served as a book and reminded me of my ingratitude and sins."[2]

At the time of the Moorish occupation, when each community lived in a separate quarter, Ávila's Jewish ghetto had been located there. The expulsion of the Jews at the end of the fifteenth century had turned it into a deserted area.

What was the origin of this Carmel? In 1479, a *beatorio* (i.e., a small community of *beata*) that welcomed pious widows and unmarried women of different social classes had been established in Ávila within the city's walls. Their vows were taken as lay tertiaries and connected them more or less to the Carmelite Order, present in Castile since the thirteenth century. The destiny of these *beata*, who subsisted on public charity, remained precarious. Independent of the Church, they sometimes had a bad reputation. Some of them were repentant prostitutes. Their mystical states, rich in unusual displays, made people distrust them, and the lower classes found therein sustenance for their superstitions.

That is why at the beginning of the sixteenth century, their young superior and benefactress, Doña Beatriz Guiera, proposed to them that, in order to escape suspicion from the Inquisition, they should adopt the Carmelite Rule. Using her inheritance, Doña Beatriz then constructed outside the walls, on the site of the old Jewish cemetery, a very unpretentious monastery. The piety of the nuns soon attracted a great many vocations. When they reached one hundred and fifty in number, they then built, this time thanks to the donations of Elvira de Medina, the still existing great monastery of the Incarnation, which was inaugurated on April 4, 1515, the very day of Teresa's baptism.

The Carmelite Order traces its origin to the twelfth century. Around 1155, Latin Christian hermits, former crusaders, settled in Palestine in some grottoes of a small valley of Mount Carmel. The view from the valley includes the plain of Nazareth, a site that would have been inhabited by Elijah († ca. 853 B.C.), the hermit prophet of the Old Testament. It was from him that the Carmelites derived their tradition of contemplation, which was also that of the ancient cenobites of Libya, Egypt, and Palestine: "He is living, the God before whom I stand!"

The brothers of Our Lady of Mount Carmel, placed under the protection of the Virgin, had received their Rule around 1209 from Albert Avogadro, the Latin patriarch of Jerusalem who had withdrawn to St. John of Acre. These ascetics aspired to be hermits, but a fraternal way of life under the guidance of a wise man, the prior, brought them together. Their Rule can be summarized as follows: solitude, silence, obedience, ascetic poverty, penance, and manual labor, with prayer remaining their principal occupation. "Go east and hide in the Wadi of Cherith; there you shall drink of the stream of living waters," Yahweh said to Elijah. The torrent of divine joy leads to ecstasy as the fruit of contemplation, declares an ancient text. The inner search for divine life furthered the fraternal exercise of charity that is its first application. This Rule humanizes spiritual exercises by taking life in common into account. "Let everyone remain alone in his cell, meditating day and night on the law of the Lord and keeping watch in prayer, unless he be legitimately occupied at something else."

We can immediately see the deviation to which this last sentence can lead. It refers to work that allows for survival, and if alms can lead to avoidance or reduction of work, the community finds itself obliged to receive its benefactors with the resulting distractions and dispersion.

But the Rule of the holy patriarch Albert forbade the use of unearned income and all forms of property. The community lived on daily alms. Eight months of fasting were prescribed (except on Sundays), and each house was to shelter no more than thirteen monks, up to twenty-one only by exception.

In the thirteenth century, after the Arab conquest chased Christians from Palestine, the Carmelites departed for Europe, where they were well received. The first Carmel was founded in Paris in 1254, and another was established in Spain in 1282. Since the Carmelites henceforth devoted themselves to the apostolate, Rome classified them among the active mendicant Orders. But these religious, distinguishable by the scapular, a piece of fabric that the monks wore over their shoulders in memory of the service apron of Mary at Nazareth, had retained a pronounced taste for contemplative life from their Oriental origin. However, invited to choose between the countryside and the city, they had chosen the latter; unlike the Cistercians, they were not from an agricultural tradition that required a large community and an abundance of manpower.

The Carmelites experienced a great expansion in the thirteenth and fourteenth centuries. Then came a period of decadence linked to the catastrophic events of the Middle Ages: plagues, famines, wars, and schisms. In 1432, Pope Eugene IV added to the Order's departure from its original observance of the Rule by authorizing unearned income and ownership of property and real estate. The number of religious per monastery was no longer restricted, fasting was made less rigorous, silence less strict, the enclosure relaxed, clothing more comfortable. Even the vow of stability, which in Orders of strict observance requires that persons remain for their entire life in the monastery where they have made their solemn profession, was no longer enforced.

In 1453, a community of Flemish Beguines was officially admitted into the Order.

They were the first women Carmelites. Not obligated to the apostolate, these cloistered nuns were obliged to keep a strict enclosure "within which they must know God alone and serve Him and pray to Him for the salvation of the world." Devotion to Mary was deepening. Owing to this voluntary confinement, but also by nature and choice, the Carmelites symbolized the contemplative Order par excellence. The first convents were built in Flanders, French Brittany, and Italian Tuscany.

In 1464, the prior general, Jean Soreth, who was attempting to maintain the early asceticism, founded in Brittany the first French Carmel for women with Françoise d'Amboise and nine nuns who had come from Liège in Belgium.

AT THE TIME OF TERESA'S ARRIVAL in 1535, the monastery of Our Lady of the Incarnation was overpopulated: one hundred and sixty choir nuns, one hundred or so lay sisters, some twenty children or very young postulants, the novitiate, and some lay boarders. Stability and enclosure were no longer rigidly observed. A person could leave to spend a few months with her family under the pretext of regaining her health, a practice that eased the pressure on the monastery's finances, whose revenues were meager. The buildings, which were poorly maintained, were evidence of their poverty. During the winter months, rain and snow, driven by the violent wind, seeped under the roof tiles and even flooded the upper floors. For lack of heat, the walls oozed with humidity.

No equality whatsoever was observed among the cloistered nuns, even those of the choir. The lay sisters, who had entered without a dowry, served the nuns supplied with revenues by taking over the manual chores: cooking, gardening, laundering, doing the housework, operating the bread oven. They slept in a dormitory. The choir nuns had, at the very minimum, a cell at their disposal, while some of them were able to occupy a small independent apartment that included a sleeping cell, an oratory, and a small kitchen. Exempted from all manual labor, they were even authorized to keep a lay servant.

No one was astonished at these inequalities so little in conformity with the spirit of Carmel. Even Teresa does not allude to them in her writings. She would tackle them only later. Life at the Incarnation, punctuated by religious services and with minor mortifications reminding a person that she was no longer in the world, was the epitome of the pious and lukewarm routine of the relaxed Rule. Here, contemplative life signified peace especially, and no risk was being taken regarding heaven. Naturally, the three vows of poverty, chastity, and obedience were respected, and the seven Offices of the day and night, sung in the chapel, were followed as best as each individual could manage.

But was the heart in it? For these ladies, it was a question of overcoming boredom, especially during the long winters. The pious routine of the Offices and the boring exhortations of the confessors did not suffice. Many of the religious who had entered without a vocation, even sometimes obliged to do so, resorted to dissipation. Their families had not been able to marry them off for various reasons and, not knowing what to do with them in the world, viewed the monastery as a means of settling them by providing them with a stable and respectable social position.

The Incarnation was spiritually dependent upon the male Carmelites of Ávila, whose monastery had been founded in the city in 1378 against a northern outer wall of the ramparts. They supplied the confessors. It was a serious community. There were no ignorant and quarrelsome monks there, as could sometimes be found in Europe, so much so that in 1515 the prior general of the Order had resigned. But neither did they burn with the fervor that animated the newer Orders, as was the case with the Jesuits. The provincial prior of Castile, residing in Toledo, arbitrated the conflicts.

In 1535, the convent of the Incarnation was not as lax as many other monasteries. It was more difficult to enter there, and it had, in any case, reached its saturation point. A small, fervent, and ascetic group quietly existed within the larger community, helping the Incarnation maintain a respectable atmosphere that was disturbed only on feast days, when some of the religious received relatives and friends to the sound of violas, harps, and songs to the rhythm of a tambourine!

Unfortunately, it bears repeating that these monasteries where the Rule was relaxed mirrored the world's social inequalities. The lay religious were often orphans or the youngest child of large, destitute, urban families. They were set apart by their white veil. They did not have access either to the choir, where the community chanted the religious services, or to the Chapter, where decisions were made and the prioress elected. Such an election, in any case, was often only symbolic. Certain noble families, from whom one expected donations or bequests, reserved the priorate for their religious daughters and even introduced children to be trained for monastic life. Little "nuns" five to ten years of age could thus be seen toddling along in the cloisters, proud of their habit made to order and often more fervent than certain nuns.

IN SPITE OF THIS UNUSUAL CONTEXT, Teresa began her novitiate in the best possible frame of mind. She had entered through strength of will, out of prudence, and by following her reason, but after some difficult days—for she neither knew how to pray nor could she chant—she was now opening herself to an authentic spiritual life: "All the things of religious life delighted me, and it is true that sometimes while sweeping, during the hours I used to spend in self-indulgence and self-adornment, I realized that I was free of all that and experienced a new joy which amazed me."[3]

How can this first conversion be explained? Teresa had been raised in a conventional religion, that of a young Catholic aristocrat, in which God reigns on his throne very high above the world as a glorious, strict, jealous, inaccessible Master. Here in the monastery, she breathed an aroma of Christ and the Virgin that reawakened in her the desire she had known in her early childhood. This desire had been a secret seed that asked only to germinate and grow, forgotten sometimes but emerging on other occasions, as during the encounter with Mother María de Briceño or the visit with her uncle at Hortigosa.

Her novitiate went well. She was reassured. She had expected to undergo a severe purgatory that would count toward eternity, a calculated insurance for a future paradise. The mitigated Rule satisfied her. This young aristocrat who had never touched a broom discovered in her novitiate the humble joys of manual labor well executed in a setting rid of worldly constraints. She exercised her natural charity by taking care of a nun stricken with a repugnant malady. In return, the sick nun by her patience granted Teresa what she lacked most: an all-trusting abandonment to God. She attentively observed a few authentic and discreet saints dedicated to an asceticism that seemed extraordinary to her. One of these individuals was Teresa de Quezada, who was of illustrious birth but compelled herself out of humility to sleep in the dormitory with the lay nuns. For the first time, Teresa was witnessing strange phenomena, such as the candle lit by a saintly nun that burned on the Virgin's altar without being consumed.

And it was with great joy that on November 3, 1537, she pronounced her vows, which were preceded by the customary question: "What are you asking for?"

"I am asking for God's mercy and the company of my sisters in perpetual enclosure. I make the vows of obedience, chastity, and poverty, which I shall keep with the grace of God and the prayers of my sisters."

"I remember the kind of profession I made and the great resolve and happiness with which I made it and the espousal that I entered into with you. I cannot speak of this without tears...."

The Incarnation was like a Spanish inn; persons found there what they had brought with them. In spite of all her faults, Teresa allowed the desire for God to grow within her. She was discovering interiority, what she would later call "a palace of immense wealth, the interior castle with its seven dwelling places." This palace was inhabited by a king before whom Charles V cut a sorry figure. The king was Jesus, the God of her childhood, today the fiancé promised to her heart.

Promised, but not yet obtained. Why was he eluding her? Did she, from desire or pride, want to go too quickly, to achieve in two years, the duration of her novitiate, what the most saintly of women spend a lifetime in attaining? Don Alonso's spoiled child realized that she had not mastered that delightful state, the prayer of quiet that is not yet union, but only the divine touch, a foretaste of the spiritual marriage. She was again finding irritating dryness in her prayer, distractions during divine services. No amount of flagellations with nettles, nor excessive fasting—which she practiced in spite of mother prioress's warning—or the spectacular penances she imposed upon herself in front of the community to tame her pride overcame all of this.

She sometimes displayed a childish pride. A Teresian legend relates that a *zahori*, or soothsayer, had predicted a "St. Teresa" to the Incarnation monastery, one who would fill a void in the liturgical calendar for that day. An elderly nun recalled this prediction on the day that young Teresa de Ahumada pronounced her solemn vows. "God grant that it be I," she murmured. And Teresa de Quezada, the mystic in the odor of sanctity, echoed: "God grant that it be I!"[4]

Why not? In her eyes, sanctity, like the conquest of the New World, was a matter of will power. But that was not working. She assumed her vocation with determination in a tragic, exhausting effort. The "divine touches" were a thing of the past—Christ remained elusive. He became for her not a friend—we cannot speak of love—but a rigorous master. It was "a combat full of bitterness, without reward" for "this frigid lover [who]...did not even know how to mimic the gestures of love." "She remained in the depths of her soul as cold as a funeral pyre touched by no flame at all."[5]

She prayed in vain. She did not think that she was on the wrong track, as her father still hoped she would decide. Besides, her honor was at stake. An Ahumada y Cepeda did not give up in the face of the first difficulty. No, Teresa would not turn back. But what if this route led nowhere?

Sometimes, a glimmer of hope touched her while reading a book or when a fired-up preacher attempted to communicate his passion to a dozing audience. In those moments, tense, almost awake, she would have liked to give herself to that mysterious Master who called to her while evading her. But she was as yet incapable of achieving within herself the emptiness required by the great leap—the complete break.

However, her will remained intact. Returning later to this uncertain period of her life, she would write:

> There is no task...no matter how hard, that I would hesitate to undertake. For I have already experienced in many ways that if I strive at the outset with determination to do it, even in this life His Majesty pays the soul in such ways that only he who has this joy understands it. Yet, since the task is for God alone, He may desire that the soul feel this fear before beginning so that it gain more merit.

Indeed, she also wrote: "Without taking into account the resistances of nature."

IT WAS AT THIS TIME that her body gave way. Already during her novitiate she had suffered from strange malaises that became more pronounced—persistent fevers, headaches, unexplainable pain: "I experienced such heart pains that this frightened any who witnessed them...the sickness was so serious that I always nearly lost consciousness, and sometimes lost it completely...." Her heart would stop, plunging her into a fainting fit that frightened her companions. Then, after recovering consciousness, through a superhuman effort she would take control of herself, leave the infirmary as pale as a dead woman, and take her place again in the chancel. To those who advised her to spare herself, she would answer: "We come here to die for Christ, and not to pamper ourselves."

Her doctors were at a loss to understand the condition. In her autobiography, *The Book of Her Life*, she evoked "the change in food and lifestyle." Did it have to do with the excessive fasting she had imposed upon herself? Or the sometimes harsh cold during the winter months in this never-heated monastery?

We shall see in Teresa's long history that, like many saints, her psychological conflicts had a pronounced physical effect on her. And by wanting to impose too much upon herself, she snapped as does a too tightly stretched bowstring.

These conflicts were numerous. Repressed carnal appetites? Unsatisfied youthful love? Despite her courage, she remained especially traumatized by family events: the death of her mother when she was thirteen, her beloved brother Rodrigo's departure when she was twenty. Then the voluntary break with her father and her feelings of guilt over the abandonment of her nine-year-old brother, Agostino, and her eight-year-old sister, Juana, whom she would one day take in and care for in her own cell at the monastery.

Another reason for her feeling of culpability was that she had finally realized that her motivations were not pure. She had not abandoned her family "just for the glory of God" but to escape the tragic destiny that had struck her mother, as it did many women of that time. She had avoided maternity, and she thought that she could pay the price for this by leading an ascetic religious life. Having entered the Incarnation to "earn salvation," that is, to escape hell, she took cognizance of the fact that life in the convent was no more disagreeable than life elsewhere! "She found the house large and full of amenities, and the apartment very much to her liking." She then developed a neurosis of dissatisfaction because of this existence within a relaxed form of the Rule that, in the final analysis, was disappointing to her. Her nature, avid for the absolute, in search of perfection, could not possibly be satisfied with the pious tranquility that reigned in that monastery. She now knew that there was something else. Not only moral perfection, an inaccessible ideal for the moment, but also "the divine touch," a relationship with the living God, which was, at the heart of the matter, what she had always sought: Love.

Would she finally achieve the spiritual breakthrough to which her deepest being aspired? In this God-fearing monastery without vices or heroism, in a word, tepid, it was as though no one pursued that ideal except for a few cloistered nuns who went unnoticed and remained discreetly in their cells. And especially not the prioress, a grand lady occupied with managing everyday life without making waves. During her novitiate, Teresa experienced joys and enthusiasm that awakened within her the desire for the divine. Then she understood that it would be difficult for her to escape mediocrity and routine and that she would have to do violence to herself to break away from it.

Was she counseled? At the Incarnation there was neither a prioress nor a mistress of novices nor a spiritual director worthy of the name. She stated the case briefly in her memoirs: "For during the twenty years after this period of which I am speaking [1535], I did not find a master, I mean a confessor, who understood me, even though I looked for one."

She had observed upon arriving that she neither knew how to chant—so much for that!—nor how to properly follow the religious services. She could not see where it all led, and her pride prevented her from asking for assistance. Nor did she really know how to pray properly, how to collect her thoughts, how to enter into the prayer of quiet, or how to concentrate on what was essential: Jesus, the Son of the living God. "I never dared to begin prayer without a book. For my soul was as fearful of being without it during prayer as it would have been should it have had to battle with a lot of people." The expression is clear. It is a question of distractions, inopportune thoughts that assail the spirit and are in opposition to necessary concentration on the life of Christ and to the trusting abandonment in God the Father that allows a person to start out on the royal way of mental prayer, which is a veritable dialogue of love. "[The book was like] a shield by which to sustain the blows of my many thoughts." Her heart was not in it.

How does one enter into the self after having cracked the shell of habit and torn off the mask? This type of spiritual exercise was not practiced at the Incarnation or in any other monastery that followed a mitigated Rule. Prayer of recollection and quiet was unknown in any of them, allowing for exceptions. The Rule required only to "meditate day and night the law of the Lord," a vague formula that avoided questioning oneself about oneself. The Divine Office was recited, Mass was attended, the mind often occupied by a thousand distractions. Vocal prayer was practiced in common. Admittedly, it was an effective aid, but it did not exempt anyone from personal prayer, which favors an intimate union, allowing a person to shake off the weight of the daily grind. Already, at the Augustinian convent, Teresa had not recognized herself in this type of conventional piety in which she felt locked up and especially limited.

Thus did she find herself caught in the trap. The "point of honor" forbade her to leave. But her body rebelled. She collapsed.

Her father was frightened. Then, in agreement with mother prioress, he took it upon himself to remove Teresa, since the doctors of Ávila who had been sent to her side could find no remedy for her ills, nor could they undo all the knots within that made her a prisoner of herself without any hope of deliverance. She had believed that her decision, her determination, could sweep it all away. Given her imperious and generous nature, she had wanted to achieve everything, right away and by herself. A spiritual director could have understood her and come to her aid. But she had not yet found one. Later she would discover, little by little, that decisiveness, reason, and determination cannot be based upon pride alone, that point of honor which reduced her to herself, but upon trust and on the love of God, upon abandoning oneself to his mercy. He alone can accomplish everything in us and with us.

CHAPTER 6

The Becedas "Cure"

(1537–1540)

During that winter of 1537–1538, the doctors, incapable of curing her, recommended sending Teresa to Becedas, a tiny, remote Castilia village in the Bejas Mountain. There, nearly forty miles from Ávila, a reputed woman healer was working wonders with plant-based treatments. They hoped the change of air, freedom, and a richer diet would do the rest.

Teresa received permission to leave the Carmel without difficulty since the mitigated Rule did not impose the vow of stability nor perpetual enclosure. She would keep her Carmelite habit, and Sister Juana Suárez would chaperone her.

Since her treatment would begin in the spring, her father decided to send her in the meantime to recover with her half-sister María at Castellanos de la Cañada. As she had done in 1535, Teresa stopped in Hortigosa at her uncle Don Pedro Sánchez de Cepeda's house on her way there.

This dear old mystic had not changed. Delighted to see once again the niece who had read to him, he questioned her at length regarding her weak spells. In his opinion, the cure could only be a spiritual one. He exclaimed: "I have what you need!"

Opening a bookcase, he took out a worn volume and handed it to her. Teresa smiled. Books had always been her passion. Unfortunately, she had not found any at the Incarnation, at least none that could have enlightened or impassioned her. This large monastery did not have a library worthy of the name, and the sisters rich enough to own books kept them for themselves. She read the title: *The Third Spiritual Alphabet* by Father Francisco de Osuna of the Friars Minor, Toledo, 1527.[1]

"What is it about?"

"It is a treatise on the prayer of quiet."

Teresa's heart began to pound harder. "Prayer?"

"Yes, the prayer of recollection. This spiritual primer is my preferred reading. The author insists on the need to make one's mind a blank in order to leave the space to God alone."

"At this moment, my mind *is* a blank. It is a desert!"

"Risk entering this desert, beyond language and ready-made ideas, in loving simplicity and trust. God likes this place outside of time. There, forget your woes."

"'Loving trust,' you said?"

"Love opens the door to contemplation. And this personal relationship to God gives access to the interior. It enlightens, inhabits, and supports it."

Teresa remained pensive. The *interior journey!* The contradiction of these two words struck her. But beyond the apparent contradiction, she guessed the essential: another mode of prayer, and another world, a spiritual one, where love and fervor reigned. During her novitiate, she had experienced it: the touch of the Divine Being. Had she not already been invited to the interior journey that she would later describe as the only adventure that deserved to be lived? But then it had been only an aroma that she had not been able to seize. She had, however, remained nostalgic about such a state, which is the humble form of desire—a mysterious desire that came from her childhood.

That night, by candlelight, she opened the book and read:

"In the prayer of quiet, the highest level of our soul rises toward God in the purest and most affectionate manner on the wings of *desire*, sustained by love."

She was engulfed by an immense joy. It was a revelation for her. No, she was not getting all worked up about it. She had read the accounts of the martyrs, but never treatises on *mysticism* that revealed these *mysteries*. Until then, religion for her had been something exterior intended to protect a person, like those massive ramparts of Ávila, a reasonable practice wherein one did not really become engaged except to respect morality. For the rest—the essential, the personal relationship to God!—one trusted the Church, its theologians and its saints. But to enter into God's intimacy! And not just any divinity. This personal God had a history, a face, a name: Jesus, the God-sent Messiah to lead us to the Father, the One from whom one awaits the truth that delivers. Was it possible to give oneself to him without an intermediary?

In a flash, she understood through infused knowledge that God loved her, that he was present in her, that he lived in her. And from then on, nothing would be like it had been before. She now had to take risks, enter into the very core of her own silence, move forward unafraid in this inhabited solitude. On that day, Teresa entered into the first dwelling of the castle of the soul. Everything remained to be done, but she sensed in herself an unlimited courage; she was strong in him who could do all things in her. She aspired, as do all true mystics, to union with the divine Spirit in the very depths of her heart so that perhaps one day he and she would form but one spirit.

Throughout the deep and silent night, she immersed herself in her reading. "And so I was very happy with this book and resolved to follow that path with all my strength."[2]

When she parted from her uncle, she handed him the book with regret.

"Keep it," he said to her. "I know it by heart."

SETTLED IN FOR THREE MONTHS at her half-sister María's, Teresa had all the leisure she needed to plunge into the book. Friar Osuna's method in the *Spiritual Alphabet* was a simple one. It addressed itself neither to reason nor to the intelligence, but to the heart. It developed the art of a personal, entirely affective prayer that can be summarized thus:

"To pray is to think of Jesus while loving Him." This treatise on mysticism is preceded by maxims presented in alphabetical order, from which the title *Alphabet* derives. A method of recollection practiced by the *Recogidos* (the contemplatives)—a tiny, fervent spiritual group—inspired the author. One first shuts oneself off from the social whirl and outside noises to the extent of "rendering oneself blind, deaf, and mute"—in short, making one's mind a blank. The person attempts to think of nothing, to flee distractions (parasitic mental images) with the aim of concentrating on God alone with love, the cutting edge of one's conscience.

This religious movement, inherited from Francis of Assisi, harks back to the German-Flemish mystics Eckhart and Ruysbroeck and anticipates Fénelon and Madame Guyon in France: "The search for a wholly interior God through unknown ways, outside any formula, any hierarchy, the vertiginous ecstasies of the *Alumbrados* of Granada: discovering Jesus just through the transport of the soul."[3]

This kind of prayer did not resemble what Teresa had been taught during her novitiate. The prayer of quiet is a personal one, different from the community prayer of the hours of the Office, not in opposition but complementary to it. The Rule of St. Albert stated: "Ponder the Lord's law day and night and keep watch at prayer." This left great freedom. In the novitiate,

Teresa had been prescribed to "meditate upon her sins and the mysteries of the passion." Now, she would write, "For God didn't give me talent for discursive thought or for a profitable use of the imagination."[4]

In the prayer of quiet, God manifests himself in the very depths of one's being (the heart); he gives himself over to be loved here and now, no longer in a future paradise that opposes the eternal hell that is the obsessive fear of anguished minds. Reason and understanding have nothing to do with it. It suffices to abandon oneself to this love, to this visage, that of Jesus. This strength is all a person could wish for; it carries one away, powerful and tender at one and the same time. Prayer of recollection is going to God with an affective disposition, giving him one's heart while forgetting the logical linkage of thoughts. Then "God manifests Himself in the intimacy of that heart, communicating to it the awareness of His presence and giving Himself to be loved. Our entire will finds itself absorbed in Him and, as though inebriated, seized by an ineffable force."[5]

For Teresa, badly weaned from family and human affections, it was a revelation. A door opened in her to an interior kingdom where, even from here below, a person can enjoy a personal God by loving him after having given oneself up to him in a disinterested manner.

Filled with wonder, she did not tire of reading and rereading Osuna, who writes:

> The Lord comes to meet us with open arms, with a more joyous and more tender contentment than that of a mother who receives her child when he comes to her seeking consolation for his grief. She opens her arms and not only embraces him, but uncovers her breast and nourishes him with her milk, and then she brings her face to his; then do tears and anguish disappear.

This young woman, who had been so ardent in the past, was dying of dryness like a plant without water. Remaining outside herself, she was depriving herself of a treasure. And, filled with wonder, she received her first favors. "The Lord...began to favor me by means of this path; so much so that He granted me the prayer of quiet. And sometimes I arrived at union, although I did not understand what the one was or the other," she would write in Chapter 4 of her *Life*.

She then discovered that this strange phenomenon had positive and lasting effects; the love of God acts in the soul to incite an ardent desire for perfection. Teresa, who had read neither Plato nor Aristotle, was discovering that contemplation of God, the necessary Existing One, is an invitation to perfection and a method of accessing the ways of sanctity. In addition, it gives support for physical sufferings, even making a lever of them. Sickness does not prevent the love of God; it is sufficient to want to accomplish his will, to identify one's own will with his.

Another discovery: the *Spiritual Alphabet* taught Teresa how to really examine her conscience. This examination was no longer the superficial one that guides too many hurried confessions, but a genuine in-depth psychological investigation to liberate hidden memories.

Thanks to this purification, would she now finally be able to fulfill her desire for the Absolute and see her contemplative vocation reinforced? Having entered into the prayer of quiet, having been touched by the Spirit, she advanced with utter trust toward the second dwelling: "I tried as hard as I could to keep Jesus Christ, our God and our Lord, present within me."[6]

Alas! "This union lasted for so short a time that I do not know if it continued for the space of a Hail Mary." No matter! The experience was there—irrefutable. And "I was left with some effects so great that...it seems I trampled the world underfoot."[7]

Spring was at hand. Leaving her sister, Teresa went to the village of Becedas, as expected, to begin her treatment. She could not foresee what awaited her there!

IN THIS ISOLATED VILLAGE surrounded by arid hills with low-roofed houses huddled up against the church, there was but a single priest, the pastor, Pedro Hernández. This young man had difficulty enduring ecclesiastical celibacy. Knowing that he was in a state of mortal sin, having lived with a woman of the village for seven years, he continued, nonetheless, to celebrate Mass and to hear confessions. Everyone in Becedas knew about this affair and had more or less come to terms with the situation. Teresa, overwhelmed by her mystical experience, was in need of a confessor. She had not been informed of the turpitude of the pastor's lifestyle, so she went to see him. Aroused by his attractive penitent, the priest fell in love with the nun, whose holy habit and Carmelite companion—supposed to protect her—were unable to defend her against him. She herself was not insensible. "The devil began to upset my soul,"[8] she writes.

Teresa, who did not say everything, could have remained silent about this meeting. Instead, she writes about it at length in her autobiography without beating about the bush. She first describes the seducer as "a cleric of excellent intelligence and social status.... He was learned, although not greatly so." "...[I]t happened that he became extremely fond of me.... His

affection for me was not bad; but since it was too great, it came to no good."
She did not worry too much about this because "he had learned from me
that I was determined not to do anything grave against God for any reason,
and he also assured me of the same...."

She was naïve enough to believe him. Immersed in the *Spiritual Alphabet*,
she was experimenting with the prayer of quiet, which put her in states near-
ing ecstasy. Quite naturally, she shared this with her strange confessor, who
was astonished to see so young a nun already intoxicated with God. Did he
experience some remorse?

Reversing roles, he admitted to her "his bad moral state." "This was no
small matter, because for about seven years he had been living in a dangerous state on account of his affection and dealings with a woman in the same
place."

Was he sincere, or did he hope that he could attract and then seduce
Teresa by gaining her sympathy? Whatever his motivation, Teresa was scandalized and dismayed. Yet such a situation was not unusual in a Church that
required of its priests the heroism of celibacy. Not imagining a trap, Teresa
attacked first things first: that is, how to rescue this pastor from hell. She
made use of her own seductive powers, responding to the priest's amorous
fervor with what she termed compassion, "for I loved him deeply." A seemingly dangerous move for so inexperienced a young woman of twenty-three,
but she was sure of herself.

Twenty-four years later, writing her *Life*, she waxed indignant: "I was so
frivolous and blind that it seemed to me a virtue to be grateful and loyal to
anyone who loved me. Damned be such loyalty that goes against the law of
God!" She should have broken off the relationship, but she did not do so.
Touched by the love that this man was expressing for her, she was determined to save him in spite of himself. Between the lines, it is possible to discern the risky game she played: "I never thought that the great affection he
bore me was wrong, although it could have been more pure. But there were
also occasions on which, if we had not remained very much in God's presence, there would have been more serious offenses."

Making inquiries in the village, Teresa learned from the God-fearing gossips of the parish that the woman who had seduced the pastor was a sorceress who kept him bewitched, using a "charm" that she had given him and
that he wore around his neck. It was "a little copper idol," a talisman or
amulet like those loved by the humble folk of the countryside. As to the
spell, Teresa did not really believe in it, but can one ever be sure? She con-
cluded that "the poor man was not so much at fault" since he was under its

influence. As to the woman and those like her, "they will stop at nothing so as to hold on to this friendship and passion the devil has placed in them."

This affair had aroused Teresa's curiosity, but she was playing with fire by becoming involved in saving "the poor man." Not only did she not have the wisdom to flee him, but to arrive at her goal, she "began to show him more love."

But Teresa was well aware of what she was doing. She spoke to him only about God! Gradually, for the sake of the affection he bore her, she asked him to give her the charm. He could not refuse. She threw it into the river.

Immediately, a miracle took place: "grieving over his bad moral state...he stopped seeing [the woman] entirely, and he never tired of thanking God for having given him light," before giving up his soul to God, dying prematurely a year later.

Teresa, whose purity of intention cannot be doubted, had won in spite of the folly of her imprudence and the risks she had taken. Won, thanks to God. For, she states: "[I] remained very much in God's presence." She had been the instrument of salvation for this priest. "He died a very good death and completely detached from that occasion," she writes. "I am certain that he is on the path of salvation."

AFTER THIS FEARSOME TEST, Teresa continued her treatment, which was based upon plants that were prescribed by an experienced and reputable healer and that could not cause her any harm. Nonetheless, her health continued to deteriorate.

> Sometimes it seemed that sharp teeth were biting into me, so much so that it was feared I had rabies. With the continuous fever and the great lack of strength (for because of nausea I wasn't able to eat anything, only drink), I was so shriveled and wasted away...that my nerves began to shrink causing such unbearable pains that I found no rest either by day or by night.

She also states, "My tongue [was] bitten to pieces...." All these symptoms strongly resemble those of a psychosomatic sickness brought on by an accumulation of conflicts.

In a complete spiral of depression, she was letting herself die. Alarmed, her father brought her back to Ávila in an extreme state of thinness, and doctors gave up hope for her.

On August 15, she asked for a confessor. Frightened by the idea of death, *her father stalled for time.* During the night, Teresa lost consciousness. She then received the last rites, but too late: she had already sunk into a coma. The doctors declared her dead. At the Incarnation, her grave was dug at the cemetery, and two Carmelites came to her father's house to claim her body. Her Carmelite brethren chanted the Office of the Dead.

Only Don Alonso still hoped against all hope. But after four days had passed, he deferred to the evidence: his beloved daughter was dead! According to custom, wax was poured on the eyelids, shut forever.

She was about to be buried when she woke up, quite astonished at being alive. Frantically sitting up in her bed, she cried out: "I asked for a confessor!"

After this statement, having finally been delivered of what was crushing her, she received Communion and seemed to liberate herself "with many tears...for the mistake I made."

What offense could she have been referring to if not what had happened at Becedas?

She then began to recount, in short phrases interspersed with sobs, what she had seen in her lethargic sleep: paradise, but hell also. And the reason she had been sent back to earth: she had a *mission to accomplish.* Her listeners were able to make out the words: "monasteries, foundations, the saving of souls." finally, she cried out: "Do not believe me to be dead until my body is covered by a *cloth of gold!*"

A mysterious phrase to which we shall return.

To the doctors, she seemed to be totally delirious. She then fell back on her bed. Not freed in the least, she continued to suffer:

[O]nly the Lord can know the unbearable torments I suffered...all shriveled and drawn together in a ball.... I was unable to stir, not an arm or a foot, neither hand nor head, unable to move as though I were dead.... Since there was no way of touching me, because I was so bruised that I couldn't endure it, they moved me about in a sheet, one of the nuns at one end and another at the other.[9]

Teresa remained in this state for seven months. Then, although there was no noticeable improvement in her condition, she insisted on being brought back to her monastery. That was her real home; it was there that she wanted to die.

TERESA EMERGED FROM THE NIGHT in which she was sinking. Her trial was not over, however. For three years, she remained more or less paralyzed, "totally resigned to the will of God," she writes. Sustained by her divine model, Christ crucified, she would purify her being like fire purifies gold ore in the crucible. Practicing mental prayer intensely, she anchored divine life in her heart. Realizing the fragile nature of her earthly existence, she saw, acting in her, the power of the Spirit, stronger than death. She drew the conviction from this that "to have life is to live in such a way that there is no fear of death or of any of life's happenings."[10]

But she was little more than a shadow of herself, thin and paralyzed. Of her radiant beauty only her brilliant gaze, her flashing black eyes, remained.

The infirmary at the Incarnation became a visiting room where the ladies of Ávila as much as her sisters in religion crowded to see her. Her patience and her incomprehensible joy filled them with wonder. "...[T]hey were amazed at the patience the Lord gave me. For if this patience had not come from the hand of His Majesty, it seemed it would have been impossible to suffer so much with so great contentment."[11]

She would always remember those terrible years. Writing one day to Father Diego de Yanguas, she stated, "Does there exist a human body which has suffered as much as mine?"

At last she rose from her bed. Sometimes she could be seen dragging herself on hands and knees in the cloister, praising God. But she was not totally resigned; in her prayers she would cry out: "My God, I would serve you much better if I were well!"[12]

Tired of being bedridden, and especially of being dependent upon others, she asked St. Joseph, whose devotion was beginning to spread in Spain, to heal her. "*Señor y padre mio* has never refused me anything," she would say. And at last, she recovered her health! A miracle! "[St. Joseph] brought it about that I could rise and walk and not be crippled...raised [me] up body and soul so that all who saw me were amazed to see me alive!"[13] She was also saved by the Christ whose love called to her and by her exceptional vitality. Contrary to Thérèse of Lisieux and Elizabeth of the Trinity, she had conquered death, "the fabulous vertigo which attracted her, allowing herself to be dissolved in the blinding suffering of Christ on the cross." "Standing up to the desire for God in order to live it and not drown in it."[14] She was cured, at least relatively speaking, for until her death her body would remain "an arsenal of ailments."

What would she now do with her life? After returning from the abyss, had she not spoken of a mission she had been sent back to accomplish?

CHAPTER 7

ʾorn ʾBetween the ʾWorld and God

(1541–1554)

*J*n the parlor or visiting room, Teresa found noblemen and beautiful ladies of Ávila—as well as all those well-read *lettrados* of whom she would later say: "I always liked educated persons"—eager to see and hear her.

The miracle of her recovery had made her fashionable. Christian Murciaux has painted this picture of her:

> This beautiful and knowledgeable cloistered nun had retained on the other side of the grille the social graces and refinements of the world. She held forth about salvation and the passions, about love as well as renunciation. Vivacity and felicitous liberty of expression. She needed only to talk in order to persuade.[1]

Alternating between irony and feminine gentleness in her exchanges, she possessed the art of intermingling the day-to-day of this earth with the eternal. Yes, she was a delight in this whirlwind of worldly vanities. But she also exercised a positive influence on some of those in distress who came to consult her. She was training for what she would later be: an incomparable directress of consciences.

However, a Carmelite nun does not have a confessor's vocation and even less so that of a preacher. Her role was not to speak of God to the world, but to speak to God about the world. Regarding her vocation, Teresa was thus falling into a bad habit. In the beginning, she had received these visits with a certain embarrassment, then she had taken more and more pleasure in them. Mother prioress found no fault in the visits, for the people in question were important persons and benefactors of the poor monastery. A grille separated the visitors from the nun. But nothing could stop the words. The parlor well deserved its name: *locutorio* ("speak room")! In spite of the grille and sometimes the prescribed presence of a third religious, not only did they talk, but they chattered, and the visitors did not hesitate to pass some pastries and other sweets through the grille. Since her profession Teresa had also had at her disposal a small apartment where she could receive the ladies and her Carmelite friends. A patio in the shape of a corridor opened out to the cloister of the ground floor. Beside it was her private oratory; above it were the large cell where she slept and a small kitchen.

What is the balance between courtesy toward visitors and the slide toward seduction, which she exerted in spite of herself through her innate charm? She did nothing that was prohibited, and that was the whole problem of this mitigated-Rule monastery that was not a school of perfection but just barely one of honorable wisdom without heroism. Moreover, as she would later write, "so much vigilance seemed to me to be impossible."

All those who knew Teresa portray her at the age of twenty-seven as *seductive* with something more—depth—brought to her by Carmel, but especially by her suffering, sickness, and contact with death. Don Antonio Aguiar describes her way of speaking as "very gracious, her conversation both soft and serious, as if emanating from her heart, glowing with such a gentle fire that it melted without burning them the hearts of those who approached her. It was as though she held in her hands the tiller which turns hearts around."

Marcelle Auclair, without granting any concession, describes her thus: "She was too well-liked, she who cared so much about being loved. Her gaiety was enchanting, her loyalty reassuring."[2]

It was impossible not to like her. She was a good religious, virtuous, and she avoided malicious gossip, that usual distraction of idle persons. Her weak point lay in vanity, which seems surprising in a soul of such quality. But she herself said: "In my craftiness I strove to be held in high esteem, although I did not advertently feign Christianity."[3] Even in the convent, she remained a woman who desired to please. Moreover, she would never change; she would use her ability to please to get her way with certain bishops, general superiors, and confessors. "I used to be very fond of being liked."[4] "She had within her an irresistible need to please, a need for affection," emphasizes Father Emmanuel Renault, a Discalced Carmelite and Teresian scholar. As a matter of fact, she constantly made use of her charm in the parlor.

What would be a trivial tendency in a person of the world handicapped one whose secret ideals were to be swallowed up in God's presence in solitude and to aim at perfection.

Of course, God was also a subject of conversation at the Incarnation parlor. Methods of prayer—Osuna's and Laredo's, as well as the merits of fashionable preachers—were compared. Then, imperceptibly, secular topics would enter. How could these be avoided? Six of Teresa's brothers were fighting in America. There wasn't a single family in Ávila without either a son, a father, or a brother combating the Turks, the French, or the Native Americans.

From mundane but serious topics, the conversation turned to more pleasant ones, such as the arts and literature. Teresa stated in her writings that the Incarnation was a rather good monastery in spite of the laxity of the Rule. Yet the *galanteo de monjas* (courting of religious) was tolerated in this Carmel. It was permitted for a nobleman to court a nun in the parlor and pass to her, through the grille or by the turn sister, short letters and poems. Even her father no longer recognized his daughter in this "laughing, prattling" nun "distracted from God."[5]

This slackening of fervor on her part, which lasted for thirteen years, can be attributed to a kind of revenge of life over the death she had come so close to experiencing. The structure of this overcrowded monastery with its mitigated Rule lent itself to this type of deviation from austerity. "They gave me as much and even more freedom than they gave to the older ones."

She would later judge herself without indulgence: "I saw very clearly...that these (virtuous things and my taste for them) were failing me because I was failing you." "I grieved very much over being held in esteem since I knew what was down deep in my heart."

The Carmelite priest, Jean Abiven, who has subtly analyzed Teresa's interior struggles, has observed: "If she judges herself harshly, it is because she perceives in a bright light the existence in herself of a dynamic of evil whose development would have led her to her perdition."[6] "I thus began to go from pastime to pastime, from vanity to vanity, from one occasion to another, to place myself so often in very serious occasions, and to allow my soul to become spoiled by many vanities.... And I was aided in this vanity by the fact that as the sins increased I began to lose joy in virtuous things and my taste for them."

And what had to happen did happen. Abandoning herself to her irresistible need to please and to be loved, she fell in love with one of the noblemen who had become enamored of her: "I engaged in these conversations

thinking that since this was the custom, my soul would not receive the harm
and distraction I afterward understood comes from such companionship."

The nobleman's name was Francisco de Guzmán. He was a member of
a noble Castilian family and related to the husband of Teresa's half-sister.
Initially, Teresa determined that she could not refuse to receive him. At first
they spoke about the family, then about war, and before long their conversations finally became more intimate. Teresa would later admit that she felt
"the deepest affection" for this man.

She had such a need for affection! Her brothers and her cousins were in
America, while she had initiated her father so well in the practice of the
prayer of quiet, she hardly saw him anymore. Distressed at seeing her lose
herself in the midst of all these garrulous visitors, he had been making fewer
and fewer visits to the Incarnation.

As she had done with the priest in Becedas, Teresa took more and more
wayward pleasure with Don Francisco. It is difficult today to believe in this
idyll, but it was the custom of the times, a kind of detour of the apostolate.
One received visitors to help "save souls" not of *suitors* but *devout persons*.
"And no one was astonished at seeing that the pretty ones attracted more
than the ugly ones to that devotion."[7]

However, only twenty years later Teresa would severely judge these
"friendships and attachments that the devil arranges in monasteries," quali-
fying these meetings in the parlor as "pestilential recreations." She ingenu-
ously underlines the fact that she would never have taken "the liberty to do
something without permission, such as giving messages through holes in the
walls, or at night," an admission suggesting that this was possible in a
Carmel under a mitigated Rule at the time.

She may have exaggerated. Regarding what she would call her "great
sins," the judges at her process of canonization would later conclude in her
favor, and Pope Urban VIII would describe them as "holy exaggerations of
her humility." The real danger for her lay elsewhere: falling short of her vocation for sanctity.

Although at the Incarnation no one cautioned Teresa except an older
nun, "a great servant of God and very religious," the warnings from above
were very precise. While she was at the parlor in the company of her gallant
companion,

> [w]ith great severity, Christ appeared before me, making me understand
> what He regretted about the friendship.... And this vision left such an
> impression on me that, though more than twenty-six years have gone by, it
> seems to me it is still present. I was left very frightened and disturbed....

She decided to sever the relationship. But the devil made her doubt her vision. "It did me much harm not to know that it was possible to see in other ways than with the bodily eyes." As Don Francisco insisted on seeing her again, and as she took pleasure in this, she again accepted to receive him, thinking that she "had fancied the vision...."

In the parlor, she received another warning:

> Once at another time, when with this same person, we saw coming toward us...something that looked like a large toad, moving much more quickly than toads usually do. In that part where it came from I cannot understand how there could have been a nasty little creature like that in the middle of the day, nor had there ever been one there before.

Taking fright, she stopped seeing Don Francisco.

Her spirit had been led astray by what she would later call "futility and vanity," and she was little by little moving away from the prayer of quiet that had been her happiness and her joy. "I was then ashamed to return to the search for God by means of a friendship as special as is that found in the intimate exchange of prayer." She was losing her fervor, contenting herself with the obligatory vocal prayers at the community's recitation of the Office.

While this back and forth between heaven and earth is surprising, it is also a sign of human freedom. One senses that Teresa was very much a woman and very fragile. Her startling reactions would later lead one of her biographers, a Carmelite sister, to state, using the words of St. Gregory on Job, that "this grand lady proved herself to be sublime even in her sins."[8]

Much, much later, Teresa would understand the difficulties of spiritual life and the reason why a young nun takes more pleasure in conversing with a gallant *hidalgo* than with an old confessor. And what was the influence of the devil, that character omnipresent in the mentality of the time?

Ah, the devil! During those thirteen years of laxity, Teresa would often find herself tempted, even persecuted by him. He appeared to her under a horrible shape, and she believed that she heard his voice menacing her. Sometimes, he attacked and tormented her directly. She attempted to escape from this nauseous infestation, banging her head and arms against the walls of her cell, and when he withdrew he left behind sulfurous odors. Hallucination? Imagination?

Under these conditions, how could she avoid returning to the question of salvation? Having entered Carmel to escape hell, was she not already damned? Earthly joys were becoming odious to her. "Neither did I enjoy God nor did I find happiness in the world."[9] But then what was she doing in this monastery? She reached the point of doubting her religious vocation.

She had been mistaken, and now it was too late; the "point of honor" prevented her from returning to the world to make a life for herself while she was still young. She continued, nonetheless, to participate in the Divine Office and all those rites, but her heart was no longer in it.

In her moments of lucidity, when the desire for the All-Encompassing Other won out over worldly vanities and sensual desire, Teresa tried to pray in depth and return to mental prayer. "Prayer is the door to favors as great as those He granted me. If this door is closed, I don't know how He will grant them."[10] In vain she resorted to her memories. "It seemed to me that in this life there could be no greater good than the practice of prayer." Not to only chant in the choir and recite psalms or pious formulas, but to simply abandon oneself, opening one's heart and allowing oneself to be overcome by Love.

But she could achieve nothing. Opening a door is not enough to gain access to the interior kingdom where the divine takes on substance, where Jesus expects presence and resemblance from us. It also requires a strong human will, a constantly renewed desire, and humility bordering on self-effacement, up to the death of one's being. But it would take Teresa twenty years to understand that.

"It seems I desired to harmonize these two contrarieties—so inimical to one another—such as are the spiritual life and sensory joys, pleasures, and pastimes."

We form self-aggrandizing images of ourselves. For this reason, we dread confrontation with the divine truth that lives in us. Teresa was refusing the metamorphosis.

However, thanks to certain divine favors and the last warning from Christ, she already had a foretaste of her future state.

How could she emerge from the mental confusion that was preventing her from taking wing, "from taking the path which opens onto the Word which liberates, while remaining in the lie which divides us in two?"[11] and from escaping "the satisfaction of our own will which leads to the vain delight in ourselves"[12]—all of this conceited exaltation that she derived from the parlor visits? She received no support at all from her ordinary confessors, who saw only venial sins in this custom. But Teresa could not be satisfied with their absolution. Later, she would be scandalized by the broad freedom she was given by her confessors, who "gave...a great pretext for...pastimes and satisfactions by saying that these were licit." And she would deplore that "so little help was found anywhere, except in God."[13]

But God himself was withdrawing! She now had to force herself to pray in her little oratory. "I was doing a great deal by being able to keep up with the choir duties." "It seemed to me that...it was better to go the way of the many, to recite what I was obligated to vocally and not to practice mental prayer and so much intimacy with God." And yet at the parlor, she continued to extol the benefits of this type of prayer that eluded her.

The death of her father on December 26, 1543, plunged Teresa into a state of desperation. "When I saw him coming to the end of his life, it seemed my soul was being wrenched from me, for I loved him dearly." He was her last friend—my "every good and joy." Teresa highlighed the sanctity of his death: "He looked like an angel. This it seems to me he was, so to speak, in soul and character, for he preserved his soul very well." She, who had passionately initiated him in mental prayer, gauged how much he must have suffered to see her abandon it.

On the human level, he left only debts. He had run through his enormous patrimony almost entirely to maintain his lifestyle as a *hidalgo* and especially to endow his daughters and arm his sons—almost all of whom would fight in the distant lands of the New World—as knights. Don Alonso de Cepeda was buried at the convent of San Francisco near the Incarnation.

This death gave Teresa the opportunity to meet at length with the Dominican Vicente Barrón, her father's confessor. Even today in the old Dominican monastery of Ávila, people visit San Tomás el Real, the chapel of Christ in agony, where this inscription can be read on a door: *Aquí se confesaba santa Teresa* (Here St. Teresa went to confession). At that time, Teresa did not leave the monastery for confession, and only mitigated Carmelites were admitted there as confessors. Her meeting with Father Barrón, a reform-minded Dominican, was a decisive one.

He listened attentively to her confession and observed that she did not attempt to exonerate herself.[14] Indulgent toward her, he understood her distress. Admittedly, it was from a sense of loyalty that she had renounced mental prayer, feeling that she was unworthy of the exceptional favors that the Lord was bestowing upon her. But this alienation deprived her of assistance and of that hope of at last fully responding to her mystical vocation.

"Jesus came to earth for the weak, the sinners. Do not refuse this hand and this heart he is holding out to you."

He ordered her to take up prayer once again and to receive Communion every two weeks. She attempted to resist: "In prayer, I understand more clearly my faults."

"That is exactly why you must take it up again and cling to it."

She accepted, but not without hesitation. "I began to return to it, although not to give up the occasions of sin.... On the one hand God was calling me; on the other hand I was following the world." She was a prisoner of these "betrayals, in which I always do evil and strive to undo the favors You've granted me."[15] Although she had renounced human love, she did not yet totally adhere to divine love—a situation fraught with every possible danger.

Three years after the death of her father, yet another tragedy plunged her once again into mourning. Her brother Antonio, who had been compelled to leave the Dominicans because of poor health, had been massacred in Peru. Antonio had gone to join his brothers in the fratricidal combat of Añaquito between the regular soldiers of the viceroy Vasco Nuñez Vela (also killed), on whose side Teresa's brothers had fought, and the partisan rebels of Gonzalo Pizarro, brother of the conquistador who massacred the Incas. A short time later, Francisco Nuñez Vela, Vasco's brother and Teresa's godfather, was also killed.[16]

WHAT WAS TERESA LIKE at thirty years of age?

As beautiful as always, torn between God and the world, she sensed that her youth was escaping her before she had been given the chance to live in her woman's body. She had lived deprived of love and natural childbirths without having truly entered into spiritual maternity, without having borne fruit.

At the parlor, she made the most of what she called "sensual pastimes" while simultaneously feeling herself to be called by God and gratified by him with mystical favors. This contradiction led her to write: "With wonderful gifts You punished my sins!" She aspired, however, to perfection, which she unconsciously knew she could achieve through mental prayer.

The years were passing between the world and God—years of "ingratitude and mischief," she would state. Father Barrón had gone, leaving her alone spiritually. She sought in vain to find around her "persons who practiced prayer" to support her in her passionate quest of the Absolute. She found only that "in falling I had many friends to help me; but in rising I found myself so alone...." And this prayer arose from her heart torn to pieces: "Help my stupidity."

The deaths of her father and her brother Antonio brutally obliged her to resituate herself, alone, faced with herself, confronted with the current of life, which goes by so quickly. She had to plunge into it without hesitation, to live it, to advance into deep waters and no longer float on the surface, to enter, at all costs, into the prayer of quiet, that is, into perfection.

CHAPTER 8

She Finally Gives Herself to Love without Reservation

(1554)

During the twenty-five years Teresa had spent at the Incarnation, the desire for God that had been placed in her when she was a child did not cease to secretly torment her. That achieving this desire took twenty years cannot possibly surprise those who believe in the freedom of God's children.

Desire was working in her like a grain of wheat buried in the earth. In that year 1554, at the Incarnation, she was searching for the face of him whom she desired obscurely. He would reveal to her her own face, who she was deep down, since humanity has been created in God's image. "Become what you are!" Unconsciously, she was addressing herself to the unknown God, "to Him who knows that I desire Him because He is Himself at the heart of this desire."[1]

"I understood clearly that I was in captivity, but I wasn't able to understand why...."[2] Then something happened. Entering the monastery's oratory, Teresa noticed the statue of a "much wounded Christ" that had just been placed there in preparation for a ceremony. Her heart was carried away. She approached. The man was still bound; he had just undergone the ordeal of the whip. His body was covered with blood, and suffering contorted his face; it was an infinite wretchedness. *Ecce Homo!*

> ...[B]eholding it I was utterly distressed in seeing Him that way, for it well represented what He suffered for us. I felt so keenly aware of how poorly I thanked Him for those wounds that, it seems to me, my heart broke. Beseeching Him to strengthen me once and for all that I might not offend

66

Him, I threw myself down before Him with the greatest outpouring of tears.[3]

In an instant, Teresa had gone from fear—the fear of death and hell that had poisoned her youth—to love. Lifting her face bathed in tears, she contemplated her Savior. She believed that she saw that pained face become animated, and she gave herself unreservedly to Love. "...I then said that I would not rise from there until He granted what I was begging Him for. I believe certainly this was beneficial to me, because from that time I went on improving."[4]

Returning to her cell transformed by the change taking effect, Teresa resumed the prayer of quiet, that intimate prayer that had brought her so much after she had discovered Osuna's *Spiritual Alphabet* seventeen years earlier. "I strove to picture Christ within me.... It seemed to me that being alone and afflicted, as a person in need, He had to accept me."[5]

She immediately felt herself welcomed. "A feeling of the presence of God would come upon me unexpectedly so that I could in no way doubt He was within me or I totally immersed in Him."[6] She then remembered with intensity the repentant sinner Mary Magdalene bathing the feet of Jesus with her tears, "welcoming his message and rendering him the homage of a listening heart,"[7] "...thinking that He would not despise my tears...."[8] She loved and admired this woman who had known how to abandon herself to him in whom she had recognized the very source of life. Teresa would take her as a role model.

In that same year, 1554, "by chance" someone presented Teresa with the *Confessions of St. Augustine*, which had just been translated at Salamanca. She recognized herself in Augustine's writings. She was immediately struck by these words, and she underlined the passage in which the saint addresses himself to Christ: "And behold, Thou wert within and I was without. I was looking for Thee out there.... Thou wert with me, yet I was not with Thee.... Thou didst touch me, and I was inflamed with desire for Thy peace." And Teresa's prayer rose with that of St. Augustine: "Give me, Lord, what You command, and command what You desire."

She then continued her reading:

When I came to the passage where he speaks about his conversion and read how he heard that voice in the garden,[9] it only seemed to me, according to what I felt in my heart, that it was I the Lord called. I remained for a long time totally dissolved in tears and feeling within myself utter distress and weariness.... The inclination to spend more time with Him began to grow.... His Majesty began to favor me again.[10]

She had crossed the invisible barrier that separated her from her God, and she felt that he was very close by. At last, she could pray as one talks to a friend, express the total gift of herself, offer the Absolute her spirit, emptied of all else and at his disposal, as well as her loving heart.

> This is another, new book from here on—I mean another, new life...the one God lived in me.... May the Lord be praised who freed me from myself.[11]

Yes, for Teresa everything was beginning with God's irruption in her life. It was no longer just the touches of the Divine Being that had already filled her with happiness, but a deeper, more stable state, a real and enduring proximity. She forgot the time of her first vows, when the motivation for living at the Carmel came not from love but from a servile fear and an egotistical desire "to achieve one's salvation." Love was taking the place of fear and at last ensuring her vocation as a contemplative religious, which is a vocation to give oneself unconditionally to Love.

BUT LET US RETURN TO INTERIOR, personal prayer, which would occupy such a large place in her life and open up to her the royal road of spiritual marriage. "Silent prayer is not a constraining affair, like a very narrow mold," emphasizes Father Abiven. "To enter into mental prayer, there must be two."[12] This type of prayer is speaking to God.

It is impossible to imagine God. Teresa would then enter into this mystery with Christ: "I saw that He was man, even though He was God.... I can speak with Him as with a friend, even though He is Lord."[13] And it is not necessary to be immersed in prayer in the choir or the oratory. This "intimate sharing between friends"[14] can prolong itself, even in the kitchen. "The important thing is not to think much but to love much,"[15] she stated.

In her prayer, she no longer imposed any method on herself. At first fixated on a given reading, she ended up detached from this practice. "In the presence of the Lord, it is sufficient to look at Him." And to listen to him. Concretely, it means to imagine a given scene of Christ's life and thereby enter into his humanity with all one's heart, to initiate meditation on precise episodes, for otherwise the imagination risks creating pipe dreams.

Such is that prayer of quiet that Teresa would later refine in *The Way of Perfection*—"a concentrated and solitary meditation which, little by little, by recreating in us the desire for Christ's existence on earth, makes Him familiar to us." It is also like "a sounding line thrown into the thick layers of the soul's mystery."[16]

Teresa would enter into the life of Jesus who, in amorous response, would then penetrate her spirit. She had often meditated in front of paintings, images, and statues without success except for the "much wounded Christ," which made her rediscover the way to mental prayer, whose secret lay in the presence of Christ resurrected in the deepest part of her being. She did not see him (not yet), but she sensed him at her side. She wrote: "I was like one who is blind or in darkness; he speaks with a person and sees that that person is with him because he knows with certainty that he is there (I mean he understands and believes he is there, but does not see him)."[17]

Why this type of prayer? "Mental prayer...is nothing else than an intimate sharing between friends; it means taking time frequently to be alone with Him who we know loves us."[18] Within it, we receive the light, which is "at our disposal for the sake of keeping the law of God with perfection."[19] Without this solid foundation, Teresa would later add in *The Way of Perfection*, the entire spiritual edifice rests on erroneous premises, be it in monastic life or in the world.

BUT SHE NEEDED TO ANSWER this love by a more radical separation from the world, and she only half succeeded in this. "Although in this matter of desires I have always had great ones, I strove...both to practice prayer and to live for my own pleasure."[20]

Nonetheless, she attempted to avoid the occasions to dissipate herself, no longer answering the call of the turn sister that used to make her heart beat: *"Doña Teresa is wanted at the parlor!"* "I started to shun the occasions of sin, because when they were avoided I then returned to loving His Majesty."[21] From these ineffable visits, she emerged "much improved and strengthened."

Unfortunately, she remained fragile, not only unable to master herself, but also unable to understand the mystical phenomena that rose up in her. Having come to Carmel to suffer and merit paradise, she was embarrassed to feel so much happiness with these favors. In *The Life*, she writes about the *pleasures* of the prayer of quiet that were "neither entirely spiritual nor entirely of the senses,"[22] and that "the sweetness and the delight are incomparably greater than that experienced in the previous prayer." Is it permissible to die "to all earthly things" and to experience an "enjoyment of God"?[23]

This apparent contradiction introduced a doubt in her mind. Were these feelings the fruits of her imagination, illusions, hallucinations? Then she doubted God himself: "Since at that time other women had fallen into serious illusions and deceptions caused by the devil, I began to be afraid. I experienced wonderful delight and sweetness and often without being able to avoid it...."[24]

At that time, fear of the devil was omnipresent. People saw him everywhere, even in the mystical phenomena of the purest. The Church shared and encouraged this obsessive fear of falling into the devil's traps. And Carmel was not shielded from this—quite the contrary! These societies of often unsatisfied virgins constituted a privileged place for the devil! To make one of them believe that God was favoring her was to make her lose her humility and to make her fall, bit by bit, into the sin of pride! The risk was real. Teresa would later write:

> You will hear some persons frequently making objections: "there are dangers"; "so-and-so went astray by such means"... "it's not for women, for they will be susceptible to illusions"; "it's better they stick to their sewing"; "they don't need these delicacies"; "the Our Father and the Hail Mary are sufficient."[25]

All convents in Spain still trembled from the enormous scandal that had shaken the country in 1546. Magdalena de la Cruz, the former Claretian abbess of Cordoba, had confessed to the court of the Inquisition that her sanctity, her ecstasies, and her miracles were feigned—not the results of a spiritual marriage but of a pact with the devil! She had been the most venerated prophet of the kingdom. Her prophesies seemed so infallible that the empress, the princes, the bishops, the pope, and even the Inquisitor General, Don Alonso Manrique, consulted her. The Holy Office quickly settled the affair. She avoided being burned at the stake by publicly making amends in the cathedral of Cordoba before being locked away for life in the monastery of Andujar.

Teresa attempted to reassure herself by invoking that voice within her: "Serve me, and don't bother about such things."[26] She knew that "these gifts were bestowed on persons who were already very advanced and mortified."[27] But, only half reassured, she wanted to ask for counsel.

Father Barrón, as already noted, had left Ávila. She did not dare to broach the subject with the ordinary confessors of the Incarnation, mitigated Carmelites who were allergic and even hostile to mysticism. Instead, Teresa decided to address herself to a relative, a family friend renowned for his piety and wisdom, Don Francisco de Salcedo, whom she calls "this blessed and holy man."[28] Shaped by Dominican theology, this layman was considered to be "the most authoritative mind in Ávila."

However, she did not dare to reveal her ecstasies to him, and her sharings with him remained in the realm of generalities that presented the facts in a false light. After listening to her, he remained perplexed, and then he sought out a reputed preacher of Ávila, Gaspar Daza. But this zealous and austere priest distrusted religious women mystics who were not content with their regular confessor. He refused to hear her confession.

"Since you are practicing the prayer of quiet, why worry about little imperfections?"

"I am perhaps very advanced in divine favors, but I am an absolute novice as to virtues."

Disconcerted, Master Daza shook his head and, pretending to have urgent occupations, left her abruptly. "He began with a holy determination to guide me as though I were a strong person—for by rights I should have been so because of the prayer he observed I was experiencing...."[29]

Evidently Master Daza was shocked by the parlor scene at the Incarnation. This monastery did not inspire his trust at all.

Once again opening up to her friend Salcedo, Teresa then admitted her ecstasies, a secret that she had not yet dared to confide to anyone. This time, the "holy gentleman" took fright. How could such a dissipated nun enjoy such divine favors?

"They are reserved to very advanced and mortified persons, which is not your case."

"What do you conclude from this?"

"I cannot help but be very fearful."

"But what then?"

"It seems to me that certain things could be the work of the devil."

This worried her. "What must I do?"

"Examine all the particularities of your prayer and give me an account in writing."

"But I am incapable of doing so!"

Since he insisted, she agreed to write up at least a brief account of her life. She gave it to him, not suspecting that this work, this effort, had laid the first stone of an immense literary and spiritual *oeuvre*. Then, despairing at being misunderstood, she buried herself in books.

Reading the *Ascent of Mount Sion*, which the Franciscan mystic Bernardino de Laredo had published in 1535, gave her courage once again. In his book, the author studies mental emptiness, intellectual vacuity—a state that, according to him, is necessary to leave all room to God. However, when the prayer of quiet introduces one to another state of consciousness, a person loses his or her footing with regard to earthly, tangible realities. Is there not danger here? Could not the devil take advantage of this to worm his way in? Laredo answered:

> This absence of thought [loss of ordinary consciousness] introduces one into a vast world [the unconscious?] which contains all that is [God], with the result that in his presence, the rest is nothing. Of the all-quiet soul occupied with God, in a union of love in contemplation, one can say that it should think of nothing, for in this absence of thought the soul possesses what is essential to all thought.

These were prophetic words that left Teresa unsatisfied. And what could be said about ecstasy, in which persons are snatched out of themselves and absorbed in God?

Meanwhile, after having closely examined the account of her life, Don Salcedo and Master Daza, whom Teresa later called an "easily offended semi-theologian," had met to rule on her case. They were not adherents of Laredo's spirituality; to them, his treatise, published in Seville, seemed to be suspect of heresy. After thoroughly discussing the situation, the two men decided it would be a good idea for Teresa to refer the matter to the Jesuits.

THE JESUITS, A NEW ORDER founded in 1540 by Ignatius of Loyola (1491–1556) and named the Society of Jesus, spearhead of the pope in the Counter-Reformation, already enjoyed a great reputation. Very much imbued with an interior life, the Jesuits differed from traditional active religious. Regular clergy dedicated to the apostolate, living in community, they were not obliged to recite the Divine Office in common and did not wear a monastic habit. Learned educators, they were also considered to be good confessors, although the Dominicans were still viewed as the guarantors of Church doctrine. But newer and more modern, the Jesuits were fashionable. In a letter to her brother Lorenzo after he returned from America, Teresa wrote:

> In my previous letters I forgot to tell you about the good facilities Ávila has for the education of children. The Jesuits have a school where they teach grammar and hear the confessions of the students once a week and make their students so virtuous that it is something to praise God for. The students also learn philosophy and afterward for their theology go to Santo Tomás. There is no reason to go elsewhere for studies and training in virtue....[30]

Don Salcedo was on excellent terms with the Jesuits of Ávila, who were established in the upper part of the city at the former St. Giles Hospital, which they had converted into a college. Their rector, Dionisio Álvarez, was a stern theologian. Salcedo advised Teresa to request that one of the Jesuits visit her after she had written out a general confession setting forth the state of her soul and the divine favors she believed were being bestowed upon her. Then everything could be understood more clearly.

In ordinary confession, a priest tries to discern the obstacles preventing one's desire for God from developing and bearing fruit. He also attempts to recognize true sin, sometimes disguised behind the avowal of a venial compromise with one's conscience.

In the sixteenth century, general confession was similar to the kind of psychoanalysis practiced today, with the spiritual dimension added (which is indeed important!). It was a question of going back as far as possible in the conscious and unconscious memories of the mind to oust the camouflages, undo the barriers, and cause the naked truth to be drawn from the well.

This prospect did not appeal to Teresa. She sensed that she was about to put everything at stake and risk losing her way in the process. The Jesuits were reputed to go to the bottom of things. What would they flush out in her? What would be raised from her passionate youth that had caused her so much difficulty as she tried to rid herself of it? And in this whirlwind, what would become of the pure jewel of contemplation that she had caught a glimpse of in mental prayer and that was such a fragile treasure?

She was also afraid of being told by a theologian that this powerful and tender force working in her was not Christ but the devil, the prince of evil acting to damn her by making her believe that she was not an ordinary nun. Nonetheless, she requested the interview and awaited it in a state of anguish while trying her best to write out her general confession in "as clear an account of my life as I knew how to give, without leaving anything out."[31]

"Doña Teresa to the parlor!"

Finally, there he was! So young! Diego de Cetina, who had only just been ordained, was no more than twenty-five years old. But from their first meeting, Teresa felt herself suffused by the spirit of God. In Cetina's soft and blazing look, her mystical soul recognized a soul friend, and she welcomed in him the one sent by God. We will never know what this general confession through the grille consisted of, for Teresa destroyed the written text. In *The Life*, she confines herself to stating: "I spoke with that servant of God...all about my soul."[32] On the other hand, she reports the reaction of the young priest: "The spirit of God is evidently acting in you."

Deliverance, happiness, joy inundated Teresa's heart. She felt herself being invited to go forward according to her loving, enthusiastic, audacious nature. The priest added: "You must take up the prayer of quiet again, but on a more solid footing. You would be very culpable if you did not respond to the favors God is granting you. Perhaps he wants to make use of you for the good of a great number of souls."

She remained puzzled. "He said other things (for it seems he prophesied what the Lord afterward did with me)."

He also said to her:

> As our Master, Brother Ignatius, teaches us, meditate each day on a partic-
> ular aspect of the passion to derive benefit from it. Concentrate upon the
> humanity of Christ. One cannot reach God without passing through the
> humanity of Jesus, the universal Mediator. That is where true humility lies.
> The results are extraordinary.

She caught her breath, remembering her revelation before the statue of the "much wounded Christ." She asked: "What must one think of divine favors?"

"Resist as much as you can these mystical comforts that gratify your feel-ings. Refrain from exaltation and illuminism. Remain in your place, the last one."

LATER TERESA WOULD UNDERSTAND the wisdom of these warnings: "It is very good for a soul that hasn't gone beyond this point to refrain from striv-ing to ascend further."[33] Contemplation cannot be forced. It is given. "Since this edifice is built entirely on humility, the closer one comes to God, the more progress there must be in this virtue; and if there is no progress in humility, everything is going to be ruined."[34] It would be prideful to want to rise higher than ourselves. And Teresa would add, "Whoever would desire to pass beyond this point and raise the spirit up to an experience of spiritu-al consolations that are not given would lose both the one and the other, in my opinion."[35] Everything takes place in small touches: "The Lord puts what He wants the soul to know very deep within it, and there He makes...known without image or explicit words, but in the manner of this vision we mentioned...great truths and mysteries."[36]

This is the way Diego de Cetina must have spoken to her. He also taught her to be on guard against her fears. She had not forgotten to ask him: "How does one distinguish between what comes from God and what might come from the devil?"

"With God, the soul receives a light that is incomparably more intense and that penetrates it with a stupefaction that reduces it to nothingness. From thence comes the desire for humility and not pride. It is then impossible to doubt the presence of God."

He added, however: "Every consolation is not safe from illusions. Mortify yourself!"

She looked at him with astonishment. "...[I]t doesn't seem to me I even understood the word."[37]

He smiled and added: "But don't be in any hurry. No excessive zeal! Allow yourself to be led by the path of love of Christ. I am not leaving you with any other instruction. You have every liberty to act without any other obligation than that which love will inspire you."[38]

SHE RETURNED TO HER CELL, her heart filled with joy, like a fiancée going to the spouse who awaits her. She was uplifted to the very depths of her being by the young Jesuit's injunction, "dwell only on the humanity"[39] of Christ, confirming what she had already received, which was most precious: "I saw that He was man, even though He was God"[40]

And suddenly everything became clear to her. Under the influence of a rapid reading of certain spiritual masters like Laredo, she had experienced the temptation to practice mental prayer without images in a kind of mental void in the Oriental manner: "Mimic through one's own effort that suspension of psychic activity that God grants in supernatural prayers."[41]

From this viewpoint, Christic meditation was put aside to attain God, an abstract God without a corporal representation. Had not Jesus himself said: "It is much better for you that I go" (Jn 16)? In fact, a person risks conjuring up a personal God based upon private phantasms. Teresa would remember this when she wrote *The Way of Perfection*: "...the soul cannot reach [the most perfect contemplation] by itself, since the work is an entirely supernatural one that the Lord effects in the soul.... We are not angels."[42]

Understanding the warning of Diego de Cetina, Teresa placed herself at the feet of Jesus in his most deeply moving humanity. In turn, she became the Samaritan woman, Veronica, and especially Mary Magdalene. She would reiterate: "I saw that He was man, even though He was God." And thanks to him, she had access to the Father through the Spirit.

She had already had, and she would again have, contacts with Christ. Like all visionaries, she cried out: "Master, who are you?" And like the apostle, she dared to ask: "Where do you dwell?" Now she knew. He dwelled with the Father in the deepest part of her heart, and she would do all in her power to keep them there. "I began to make many changes, although my confessor didn't press me.... And this urged me more because he guided my soul by stressing the love of God and allowed [me] freedom and used no pressure if I didn't set about doing things out of love."[43]

However, one of Father de Cetina's counsels worried her. He had spoken of mortifications. Was he alluding to those parlor visits that had deprived Teresa of the benefits of mental prayer as taught by Osuna? She reduced the number of visits to what seemed to be the lowest possible level. Wanting to identify with the sufferings of Christ, Teresa, who had already suffered so much, also mortified herself harshly to vanquish her body. She wore a hair shirt made of iron, spread thorns and nettles on her bed to keep herself awake, and scourged herself to the point of spattering the wall with her blood.

But was this really the solution to her conflict between the flesh and the spirit, between the world and God? She aspired to find her equilibrium between dryness and fervor, which can lead to those two extremes of spirituality, the night of the soul and mystical exaltation. "The love of God," she would wisely write later on, "does not consist of tears or in this delight and tenderness, which for the greater part we desire and find consolation in; but it consists in serving with justice and fortitude of soul and in humility."[44] With hidden regret, she emphasized that ecstasy is not the human vocation here below: "We are not angels.... To desire to be like angels while we are on earth...is foolishness."[45]

But in 1554, everything in her aspired to this sacred madness that would lead her to the highest summits of mystical life.

GUIDED BY FATHER DE CETINA, she happily took up mental prayer once again, and this intimate prayer fulfilled all her wishes. No doubt he initiated her in the *Spiritual Exercises* of St. Ignatius, which are an invitation to contemplate the mysteries of Christ in his sacred humanity, his incarnation. But this time, she entered mental prayer with the wisdom of an informed nun. With constancy, humility, and perhaps not without an ulterior motive of secretly soliciting the Lord—"*if it is You, I am bound to end up being sure of it*"—she went to great lengths to follow Father de Centina's advice. She strove to resist the perceptible manifestations of the prayer of union that sometimes follow the prayer of quiet: those great "delights" and other favors from God. Although they made her happy, they still remained suspect in the mind of the Church—and thus to ordinary confessors—as if, when it is a question of God, it is more prudent and certain to suffer in imitation of the Crucified than to rejoice with the Resurrected One!

Notwithstanding all this, the "favors" continued to manifest themselves. And even more so, as if the Absolute wanted to reward her for her renunciation and her humility. She understood then that these favors did not depend upon her but came from the sole will of God. "When it comes, I say that we neither act nor do anything...."[46] The more she resisted what she called "the delights" of God, the more was she enthralled by him. Not only an experience confined to her Incarnation oratory, rapture could surprise her elsewhere: in her work, at various occupations, and, naturally, at chapel during the hours of the Office.

This worried Father de Cetina, who continued to visit her at the Incarnation. It crossed his mind that he should have scruples. Was his first intuition regarding Teresa correct? In these mystical affairs, one can never be too prudent. That is why in May 1554, when the Jesuit college of Ávila received the visit of the apostolic visitator, Father de Cetina unburdened himself of too heavy a weight by speaking with him.

This individual, arriving from Tordecillas where he had spoken with Queen Joan, bore a famous name in Christendom: Borgia. He was the most eminent Jesuit of the Society of Jesus. Extraordinary meeting! Teresa was decidedly favored by God. Son of the Duke of Gandia and Joanna of Aragón, great-grandson of Pope Alexander VI, this brilliant nobleman had been the Master of the Horse of Empress Isabella and the close friend of her husband, Charles V, who had named him viceroy of Catalonia. It was said that upon seeing the decomposed body of Empress Isabella, Francisco Borgia had vowed never again to serve a mortal being. Renouncing his titles and his fortune shortly after the death of his wife, he had entered the Jesuits in 1548. Teresa would later say: "He was advancing in the favors and gifts of God."[47] The former Duke of Gandia, who had refused a cardinal's red hat, fulfilled important functions in the new Society of Jesus. Ignatius of Loyola had named him Apostolic Commissioner of the Society for Spain and America.[48]

Naturally, Father de Cetina had first spoken at length about Teresa to his rector, who had decided to have her meet the holy former duke when he came through Ávila.

Borgia was immediately dazzled by this impassioned Carmelite. She confided in him without any embarrassment whatsoever, hiding nothing from him about the secrets of her interior life. These two persons, familiar with supernatural states, conversed at length about divine favors. Then the former viceroy exclaimed: "It is truly the spirit of God that drives you! Do not resist any longer the attractions of divine grace. Allow yourself to be transported by His Majesty and rejoice in him since he wants to rejoice in you."

CHAPTER 9

Voices in the Night

(1555–1558)

At forty, an age when a sixteenth-century woman had reached her hoped-for lifespan, Teresa once again found her child's heart. Instead of locking herself away within her failures, her twenty years of hesitations, she opened herself freely to the Mystery that would make a new woman of her, open to the beyond, thanks to the prayer of quiet:

> All this that takes place here brings with it the greatest consolation and with so little labor that prayer does not tire one...for the soul is now ascending above its misery and receiving a little knowledge of the delights of glory.... His Majesty is beginning to communicate Himself to this soul.... It sees clearly that one moment of the enjoyment of glory cannot be experienced here below, neither are there riches, or sovereignties, or honors, or delights that are able to provide a brief moment of that happiness ...that...satisfies us.... It seems it [the soul] has found everything at once and doesn't know what it has found.[1]

What was this miracle?

Teresa's conversion began with an act of faith in God's call and a thirst for God. Then suddenly light permeated her with the presence of Christ. She recognized him who watched within her, and the secret desire that she had for him finally coincided with the divine will to give of itself. Discovering that she had been loved even before loving, she allowed her joy to shine forth and in a boundless movement of love gave herself to him who was awaiting her.

But without this direct mediation of Christ, Teresa might have failed in her search for truth. That is why she passionately attached herself to him.

From that moment on, she asked herself a new question: What was the meaning of this irruption? What was God's will for her, a miniscule particle of creation whom he had given a vocation for the infinite? St. John has said: "God is love." This being the case, "to love God is to want as love wants. Allowing our will to organize itself according to a request for love replaces our spirit on the trajectory of unconscious desire."[2] And this reconciles us with ourselves, all the while converting us to what already exists within us.

How does one achieve harmony with love? Through humility, faith, and reason. We must humbly ask God to realize in us what he wants, which faith tells us is true life, the purpose for which we are created. Reason tells us that absurdity leads to nothing and that life has meaning. To conform ourselves to the Creator's plan for us, a plan revealed by Christ, is a reasonable wager. We risk nothing in risking this since the other choice leads only to nothingness.[3]

In the second dwelling of *The Interior Castle*, Teresa would invite her sisters to risk the wager:

> The whole aim of any person who is beginning prayer...should be that he work and prepare himself with determination and every possible effort to bring his will into conformity with God's will.... The greatest perfection attainable along the spiritual path lies in this conformity.

Then, as St. Paul says, we shall judge the result according to the fruits. What are the fruits of love? If pleasure and joy coincide with desire, illumination takes place, and we become our true and eternal selves.

Some residual vanities, and sometimes pride, remain. Teresa would invite her sisters to "strive to do what lies in our power and guard ourselves against these poisonous little reptiles, for the Lord often desires that dryness and bad thoughts afflict and pursue us without our being able to get rid of them, and trust in the mercy of God."[4] This often takes place in suffering, and no one is spared from the night of the spirit. Suffering is necessary for the spirit to divest itself of its own will, to deify itself. ("You will be like gods," Satan said to Eve.) At Golgotha, Jesus sacrificed himself so that the spirit of God could triumph in him.

That is why, at the start of her conversion in 1555, Teresa still felt very dependent upon a spiritual director who could understand and guide her without restraining her impulses. When Father Diego de Cetina was transferred to Salamanca that same year, she felt helpless: "I thought I would return to my wretchedness...my soul was...very disconsolate and fearful."[5]

One day, her prioress asked her to accompany a young boarder at the Incarnation on a visit to her mother's house. The mother of the boarder,

Doña Guiomar de Ulloa, who belonged to a great family of Ávila, had just lost her husband, Don Francisco Dávila, Lord of Villatoro. Before the visit, Teresa had already noticed Doña Guiomar at St. Giles, the Jesuit church near her palace. Teresa had been struck by her youth—she was twenty-five— her beauty, her piety, and her humility.

Doña Guiomar invited Teresa to stay with her for a short time. Teresa accepted with pleasure, not for the comfort she would find there, but for the silence and the solitude, which, more than at the Incarnation, would allow her to devote herself to mental prayer. A great friendship immediately united the two women, and we shall shortly see the important role that Doña Guiomar would play in the Teresian Reform.

The Carmelite not only found silence and peace in this palace, but she also met an excellent confessor in the young widow's director. At only twenty-eight years old, Father Juan de Prádanos was the vice rector of St. Giles, the Jesuit college in Ávila. As his colleague Cetina had done, he encouraged Teresa to pursue the prayer of quiet. He did not insist on bodily mortifications, but he urged her to restrict her parlor visits—Teresa's weak point. Thinking of an intense friendship, she resisted: "I do not offend God there, and I also would not know how to break off certain friendships without seeming ungrateful."

"Reflect on this problem. For a Carmelite there can be no sharing between God and the world. He wants you all to himself."

"HE TOLD ME TO COMMEND the matter to God for some days and to recite the *Veni Creator* so that God might give me light about the best course of action."[6]

Teresa obeyed. A few days later, after a long period of mental prayer, the answer was given to her with a precision that stunned her:

> One day, having spent a long time in prayer and begging the Lord to help me please Him in all things, I began the hymn; while saying it, a rapture came upon me so suddenly that it almost carried me out of myself.... I heard these words: "*No longer do I want you to converse with men, but with angels.*"

In her account, Teresa insists:

> It was something I could not doubt, because it was very obvious. It was the first time the Lord granted me this favor of rapture.... This experience terrified me because the movement of the soul was powerful and these words were spoken to me deep within [my] spirit.... From that day on I was

very courageous in abandoning all for God, as one who had wanted from
that moment...to change completely.[7]

Regarding this ecstasy, Teresa speaks of a "first time" and "something
new." She had experienced other ecstasies: the divine touch, the prayer of
quiet, the prayer of union. As she would explain later in *The Interior Castle,*
this ecstasy was different, a higher level of a mystical state than she had experienced before.

This heightenend state had visible effects; while previously she could not
bring herself to break off a certain friendship (among others), suddenly she
found it amazingly easy to free herself of it. This filled her with wonder: "...in
an instant He gave me the freedom that I with all the efforts of many years
could not attain by myself."[8]

She thus found herself detached from useless friendships. Breaking with
the vanities of the world and its sometimes dangerous distractions, she
intended from then on to place human relations at the service of her action
for God. For she did not advocate a closing off of an eremitic type: "I would
counsel those who practice prayer to seek, at least in the beginning, friendship and association with other persons having the same interest."[9] Like
Doña Guiomar.

But let us return for an instant to the subject of that *ecstasy,* that rapture,
that abduction, the marvelous fruit of mental prayer. She explains it all at
length for the first time in Chapter 20 of *The Life*: "the difference there is
between *union* and *rapture* or, as they call it, elevation or flight of the spirit,
or transport...it is also called *ecstasy.*"

Although Teresa does not make it clear, as she would later, it seems that
this first great ecstasy had provoked in her both a physical and a mental
upheaval that must have worried her sisters:

> The Lord gathers up the soul...in the way the clouds gather up the earthly
> vapors and raises it completely out of itself. The cloud ascends to heaven
> and brings the soul along, and begins to show it the things of the kingdom
> that He prepared for it.... In these raptures it seems that the soul is not ani-
> mating the body. Thus there is a very strong feeling that the natural bodi-
> ly heat is failing it. The body gradually grows cold, although this happens
> with the greatest ease and delight.[10]

In mental prayer, ecstasy is not in the least inevitable. It is even the
exception. The person praying is usually like a swimmer who advances on
the surface. He or she bathes in the water but still belongs to the world of
the atmosphere. In ecstasy, he or she suddenly plummets as though drawn
under by the depths. The person should suffocate. But, taken over by the

abyssal entity calling out to him or her, the person survives, for a limited time, perhaps, but long enough to discover the supernatural realities underlying the world.

Teresa invents nothing; she only records the phenomena. In ecstasy, "there is no remedy that can be used to resist,"[11] she wrote. A person in ecstasy is seized in the inmost depths of his or her being, all psychic activity is suspended, and the person loses awareness of both self and surroundings. It is not like a fainting spell or a coma, a physical blackout. It is a mysterious phenomenon of a religious nature that occurs abruptly, unexpectedly, and anywhere.

As to the voices (the phenomenon of locution), they do not proceed from vibrations affecting the eardrums. They are directly perceived by the conscious. Where do they come from? They occur when the person does not expect them and therefore cannot be the result of autosuggestion. Besides, the answers one hears are not always those one expects. In addition, "they at once carry out what they signify."[12] Often when she was in a state of anguish, Teresa would hear: *"Do not fear."* And she would immediately feel appeased and confident. The fruits of the unconscious never act in this manner. On the contrary, according to Freud, the unconscious expresses repressed anguish; in attempting to deliver itself from this anguish, the unconscious provokes a release in which repressed emotions come to the field of consciousness—always a painful phenomenon.

Teresa's new ecstasy was an essential turning point in her life. This *rapture*, which left her so taken aback at the time, did not come by chance; God granted this to allow her to detach herself from the last bonds detaining her in the world. Then she could give herself entirely to Love, to the Christ who had answered her prayer.

IN THE FEW YEARS THAT FOLLOWED, Teresa, with the kindly agreement of her prioress, would make long sojourns at Doña Guiomar's. It was said that Doña Guiomar had transformed her palace into a convent. There, Teresa met Mother María Diaz, a quite remarkable *beata*. Doña Guiomar venerated and lodged this woman called "the saint of Ávila," and her hospitality to a person of such humble birth caused great scandal among the house staff and the aristocrats of Ávila. Shut away in a room, dressed like a very poor wretch, Mother María Diaz fasted and mortified herself, praying constantly. Sometimes she would discreetly complain of the dryness of her soul: "Lord! After having stripped me of everything, is this the way you leave me?"

She set an example before Teresa, who was astonished by this problem of the night of the soul. Teresa asked her: "Do you not desire, as I do, to die in order to enjoy Christ?"

"Here below, I have something better to do: suffer through Christ."

But Teresa had no desire to suffer for the sake of suffering. Her only ambition was to love and to do the will of the God of love. María Diaz constantly surprised Teresa, for she experienced neither ecstasy nor other divine favors, a reassurance to theologians who were scandalized by the idea that a woman, albeit a saint, could take pleasure in Christ! But why not? Teresa would dare to write, "The Lord sometimes desires, as I say, that the body enjoy [the experience of ecstasy] since the body is now obedient to what the soul desires."[13]

AFTER RETURNING TO THE INCARNATION, Teresa had some difficulty settling into the routine of the monastery, so much was her soul aflame for something else. Her ecstasy had given her an acuteness of discernment difficult to support for most of these religious women, who were scandalized or frightened by her raptures and penances. Already, the Reform was secretly maturing in her: "the world [is intolerant] of faults in the good, forcing them to be perfect through its criticisms.... Seeing the soul begin, the world wants it to be perfect."[14]

At the monastery, all those who saw that they were targets because of their lukewarm and relaxed lifestyles felt threatened. Teresa was disturbing. Was she going too far in her radical detachment? No more worldly parlor visits! Her words could not have been harsher: "I have never again been able to tie myself to any friendship or to find consolation in or bear particular love for any other persons...nor does it matter whether they are friends or relatives.... It is a painful cross for me to deal with [them]." In such situations she felt like a person sold into slavery.

It should be repeated that she was not seeking the solitude of a hermit, for she adds, "[unless] the persons seek to love and serve God or to speak about prayer...."[15] In her *Spiritual Testimonies,* she underscores the fact that "I feel as though I am among strangers, except when I am with those to whom I speak about prayer and the soul, for with these persons I am happy and consoled."[16]

In those transition years of 1555 to 1558, she was seeking her God, who had already found her.

Outside of religious services and periods of meditation, how did she occupy herself during the long hours of the day? She kept both feet on the ground. She sat before her spinning wheel or she sewed and darned. Impelled by her devotion for holy cleanliness—quite rare in her day—she hunted down dust in every little nook as though she wanted to sweep from her life everything that still tarnished it. She put together bouquets to decorate the altar, bouquets that were always different according to the feast days and the liturgical period and that resembled her, alive and fragile at the same time. In her large cell, she also received the sisters who wished to spend a moment with her to relax, confide in her, or speak of God.

But especially when night came, pressed to do so by her confessors, she wrote in the great silence, disturbed only by the distant roar of waters. For the sake of obedience—though she would later take pleasure in doing so—she related the story of her tormented life, attempting to clarify her states of conscience. At times she was tortured by this, for she found it repugnant to reveal herself in this way, to bare her soul. Her writing, her will to see herself clearly, to analyze herself, to be precise about nuances, helped to build her up. She was stronger for having lived through these experiences, though the shock of them still remained with her. These analyses of her interior life are so clear and profound that they still remain true for those who seek God. And she went forward, refining her thinking, more and more certain of the presence of Jesus in her, of the Christ for whom she lived.

Naturally, this art of writing was not given to her all at once. As a realist, she despaired of defining union "without making it sound like Greek."[17] But she was a born observer of psychological states, at that time a quality that was not only unfashionable, but was also becoming suspect. Even in her ecstasies she remained an objective observer, refusing to passively abandon herself to celestial favors and other raptures of the spirit.

She experienced the sensation of advancing into unknown territory bordered by dangerous precipices! The interior adventure is not without risks, for no one knows where it leads and if it leads. Why these strange manifestations—such as the catatonic state that she called "a sleep of the faculties"?[18] And why these nights of the spirit? For she, like María Diaz, would also experience the dryness that sometimes followed her ecstasies and in which "the soul is crucified since no consolation comes to it from heaven...nor does it desire any from earth.... Receiving no help from either side, it is as though crucified between heaven and earth."[19]

To meditate upon each scene from the life of Christ and to attempt to insert oneself in it entails taking significant risks. A life entirely given over to God leads to Calvary. It would be too easy to be content with imitating St. John and to rest on Christ's heart like a gratified lover. Jesus called Teresa to the most secret level of his spirit, where burns the anguish of the Mount of Olives, the suffering of Golgotha, and the ultimate question: *"Father, why have you abandoned me?"* Contemplating the adorable face of her humiliated God, she wiped the sweat and the tears of blood from his visage. He asks only for a bit of love, but she wanted to give herself totally.

Her wish was granted. She was now in the dark night herself. A mortal sadness had taken hold of her. Interior prayer was no longer of any use. Her soul shriveled up from dryness. She could no longer pray. She now awaited as a deliverance the shrill sound of the small bell that announced the end of meditation, which only the day before had been for her a pure instant of happiness.

Like a swarm of large black flies, a multitude of parasitic thoughts swooped down upon her spirit, solicited her attention, and troubled her. They made it impossible for her to achieve the concentration necessary for meditation and deep interior prayer. She who had fled from the world found herself chained to it once again in the most humiliating manner. Faced with this assault, any attempt aimed at mastering meditation seemed useless.

Where was Christ? "Where are you, my love and my God?" She could no longer see in the black darkness. There he was, up there, suspended from his cross, agonizing. *"Why have you abandoned me?"* What can his spirit do in a body ground down by suffering and facing death?

Suffering? In her flight forward, Teresa hurled herself into it. Suffering, "the most rapid beast that can take us to God," whispered a Flemish mystic to her. Clutching the neck of this insane horse, she tore along. She asked for suffering in order to identify herself with the Crucified One, and it was given to her. "I determined to pay no attention to the body or to my health.... Lord, either to die or to suffer,"[20] she writes. Is this not the extreme manner of proving to the one you love that you still have something to give him when you thought you had given him everything? This pathetic body, this dust!

Teresa was spared nothing. Fever, nausea, headaches no longer left her. She emerged from these symptoms as from a bad dream, her spirit distraught. She seemed to be hearing in the shadows something like a snicker. Yes, she had forgotten *the villain deprived of love* whose screeching and rage still poisoned the happiness of the elect. "It seemed," she wrote, "the devils were playing ball with my soul."[21]

The devils! That was exactly where her detractors, disturbed in their habits, awaited her. But, anchored in faith, she was advancing step by step, knowing that she was the docile instrument of God. She, a weak woman? "Others were women, and they have done heroic things for love of you."[22]

SHE WOULD NEED HEROISM. It is difficult for us today to imagine sixteenth-century Spain. The majority of the population felt a burning faith. Rich and poor understood that another world would follow their earthly sojourn. But watch out! If many were called to paradise, few were chosen. Christ had denounced the rich; fortunately, they could redeem themselves through their good works. An ingenious system of sharing corrected the social inequalities a little—very little. The Church had arranged all that, and the organization of *indulgences,* which scandalized the Reformed, was flourishing.

The condemnation of the repentant prophetess, Magdalena de la Cruz, had barely dampened popular belief. Everywhere in Spain, faith merged with the marvelous, which should not come as a surprise, since by his very essence God is *marvelous* ("that which stimulates admiration"). Teresa of Ávila's ecstasies should be studied in their specific context. It was customary in churches—and elsewhere—to see some of the faithful publicly accusing themselves of their sins, bursting into tears, flogging themselves in processions, and kissing the ground or crawling along on their knees while imploring the Lord's mercy. Displays of emotion such as raptures in front of a statue or a painting were a usual occurrence, not an exception. The faith of these people was deep and alive; it expressed itself outwardly, and it sometimes exploded. And Someone answered. Rejecting the religious formalism of a petrified dogma, some persons went forward toward a unifying mysticism. The movement of illuminism affecting the people dated back to the beginning of the sixteenth century in Spain with the *Alumbrados* (the Illuminated). People strove for spiritual perfection through interior illumination. God gives himself to be loved by manifesting himself in the deepest regions of the heart. Personal prayer (*oraison*) was practiced, and although this movement was admittedly based upon the Gospels and the Catholic masters, it granted decisive importance to affectivity.

To the question: "Why?" Father Abiven answers:

These prophetic graces called charisms are intended for use by people of faith. God [has persons] experience in a quasi-experimental manner, and with extraordinary intensity, the realities of the faith lived by the average faithful person in obscurity or in a minor psychological mode. The witness, burned and burning, tells us: "These realities are not an illusion. I have actually touched them personally."[23]

The Church approved this burning religiosity on the condition that the Church could keep it within bounds. The *Alumbrados* advocated the free examination of Scripture and its accessibility in the language of the people. Why restrict the sacred text only to clerics who could read Greek and Latin?

At that time, two religious currents could be distinguished from one another. The *Recogidos* (the contemplatives) advocated rules to obtain interior peace and master mental prayer, and the Church encouraged this reasonable devotion. On the other hand, the *Alumbrados*, also called *Dejados* (the abandoned), required total renunciation in God, the crushing of the ego, and the refusal of activity. They were seeking extraordinary states of prayer. Because of their excesses, they cut themselves off from the Church, a reasonable institution that seeks to reconcile the spiritual and the temporal.

The Church had its work cut out for it! The world was exploding, coming apart at its old seams. In the 1550s, Rome's great worry was not so much the *Alumbrados* as their antithesis. The Protestant Reformation, which the Council of Trent was attempting to check, was sweeping over northern Europe. To combat the heresies, the Holy See, which was trying hard to restore discipline in the Church, had instituted the Inquisition tribunal, active in Spain since 1484. The Inquisition tribunal's power and prestige, and the fear it inspired, did not stem only from the spiritual sanction of excommunication (deprival of the sacraments) but also from the physical means it employed. The tribunal used retaliatory measures, including death, that were put in place by the executive royal power and closely associated with the spiritual power of the Roman Holy See.

Thanks to a ruthless repression, the Protestant Reformation never took hold in Spain. For lack of a clash of swords with the Protestants, the tribunals of the Holy Office fell back upon the *Alumbrados*. Feeling itself overwhelmed, the Church of Spain sought to retake control of the people and keep the too highly emotional manifestations of love of God in check. Since it would have been illusory to employ rational arguments, the Inquisition used the threat of demonic menace. "The devil was seen everywhere that the Lord was believed to have been seen."[24] *Alumbrados* and *Dejados* became as suspect as the followers of Lutheranism. Trials grew in number, sometimes followed by *auto-da-fés*, namely, burnings at the stake. The heretics, dressed in the ignominious yellow tunics of the repented, wearing ridiculous pointed hats, and holding candles, were seen marching through the streets. They emerged onto squares crowded with thousands of people eager for the spectacle, while the aristocrats watched from the balconies. Even Father Cazalla,

Charles V's former preacher, was imprisoned and burned in 1559 along with 110 supposed heretics.

It was in this worrisome context that a Carmelite of Ávila, discreet up to that time, manifested the divine favors she believed the Lord was bestowing upon her through visible signs. Teresa's manifestations continued despite repeated warnings from the most prudent among her friends: Salcedo, the pious gentleman; Daza, the learned priest; and Ibáñez, the Dominican. One day, called to the parlor, she recognized Don Alonso de Quiñones, an aristocrat of Ávila, through the grille. With a reproving eye, he greeted her coldly and simply uttered the following: "Remember Magdalena de la Cruz. Spain thought her a saint; she was the slave of the devil."

After a heavily menacing silence, Teresa answered in a toneless voice: "I never remember her without trembling."

Shaken by the Carmelite's humble tone, the nobleman withdrew.

Others did not disarm. In Ávila, a person of distinction declared: "I hope to live to be old enough to see this nun end up as she deserves, on the stake of the Inquisition." After all was said and done, just how far would this woman go, plunged in her "mental prayer" rather than being content with the common vocal prayer and the liturgy?

Teresa worried so much that she might unwittingly be a victim of the devil that she continued to solicit the opinions of those who had cautioned her to be on guard. She had unfortunately just lost Father de Prádanos, who had fallen gravely ill, and had received as a confessor a twenty-five-year-old Jesuit, Baltasar Álvarez. Incapable of understanding her, he subjected her mystical flights to various vexations. She would later declare that he "mortified me very much and...disturbed me exceedingly."[25] For example, he imposed upon her a general confession at the Jesuit college without a veil, her face exposed, which was humiliating. Whenever she asked him questions in writing and requested an urgent answer, he responded by writing his reply on the envelope: "Not to be opened for a month." And she obeyed.

Who was this young Jesuit intervening in her life at such a crucial moment? Of an open enough mind, Álvarez lacked experience. He was a good theologian but intransigent on dogmatic truths. He had neither the gifts of mind nor the qualities of heart to understand and direct a mystic. In addition, he did not succeed in conquering the natural harshness of his character even though he went to great lengths to do so by dint of mortifications. Living in a narrow cell cluttered with books, he asserted that "suffering in a thousand ways without being guilty is a mouthful of tender meat without bones." In entrusting Teresa to him, his rector, the stern

Father Dionisio Álvarez, had recommended that she be treated with firmness, like an exalted novice—which she was not.

Father Baltasar Álvarez preferred nuns without problems, and especially without ecstasies! With him, Teresa found her scruples and her fears vis-à-vis the devil returning once again. She was tempted to leave this confessor, but she refused to in order to avoid offending him and, especially, to mortify herself. "All this was necessary because my will did not easily bend. The Lord told me once that it wasn't obedience if I wasn't resolved to suffer, that I should fix my eyes on what he suffered, and that all would be easy."[26]

Criticized in the city, isolated in her own monastery, she thought of going away, perhaps to Flanders or to Brittany. It was the first spark of desire for a convent that was pure, strict, arranged for religious life, and entirely given up to divine love through interiority.

When Teresa consulted Father Baltasar Álvarez, he opposed to this idea.

Was he the one who was inciting the city against her? He had given up on being able to keep her on a tight leash and had consulted her friends Don Salcedo and Daza along with a few Jesuits of the college. Teresa later reproached them "with not having kept the secret," of having divulged to the public the secrets of her ecstasies. How could such secrets be kept in this monastery that was like a sieve? Teresa herself asked people to pray for her.

Then the sentence was pronounced: "He then assured me, I believe there were five or six of them, all great servants of God; and my confessor told me that they all came to the decision that my experience was from the devil, that I shouldn't receive Communion so often, and that I should try to *distract* myself in such a way that I would not be alone." But for her this meant returning to the mitigated situation in which she had frittered away twenty years! And they were going to deprive her of Communion! Once again she was thrust into darkness. In vain she "begged His Majesty to lead me by another path."

However, she decided to obey. All of these persons who were advising her "lived a good life—incomparably better than I—and they were learned men. Why shouldn't I believe them?" Father Baltasar Álvarez repeated to her that all these measures were necessary to break her will—which today we would call her ego. She obeyed him with such humble submission that, moved, he confided to a friend: "She obeys like a little child."

This situation lasted for two years. Teresa despaired of ever being understood. She had limited her meetings with Father Álvarez, no doubt at his request. It is said that she had gone to his college and he had refused to receive her. "I was alone then without any person in whom I could find some support, unable to pray vocally or read, but terrified by so much tribulation and fear as to whether the devil would deceive me...."

If she had to do without a confessor, she knew that she at least needed a director of conscience. "The soul itself doesn't understand them [its first ecstasies] nor does it know what to do with itself."[27] "A master is very necessary providing he has experience.... If he doesn't, he can be greatly mistaken and lead a soul without understanding it nor allowing it to understand itself.... These masters afflict soul and body and obstruct progress."[28] In spite of her dazzling intuitions and her experience of mystical states, she could not do without theologians to conceptualize her experiences within the dogmatic framework of the Church. "I am a daughter of the Church"—throughout her life, she would always remain faithful to this statement that she pronounced at her death.

But during these uncertain years, everyone was against her!

> I went out of the church with this affliction and entered an oratory.... I remained in this condition for four or five hours, because there was no consolation for me either from heaven or from earth; the Lord left me to suffer and to fear a thousand dangers.

A prayer then welled up in her heart: "O my Lord, how You are the true friend; and how powerful! ...and You never stop loving those who love You!" She received this answer in her heart: "Do not fear, my daughter; for I am and I will not abandon you; do not fear."

"And behold, by these words alone I was given calm together with fortitude, courage, security, quietude, and light so that in one moment I saw my soul become another."

Naturally, some good people took offense at this. Was this voice not once again a snare of the devil? Teresa was too prudent to take lightly this question that haunted the people of her era, the rich as well as the poor, learned persons as well as the unlearned. Admittedly, the devil existed. But this voice that spoke in her did not come from him.

How could she be sure of this? The devil's words cause nasty results. The soul becomes dry, arid, and anguished. "It is left as though frightened and very grieved." In addition, he pushes aside the teachings of Scripture. With her, there were none of those symptoms.

Henceforth, she did not hesitate to defy the devils, the only way to exorcise them:

> I took a cross in my hand, and it seemed to me truly that God gave me courage because in a short while I saw that I was another person and that I wouldn't fear bodily combat with them; for I thought that with that cross

I would easily conquer all of them. So I said: "Come now, all of you, for, being a servant of the Lord, I want to see what you can do to me."

From then on, all fear of the devils and hell was expunged from her. "I was left with a mastery over them truly given by the Lord of all; I pay no more attention to them than to flies." She proceeded to criticize her confessors and fainthearted friends who had plunged her into fear and scruples:

> Without doubt, I fear those who have such great fear of the devil more than I do the devil himself, for he can't do anything to me. Whereas these others, especially if they are confessors, cause severe disturbance; I have undergone some years of such great trial that I am amazed now at how I was able to suffer it.

But this was written a few years later. In 1558, she was closely dependent upon her spiritual counselors—Salcedo, Daza, and the rector of the Jesuit college, Dionisio Álvarez, who did not like her and judged that it was necessary to break this impassioned woman. They would soon find out what she was worth. Teresa was charitable in judging her persecutors: "They spoke harshly and scolded me.... They must have meant to mortify me."[29] And she was especially forgiving of the "holy gentleman" Salcedo, whom Teresa describes in *The Life*: "As the one who felt the greatest good will toward me, this gentleman waged the whole opposition. He is a God-fearing and holy man; but since he had seen that I had so recently been so wretched, he wasn't able to feel assured."[30]

The lesson she drew from this painful episode is that a person has nothing to fear from the devil "if one walks...in the truth in the presence of His Majesty and with a pure conscience."[31] In her first *Spiritual Testimony*, Teresa had written:

> If when I'm in prayer or on the days in which I am quiet and my thoughts are on God, all the learned men and saints in the world were to join together and torture me with all the torments imaginable, and I wanted to believe them, I wouldn't be able to make myself believe that these things come from the devil; for I cannot.

SO IT WAS NOT THE DEVIL. But her prudent counselors then said that those words she heard (locutions) could be merely an illusion provoked by what we would call autosuggestion today.

Teresa, who had asked herself this same question, refuted this explanation at length in Chapter 25 of *The Life*:

> He who can do all things wants us to understand that He must do what He wants.... It is in our power to divert our attention from these words of the

intellect...in the case of those words that are from God there is no way of diverting one's attention.... In those [words] from God the voice is so clear that you don't lose a syllable of what is said.

The words that she heard often had a prophetic character: "about things of the future—three or four years in advance very often—all of which have been fulfilled."

In autosuggestion, if the words

are something the intellect fabricates, no matter how subtly it works, a person will know that it is the intellect that is composing something and speaking.... And the words it fabricates are as though muffled, fancied, and without the clarity of those that come from God.

And these words are recognizable, for they spur one to action:

Those the Lord speaks are both words and works.... They dispose the soul and prepare it from the very beginning, and they touch it, give it light, favor it and bring it quiet. And if the soul suffers dryness, agitation and worry, these are taken away as though by a stroke of the hand since it seems the Lord wants it to understand that He is powerful and that His words are works.

Teresa, who had read the *Confessions of St. Augustine*, meditated upon this passage: "My mother used to say that she could distinguish by means of some sort of savor, which she could not explain in words, the difference between God's revelation and the dreaming of her own soul."

With God, "[the soul] finds that long sentences all prepared are spoken to it, which even though it were deeply recollected it wouldn't be able to compose. And in hearing the first word, as I mentioned, the soul is changed completely."

For these words at times bear with them such majesty that even though one does not call to mind who it is that speaks them, they make one tremble—if they are words of reproof; and if they are words of love, they make one dissolve in love.

But what does one do when there is a contradiction between a word from God and a command from one's confessor? Throughout her life, Teresa was confronted with this problem, and malicious gossips said that she resolved it by choosing confessors who suited her. For the time being, however, that was not the case. And she complained only slightly about those who persecuted her. In Chapter 26 of her *Life*, she emphasized that her disagreement with her confessor brought her a mortification capable of leading her to a more perfect humility:

As often as the Lord commanded something of me in prayer and my confessor told me to do otherwise, the Lord returned and told me to obey my confessor; afterward His Majesty would change the confessor's mind, and he would agree with the Lord's command.

Such a conflict could be traced back even further. Teresa delighted in reading Sacred Scripture translated into Castilian. So she was distraught when the Inquisitor General Fernando de Valdés, following the recommendations of the Council of Trent, banned such translations, arguing that the vernacular languages promoted heretical interpretations. More than seven hundred works were thus burned in Spain in the year 1559. We should remember that Teresa read neither Latin nor Greek, languages reserved to academics and ecclesiastics.

"When they forbade the reading of many books in the vernacular, I felt that prohibition very much because reading some of them was an enjoyment for me...." Deprived of a confessor and books, Teresa found herself constrained to seek within herself the answers to her questions. And the answer was given to her: "The Lord said to me: 'Don't be sad, for I shall give you a living book.'"

And illustrated! This time, it was not only a question of a voice, but also of visions!

CHAPTER 10

Visions of Light

(1559–1560)

Teresa received her first "vision"[1] on June 29, 1559. "Being in prayer on the feast day of the glorious St. Peter, I saw or, to put it better, I felt Christ beside me; I saw nothing with my bodily eyes or with my soul, but it seemed to me that Christ was at my side...speaking to me."

Astounded, not understanding what was happening within her, she was stricken with a deep fear. Then she heard his voice reassuring her. Following this, "...the Lord left me feeling as I usually did: quiet, favored, and without any fear."[2]

However, it was with some apprehension that she went to confide in her confessor. Father Baltasar Álvarez stared at her in consternation. First voices, now visions!

"In what form do you see our Lord?"

"I do not see him."

"Then, how do you know that it is he?"

"It seemed to me that Jesus Christ was always present at my side; but since this wasn't an imaginative vision, I didn't see any form. Yet I felt very clearly that He was always present at my right side and that He was the witness of everything I did.... He [was] more certainly at my side than if I saw Him."[3]

"As if you perceived the presence of the other through the senses; heard him speak, move; could touch him?"

"No, it is not that, *Padre*. The Savior made his presence known to me in a manner clearer than sunlight. I was not seeing the sun but a light which, while being imperceptible to my sight, illuminated my understanding and provided my soul with an incomparable pleasure."

"Ah! Always pleasure, Doña Teresa!"

"Ardent love but also acute faith, resolutions full of sweetness! One understands that God is present by the effects produced in the soul."

Father Álvarez remained perplexed. He did not doubt Teresa's sincerity, but he wanted to help her to see herself clearly and to thwart the snares of the imagination and the devil.

"God? Really?"

"I clearly recognized Jesus Christ, son of the Virgin, in his very holy humanity, desirous of accompanying us and showering his favors upon us."

"But, who told you that it was Christ Jesus?"

"He himself tells me so, often. In this instance, before he told me, I knew that it was he. He told me he was present—but I didn't see him."

"Well then, how can you be sure that it was truly he?"

"In this case, I did not see the object; but the knowledge of it was 'impressed' within me in such a clear manner that doubt seems to me to be impossible. It is a certainty equal, superior even, to that of sight, which can be illusory. And should doubt present itself, my soul would remain in possession of 'such great certitude' that this doubt would have no hold over it."

"You spoke of light?"

"Yes, it is a light that has no shadow and that nothing clouds. I do not pretend to explain how such a strong light can manifest itself to our interior sense and be an image so clear in our understanding that it seems to be really there. The explanation is up to learned men."

The learned man still speechless, she added: "I have no idea how this knowledge is in me; for I saw nothing, nor heard anything. Never have I had the slightest desire for this, nor even the thought that this could be possible."

"You said knowledge?"

"Yes. In an instant, the soul finds itself to be learned. It discovers in a clear light the mystery of the Trinity and other very sublime mysteries."

"Would knowledge be the unique goal of this manifestation?"

"I note that it brings about a complete transformation of the soul. It can then no longer love anything unless it is he who makes it capable of such great good fortune, without 'any effort of its own'—an inexpressible testimony of love."

"Some of these favors could, however, give rise to doubt, precisely because they are so admirable, and granted to a soul so little worthy of receiving them."

"Here the soul does not act at all, *Padre*. It finds everything prepared. It has nothing else to do than to take pleasure in it. The Lord wants to give to this soul some knowledge of what takes place in heaven, where one understands the other without speaking. And if He has deigned to allow Himself to be seen by eyes as guilty as mine, it is because 'He shows no partiality; He loves everyone, no matter how contemptible.'"

"What do you conclude from this?"

"Knowing from experience the truth of what I assert, I could never again seek satisfaction elsewhere. What treasures comparable to the least of these favors could I henceforth aspire to in this life? And these favors are but a drop of this torrent of delights that the Lord has prepared for us at the price of His sufferings."

Her face took on a sorrowful expression. She added: "But I see this world living in such a state of perdition!"[4]

Impressed, the priest withdrew. Everything this nun was saying seemed to be in conformity with the sound doctrine of the Church. Returning to the College of St. Giles, he shut himself up in his cell. And there, raising his head, he saw Christ and was struck with amazement.

The next day, he ran to see Teresa.

"*Madre!* I have seen Christ!"

"Do not believe it, *Padre.* Christ would appear to you? It would not be Christ. Look at him carefully."

"And yet, it was Christ!"

"Is this your firm belief, *Padre?* Then it is also that of those who come to you."[5]

Was the confessor the victim of a hallucination? Teresa saw as clearly in him as he in her. Whatever the case may be, from that day forward he changed his opinion of her. He took her seriously, all the while remaining on his guard, haunted by the possibility of illusions or demonic temptations.

FOR TERESA, THIS NEW DEGREE of divine knowledge was a matter of the presence of Christ in her, which she experienced in a type of vision theologians call an "intellectual vision" without images. She clarifies her experience in Chapter 28 of *The Life*: "I passed some days—a few—in which I experienced this vision continually; it did me so much good that I never left prayer [contemplation]." And whenever a doubt occurred to her while she reflected on the reticence of Father Baltasar Álvarez, "this fear didn't last long, because the Lord was giving me assurance." As he had promised her—*I shall give you a living book*[6]—Christ was instructing her on the truths of faith. "In symbols of fire she conveyed the letter of dogma."[7] Jesus accompanied her in her life, reassured her, encouraged and enlightened her. Thirsting for God, this woman was attesting to a hidden God desirous of sharing his love with us. Her charisms were the magnifying mirrors of divine revelation dulled by the passage of time. It was as if a ray of sunshine or a flash of lightning suddenly brought to the fore what dozing clerics and the people had read and heard a hundred times with indifference.

However much one may be a believer, one cannot help questioning the nature of this mystical phenomenon as Father Álvarez did. Reality was being called into question.

Regarding supernatural reality, the Catholic philosopher Jean Guitton has said to me:

> Our senses can be oriented toward external objects, but they can also put us in contact with a transcendent reality, hidden to others. For the one who sees, consciousness of the universe is modified. He has the impression of emerging from a dream, that of life, to enter into the real.[8]

The vision is outside the time and space in which it manifests itself. Theologians distinguish between vision and apparition, the latter being a vision that affects the senses. A vision is generally the outcome of contemplation. It places one in contact with a supernatural entity: Christ or the saints, who have a message to give. According to the Carmelite Father Marie-Eugène de l'Enfant-Jésus, these extraordinary favors are produced "by an infusion of light into the intelligence or by the impression of an image or a perception in the senses."

The vision can be a *sign* of the divinity given to the sleeping or rebellious creature. With the mystic, it invites union. At the highest degree, the intuitive or beatific vision given by God is an immediate seeing of his essence. In that case there are no images.

As we shall see in Teresa, ecstasy is often associated with a vision for, as Yvan Gobry has written in *L'Expérience mystique*, "the vision indicates that one knows at a distance the supernatural world; ecstasy signifies that one is there."

A healthy, rational, and sincere subject like Teresa can distinguish the difference between a vision and an ordinary reality, for between the perception and the representation the difference is not of degree but of kind. Such a person can also differentiate between a hallucination; a mental phenomenon like a dream, which maintains itself and is not provoked by a real object or an entity; and a vision, the message of an exterior entity.

The visionary not only sees but he or she knows, and nothing will make him or her budge from this, for the object of the vision is more real than ordinary perceptions. The vision is characterized by an extreme intensity, an extraordinary sensation of presence. For her part, Teresa received superior information concerning ordinarily hidden things. Seeing then becomes clairvoyance, and hearing *clairaudience*. It is a gift of God par excellence.

For Jean Guitton, the vision is a furtive coincidence of the consciousness of the "see-er" with the divine Mystery, a consciousness sundered from space and time. Beyond images, there remains the incomparable force of the *presence,* a fundamental mystical experience that manifests itself through intimate vibrations that sometimes absorb the entire being and reach as far as union, the mystical marriage. But who can describe it?

AFTER HER INTELLECTUAL VISIONS came the visions of images,[9] "furtive, rapid, interior, of an extraordinary brilliance and laden with unsuspected depth of significance."[10]

"One day, while I was in prayer, the Lord desired to show me only his hands, which were so very beautiful that I would be unable to exaggerate the beauty." "After a few days, I saw also that divine face, which it seems left me completely absorbed."

She was astounded. Why this progressive manner of revealing himself? "...[L]ater I understood that His Majesty was leading me in accordance with my natural weakness...the merciful Lord was preparing me." As though he wanted to habituate his elected one, to "accustom her to sustain the brilliance of an unbearable majesty."[11]

At first she was frightened, troubled, overwhelmed: "Glorified bodies have such beauty that the sight of so supernatural a beauty deriving from glory causes confusion. Thus the vision caused me a fear so great that I was completely agitated and disturbed...." Then, "...afterward I remained so certain and secure and felt such other effects that I immediately lost the fear."

Finally, on the feast day of St. Paul while she was at Mass, a vision of the risen Christ was granted to her. Here, she felt so out of her depth that words failed. She said, "One cannot describe this vision without ruining it." She spoke of "the exalted beauty of glorified bodies." She made clear that it was a vision in which the senses were not involved as they can be in an apparition. "I never saw this vision—nor any other—with my bodily eyes...." For someone who has not benefited from such favors, the distinction is difficult. It was not so for Teresa, in whom, notwithstanding, the doubt of having imagined things left her. How could she imagine such a vision that "surpasses everything imaginable here on earth," all that the human being is capable of conceiving, even the greatest painter in the world? "The splendor is not one that dazzles; it has a soft whiteness, is infused, gives the most intense delight to the sight, and doesn't tire it; neither does the brilliance, in which is seen the vision of so divine a beauty, tire it."

By way of comparison, "the sun's brightness…appears very tarnished …and the sunlight seems artificial." The light that emanates from the Lord "has no night; nothing troubles it. In sum, it is of such a kind that a person couldn't imagine what it is like all the days of his life, no matter how powerful an intellect he might have."

The vision was given in a strange fashion. "God gives it so suddenly that there wouldn't even be time to open your eyes, if it were necessary to open them." No matter: "For when the Lord desires to give the vision…even if we do not desire to see the vision, it is seen. No distraction is enough to resist it…."

How does one describe the indescribable? "I don't mean that I shall explain how such a strong light can be put in the interior faculty and so clear an image [of himself] put in the intellect…that He seems to be truly present to us."

In *The Life*, Teresa endeavored to describe her visions—there are a great number of them—and one can imagine the bafflement and then the impassioned curiosity of her confessor who, in the end, took her seriously, recognizing that everything in her was truth. She declared herself an objective witness in the most scientific meaning of the term. She was indeed one of those rare witnesses who expressed herself clearly, even if she believed that she was ignorant and incapable of understanding the simplest of things.

"It seemed clear to me in some cases that what I saw was an image, but in many other instances, no; rather it was Christ Himself by reason of the clarity with which He was pleased to reveal Himself to me."

Even the image is incomparable: "It does not resemble paintings here on earth, no matter how perfect they are." It is "not like an earthly drawing no matter how perfect it may be…for what is seen is an image, it is a living image…." Her enthusiasm bursts forth: "[It is] the living Christ. And He makes it known that He is both man and God, not as He was in the tomb but as He was when He came out of the tomb after His resurrection."

Thus does "the imaginary vision overlay the intellectual vision by dressing it up with living and resplendent forms." As to the light, "it explains the image and the image firmly fixes the light in sentient and precise forms," writes Father Marie-Eugène, who adds that the intellectual vision is "a direct infusion by God of a light into the soul," then "the light is illustrated by an image which encapsulates the meaning."[12]

What effects did these visions produce in Teresa? "He reveals Himself as so much the lord of this dwelling that it seems the soul is completely dissolved; and it sees itself consumed in Christ."

The confessor's impassioned questioning is understandable: Why such an action?

She answered: So that the soul may

> know how tremendous this majesty is and the power that this most sacred humanity joined with the Divinity has. In this vision there is a clear representation of what it will be like on Judgment Day.... This vision is the source of the true humility left in the soul when it sees its misery, which it cannot ignore.

This is a great theme that Teresa would continue to develop and that is the key to her future sanctity: "Although the soul sees that He shows love, it doesn't know where to hide, and so it is completely consumed."

It was through her words, which seemed to be dictated by her visions, that Teresa would, in the end, convince her confessors both of the reality of her visions and of their supernatural and divine—not demonic—character. If the visions had been demonic, pride would have taken possession of her rather than humility. A few centuries later, the proud Viscount Charles de Foucauld, after his "...illumination" in the Church of St. Augustin in Paris, declared himself to be "the least and the most miserable of men." Teresa saw herself as *consumed*, reduced to nothingness in comparison to the splendor of the vision of the resurrected Christ from which shone forth celestial perfection. As a consequence, she added, "this vision is the source of confusion and true repentance for sins." Thus, the Lord was inviting her to a radical conversion.

Consumed? No. She escaped this thanks to ecstasy.

> When the Lord desires to show the soul a great part of His grandeur and majesty...it would be impossible for any subject to endure it—unless the Lord should want to help it very supernaturally by placing it in rapture and ecstasy since in the enjoyment of that divine presence the vision of it is lost.

Here at last is an explanation of the role of the lethargic state in ecstasy. All the great mystics since Moses have stated that a person cannot possibly see God without dying. This apparent and temporary death, this "sleep of the powers," preserves the body and the mind.

Upon awaking, states Teresa, "that majesty and beauty remain so impressed that they are unforgettable," except in the night of the spirit. These nights seem to be imposed upon human beings to remind them of their dependence and to avoid inflating their pride, an ever-present temptation that could break the miracle of union.

Besides, can one really speak of lethargy in ecstasy? Lethargic sleep is a state in which the life functions are so reduced that they seem to be suspended. In the case of ecstasy, lethargy is a reaction of weakness that protects the human body overcome by divine power. During a thunderstorm, when there is too much energy, fuses blow up. But in the mystical experience, the thought process is not annihilated as much as it is totally absorbed by God.

In analyzing the extraordinary phenomena of which she was the object, Teresa finally understood the reason for the vision without images (called intellectual) and the one with images (called imaginative). In both cases, God was present in her. But "a wonderful thing happens when so divine a presence is represented in the imagination so that, in conformity with our weakness, this presence can last in the memory and keep the thought well occupied."

God cannot be represented by an image; he cannot be seen with the eyes of the body. But it is possible to have an idea of him thanks to Christ's humanity, God incarnate. *"Whoever sees me sees the Father."* Teresa states:

> With the eyes of the soul we see the excellence, beauty, and glory of the most holy humanity; and through the intellectual vision...we are given an understanding of how God is powerful, that He can do all things, that He commands all and governs all, and that His love permeates all things.

For her, doubt was not allowed. The visions were truly he, "an evanescent image, but of an incomparable brilliance which awakened fervor in her soul."[13]

However, in answer to the harassment of her detractors and the legitimate reservations of some confessors, Teresa did not hesitate to call herself into question and carefully sift out the facts of her visions.

The devil? He was powerless. She knew how to recognize him and admitted that when she first began her prayer of quiet, he had sought to mislead her, to divert her. "He takes the form of flesh, but he can't counterfeit the image by giving it the glory it has when it comes from God."

She added that when a vision comes from the devil, "[the delight] does not have the appearance of pure and chaste love." It is not a divine joy, but a suspect pleasure. Too sensual and human, it does not uplift, but debases, reducing the person to animal instincts. The inquisitors often would not be able to make heads or tails of it!

IF WE EXCLUDE THE HYPOTHESIS of the devil, could not a vision be the product of our imagination? Teresa had already refuted this by insisting:

> That this vision from God could be the work of the imagination is the most impossible of impossible things; it is utter nonsense to think so, for the beauty and the whiteness of one hand alone is completely beyond our imagination.... For if the vision were represented by means of the intellect, apart from the fact that it wouldn't produce any of the great effects that a true [vision] produces, the soul would be left exhausted.

Instead of being exhausted by a false vision, "One cannot exaggerate the richness that the true vision leaves; it even gives health to the body and leaves it comforted"–comforting strength for the mission awaiting her.

She was convinced of the truth of her vision because she had experienced it herself: joy had possessed her, a divine joy that could not deceive, and nothing could wrest it from her. And this God who gives himself (this Love) remained in her, even if the image she had of herself (her ego) obscured it, going so far as to provoke a night of the spirit in her conscience.

But at the time of the ecstasy, it is rare for the ego to resist. Teresa clearly stated in the first of her *Spiritual Testimonies*:

> I am seldom able while in prayer to use my intellect in a discursive way [reason with my intelligence], for my soul immediately begins to grow recollected; and it remains in quiet or rapture to the extent that I cannot make any use of the senses. This recollection reaches such a point that if it were not for hearing...none of the senses would be of any avail.

She insists: "and this hearing does not include understanding." In the second chapter of the seventh dwelling of *The Interior Castle*, she even explained herself to her sisters: "This *center of our soul*, or this spirit, is something so difficult to explain, and even believe in...for I do not know how to explain this center. ...I know that I'm speaking the truth in what I say."

Teresa of Ávila discovered the unconscious 350 years before Freud! But she understood the unconscious as a receiving space open to the Infinite and not, as the Viennese doctor suggests, simply bogged down in the swamp and garbage dump of the human spirit.

IN THE VISION OF IMAGES, the soul *sees* Christ and contemplates his mysterious humanity. The intellectual vision without images shows the sovereign
God to the soul. Time is then abolished. A fraction of a second seems eternal. This vision being unbearable, Teresa would lose control of her senses
and fall into ecstasy; more precisely, her spirit would escape toward the
heights. In the sixth dwelling, she wrote:

> Thus, while the soul remains in its place, the superior part rises above it....
> What is true, is that with the speed of a ball shot from an arquebus, when
> fire is applied, an interior flight is experienced...which, though noiseless, is
> so clearly a movement that it cannot be the work of the imagination. And
> while the spirit is far outside itself, from all it can understand, great things
> are shown to it.[14]

Teresa's rational mind must be emphasized. Unlike other visionaries
who preceded her, such as Angela of Foligno and Catherine of Siena, she
constantly questioned herself. Was not a given vision an image created by
the brain? No, for the vision would be dead in comparison to the vision
given by God. Teresa had known this natural phenomenon, later described
by Carl Jung, of the waking dream. She did not confuse it with the mystical
vision. She stated:

> It happens to some persons...that their imagination is so weak, or their
> intellect so effective, or I don't know what the cause is, that they become
> so absorbed in their imagination to the extent that everything they think
> about seems to be clearly seen. Yet, if they were to see a real vision, they
> would know without any doubt whatsoever their mistake....[15]

Hallucinations have no object. They are only imaginary creations gener-
ated by the person who perceives them. Vision refers to an object or an exterior being who delivers a message. The distinction is made through concrete
proofs: conversion, prophecies, healings, illuminations. Later, Teresa would
show in *The Interior Castle* that the more a person plunges into the depths of
the psyche, the more one is capable of attaining a concrete, transcendent
reality. In this way, the subconscious space serves as an intermediary
between heaven and earth. The supernatural vision is as real; it is a knowledge similar to ordinary optical vision, although it is a different kind.

   In the mystic vision, Christ appears without advance notice, filling the
senses with fear and disturbance that soon give way to an unalloyed happiness and love.

   Teresa spoke of "inestimable treasures." In these extraordinary matters
of ecstasy, we remain on the cutting edge. But Teresa did not escape before
all else the importance of knowing how to discern what is the real presence

of God and what is an illusion via projection of the ego or the devil's temptation. In *The Life*,[16] she distinguishes three degrees of discernment: 1) *Motions*: God speaks in me; this is the mystical experience. 2) *Comprehension*: The favors are recognized, "the purest gold of the divine wisdom...the faculties are not united but absorbed and looking as though in wonder at what they see."[17] 3) *The Testimony*: One knows how to speak about the experience.

Actually, the richness of the results of her experiences would finally completely convince her confessor. She dared to write this herself:

> ...all who knew me saw clearly that my soul was changed, and my confessor told me so. The difference in all things was very great; it was not feigned, but all could see it very clearly. I said that since I was previously so wretched I couldn't believe that if the devil did this to deceive me and bring me to hell he would have taken a means as contrary as was that of removing vices and bestowing virtues and fortitude.[18]

She is just as clear in her first *Spiritual Testimony*:

> ...In a moment, I receive the effects and benefits.... But while it seems to me that my soul is getting lost, I see what it gains, so that should I have desired to obtain these blessings myself in the course of a year I don't think it would have been possible to have acquired them.... I am amazed to see so many truths and so clearly, for the things of the world appear to me to be nonsense.

These favors were given to her so that she would start out on the way to perfection. Later, she would draw from them the strength for her missions as a foundress: "Some desires to serve God come upon me...and there is also pain in seeing of what little use I am." But, suddenly, an irresistible force lifted her up despite the risks of martyrdom and death. "This, too, occurs without reflection; but in an instant it changes me completely, and I don't know where I get so much strength."[19]

UNFORTUNATELY, THE OPPOSITION was not slackening. Who stood against Teresa? Perhaps some relatives and friends of the mitigated religious of the Incarnation, who had heard Teresa take issue with the downhill drift of the parlor visits and other breaches of monastic rigor. Indeed, some may have objected to her radicalism, which required that one break with the world in order to achieve the conversion necessary to contemplation. Another possible force of opposition was the many haughty, jealous theologians. At the very least, these men felt scandalized that a simple nun—a woman—incapable of even reading Latin, seemingly questioned their authority by receiving enlightenment directly from heaven rather than contenting herself with the teachings of the Church. Of course, it was this same Church that, by depriving Teresa of being able to read Sacred Scripture in the Castilian language, had pushed her headlong into her interior world that opened directly onto the Absolute.

Almost all the holy mystics encountered this problem in their lives. Before canonizing them, theologians contest their enlightenment and inordinate power to "review dogma in letters of fire." Prudence, no doubt; jealousy sometimes. In her humility, Teresa would even write: "Since there were very holy persons in this place—and compared to them I was a wretched person—and God was not leading them by this path, they immediately became fearful."

None of this is insignificant. As Father Pierre Lauzeral writes, "Daza and Salcedo cast over the budding reformer a cloud of suspicion that would follow her even beyond her death."[20]

Teresa's voices, and now her visions, were known throughout Ávila. If some people marveled at them, others were irritated or mocked them. Teresa was deeply saddened by this. "For it seems that because of my sins, my secrets and confidences, which they came to know of, were spread around, although I spoke to no one about them except to my confessor or anyone he told me to tell."[21]

Later on, Teresa acknowledged that her radical transformation could not go unnoticed by anyone, least of all her sisters.

> All who knew me saw clearly that my soul was changed, and my confessor told me so. The difference in all things was very great; it was not feigned, but all could see it very clearly.

And that change bothered the Pharisees of Ávila. María Diaz, the *beata* without ecstasies or visions, without literary talent, troubled no one. Not only was Teresa challenging monastic standards but also the exclusive spiritual power of the clerics, at least certain clerics who held this power not because of their sanctity, but because of their theological studies or their family and social position.

Father Baltasar Álvarez found himself harassed by outside pressures from the moment he took Teresa seriously. "I knew that they told him to be careful of me, that he shouldn't let the devil deceive him by anything I told him."[22]

The priest hesitated. Did some of his Jesuit colleagues pressure him? Teresa was frightened that he was being forced to abandon her. "I feared that

I would have no one who would hear my confession, but that all would run from me. I did nothing but weep."[23]

But the more Father Álvarez listened to Teresa, the more he marveled. From then on, "This Father strove for my soul's perfection in every way he could. Since I had so much fear, I obeyed him in everything."

Would this protect her from the Inquisition? Teresa stresses that Father Álvarez "suffered a great deal during the three years or more that he was my confessor." She speaks of "great persecutions." "Everyone came to him, and he was blamed without any fault on his part." Teresa also had to endure visits from her opponents, several of whom, as she points out, were saints. She was no doubt alluding to her friend Don Salcedo, the holy gentleman. "...[H]e didn't understand me; he strongly desired that I might advance and that the Lord might give me light."[24] For this reason she would, nonetheless, maintain her friendship with him until death.

Due to these outside pressures, and because of his personal doubts, Father Álvarez did not support Teresa as much as she wished. Fortunately, she had God to sustain her. God visited her with such regularity that we must suppose he had a precise plan for her, a new orientation for her life.

She could not yet imagine, however, what God expected of her, the "little nothing" she believed herself to be.

CHAPTER 11

Visions, Ecstasies, Such Delightful Wounds

(1560)

or two and a half years, Teresa received visions of Christ without being able to cause or stop them. It would be impossible to state it more clearly: a supernatural vision is as much given as it can be taken away. We can do nothing but desire it with love and welcome it with fervor and humility. And when Teresa wanted "to describe these things...by trying to do so, I would lose the vision entirely."[1]

In speaking of these supernatural visions, Teresa used the language of a person in love, and she desired to see more. If she saw "His most beautiful and divine mouth," she admitted that she was never able "to know the color of His eyes!" As soon as she tried, the vision would disappear. It was always Christ who acted and not she. But he showed her the wounds of his passion. "Sometimes He appeared on the cross or in the garden, and a few times with the crown of thorns; sometimes He also appeared carrying the cross." At those times, she would be deeply distressed and moved to tears.

Obedient to the demands of Father Baltasar Álvarez, Teresa told him everything, and the young Jesuit listened, filled with wonder. Despite the warnings of his stern rector, Álvarez found it impossible to contest the Carmelite's sincerity. However, when these accounts were too heavy for him to bear, he asked Teresa to repeat them to her ordinary counselors, Don Salcedo and Master Daza. It would have been better, no doubt, for her to remain silent. "I suffered numerous affronts and trials in speaking about these visions, and very many persecutions. It seemed so certain to them that I had a devil that some persons wanted to exorcize me."

At that time, the Inquisition pyres were burning throughout Spain. But now, being certain of the origin of her ecstasies, she disregarded these menaces, disappointed only by the doubt of so many friends. Why was she unable to convince them? Such visions cannot be communicated with words, and she stopped telling these men about her visions, limiting her accounts to her confessor. Unfortunately, Father Dionisio Álvarez considered it wise to send him away. He entrusted Teresa to another Jesuit, Father de Águila, brother of the Incarnation's prioress. It could not have been a worse choice. He listened to Teresa and, influenced by the city's rumors, decided to put her in her place. In no uncertain terms, Father de Águila informed Teresa that her visions and locutions were illusions created by the devil. He instructed her to respond to them by making a gesture of scorn with her fingers—*las higas* (the horns)—to show her contempt.[2]

"Making [horns] at this vision of the Lord caused me the greatest pain.... It was a kind of severe penance for me.... I recalled the injuries the Jews caused Him and begged Him to pardon me."

Christ answered that she should not "worry," that she did well by obeying. And he added: "I shall make the truth known."

Afterward, rather than multiplying the Signs of the Cross as she had been ordered to do, she got into the habit of holding the ebony cross of her rosary out toward him. "Once...He took it from me with His own hands; when He gave it back to me, it was made of four large stones incomparably more precious than diamonds.... The representation of the five wounds was of very delicate workmanship."

Teresa was the only one to see them, a phenomenon of selective vision that is sometimes encountered in mystics. One day, her sister Juana asked Teresa to give her this cross. She gave it to her with great sorrow. It can be seen today at the Carmelite convent of Alba de Tormes, where it is said to have worked miraculous healings.

Since the visions did not stop, her new confessor ordered her to cease practicing mental prayer. She obeyed him, but without ever being able to prevent the visions. When she complained interiorly of her confessor, Christ said to her: "What they are doing is tyranny."

Father de Águila had also ordered her to "enjoy herself." She tried to do so, but she does not say how: through reading, visits, outings?

> In seeking to distract myself, I never got free from prayer. It even seemed to me that I was in prayer while sleeping.... Love of God [was increasing] in me to such a degree that I didn't know where it came from (for it was very supernatural); nor did I procure it. I saw that I was dying with desire to see God, and I didn't know where to seek this life except in death.

Death was the only way to put an end to the torture, since those whom she loved and respected did not believe her and put her on guard against God himself!

Then, upon returning to her cell, she abandoned herself to Love, which plunged her into "a death so delightful that the soul would never want to escape from it." But why this mixture of suffering and joy? "The pain and glory joined together left me confused; I couldn't understand how such a combination was possible."

Her grounds for suffering were numerous: identification with the passion of Christ, a sense of her own indignity, intervals of divine withdrawal causing her to feel deprived. Added to these were her habitual physical sufferings and the lack of understanding of her friends and even of the people of Ávila, many of whom were accusing her of trying to gain notice by pretending to be a saint.

This amorous exaltation, alternately fulfilled by the presence and then anguished by the absence of the Beloved, worried her confessors. She paid no attention: "It's impossible for anyone who has not experienced them to be able to understand these impulses, which are so vehement." And she refuted in advance any comparison of the impulses she experienced with human emotional impulses, which would be considered too carnal:

> [These impulses] are not a disquiet of the heart. Neither are they the certain devotional feelings that often occur and seem to suffocate the spirit because they can't be contained. These devotional feelings belong to a lower form of prayer and their impetuous stirrings should be avoided by trying gently to gather them within oneself and by quieting the soul.... *Reason* should bridle these feelings because they could be caused by our own natural weakness.

It would seem, however, that she had been close to succumbing:

> We should consider with fear that they are not totally perfect but can pertain in great part to the sensory portion of the soul.... Let this love be held within and not resemble the pot that heats up too fast and boils over because too much wood was put on the fire.

But who threw the wood? Who lit the fire that she spoke of striving "to put out with gentle and not arduous tears"? "The soul did not cause this love, but...seemingly a spark from the very great love the Lord has for it suddenly fell upon it, making it burn all over."

In Chapter 20 of *The Life*, she would express herself directly:

> The suffering bears along with it such great happiness that I don't know what to compare it to. It is an arduous, delightful martyrdom since it

admits no earthly thing representable to the soul, even if this be what is usually more pleasing to it. It clearly understands that it desires only its God.

She concludes by suggesting that one should not get carried away in the beginning, but "great discretion is necessary...so that everything may proceed gently and the spirit may be shown how to work interiorly. One should strive earnestly to avoid exterior feelings." Later, the foundress-prioress would warn her sisters against the excesses of sentimental devotion, something repugnant to her proud and noble Castilian soul, as was everything that could make her similar to the *Alumbrados* and their savage, irrational devotions. But did she really escape this in the beginning? She spoke too well about it! Can a person really resist? "We ourselves don't put the wood on the fire, but it seems that once the fire is lit we are suddenly thrown into it so as to be burned up."

On many occasions she was put to the test by one temptation after another, including the situation with the pastor of Becedas and some more or less flirtatious parlor visits. To avoid losing herself and liberating the vital powers besieging her, she had only one way out. She invested them in the only masculine being whom she was authorized to love: Christ—not a sublimated Christ, but a Christ in his full humanity.

She then took Mary Magdalene, the great forgiven lover in the Gospels, as a model. Like her, "thinking that He would not despise my tears, [I] placed myself at His feet."[3]

She had experienced this amorous conversion in 1554 when she was faced with "the much wounded Christ." And the miracle had taken place; her heart had been moved, and she loved and felt loved in return:

> I had such little ability to represent things with my intellect...I could only think about Christ as He was as man....[4]

However, her troubles were not over:

> I clearly understood that I loved Him; but I did not understand as I should have [in] what true love of God consists.[5]

That is why she came up against the mystery of simultaneous suffering and pleasure. God grants us his love and calls for our love in exchange. But if to love is happiness, it is also suffering. To love truly is to abandon a portion of one's ego. And to love God, the Infinite Being, is to desire to give him everything, to cast oneself aside, to renounce one's being day after day. "To love is to suffer; it is allowing appearances to destroy our appearance so that the truth of ourselves can be born."[6]

This is what St. John of the Cross, thinking of Teresa, would later express in paragraph thirteen of his commentary on the second stanza of *The Living Flame of Love*: "This happens because these souls are purified and established in God, and that which is a cause of pain and torment to their corruptible flesh is sweet and delectable to their strong and healthy spirit."

SUFFERING AND PLEASURE! Everything became polarized one day in April 1560. Coming out of an ecstasy, Teresa suffered cruelly when she saw that she had been abruptly abandoned by her God. "As a deer longs for flowing streams, so my soul longs for you, O God!"[7] Suddenly,

> I saw close to me toward my left side an angel in bodily form.... The angel was not large but small; he was very beautiful and his face was so aflame that he seemed to be one of those very sublime angels that appear to be all afire.... I saw in his hands a large golden dart and at the end of the iron tip there appeared to be a little fire. It seemed to me this angel plunged the dart several times into my heart and that it reached deep within me. When he drew it out, I thought he was carrying off with him the deepest part of me; and he left me all on fire with great love of God.[8]
>
> The pain was so great that it made me moan, and the sweetness this greatest pain caused me was so superabundant that there is no desire capable of taking it away; nor is the soul content with less than God. The pain is not bodily but spiritual, although the body doesn't fail to share in some of it, and even a great deal. The loving exchange that takes place between the soul and God is so sweet....[9]

In another passage, she explains more clearly the conjunction of torment with pleasure. The torment comes from seeing one's "sins," one's "entrails"— that is, the self, its egotism, and its sensuality—torn out. Happiness is to be united with God:

> At times, an arrow is thrust into the deepest and most living recesses of the heart in such a way that the soul doesn't know what has happened or what it wants. It well understands that it wants God and that the arrow seems to have been dipped in a poisonous herb so that for the love of this Lord it might despise itself; and it would gladly lose its life for Him. You can't exaggerate or describe the way in which God wounds the soul and the extreme pain this wound produces, for it causes the soul to forget itself. Yet this pain is so delightful that there is no other pleasure in life that gives greater happiness. The soul would always want...to be dying of this sickness.... I went about as though stupefied. I desired neither to see nor to speak, but to clasp my suffering close to me, for to me it was greater glory than all creation.[10]

In *The Life*, she concludes: "Such was the grace which the Lord showered on me." A grace that was repeated numerous times.

Sister Ana Gutiérrez, who witnessed one of these raptures, stated that during the rapture, Teresa's face was illuminated. Regaining consciousness, Teresa reassured the young religious: "Did I frighten you, Ana? Ah! I wish you as much!"

Another time she complained of a great heat that seemed to be irradiating her heart,[11] and she asked Ana to cut her hair. Marveling at the sweet scent emanating from the shorn locks, Sister Ana spirited one away. Teresa noticed it and scolded her: "Do not think any more of these foolish things and go throw that out."

Two centuries later, on August 8, 1744, in his brief, *Dominici gregis*, Pope Benedict XIV instituted the feast of the Transverberation of St. Teresa's heart.

LET US TRY TO UNDERSTAND what was taking place in Teresa, which she herself attempted to express in pages that remain a model of mystical literature:

> I saw that I was dying with desire to see God, and I didn't know where to seek this life except in death.... For nothing satisfied me, nor could I put up with myself; it truly seemed as if my soul were being wrested from me.

Teresa never ceased speaking of love, but she was never totally satisfied. J.-N. Vuarnet emphasizes the fact that "anguish always exists side by side with ecstasy, pain with desire."[12]

If love is madness, what can be said of divine love? "Give me a heart which loves, a heart ravenous for God," St. Augustine cried out.

This state of consciousness, difficult to define, consists of many levels. In the state of quietude that Teresa had known in her youth, the subject retains consciousness. In this state, there is only a slight alienation of the senses. But in the more elevated state known as "rapture," there is a loss of consciousness (although not always, for Teresa stated that she felt and saw herself lifted up while in this state). The alienation is imperious, irresistible, beatific. Speaking of himself in his Second Letter to the Corinthians, St. Paul wrote: "I know someone in Christ who, (whether in the body or out of the body, I do not know, God knows) was caught up to the third heaven...was caught up into paradise and heard ineffable things, which no one may utter."

Finally, there is the transport of love, a truly mystical blaze that represents the extreme state, the mystical marriage.

The severe ecstasies seem to be born of a burning desire for union to which God suddenly responds. They can favor simple novices and lay people living in the world. Restful ecstasies are linked to detachment and silence, to concentration. In this "ecstasy" (interiority), the pure essence of Love, "in which grace and nature are not in opposition, but in concert,"[13] is revealed.

With Teresa, the motivation for ecstasy was religious: a loving search for God that reached mystical union. In the light of her love, Christ illuminated her soul in its poverty and urged her on, granting her the grace to dare to have the courage to undertake a real change. This experience, to which her life gave witness, is what spiritual masters call transforming union.

Ecstasy is the outcome of divine love. It is, therefore, not by accident that women have an important part in it. It is a "transport of love," repeat the mystics. It is a state of joy that so enlarges and dilates the human heart that sometimes a person dies from it, and the bodily state always finds itself disrupted by it: levitation, light, fire of love. It is like "an amorous furnace," wrote the Franciscan mystic Jacopone de Todi. At its extreme, stigmatization manifests a will to identify with the passion of Christ. The angel's dart piercing Teresa's heart is also the centurion's lance giving Christ the *coup de grâce*.

Desire, deprivation, love, union. Here Eastern and Christian mystics diverge as to the meaning that should be given to the term *fusion*. For the Catholic, the person is not annihilated but retains one's humanity. "He has not changed his own substance," emphasizes Angela de Foligno. A person is "absorbed in God through participation," adds John of the Cross, but "we cannot change ourselves substantially into Him," leaving the person's unity after death, while a drop of water is lost in the ocean where its molecules are dispersed.

Whatever the case may be, it is love that makes us like God, for "God is love," says St. John. This fundamental affidavit is confirmed by all mystics. Ecstasy brings an intimate knowledge of God, a nonintellectual but emotional knowledge, as in true human love. "It is a very delectable science because it is a science entirely of love," John of the Cross also states in *The Spiritual Canticle*. "It is love which teaches, it is love which renders it delightful. God himself communicates this science, and he communicates it in the love with which He gives himself." "O Love that loves me more than I can love myself or understand!" Teresa cries out.[14]

Love thus accomplishes the union of two spirits in this participation. "To be completely united and transformed through love in the always adorable will of the heavenly Father," wrote John of the Cross.[15]

Mystics are also unanimous in recognizing that ecstatic union is not acquired by the human will. It is always a free gift from God. "God is the source," writes Teresa in *The Interior Castle* (IV:2). "And since His Majesty desires to do so—when He is pleased to grant some supernatural favor—He produces this delight with the greatest peace and quiet and sweetness in the very interior part of ourselves."

However, ecstasy is generally given only at the end of the long toil of self-purification and only where there is a humble will for contemplation. They who have decided, following a call, to consecrate themselves to God alone must prepare and keep themselves in a state of adherence so that God may work in them without impediment. The desire they have for him is the most efficacious of prayers to prepare themselves for this gift.

The summit of ecstasy—the spiritual marriage—is thus described by John of the Cross in stanza 2, paragraph 21 of his commentary on *The Living Flame of Love:*

> Although that which the soul tastes in this touch of God is not perfect, it does in fact have a certain savor of eternal life.... And this is not incredible if we believe, as we should, that this is a touch of substances, that is, of the substance of God in the substance of the soul.... The delicateness of delight felt in this contact is inexpressible.... There is no way to catch in words the sublime things of God which happen in these souls. The appropriate language for the person receiving these favors is that he understand them, experience them within himself, enjoy them, and be silent.

But Teresa, carried away by her Castilian blood, could not remain silent. Having seen the resurrected Christ, she had seen God. Would she manage to describe him?

CHAPTER 12

"Gravity and Grace"

(1560)

he year 1560 was a remarkable one for Spain. Madrid was designated its capital city, Philip II married Elisabeth of France, and gold continued to pour in from America. It was also an extraordinary year for Teresa. In January, she had seen the resurrected Christ. In April, she had experienced the transverberation. Her numerous ecstasies sometimes left her cut off from the world for many days, "dialoguing with the angels," as Christ asked her to do. Receiving prophetic visions, she was mysteriously informed in advance of the death of certain persons. After one of her friends, the Dominican theologian Pedro Ibáñez, had been slandered, the Virgin appeared to Teresa in a vision and covered the religious in a cloak of dazzling whiteness. Moreover, at Teresa's request, Christ restored sight to a blind man.

Another unusual phenomenon occurred: she levitated! Her body escaped gravity, a striking sign of the detachment of the being vis-à-vis earthly contingencies. A new threshold had just been crossed. It was not only her spirit that rose, it was her body also; her entire being stretched toward God.

How can a person go from ecstasy to levitation, the physical expression of mystical elevation? In Chapter 20 of *The Life*, while deploring them, Teresa describes these phenomenal states that drew attention to her despite herself.

First, everything begins with an ecstasy. The body is eclipsed, reduced to a lethargic state: pulse and breathing slowing considerably, internal temperature plummeting, limbs becoming rigid. Vital functions are reduced to the point where they seem to be suspended. "At this stage there is no remedy that can be used to resist...rather, without any forethought or any help there frequently comes a force so swift and powerful that one sees and feels this cloud or mighty eagle raise it up and carry it aloft on its wings."[1]

The spirit then carries the body along behind it:

> Yet I confess that the favor greatly frightened me; at first the fear is extreme. When one sees one's body so elevated from the ground that even though the spirit carries it along after itself, and does so very gently if one does not resist, one's feelings are not lost. At least I was conscious in such a way that I could understand I was being elevated.

At first, Teresa was seized with terror. "It is necessary that the soul be resolute and courageous...in order to risk all, come what may, and abandon itself into the hands of God and go willingly wherever it is brought."

But did she have a choice? No. She was carried along in spite of herself:

> So forceful is this enrapturing that very many times I wanted to resist and used all my energy, especially sometimes when it happened in public.... At times I was able to accomplish something, but with a great loss of energy, as when someone fights with a giant and afterward is worn out.

The scene in the Incarnation chapel can be imagined:

> At other times it was impossible for me to resist, but it carried off my soul and usually, too, my head along with it without my being able to hold back—and sometimes the whole body until it was raised from the ground.... Once it happened when we were together in the choir ready to go up and receive communion and while I was kneeling. I was very distressed.... At other times when I began to see the Lord was going to do the same (and once when there were some ladies of nobility present in order to hear a sermon, for it was our titular feast), I stretched out on the floor and the nuns came and held me down.... When I desired to resist them, such great powers raised me up from the very soles of my feet that I don't know what to compare these powers to; they were much greater than in the other spiritual experiences—and so I was worn out. The struggle is a fierce one, and in the end struggle is of little avail against the Lord's desire; there is no power against His power.

She was now totally conscious of the phenomenon when it took her by surprise:

> In these raptures...without any forethought or any help they frequently come as a force so swift and powerful.... I say that often, it seemed to me, the body was left so light that all its weight was gone, and sometimes this feeling reached such a point that I almost didn't know how to put my feet on the ground.

The phenomenon could not be self-induced, since she fought against the rapture.

But there is confusion in her use of the word *rapture*. Happy confusion, since it concerns the body as well as the spirit, one carrying the other along with it. Teresa says: "Union and rapture, or, as they call it, elevation or flight of the spirit, or transport, which are all the same. I mean that these latter terms, though different, refer to the same thing; it is also called ecstasy."

The "mystical flight," or levitation, is the physical effect (exceptional) of ecstasy. An accident. Or a sign?

Teresa emphasized that she used all her energy to resist the physical effects of rapture and ended by admitting she was no longer mistress of her body, "since, like it or not, one is taken away." All the while, she was conscious of the phenomenon she could not explain beyond that God had chosen to give it to her: "It doesn't seem He is satisfied in truly bringing the soul to Himself, but it seems He desires the body even though it is mortal and, on account of the many offenses it has committed, made of such foul clay."

The primary cause of the rapture could be *the desire* to reach God in that extreme degree where our love matches his: "I am oblivious of everything in that anxious longing to see God." And when the desire is fulfilled—the sight of God in ecstasy—it is as if the body were carried along. Why is it brought along? Because the body and soul do not wish to be separated. Because such a separation, if it should last, would risk leading to death, and Teresa's body, in spite of what she said (*"I die because I do not die"*), clung to life! She was not yet sufficiently detached to think, as she would say in Chapter 20 of *The Life*, "...the Lord would be served if my life came to an end. In my opinion, a pain as great as this is sufficient to put an end to life, but I don't merit death." These statements were the expression of her perfect obedience to the will of God.

Be that as it may, it is difficult to believe this explanation of levitation. Doctor Herbert Thurston, a Jesuit medical specialist of paranormal states and a scientist very critical of hagiographic accounts of the saints, after having read and analyzed a facsimile of the authentic manuscript of *The Life*, places his trust in Teresa.[2] Scientific proof of the veracity of her testimony is here combined: Teresa, whose morality was of the highest order, was incapable of lying; she was conscious of the phenomenon that repeated itself; she fought against its effects with persistence before abandoning herself; out of modesty she attempted to hide it; and finally, she wrote about it only when ordered to do so by her superiors and with the sole aim of "giving witness to the grandeur of God," who had accomplished such marvels in her.

Of course, where this type of extraordinary phenomena is concerned, other trustworthy testimonies are indispensable. They are to be found in abundance in the dossier of her canonization trial: ten or so depositions given under oath, like that of Sister Ana of the Incarnation, a Carmelite from Segovia:

> I was in the choir when our holy mother came in and knelt. As I was look-ing at her, she was raised about half an ell [twenty-four inches] above the floor without her feet touching it. On seeing that, I was terrified. She was trembling in all her being. I approached her gently and placed my hands under her feet, which I bathed with my tears, as long as the ecstasy lasted, maybe about half an hour. Then suddenly she fell down and set herself on her feet. She ordered me to say nothing of what I had seen.

In his *Vida de santa Teresa*, her contemporary Diego de Yepes, confessor of Philip II and later a bishop, reports the saint's struggle against a rapture swooping down upon her with physical consequences that she dreaded hap-pening in public: "I begged the Lord very much not to give me any more favors that would involve any outward show." She would suddenly sense her body escaping gravity. In a desperate effort, she would grip the bars of the grille, but in vain. She rose into the air, and this cry escaped her lips: "Lord, for a thing of such little importance as my being, do not permit that a crea-ture as vile as I am be honored like a holy woman!"

The witness was still amazed. He related that on another day she was seized by a rapture in the choir. Teresa, in interior prayer, prostrated on the floor covered with mats, suddenly felt herself being carried upward and grabbed hold of the mats, taking them with her in the air.

TERESA OF ÁVILA IS NOT the only example of levitation. Although rare, sim-ilar cases have been recorded throughout the centuries.[3] Hagiographers of Christian saints have noted more than one thousand known cases, one hun-dred of which are validated by serious inquiries for canonization and eyewit-nesses. In our own day, skeptical though we may be, some cases have been noted. Paul Lesourd quotes these words of Padre Pio: "Jesus is always gener-ous toward me; it even happens that he lifts me from the ground and lays me on my bed."

In *The Dark Night of the Soul* (Book 2, Chapter 1, Paragraph 2), St. John of the Cross, who levitated, attributes the physical phenomena of mysticism to "the weakness and corruption of the senses." Since the senses would obstruct the revolutionary action of God in the spirit, God invites the human being to an evolutionary mutation. The phenomena cease when the purification is completed thanks to the night of the spirit. Then, "[the per-

fect] enjoy freedom of spirit without detriment to or transport of their
senses."

How did Teresa judge this phenomenon? For her, it was a grace, a favor
manifesting the Lord's tremendous power—"These favors are given by
Him"—which prompted in her a deep humility, a break with regard to the
world, which would give her the power to serve Christ in a way she could
never have previously done.

> From this prayer comes the pain of having to return to everyday life; in this
> prayer wings sprout enabling one to fly with ease; the fledgeling has shed
> its down; in this prayer Christ's banner is now completely raised. It seems
> just as though the custodian of this fortress climbs, or is taken up, to the
> hightest tower to raise the banner for God.

For her, it was thus a sort of invitation to deploy, to found, despite her
initial vocation to remain buried in the silence of a Carmel.

Having penetrated to the very depths of her interior castle, Teresa
became aware of the futility and fragility of worldly things; she was now
ready to do battle for Christ. She had renounced her own will and all material possessions. Henceforth, she would have no other ambition but to
accomplish the will of God. She had acquired a sovereign freedom, such that
she no longer recognized herself. "It is clearly understood that the flight is
given to the spirit so that it may be elevated above every creature—and above
itself first of all. The flight is an easy flight, a delightful one, a flight without
noise."

WITHOUT NOISE? These extraordinary manifestations—ecstasies, lethargy,
prophecies, and levitations—could not pass unnoticed, however discreet her
confessor. Her Carmelite sisters were direct witnesses and did not refrain
from speaking about what they saw. Upon emerging from her ecstasies,
Teresa took on again the humble face of an ordinary Carmelite, but interiorly she remained so consumed with love that the intensity of her glance
betrayed her.

Gradually the monastery reached a state of ferment. Thanks to the parlor visitations, which acted like sieves between the convent and the world,
all of Ávila, already alerted in part by Don Francisco de Salcedo, soon knew
that supernatural incidents were taking place at the Incarnation. Also, they
soon found out that "the saint of Ávila" was not the woeful and sorrowful
María Diaz, but indeed, against all logic, the resplendent Teresa de Jesús who
in the past had dazzled Ávilan society for other reasons.

People rushed to the monastery chapel to witness the spectacular ecstasies, the lethargic collapses, and perhaps the levitations. Many were those who saw her one day after Communion "raised by two or three palm widths above the earth."[4]

Naturally, her superiors and the religious authorities worried about this—and, first and foremost, Teresa herself—as they saw her body, her spirit, and her soul escape from her. "So forceful is this enrapturing that very many times I wanted to resist, especially sometimes when it happened in public...." She felt great sorrow when the matter began to be known publicly.

AMONG THE "RECREATIONAL ACTIVITIES" that her confessor imposed upon her, Teresa loved her long stays with Doña Guiomar de Ulloa. This grand, mystical lady understood Teresa; she sometimes shared Teresa's interior prayers and experienced ecstasies. Teresa confided to her the difficulties she encountered with most of her spiritual advisors and even with Father Baltasar Álvarez, who had returned to Ávila.

That summer of 1560, an eminent man, Peter of Alcántara, was staying in the city. [5] The Franciscan reformer of his Order was also a mystic and acting as general commissioner for his Franciscan provincial. Teresa, who had already read his treatises on the prayer of quiet, spoke of him with enthusiasm in Chapter 27 of *The Life*. She described him as "a very holy and spiritual man." "His spirit is large, as in times past.... He told me that for forty years he slept only an hour and a half during the night...and that to [conquer sleep] he was always either on his knees or standing." Poorly clothed,

> he wore nothing on his feet, nor did he wear any clothes other than a coarse serge habit with nothing else to cover the body.... Eating every third day was a very common practice for him.... His practice of poverty and mortification...was extreme.... Yet with all this sanctity he was very affable....

But, especially, "he experienced great raptures and impulses of love of God, of which I was once a witness."

Teresa also stated quite seriously that "he never looked at women for many years!" But at the instigation of Doña Guiomar, with whom he had come to discuss a foundation, he met and looked at Teresa. "He told me that it no longer made any difference whether he saw or did not see [women]. But he was very old when I came to know him and so extremely weak that it seemed he was made of nothing but tree roots."

These two mystics recognized one another from their very first encounter at Doña Guiomar's. "His words were few unless he was questioned. He was very pleasant in his speech because he had a bright mind."

Teresa did not fail to question him, and "without any duplicity or covering over [she] discussed [her] soul with him."[6] She also had the reputation of levitating. They surely conversed about this extraordinary phenomenon. At that time in her life, Teresa did not yet clearly grasp what was happening to her. He reassured her. As to her visions, they too came from God for a particular end.

This conversation between the two saints, each conscious of living an incredible adventure, can be reconstituted in light of Chapter 30 of *The Life*, Teresa's deeply moving confession. She did not understand her nights of the spirit when she found herself as if between heaven and earth, having left this world without truly finding support in the supernatural!

The saint explained to Teresa that in those somber intervals during which she would lose her footing, she had to resume her march by participating in the Calvary of Christ, who had experienced this terrifying ordeal. The night of the spirit is given to purify the mental state as fire purifies gold.

When she told him that to see the living Christ was her unique passion, he recognized himself. She had finally seen Christ, seen him in the splendor of the resurrection. It remained only to meet head-on the final test, the spiritual marriage, the union with the Spirit, the admitted dream of these two adventurers of the interior journey.

"*Padre!* Can the human soul identify itself with the founding divinity without dying?"

He smiled, knowing that he had fewer than two years to live. Teresa knew it also. But she knew nothing of her own destiny, convinced only that an immense amount of work, for which she was now being prepared, was awaiting her.

"Given where you are, *Madre*, you have nothing more to lose. And it is impossible for you to back away. You must go to the very limit of your experience. For it is in the contemplation of God, the necessary Existing One, that perfection lies."

His look lost itself in the infinite. She saw that he was about to lift up from the earth, and she felt a sacred terror. But he controlled himself. He still had questions to ask her.

"*Madre!* You have reached the level of pure essence. What have you to say of this?"

"That all things are seen and are contained in God."

"But what else?"

"That divinity is like a diamond of a supremely limpid transparency which expresses light, the essence of God. Each one of our actions is reflected in this diamond, for nothing could possibly exist outside of a grandeur which contains everything within itself and upon which our sins alone imprint horrible stains."

He cried out: "So God is therefore light! I knew it!"

Now it was his turn to contemplate this woman to whom God had revealed his essence in the image of a diamond of perfect purity, a vision clouded only by our imperfections. Incommensurable mystery! It confirmed the union of the human being with its Creator, a dependence both reassuring and terrifying. In the end, according to the image of the Song of Songs, the wounded and thirsting doe could drink at the source of living waters. In God's tabernacle, Teresa, the beloved, was finally savoring ineffable delights.

"To live or to die, henceforth for me it's all the same," she said.

"The spirit of God is acting in you, Teresa! You will live. And you will do great things for him."

She was startled. Yes, she felt that she had been regenerated by the sharing of divine light. The Carmelite Father Marie-Eugène Grialou has written, "The distinctive effect of extraordinary favors is light; and a light of such a quality that it can have an extraordinary influence on spiritual life; it is a light at one and the same time clear and transcendent, adapted and unbounded."[7]

But she still suffered from these alternations of exaltation and depression. Night followed the light as in the cycle of day and night. She suddenly felt weak and miserable. Once again, her body pulled her down with an intolerable weight. The saint listened to her with kindness as she complained about the lack of comprehension she encountered. He shook his beautiful white beard.

"One of the greatest trials here below is the opposition of well-meaning people. You have yet to suffer a great deal, for you need continual help, and there is no one here who understands you."

She admitted to him that in the clan of the devout, which was hostile to her, it was Don Francisco de Salcedo who caused her to suffer the most, but she was dependent upon these men because the Church trusted them. "After having seen me so imperfect not long ago, he cannot manage to be reassured about my state. He sees the devil everywhere."

"I will speak to him. Continue your interior prayer without respite, and be assured that you are guided by the Spirit of God."

He left her, asking her to pray for him and to write to him. "He left me with the greatest consolation and happiness and the ability to feel secure in my prayer."[8]

Peter of Alcántara brought together Teresa's opponents and all those who were speaking of exorcism and he declared to them: "After Holy Scripture, there is nothing more true than the divine origin of what this woman is seeing."

Fray Peter was venerated in Ávila, as he was throughout Spain. Criticism of Teresa became less virulent. The clan of the devout drew in its claws. Don Salcedo, the holy gentleman, was brought around. He was even heard to declare: "If I were told that St. John the Baptist was at the gate of Ávila and *Madre* Teresa was in another part of the city, I would renounce seeing John the Baptist to throw myself at the feet of *la Madre!*"

Those who had always believed in Teresa came out of the shadows where fear of the Inquisition had driven them. Among them was Father Pedro Ibáñez, the brilliant Dominican theologian whom she had already consulted in his monastery of San Tomás. He had then deemed that she was going too far in interior prayer; he had feared the abyss for her. And she was in it! When he saw her again, he was dazzled: "I cannot but consider her a saint."

How she had changed, Teresa de Jesús! Still beautiful, as always, at the age of forty-five, in the full bloom of both her spirit and her body, "she was emerging from these trials and the torrent of her graces, standing tall with an admirable lucidity and a stalwart equilibrium."[9] Transfigured by love of the Absolute, she was becoming the one whom all of Spain would call "*la Madre*," an exceptional personality springing from her desire for effacement, to withdraw as a simple and anonymous lay sister in a small, obscure, and remote monastery! There to enjoy his love! No. She exclaimed: "*Padre!* I now have such an imperious desire to serve God that I would like to cry out to everyone, saying how important it is not to be content with little—a desire so intense that the idea of my powerlessness shatters me internally. This body ties me down. Were it not for it, I would do great things."

He was startled. But no. In this look—pure, almost unbearable—there was not the least trace of pride.

These strange words had escaped Teresa as if someone inside her had pronounced them for her. And yet it would be so good to leave this world and this body, crippled with suffering, to rejoin the Beloved without delay. Yet Christ had gone to the very end of his Calvary. And so she would live to share her secret, her happiness, with her own, since that was her mission. Of this she was now certain.

He asked with a quiver in his voice: "You said 'great things,' *Madre?*"

"Reform the Carmel as Fray Peter of Alcántara is doing with the Franciscans."

He remained pensive.

"This is in line with the aim of the Council of Trent. Yes, the saint of Alcántara is reforming the Franciscan Order. But the Carmel! There would be fierce opposition!"

"The state of powerlessness to serve God in which I am in causes me unbearable sorrow."

"Patience, daughter! Your time will come."

"It has come. What do you order me to do?"

"Obey him who lives in you. To see more clearly in this, write your spiritual testimonies setting forth the state of your soul, divine favors, the trials."[10]

Teresa got to work. She met again with Peter of Alcántara. He taught her how to write about and describe her ecstasies without distorting them. After Francis Borgia, he was the second saint that she had the benefit of knowing. He guided her to give birth to herself, enabling Teresa de Jesús to finally become *la Madre fundadora*, the Mother foundress. By explaining to her his reform and the Rule of the tiny convent of Palancar he had just founded with ten brothers, he gave her the model for the future tiny community of Discalced Carmelites of which she dreamed. And the idea was growing in her heart. Reform the Carmel! Give it once again the purity, the strength, and the vigor of the first ascetics!

Thus interior prayer and ecstatic states were not cutting her off from the world. On the contrary, they were moving her to action. "It is here that resolutions, burning desires, heroic works are born."[11] From the contemplation of Christ, the divine model, was born an ardent desire for perfection and for making known the Love that was giving itself to her.

CHAPTER 13

The Break

(1560)

*I*n August 1560, a terrible vision upset Teresa's existence. She recounted it in Chapter 32 of *The Life*:

> While I was in prayer one day, I suddenly found that, without knowing how, I had seemingly been put in hell.... The entrance it seems to me was similar to a very long and narrow alleyway, like an oven, low and dark and confined; the floor seemed to me to consist of dirty, muddy water emitting a foul stench and swarming with putrid vermin. At the end of the alleyway a hole that looked like a small cupboard was hollowed out in the wall; there I found I was placed in a cramped condition.... Those walls, which were terrifying to see, closed in on themselves and suffocated everything. There was no light, but all was enveloped in the blackest darkness.

She was immediately submerged in suffering.

> I experienced a fire in [my] soul.... The bodily pains were so unbearable that though I had suffered excruciating ones in this life...these were all nothing in comparison with the ones I experienced there. I saw furthermore that they would go on without end and without ever ceasing. This, however, was nothing next to the soul's agonizing: a constriction, a suffocation, an affliction so keenly felt and with such a despairing and tormenting unhappiness...the experience is as though the soul were continually being wrested from the body...it is the soul itself that tears itself in pieces. The fact is that I don't know how to give a sufficiently powerful description of that interior fire and that despair.... I felt myself burning and crumbling.... Being in such an unwholesome place, so unable to hope for any consolation.... I don't understand how this could be, that everything painful to see was visible.

126

Teresa insisted on the realistic side of this ordeal, this *experience*: "I understood that the Lord wanted me to see the place the devils had prepared for me.... The Lord wanted me actually to feel those spiritual torments and afflictions, as though the body were suffering."

For Teresa, there was no doubt at all: the devil, master of hell, is a person, and he exists to destroy us. This fear was at that time omnipresent in the Christian world. Preachers used and abused it to maintain moral and political order; it is clear that they believed in it. Objective proofs were not lacking, and Teresa quotes them at length in Chapter 31 of *The Life*:

> I was once in an oratory; and [the devil] appeared to me in an abominable form at my left side.... It seemed that a great flame, all bright without shadow, came forth from his body. He told me in a terrifying way that I had really freed myself from his hands but that he would catch me with them again.

Some of these sisters smelled "a foul stench like that of brimstone" in her cell. Sometimes she heard "the striking of loud blows near the place where I was; I heard some coarse words next to me as though the devils were plotting something."

This caused her a suffering full of anguish: "I was tormented for five hours with such terrible interior and exterior pains and disturbance that it didn't seem to me I could suffer them any longer." At this point, we cannot help but think of the diabolic infestations that would poison the life of the Curé d'Ars three and a half centuries later, and, closer to our time, the life of Padre Pio.

There are two plausible interpretations of Teresa's vision of hell. For the Carmelite Father Jean Abiven, it symbolizes "what would await us if we refused the gift of God." After all, we carry within us (as did Teresa in her youth) a "dynamic of evil from which divine grace delivers us if we accept it." On the other hand, if we allow it to develop, this dynamic of evil "can lead us to a hardened refusal of what God-Love is, which is hell."[1]

Dazzling divine light reveals repressed complexes, obscure corners of the human soul full of foul beasts: sins and other wounds that were not assumed in childhood. Father Abiven evokes "all of man's misery, all that in him is opposition to God, refusal of his love."[2]

This vision was preparing Teresa for her apostolic mission. First, begin with oneself, then stir up the unfaithful, even at the heart of religious establishments like the Incarnation, relaxed in its Rule.

Beyond this classic interpretation, the vision could be analyzed in the light of today's depth psychology. Teresa saw herself in hell as really there, a vision all the more unusual because she was enjoying the greatest of divine favors. But did she really deserve hell, the eternal punishment of those who had committed "mortal sins" by transgressing divine law?

Long before Freud, as we have said, Teresa discovered the unconscious. This visionary phenomenon is an illustration of her discovery, the fruit of an intense preparation, an introspection. What is general confession, practiced by Teresa out of obedience and with remarkable assiduity, if not a psychoanalysis with spiritual dimensions? And what is interior prayer if not a loving dialogue after a patient, progressive march consisting of trust and waiting in contemplation? It is a heart-to-heart dialogue with Jesus. A presence to him who never ceases calling us to live day after day the great adventure of his love. Teresa explains this progression in the seven dwellings of the *Interior Castle*: a literary, spiritual, and psychological masterpiece that would at one and the same time make her famous and a Doctor of the Church.

Unknown to Teresa, her general confession introduced her into that strange, unconscious, mental world—the basement of our conscious space. From this space emerged the vision of hell that seemed to slap her in the face, an archaic vision that takes root in the deepest layers of human history. It was thus given to her to seize the breadth of the destruction from which she had escaped. Not "eternal flames," a symbolic image, but the impulsion of death, *thanatos*, as opposed to the *eros* to which her destiny was leading her. Death was omnipresent in her life: her father's first wife carried off by the plague in the flower of her youth, then in gradual succession her own mother, her father, followed by three of her brothers and her half-brother caught up in the spiral of the violence of war.

Given her psychological constitution, alternating between exaltation and depression, Teresa verged on psychosis that can lead to death, a useless death that she narrowly escaped in 1540.

This is the argument put forth by the Catholic psychologist Bernadette Lorenzo, who then asks: "Why is it that those who have something to do with God have to be convulsed in their bodily experience?" "Ground *like the grain of wheat*," Bernadette Soubirous would say. Why suffering? Dr. Lorenzo's response is that "pain opens up unknown zones of biological individuality, extends the field of perceptions and intuitions. Is it a required voyage for whoever wants to seek the unknown?"

On several occasions, Teresa insisted on the suffering that crushed her body with "an arsenal of infirmities."

ALL MYSTICS HAVE SUFFERED. The mystic, humbly recognizing himself or herself as the voluntary instrument of the divine project in view of evolving humanity, makes use of suffering and the knowledge that results from it to advance toward his or her goal: God. For Teresa, the goal was Christ, sent by his Father to make his love known to us, to induce our love and make us love one another. But this journey passes through Calvary, the unjust, ignominious death of him who dared to proclaim the truth of God to the limit of his strength and at the price of his life out of love and obedience.

This explains why, with Teresa, suffering was mixed with pleasure. Suffering, if refused, would lead to "hell." Suffering accepted with love would lead to the joy of the resurrection with certain inevitable empty stretches, the nights of the soul.

The grand word has been pronounced: "night of the spirit." No one has analyzed it better than the Spanish Carmelite St. John of the Cross (1542–1591), who would soon make his dazzling appearance in the life of Teresa. The night, he stated, results from divine invasions; it is "an inflow of God into the soul, which purges it of its habitual ignorances and imperfections."[3] It is a question of "inclining the soul to a union of love with Him by purifying and enlightening it."[4]

The obscurity and the suffering that result do not come from God but from the still imperfect soul, for "the height of the divine wisdom...exceeds the abilities of the soul."[5] The soul's impurity makes this light painful; it is painful because of the bedazzlement it provokes. Whoever looks directly at the sun is blinded and sinks into obscurity. This strength also paralyzes. "The divine torrent bumps against the rock that stops it or curbs its course," writes Father Marie-Eugène.

John of the Cross attributed raptures and mystical ecstasies (catatonia) to the night of the soul, a painful phenomenon provoked by the breakdown of the ego. But the night leads to a psychological turnaround that is necessary for conversion. In the sixth dwelling, Teresa described the dimming of understanding, the disruption caused by the memory that falters.

Regardless of the phenomena, which differ from mystic to mystic, if God is truly at the origin of the trauma, like a surgeon, he injures only to heal.

TERESA HAD THUS RISEN above the ordeal; and what an ordeal!

> It seems to me I neither live, nor speak, nor have any desire but that He who strengthens and governs me might live in me. I go about as though outside myself, and so life is the severest pain for me. And the greatest

thing I offer God as a principal service to Him is that, since it is so painful for me to live separated from Him, I desire to live, but out of love for Him.[6]

Wanting to live for what? "Since I am no good for being of any help to anyone, I should like to be good for suffering...by a better fulfillment of His will." She declared that she was being crucified between heaven, which she did not yet have, and earth, where she was no longer satisfied with life in that monastery following the mitigated Rule. "Receiving no help from either side, [the soul] is as though crucified between heaven and earth. That which comes from heaven...causes more torment because the desire increases...."[7]

During that decisive year of 1560, when Teresa found herself torn between the pleasure of contemplation and the suffering of the purifying night, she turned the corner of "conversion" by detaching herself from herself. And, wonder of wonders, proof of the reality of the divine phenomenon, she "enters into perfection," where she could no longer stand the hypocrisy and the thousand venial sins of her life at the Incarnation. Rather *die*, she said, still marked by the urge of death. But this God of love wanted her to live. He asked her for this conversion, this metamorphosis. She could not refuse him anything. And so she advanced along the road between two abysses: follow the will of God or renounce it, which for her would have been to betray herself and all those who awaited her aid.

Thanks to prayer, Teresa began to understand the role of contemplative nuns, but also to see this vocation as linked to an austere, even ascetic life. She then formulated "the most perfect vow," the search for the greatest possible perfection.

Everything was in keeping with the direction of the Reform that, little by little, was taking shape in her mind. Unfortunately, the lifestyle at the Incarnation was incompatible with the search for a perfect life; it was an overcrowded community with doubtful vocations and relaxed discipline. Teresa was finally becoming aware of the excessive liberty she was enjoying in this monastery where she had felt at ease, but too much so! In the midst of interior prayer, she was troubled by frivolities, as if the outside world or the body or some demon wanted to pull her back. Teresa could no longer even concentrate on a reading.

The aspiration for a small community of cloistered nuns, ardent in their love of Christ, eager for perfection, and praying for the salvation of the world, was taking root in her. She also became aware that "provided I'm not against God...the powers of the devils are nothing."[8] Yet she was conscious of running the ever-present risk of pride when others took her for a saint.

She felt more reassured in the midst of persecutions, which made her feel that she was at last being taken for what she was: less than nothing!

Father Ibáñez advised her to detach herself from her preoccupations. What good there was in her did not come from her but from God. It was sufficient to leave everything up to him.

That was not enough for her. Virtuous passivity did not correspond to her active character. Once again, she thought of leaving, since she was not tied to the Incarnation by the vow of stability. But where could she go? In spite of the attempts made in the fifteenth century by Jean Soreth, the founder of the female branch, Spain did not have a Carmel of strict observance. There was talk of small pockets in Flanders and also in Brittany, like Notre-Dame-du-Couët, near Nantes, founded in 1477 by the Duchess of Brittany. Teresa could already see herself there as an anonymous, simple lay sister, forgotten by everyone. But her confessor dissuaded her.

"You would only be transporting your scruples elsewhere. As to the devil, he can act everywhere!"

However, the idea was making headway in Teresa's mind. Perfection is a long patience. Having consecrated herself to a contemplative life to avoid temptations and give herself to Love, she had to separate herself more radically from the world without forgetting to serve it.

ONE SEPTEMBER EVENING IN 1560, Teresa had gathered in her room at the Incarnation a few relatives and friends. They already formed a faithful group of people who were inspired by her: her two cousins Ana and Inés de Tapia, who had just received the veil as professed nuns; her two young relatives Leonora and María de Ocampo (daughters of her cousin Didace de Cepeda), whom Teresa had welcomed at the Incarnation as lay boarders after the marriage of her young sister, Juana de Ahumada. María, who was seventeen and already exhibiting a strong personality, was thinking of taking the veil, but not at the Incarnation. Juana Suárez, Teresa's longtime friend, was also there.

They all admired Teresa's faith and radiance, her joy, her desire to share with them her confidence and her faith in God. They felt her ardent desire to begin to live—and have them live—all that she had received of light and love, not her exceptional graces but that road to perfection that passed through obedience and self-forgetfulness.

In this large monastery, only a tiny third of the religious around her were applying themselves to this ideal. The majority remained hostile to any change. In her cell that opened onto the cloister, Teresa sometimes heard melodies played on the flute, drumming on the tambourine, and the call so often repeated for one or another sister to proceed to the parlor. This Incarnation monastery was not an auspicious place for the meditation, prayer, and contemplation that open wide the door to the interior life.

Suddenly, María de Ocampo exclaimed: "Let's leave and organize for ourselves a solitary life, under the primitive Rule of Carmel, in the spirit of the desert: silence, poverty, strict enclosure—everything that favors prayer and union with God."

Teresa looked at her, smiling, amazed that the idea she had been secretly pursuing for so many years would come at last from the lips of this young girl not bound by any vow. "From one word to another," she recounts, "the night passed inventing means to create a small monastery and what it would cost."

"Make the foundation!" cried out the enthusiastic María. "I will help you with my 'legitimate,' the inheritance that has been promised to me: one thousand ducats!"

This important sum, which would allow them to purchase a small house, left them musing. The problem of revenues remained. What would they live on?

They parted, each one returning to her own cell.[9]

CHAPTER 14

The St. Joseph Conspiracy

(1560–1561)

The next day, Teresa, still in a state of shock, was visited by Doña Guiomar. Neither woman kept back any secrets.

"Yesterday, we amused ourselves imagining that we were founding a very tiny monastery on the model of the Discalced Franciscan sisters."

"Don't imagine any longer, Teresa! Found it! I will help you."

Thus began what would come to be called "the St. Joseph conspiracy," named for the future St. Joseph monastery.

Doña Guiomar immediately perceived the timeliness of this project. It was a good idea coming at the right moment. The pope was urging relaxed monasteries to reform, the only evangelical answer to the Lutheran Reformation. Already in Spain, the Dominicans had undertaken their reform, as had the Franciscans. With the Society of Jesus there was an army of "Companions of Jesus" under the direct command of the pope. King Philip II himself not only supported the pope, but he had also been given the mission of fighting against the division between Catholics and Lutherans in his kingdoms. Only the Carmelites were dragging their feet, despite the timid attempts of their prior general, Rubeo de Ravenna.

Thus had María de Ocampo, with the enthusiasm of her youth, been the spark that would set alight the burning fire of the Reform smoldering in Teresa's mind and heart.

After twenty-five years of doubts and erring ways followed by resounding graces, everything was at last becoming clear for Teresa. In Chapter 21 of *The Life*, recognizing the graces that she had received from God, she wrote:

> Fortify my soul and dispose it first, Good of all goods and my Jesus, and
> then ordain ways in which I might do something for You, for there is no

longer anyone who can suffer to receive so much and not repay anything. Alas! I'm not good for anything but talk...everything adds up to just words and desires...and even in this I don't have freedom....

And she concludes: "Cost what it may, Lord, do not desire that I come into Your presence with hands so empty.... Here is my life, here is my honor and my will. I have given all to You, I am Yours...."

She, a woman, felt herself to be such a little thing! However, with Christ at her side, she was capable of the greatest actions: "I see clearly, Lord, the little I am capable of. But having reached You, having climbed to this watchtower, I see truths. I can do all things, providing You do not leave me."

Faced with the scale of the task, however, she dared not commit herself. It wasn't only a matter of money, recruits, and the house; centuries of routine had to be uprooted, and ecclesiastical authorizations had to be obtained. Once again, she turned toward Christ, asking for a sign.

> One day after Communion, His Majesty earnestly commanded me to strive for this new monastery with all my powers, and He made great promises that it would be founded and that He would be highly served in it. He said it should be called Saint Joseph and that this saint would keep watch over us at one door, and our Lady at the other, that Christ would remain with us, and that it would be a star shining with great splendor.... He asked what would become of the world if it were not for religious.... This vision had such great effects, and this locution the Lord granted was of such a nature, that I couldn't doubt it was from God.[1]

The project had an evangelical simplicity: return to the primitive Rule starting with a small, poor community—both fervent and fraternal, protected from distractions—in order to further the prayer of quiet and the interior voyage and lead a life in common as perfectly as possible according to evangelical counsels practiced to the letter. Teresa could measure all the difficulties she faced. Her mission was a challenge in this Spanish Golden Age in which the frenzied pursuit of America's riches, power, and honors was leading the world to its demise. A challenge whose profound aim was to *touch* God!

Before going forward, Teresa had to obtain the agreement of her confessor, the Jesuit Father Baltasar Álvarez, who was reluctant, especially for financial reasons. The hope of benefiting from María de Ocampo's inheritance was already causing a problem. Her parents did not care to see her shut herself away in such an austere and precarious new foundation. As to the revenues promised by Doña Guiomar, they proved to be insufficient. By dint of giving here and there without counting, this grand and generous lady ended up ruining herself. Teresa replied to her confessors: "Teresa and three ducats—that is not much. But, Teresa, three ducats, and God—that is everything. It is not a question of knowing what the religious will live on, but how they will pray. If the community is fervent, alms will come pouring in."

Only half convinced, the Jesuit shied away: "Speak about it to Father Gregorio Hernández, your provincial superior. And act according to his decision."

Teresa, ordinarily so daring, did not dare to speak to her superior. She also feared confronting the prioress of her monastery. The project for which she was preparing was nothing less than the introduction of a radical reform in the Order, and Father Hernández was known to be in favor of the mitigated Rule. He had been elected provincial of the Carmelites of Castile for that reason. It is true that St. Peter of Alcántara, having been consulted, had given Teresa a favorable opinion, as had St. Francis Borgia. But the first was a Franciscan and the second a Jesuit. They could not intervene in the affairs of the Carmel. She then asked Doña Guiomar to go in her place to the provincial in Toledo and lay out the plan to him.

A few days later, as though it was the most natural thing in the world, Teresa announced to her friends: "Our Father Provincial, who is a friend of religious perfection, has welcomed our project very favorably."

It is quite evident that he had not measured the consequences. A return to the primitive Rule? Why not? "It seems to me that a monastery of women that allows freedom is a tremendous danger,"[2] Teresa maintained. He was of course entirely in agreement! A very tiny monastery with a maximum of thirteen religious? That would make very little noise in the Order while going in the direction of the Council's Reform. The Incarnation, which numbered more than one hundred professed nuns and as many lay religious, could sustain such a small amputation. Naturally, Father Hernández would keep the new foundation under his jurisdiction. Administratively speaking, nothing would be changed. As St. Paul had advised, everything had to be tried; what was good would remain.

That is when the sky fell around them: "Hardly had the knowledge of it begun to spread throughout the city when the great persecution...came upon us: gossip, derision, saying that it was foolishness."

Teresa had committed an error in not soliciting the agreement of the Incarnation's prioress. But was this conceivable? This grand lady of the local aristocracy (whom Teresa never quotes) did not want to hear of it. To establish in the very city of Ávila a Carmel of strict observance would have underscored her convent's imperfections. Through Teresa's proposed Reform, all the mitigated felt they were being judged. Teresa's project was menacing the community with being broken up. The financial problem also had to be taken into account. All of these donations and dowries that would be going elsewhere would deprive the Incarnation, which was already in financial straits.

In the city, people were mocking the whole idea. They were talking about Teresa de Ahumada once again! After the visions, the ecstasies, and the levitations, a new foundation! Just who did she think she was? Evidently, many—both clergy and lay—felt threatened by the requirement of purity and austerity that this new program carried with it.

Doña Guiomar herself had to endure "so much persecution that she became very upset." "They didn't want to give her absolution unless she gave up the idea, because they said she was obliged to remove the scandal."

But what scandal? Was not the real scandal, rather, the lax discipline of the Carmels?

Unfortunately, in this confrontation between the mitigated and those who wanted a Reform, the city sided in favor of the Incarnation. The Carmelites' families took an unfavorable view of the Reform. Strict parlor visits reduced to a minimum? More austerities? The city councilors themselves were not in favor of a new foundation. There were already too many monasteries in the city. And Spain—between the plague and its many wars— needed its women to bear children.

Faced with the tumult, Father Provincial Hernández hesitated, deeming it imprudent to go against the tide of opposition, not to mention the problems of the insecure finances and size of the endeavor.

In the face of these difficulties, Teresa should have given up. Instead, she prayed, and immediately

> His Majesty began to console and encourage me. He told me that in this I would see what the saints who had founded religious orders had suffered, that I would have to suffer much more persecution than I could imagine, and that we shouldn't let it bother us.

Then, searching for support in the city, she asked her Dominican friend, Pedro Ibáñez, for his advice, considering him to be "a most learned man, a very great servant of God." Doña Guiomar had informed him beforehand of the project. Unfortunately, Father Ibáñez had already been contacted by the opposition. He greeted Teresa with reserve.

"A foundation? Why? Aren't there already too many convents in this city?"

"Our Lord invites me to do it."

The Dominican remained puzzled. Having heard Teresa's confession, he considered her a saint, but given the uproar in the city, he hesitated. He then put her to the test:

"Are you determined to do what I shall tell you?"

"Yes, *Padre*."

"I will reflect and give you my answer in a week."

Teresa departed. She prayed with all her soul. A week later, she was summoned by Father Ibáñez, who seemed deeply upset.

"Go ahead, *Madre!* Your plan, which returns to the primitive Rule, seems to me to be agreeable to God. Hurry to accomplish it in order to place the authorities before a *fait accompli*. Your revenues seem to be insufficient, but one must abandon oneself to divine Providence. As to those who would oppose your plan, send them to me. I'll know how to persuade them."

For their part, Don Francisco de Salcedo and Father Gaspar Daza, both of whom had been so hostile regarding Teresa's visions, approved the project. Without further hesitation, Teresa went forward. A house was sought with the aim of buying it. A modest building, "poor and small," was found outside the ramparts in the working-class area to the north of the city.

Unfortunately, the authorities, far from giving way, hardened their stance. In Toledo, Father Provincial Hernández, subjected to civilian and religious pressures, withdrew his approval for a foundation. Teresa's confessor, Baltasar Álvarez, followed suit. An ordinary nun with no position in the Order, Teresa had to submit. Father Ibáñez was also shaken as he realized that by approving this woman, a nuisance to say the least, he had taken on a heavy responsibility. He attempted to change course:

"Rumor in Ávila has it that you might be having visions, revelations? This is not the moment to report them; that would condemn you. In 1559, three decisions of the Inquisition in Valladolid and Seville led innovative heretics and other false mystics to the stake. The archbishop of Toledo himself was imprisoned!"

"I am not a heretic, *Padre!* I am a daughter of the Church!"

"No doubt. But the miracles, the visions.... The devil is hiding everywhere. The Holy Inquisition and the Royal Council are keeping watch to flush him out."

He hesitated. She felt the weight of his eyes on her. Was he not a consultant of the Inquisition and, as such, entrusted with responsibilities? She became troubled. She had not yet dared to admit to him the new divine favors that were being bestowed upon her. He guessed that she was hiding something from him.

"May I hear your confession?"

She knelt before him and opened her limpid soul to him. He was amazed by it all.

"Nothing in your interior life or in your doctrine seems to me to be contrary to holy Scripture. However, you must submit to the order of your provincial and your usual confessor."

With a humility that was all he needed to be completely convinced, she submitted.

BUT IT WAS TOO LATE. Her situation at the Incarnation was becoming unbearable. The mutterings against her intensified.

> I was very much disliked throughout my monastery because I had wanted to found a more enclosed monastery. They said I was insulting them; that in my own monastery I could also serve God since there were others in it better than I; that I had no love for the house; that it would be better to procure income for this place than for some other.[3]

At the Incarnation there was a kind of prison cell, a dungeon for recalcitrant members. There was talk of locking her away in it. Teresa was threatened with being denounced to the Inquisition. She was especially shaken by a stern letter from her confessor, Baltasar Álvarez, prompted by the rector of the Jesuit college, Dionisio Vaquez.

> He wrote me that I should now be able to see from what had happened that the project had been all a dream, that I should make amends from then on by not desiring to go out for anything or to speak any more about it since I had seen the scandal that had occurred.

She wavered. Then she remembered the vision in which the Lord urged her to persist. "If these visions had been illusions, all the prayer I had experienced was self-deception, and...I was being misled and going astray. This made me so extremely distressed I was thrown into complete confusion and severely afflicted."

Turning toward Christ, she asked him: "My Lord, how is it You command things that seem impossible? For if I were at least free, even though I am a woman!"

Having begun again to pray, she heard Christ's voice. He consoled her. Then, he ordered her to submit, "by being silent for the present, until it would come time to return to the task."

She felt at peace. "The increase of love of God I saw in my soul and many other things reached such a point that I was amazed.... I remained silent...

since I didn't want...to go against obedience to my confessor." However, hope remained; she felt certain that the foundation would be realized.

She then wrote the following poem to the grace of God:

Let nothing trouble you,
Let nothing scare you.
All is fleeting,
God alone is unchanging.
Patience
Everything obtains.
Whoever possesses God
Nothing wants
God alone suffices.[4]

Patience obtains everything. Patience and a certain daring. In 1561, Teresa, more and more rejected at the Incarnation, obtained from her prioress the authorization to reside for a long period of time at the home of her friend, Doña Guiomar. This gave her great liberty to act.

Another positive change occurred: Dionisio Vaquez, who was hostile to Teresa and was influencing her confessor, Baltasar Álvarez,[5] was replaced by Father Gaspar de Salazar. Father de Salazar arrived from Madrid, where he had been the confessor of Princess Juana, the king's sister. Of him, Teresa wrote, "His soul was a pure and holy one, and he had a special gift from the Lord for discerning spirits." He immediately fell under the spell of Teresa's grace and spiritual radiance. Moreover, the spell was mutual: "I felt in my spirit I don't know what that I never recall having felt with anyone," she writes, "a spiritual joy and understanding within my soul that his soul would understand mine and that mine would be in harmony with his."

He approved her project on the condition that she act discreetly. Baltasar Álvarez was thus rendered harmless, until such time when he could be convinced.

[He] told him to console me; that there was no reason for fear, and not to lead me by so confining a path; that he should let the spirit of the Lord work, for at times it seemed with these great spiritual impulses that my soul couldn't even breathe....

It seemed to Teresa that the rector had been sent by Providence, so much did he understand her soul. Not only did he not urge her to be reserved, but she said, "he [made me] run rather than walk with measured step."

A real conspiracy was hatched. It was impossible to found a community without ecclesiastical authorization. They could not obtain it from the

Carmelite province, with its seat in Toledo. Never mind that! Teresa, on the advice of Father Ibáñez, had Doña Guiomar act in her stead. The young widow simply asked Rome, on her own account, for the authorization to found in Ávila a convent subjected to the primitive Rule of the Carmel, suggesting that it be placed under the direct authority of the bishop of Ávila, who was not even consulted! Was Father Ibáñez really behind this bold and, at the very least, subversive idea? St. Peter of Alcántara may have suggested to Teresa that she disengage herself from the provincial authority of the mitigated Rule. But this casualness toward legitimate superiors entailed numerous risks that Teresa, swept along by her visions, did not take into account.

The little house outside the city's ramparts—intended to shelter the future monastery according to the primitive Rule of the Carmel—had been found. But whose name would be used for registering the documents of ownership? Certainly not Teresa de Ahumada's, since she had taken the vow of poverty.

In August 1561, Teresa's youngest sister, Juana, whom she had raised at the Incarnation until her marriage to Juan de Ovalle—a poor nobleman from Alba de Tormes—agreed to return to live for a time in Ávila with her small family. Juana, at age thirty-three, was pregnant and already had a four-year-old child. The family would settle in the little house whose documents of ownership carried the Ovalle name. "This is just like Teresa and her art of going her own way without actually disobeying."[6] In reality, she wanted to obey her voices without confronting her superiors head-on. With the passage of time, she hoped the Lord would make them change their minds. She did not even seem embarrassed by this subterfuge. "I took great care not to do anything against obedience. But I knew that if I said anything to my superiors, everything would be lost...." She was practicing the art of mental reservation dear to the Jesuits. You do not lie, but you also do not say everything!

Where would she find the money to begin the foundation, since her own family revenues—her dowry—were paid to the Incarnation in the form of a pension? Neither María de Ocampo nor Doña Guiomar had yet been able to honor her promise. Among the postulants, two had offered their dowries, which had allowed her to pay for the purchase of the house. As to what would follow:

> Once when in need, for I didn't know what to do or how to pay some workmen, St. Joseph, my true father and lord, appeared to me and revealed to me that I would not be lacking, that I should hire them. And so I did, without so much as a penny, and the Lord in ways that amazed those who heard about it provided for me.

"Patience obtains everything...."[7] So they waited for the workers and the building materials. Then gold fell from the sky or, rather, from the ocean: the gold would come to her from America! Even before Teresa asked her brother Lorenzo for help, the conquistador in charge of the Royal Treasury in Ecuador was coming generously to her aid.

The gold ingots had been unloaded at Seville, where a messenger conveyed them as far as Madrid. There they were "sold to the highest bidder and free of charges" and converted to Spanish currency. Don Lorenzo's messenger was entrusted with bringing them to Ávila, along with a marvelous statue of the Virgin covered in finery and jewels. His other sisters, Juana de Ovalle and María de Guzmán, were not forgotten by the generous brother whom Teresa thanked in these terms:

> I believe that it was God who stirred you to send me so much.... [S]aintly and learned persons think I am obliged not to be cowardly but to do all I can for this project—a monastery of nuns. There will be no more than fifteen nuns in it, who will practice very strict enclosure, never going out or allowing themselves to be seen without veils covering their faces. Their life will be one of prayer and mortification.... I did not have the means to pay for the work that still needed to be done. So by trusting in God alone (for God wants it to be done and will provide), I entered into an agreement with the workers. It seemed a foolish thing to do. But then His Majesty comes along and moves Your Grace to provide for it.[8]

It would now be possible, at last, to pay the workers, and Teresa was able to breathe again. She was busy on the building site and, to obey Father Ibáñez, she began to write her autobiography, *The Life,* to which all of her biographers would refer in the future. It is truly a confession that completed her liberation, and even more than that, it is "the most lucid description ever written about supernatural states and done in the most natural style."[9]

In the midst of this ongoing ferment, Teresa remained entirely given over to Love. She was radiant from the peace she derived from her long periods devoted to the prayer of quiet, which she spent in dialogue with Christ, "speaking only of him, writing about his marvels," according to the testimony of Father Ibáñez. When he expressed his astonishment at this, knowing of the Carmelite's numerous activities and concerns, she responded: "Imagine a person so enamored of another that she could not spend an instant away from the presence of the person she loves."

THE WORK OF CONSTRUCTION was far from finished when the Ovalles and their child Gonzalito, who was four years old, settled into the future monastery's outer buildings. Teresa dearly loved her sister Juana, and she patiently endured Juana's husband, a narrow-minded *hidalgo*, easily offended and jealous, but completely devoted to Teresa, whom he admired.

Juana was in the ninth month of her pregnancy when a dramatic accident occurred at St. Joseph. Gonzalito, playing at a distance among the building materials stockpiled for the construction work, was struck by a section of the wall being built that broke away. The child had the strength to drag himself to the threshold of the house, where he fell unconscious. Upon his return, Juan Ovalle found Gonzalito bloodied and his body rigid. Dead.

He brought the child to Teresa and placed him on her lap while raising loud cries. Juana also shrieked with sorrow as Doña Guiomar, who had tried in vain to keep her in her room, held her up. "Stop crying and leave," Teresa said to them. Seeing her illuminated face, the parents calmed down and closed the door as they left the room.

> They were all breathless, awaiting what would happen. Teresa lifted her veil and, calling out to God, she bent over the child. She stayed this way for some time until the child came back to life. She then caressed his face with her hands. And as he awakened from what seemed to be an ordinary sleep, she gave the child back to his mother.[10]

Having witnessed the miracle, Doña Guiomar exclaimed: "The child was dead! How can it be that he is alive?"

Smiling, Teresa ordered them to be silent. "The child was scampering about the room, running toward his aunt and embracing her."[11]

Juana gave birth to a son whom they named José at his baptism in honor of St. Joseph, the patron of the future monastery. Doña Guiomar was his godmother and Francisco de Salcedo his godfather. Strangely enough, Teresa could be seen holding the child tightly in her arms and murmuring in what sounded like a lullaby: "Should you not become a good man, little angel, I pray to God that he take you before you offend him."

He died a few months later. Teresa took him on her knees, covered him with her veil, and went into ecstasy. Juana could see that her child was dead, but she did not dare move, convinced that her sister was about to perform a new miracle. When Teresa came out of her ecstasy, she arose without saying a word and, carrying the dead child, she left the room.

"Where are you going?" cried Juana. "Why aren't you telling me that my child is dead?"

The saint's face was resplendent with light. "Let us give thanks to God. I saw his soul go up to heaven and the angels come to get him."[12]

CONSTRUCTION ADVANCED SLOWLY. In this atmosphere of daily miracles, Teresa's visions succeeded each other, and she also heard the voice of Christ encouraging her. Among her visions, one of St. Clare troubled her to the very depths of her being.

"On her feast day, while I was going to Communion, St. Clare appeared to me with striking beauty. She told me to take courage and to continue with what I had begun, that she would help me."

That vision was not without significance. Born in 1193 in Assisi, like Teresa, Clare had escaped from her father's house at the age of eighteen when he wanted to marry her off. She had made the vows of chastity and poverty and placed herself under the protection of St. Francis of Assisi. A year later, she founded the Poor Clares, the Franciscan "poor ladies," becoming the first woman to found a religious Order. Following the example of St. Francis, she fought to impose strict poverty in a monastery without revenues or property; the nuns lived on payment from their work and occasional alms. The first Poor Clares remained in intimate union with Christ, whom they were called not only to contemplate but to imitate. As the Poor Clares were living Teresa's very ideal, the vision of their founder stunned her.

It so happened that there was a monastery of Poor Clares near St. Joseph. There Teresa received the most sisterly welcome and often material aid. In 1562, she wrote the following in *The Life*: "Little by little, she [St. Clare] brought this desire of mine to such perfection that the poverty the blessed saint practiced in her house is practiced in this one, and we are living on alms." This was tantamount to founding the community on an insecure basis, which creates a kind of emptiness that can only be filled by an absolute confidence in God, which is the fountain of all spiritual favors.

Whenever she was discouraged by material difficulties, and especially when she was overtaken by doubt regarding her foundation—which implied a break, even a sort of treason vis-à-vis the Incarnation—Teresa found comfort in her cordial correspondence with St. Peter of Alcántara. Then she received a message from on high. On August 15, 1561, in the Dominican church near St. Joseph where she had once confessed the sins of her youth, "a rapture came upon me so great that it almost took me out of myself." A marvelous vision was then given to her: that of the Virgin Mary and St. Joseph.

> I saw myself vested in a white robe of shining brightness.... I saw our Lady at my right side and my father Saint Joseph at the left, for they were putting that robe on me. I was given to understand that I was now cleansed of

my sins.... The beauty I saw in our Lady was extraordinary...her garment
was of the most brilliant white, not dazzling but soft.... [She] seemed to me
to be a very young girl.

This reference to Teresa's sins is an allusion to her past, but also to the
guilt complex growing in her at the prospect of the impasse she seemed to
be headed toward, the inevitable and dramatic confrontation between the
mitigated and the future Discalced Carmelites. In *The Life*, Teresa confirmed
the fact that she had committed this folly impelled by an irresistible injunction from heaven. She, a simple religious without the slightest power,
addressed herself indirectly to the supreme authority of the Church without
referring to her superiors: her prioress, her provincial, her confessor. With
a stroke of the pen, she swept away her scruples:

> The Lord had told me it wasn't suitable to give [obedience] to my superiors
> [of the mitigated Order].... He told me I should petition Rome in a certain
> way [Doña Guiomar], which He also indicated to me, and that He would
> take care that we get our request. And so it came about, for the petition
> was made the way the Lord told me and it was granted easily, whereas we
> had been unable to obtain it.

It will be remembered that Doña Guiomar had asked that the new
monastery be placed under the authority of the bishop of Ávila, the grand
and powerful Don Álvaro de Mendoza. "At that time I wasn't acquainted
with the prelate," admits Teresa, "nor did I know who he would be." She
was acting as though everything had already been worked out!

> After being clothed and while experiencing the most marvelous delight
> and glory, it seemed to me then that our Lady took me by the hands. She
> told me I made her very happy in serving the glorious Saint Joseph, that I
> should believe that what I was striving for in regard to the monastery
> would be accomplished.... As a sign that this was true she was giving me a
> jewel. It seemed to me she placed around my neck a very beautiful golden
> necklace to which was attached a highly valuable cross. This gold and these
> stones are incomparably different from earthly ones.... They were with me
> a little while; and I was in a state of wonderful glory and happiness...then
> it seemed to me I saw them ascend to heaven with a great multitude of
> angels.

After the vision, Teresa's body remained "some time without being able
to stir or speak...almost outside myself." But her spirit was jubilant! She was
consoled, for her trials and her doubts were vindicated. An unparalleled
strength carried her along. "I was left with a great impulse to be dissolved
for God and with similar effects. And everything happened in such a way

that I could never doubt, no matter how much I tried, that the vision was from God."

Meanwhile, clouds were gathering over her head. The brief from Rome to authorize the new foundation by placing it under the authority of the bishop of Ávila had not arrived.

Two days later, in the middle of Christmas night, Teresa received a peremptory order from Ángel de Salazar, who had just succeeded Father Gregorio Hernández in his position as provincial prior.[13] She must go to Toledo to assist his friend, a grand lady of the aristocracy. His choice of this moment, when Teresa was absolutely needed in Ávila to put the finishing touches on her foundation, is significant. It seems that the new Carmelite provincial, alerted by the prioress of the Incarnation, ordered this visit with the hope that it would break the momentum of Teresa's so-very-disruptive founding.

A few days earlier during a homily in the church of the Dominicans, the preacher, turning to her, had heaped reproaches upon her, asking her why she had deserted her monastery—a foreboding of the catastrophes whose portents were accumulating.

CHAPTER 15

Difficult Mission in Toledo

(1562)

oña Luisa de la Cerda, a lady "well acquainted with the provincial...[and] a person of the nobility,"[1] had called Teresa to her side for consolation in grief. Doña Luisa had heard of Teresa from her Dominican friend García de Toledo, who had had the opportunity to hear Teresa's confession in Ávila and who held her in high esteem.

One did not resist the wishes of such a grand lady related to the monarchs of Spain. She was the daughter of the second Duke of Medinaceli, the niece of Cardinal Tavera, and the extremely rich widow of the Marshal of Castile, Don Arias Pardo de Saavedra, who had been dead for a year. She had remained inconsolable over his death, and no one in her entourage—neither her children nor her friends in the Church nor the great of this world—had been able to lead her from her despair.

The summons Teresa received from Father de Salazar was terse: "He sent me an order, under precept of obedience, to go immediately...."[2]

Still, she was hesitant. This abrupt departure risked delivering a fatal blow to the St. Joseph foundation. Her first reaction was to refuse or at least to defer, for it seemed that the stay in Toledo could be a long one. She could put forward valid motives: such a trip in the middle of winter on the terrible roads of Castile would be full of risk, and her health remained fragile. But in the middle of the night when she went to chapel for the office of Matins, she says:

> I spent all of Matins, or a great part of it, in a deep rapture. The Lord told me to go and not listen to opinions, because few would counsel me prudently; that even though I would have trials, God would be greatly served;

that for the business concerning the monastery it was fitting I be absent
until the brief arrive....

Others told her not to leave, that she should write to the provincial. But
the Jesuit rector encouraged her to obey. In his opinion, it was in Teresa's
interest to be forgotten in Ávila while the passions stirred up by her foundation subsided.

Escorted by her brother-in-law, Juan de Ovalle, Teresa set forth in an
uncomfortable wagon to cross the desert-like plateaus of Castile, where
razor-sharp winds blew. Juana Suaráz accompanied her. The trip was long.
They reached the famous city of Toledo, with its citadel and gothic cathedral
towering over the river Tagus. Teresa had never seen a large city and was
astounded by it. Toledo, which had eighty thousand inhabitants in 1562,
remained the "imperial and crowned city" where Charles V, then Philip II,
had reigned before the latter left it for Madrid after the festivities for his marriage to the young French princess Elisabeth of Valois.

The large city hummed with the crafts of the artisans who had shaped
its reputation and built its wealth—among them, the forging of swords and
the weaving of precious cloth, the craft from which her grandfather, Juan
Sánchez de Toledo, had made his fortune. Among the crowd of merchants,
customers, and people, sumptuous carriages passed each other. They
belonged to noble *hidalgos* who had not yet deserted the former imperial capital for Madrid. Teresa was astonished to see in the Toledan architecture the
profound stamp of Mozarabic civilization. Her heart thrilled at the light of
this incomparable city in which she would later say she felt better than anywhere else.

At first glance the splendor of the palace where Doña Luisa de la Cerda
was dying of grief revealed the pride and vanity of the world. And the prince-
ly welcome, the swarm of servants showing her the deepest respect, appalled
Teresa by highlighting all that was expected of her and the little that she felt
capable of doing.

Teresa remained in the palace of Luisa de la Cerda for six months, frightened at first by the attention given her and uncomfortable with "sheer
embarrassment in considering the title under which they were bringing me
there and how much they were being deceived.... Almost everything was a
cross for me because the comfort caused me great torments." She also worried about adapting herself to the ceremony imposed on everyday life by the
rigorous etiquette in this palace.

But she soon became free of these constraints thanks to the sincere
friendship that Doña Luisa showed her. "She grew deeply fond of me,"

wrote Teresa. In *The Life*, she could not stop praising this noblewoman who would play a great role in the Reform: "[She was] so good that her abundant Christian spirit supplied for all that was lacking in me." And how they resembled each other in some respects! "I realized that she was a woman and as subject to passions and weaknesses as I...." Seeing Doña Luisa the slave of her riches and her rank, Teresa understood her own good fortune at being only a poor cloistered nun.

It is difficult to imagine the humble Carmelite settled with her companion Juana Suárez in a wing of the luxuriant palace peopled with a court composed of noblemen, ladies-in-waiting, duennas and attendants, equerries and pages, and served by a multitude of valets and chambermaids. She made an enormous impression there in her poor, mended, coarse wool habit, consoling the mistress of the house in her grief and transforming the personnel with the radiance that emanated from her.

Teresa avoided social events by fleeing from parlor to parlor and shutting herself away in the oratory that she had set up in her somewhat isolated apartment. She did not realize that the domestic staff was very much aware of her ecstasies, the accounts of which were spread even into the kitchens, nourishing the fervor that the entire palace felt for her whom they were already calling "the saint of Ávila."

> The raptures have increased. At times they come with an impulse and in such a way that without my being able to help myself they are noticeable externally, and they come even while I am in the company of others. They are of such a kind that they cannot be concealed, unless—since I suffer from heart sickness—I let it be thought I'm having some fainting spell.[3]

But this deluded no one. She was making a huge impression, healing the sick and even converting a Turk!

One day, a maidservant, a member of the palace's domestic staff, came to her. She was suffering from such violent pain in her teeth and ears that nothing seemed to ease her discomfort.

"*Santa Madre!* Make a Sign of the Cross on me and I shall be healed."

"What are you saying, my girl? Make the Sign of the Cross yourself, for the cross derives its healing property from itself and not from my hand."

But, in pushing her away gently, Teresa's hand brushed the woman's head. "And the poor woman was immediately healed."[4]

Doña Luisa did not want Teresa to go. Soon all the great minds of Toledo flocked to see her, to listen to her speak so eloquently of God and denounce the vanities of the world! "I conversed with those noble ladies, whom it would have been an honor for me to serve, with the freedom I would have felt had I been their equal." She established powerful relationships that would serve her all of her life.

One of Doña Luisa's nieces, who was twenty years old, was drawing attention to herself with her somewhat showy beauty. Ana de la Cerda, princess of Éboli, boasted to Teresa that she was a close friend of the queen and, as such, was able to obtain everything at court. Unperturbed, Teresa replied: "I give thanks to Your Ladyship; but to a daughter of God, God is enough."

No, Teresa was not allowing herself to be contaminated by all this luxury. She wrote to Father Ibáñez that it all seemed a dream that would be nothing when she awoke.

She naturally exerted a great influence among the young girls being brought up in the palace. That is how she discovered María de Salazar, who would later become her best disciple (María de San José). A niece of Doña Luisa, she was sixteen years old and destined for a brilliant marriage she did not want. Teresa had noticed that she was equal to the other young women in finery, the arts, and games of wit. But Teresa saw through all of this. One day, taking her aside, she gently said to her: "María, all this finery, these jewels, these ornaments are not suitable for a person who wants to wear the veil of a religious."

Blushing, María turned away, then she faced her destiny. "*Madre*, how were you able to fathom the most intimate secret of my heart?"

In the days that followed, Teresa disclosed to her the plan for the foundation. María was afire with the desire to join her, but Teresa had to test her mettle.

Teresa also had another important encounter: "While I was there it happened that a certain religious came to that city, a person from the nobility with whom I had sometimes conversed many years previously." García de Toledo was a famous Dominican, a nephew of the viceroy of Peru (Francisco de Toledo), and a relative of the Duke of Alba. At the request of Father Ibáñez, his colleague in Ávila, this renowned theologian had agreed to read the autobiographical manuscript that Teresa was in the process of completing. For her part, Teresa was eager to see him again.

The conversation took place in the confessional of the Dominican church. Astonished at first to see this Carmelite with a reputation as an ascetic residing in one of the most glittering palaces of Spain, he listened to and questioned her. Then, taken by the charm and radiance emanating from her soul, he opened his heart to her with confidence. Thus was born one of Teresa's privileged relationships. Struck by the Dominican's personality, she wanted him to be entirely God's. "He seemed to me wiser than ever, although I always thought he had a great mind. I considered the wonderful talents and gifts he had for doing much good were he to give himself totally to God."

They spoke of interior prayer, and Teresa did not hide anything regarding her ecstasies from him. She then reproached him for the superficial life he was leading in Toledo. He was deeply troubled when they parted.

She recognized herself in García de Toledo. Twenty years earlier, though transported by divine love, she also had been unable to pull herself away from the social whirl that had enslaved her youth. And she wanted to spare him this lack of focus. He accepted her admonition. Breaking with his habits, he immersed himself in mental prayer and derived profit from it. He would soon be able to show his gratitude to the one who had enlightened him; as promised, he read the manuscript of *The Life*, which Teresa finished during her stay in Toledo. This first version did not satisfy him; strict critic that he was, he would make her rewrite it.

TERESA'S REPUTATION HAD SPREAD in Toledo and far beyond. One day, a poor woman of about forty knocked at the palace door. The porter was no longer astonished at anything. He ran to *la Madre* and informed her that a beggar who claimed to have arrived on foot from Madrid insisted on seeing her. Teresa received her immediately. Recognizing her dusty robe as the homespun habit of the Carmelite *beata,* she embraced the woman cordially, led her to her room, offered her a glass of water, and urged her to speak.

"My name is María de Yepes. Born in Granada, I was married. Becoming a widow at a young age, I then entered the Carmel of Granada, but I left it before making my solemn profession."

"And whatever for?"

"It is a relaxed Carmel, where the holy Rule of the founder is not respected."

Teresa was listening closely. María continued: "I had a revelation from Christ. He ordered me to found a monastery in conformity with our ancient traditions: enclosure, penance, silence, prayer, and especially poverty."

"A revelation, you say? And when did you receive it?"

"Last September."

Teresa was dumbfounded. It was the year and the month that Christ, whom she had contemplated "completely poor and stripped," had asked her also to open such a foundation.

"And so, María, what did you do?"

"I gave all my worldly possessions to the poor, I put on a robe of sack-cloth, and I started out for Rome."

"On foot?"

"On foot and barefooted."

"And in Rome, you saw...."

"...the pope. I was exhausted, my garment in tatters, and on the marble tiles of the Vatican palace each one of my steps left traces of blood. Pius IV welcomed me like a father."

"He is said to be in favor of reforming Carmel. We have written to him, but he has not yet answered...."

"After hearing me out, he exclaimed: 'Virile woman! Do whatever she asks!' A few days later, he signed for me a brief of approval authorizing the Reform."

"A brief? But then...." Teresa's eyes shone with hope. She urged María to continue.

"I was invited to stay at the Italian Carmel of Mantua, the only one to have kept the strictest Rule, that of the founders. Those women are called 'the walled-up ones.' Having studied their lifestyle and their Constitutions, I am hoping to found at Alcalá de Henares, in a house which has been offered to us by Doña Leonor de Mascarenhas, the former governess of the *Infante* Philip. Knowing that you were in Toledo, I wanted to meet you."

"What will be the name of your monastery?"

"La Imagen. The image of Our Lady!"

"You have been sent to Toledo by heaven, María!"[5]

THIS MEETING, THIS COINCIDENCE, seemed astounding. The *beata* remained for fifteen days with Teresa, who drank in her words, assembling in her mind everything on which her future Carmel at Ávila would be founded. In the process, she was gathering precious information on how to deal with the punctilious pontifical administration. She rejoiced that this providential encounter had taken place:

> She is a woman who practices much penance and prayer; the Lord has granted her many favors and our blessed Lady appeared to her and ordered her to make the foundation. She was so far ahead of me in serving the Lord that I was ashamed to stand in her presence.

For Teresa, María de Yepes was an example of courage and humility, though she herself was not lacking in either. Not only was María giving

Teresa the original Rule, she was also sharing her experience of that Rule while living with the sisters in Mantua.

As for Luisa de la Cerda, she now had two saints—both women of fire and light—to console her and help her rebuild her life.

Although born into a grand family of Granada, María de Yepes could neither read nor write. She had, however, learned by heart and put into practice the original Rule of Carmel kept alive at the Mantuan Carmel. Teresa was astonished to learn that the Rule forbade the possession of revenues—an element she had already considered, following the example of the Poor Clares. But St. Francis and St. Clare themselves had not been able to impose it in a permanent way. Even now Peter of Alcántara was obliged to fight to have this Franciscan tradition flourish once again.

"That we own nothing...to found the house without an income.... As she told me about it, it seemed to me to be right...." Do away with dowries and pensions. Live from day to day from small alms only, according to what God would send—was this not the perfect act of faith, without the least restriction? And it especially mattered not to give way on this point so contested by the theologians and the mitigated religious.

Teresa hesitated, however. Could she impose this fearsome ideal on the companions who would share her life? Would this not provoke an anguish and disarray that would adversely affect the peace needed in their search for God? She remembered that at the Incarnation, even though it was endowed with revenues and dowries, they had suffered from lack of food. This shortage was sometimes so severe that the most fragile members would have to be sent home to recover their health while the monastery awaited donations from some rich aristocrats or bourgeois, which inevitably resulted in a subjection that disrupted their spiritual lives.

In the second of her *Spiritual Testimonies*, Teresa clearly reveals her preference:

> I wouldn't even want to keep what is necessary, unless it were an alms. And so I have a strong desire to be in a place where I live only on alms. It seems to me that when I'm in a place where I'm certain I shall not be lacking food and clothing, I don't fulfill as perfectly the vow, or the counsel of Christ....

Now this ran counter to the monastic customs of the time. Because they were supposed to consecrate themselves entirely to divine praise and prayers of intercession, Carmelite contemplatives did not work. They were even spared domestic chores, which were taken care of by the lay sisters. Of course, the cloistered nuns could not assume the roles of their male counterparts, who could bring in justifiable remuneration through spiritual direction, celebration of religious services, and dispensing the sacraments. Only a few women among them, the most educated, taught young girls who lived in the monastery as privileged lay boarders. For a century, the Carmelites had depended upon dowries and revenues with all of the inconveniences this entailed.

The project of María de Yepes was thus not without flaws. If the ideal framework of contemplation—that is, a personal relationship with God—requires voluntary deprivation in the form of poverty, silence, and enclosure, a person still cannot live without eating, and a community still must look after its sick. Recourse to unpredictable alms, which the original Rule for the monks prescribed, did not constitute a viable solution for the nuns. Regular work seemed to be preferable. Was it always compatible with the nuns' strict enclosure, however? St. Benedict had indeed set down its limits, but he was referring to large autonomous monasteries based upon agricultural activities, whereas the Carmels of the primitive Rule were small urban communities very dependent upon their surroundings.

By refusing dowries and income that would ensure a steady if not comfortable security, Teresa nevertheless believed that she was on the right track, "the more perfect thing to do," although she did not really know how she would manage. The house that was meant to shelter the St. Joseph community had been purchased with the dowries of two postulants; Doña Guiomar's promised pension was awaited in order to subsist. What work would they do in a city where one quarter of the population suffered from malnutrition for lack of stable employment? Manual laborers were needed in the countryside, and workmen and journeymen were needed for building sites in the cities. But what could a woman, and cloistered besides, do? Spinning wool, embroidering, and weaving were not sufficient or profitable, since all women and even children did these at home.

Teresa, conscious of a problem that concerns all founders, decided to consult learned persons, the *letrados*, and not only Father García de Toledo, who had retired to the desert. She decided to solicit the holy Franciscan Peter of Alcántara, the arbiter par excellence, whose coming to Toledo had been announced. While awaiting his arrival, Teresa wrote to her counselor in Ávila, Pedro Ibáñez, who had always supported her. Could a small, fervent, and poor community place itself solely in the hands of divine Providence for its subsistence? And what answer could be given to those worried families who would entrust their children to it?

He replied immediately with a confidence born of experience. The total abnegation reserved for hermits presented too many risks for a community of cloistered nuns. Deeply disappointed, Teresa decided to disregard his advice. She suffered from her friend's stern attitude. Was he holding a grudge for the scandal she had caused in Ávila by disrupting Carmel hierarchy? He could not have been unaware of the fact that she was acting without the agreement of her provincial.

> He sent me two pages with objections and theology written on both sides on why I shouldn't do it.... I answered him that I didn't want to benefit from theology if it wasn't conducive to my following my vocation, my vow of poverty, and the counsels of Christ with total perfection, and that in this case he did me no favor with his learning.

Astounding! Not only was she opposed to her prioress and her provincial, she was also dismissing the advice of one of the most respected theologians in Ávila. It is to be noted that, once again, Teresa acted only according to her own idea. But she felt that she was directed by her visions and driven by the Holy Spirit.

There remained Peter of Alcántara, the "true lover of poverty." Invited by Doña Luisa, he came to visit soon after his arrival in Toledo. Teresa found that he had aged physically and seemed close to death, but his spirit was as ardent as always and not in the least removed from this world. She showed him her correspondence with Father Ibáñez and other theologians from Ávila. He became indignant: "I am surprised that you submitted to theologians for advice on something that falls outside their competence. When it is a matter of a trial or in cases of conscience, you can certainly have recourse to lawyers and theologians. With regard to perfection, you must consult only those who practice it."

She smiled. She was there before him like a little child awaiting the word of life. Poorly mastering his indignation, he went on: "It is a kind of infidelity to examine if it is good to follow the evangelical counsels. The counsel of God can never fail to be the best."

"I have sought it, *Padre!*"

"And what did Christ, our Master, answer you?"

"One day while praying intensely to God about this matter, the Lord told me I shouldn't in any way fail to found the monastery in poverty, that this was both the will of his Father and his own, that he would help me."[6]

"It is his infinite wisdom that is being given to you, *Madre.* Follow his very perfect counsel relative to poverty; it concerns women as well as men. If, on the other hand, you want to follow the advice of theologians devoid of spirituality, procure good income and then see if it is more useful than poverty embraced for Christ."

"Yet, some say that the monasteries' relaxation comes from their lack of resources. I know some very poor ones that aren't contemplative in the least."

"That is because they are poor in a grudging fashion and by necessity and not from a desire to follow the evangelical counsel: poverty desired and sought for the love of Christ. Those who are poor with all their heart lead a blessed life."

"I desire nothing else."

"Go, Teresa. May God give you the light to understand these truths and put them into practice. Go to Ávila and found that little nest of doves of the Lord. And do not listen any longer to the theologians who are opposed to this. The omnipotence of Christ will give you the strength and the means to accomplish this mission. By drawing closer to the destitution of the manger and the cross, you cannot go wrong."

"So then I must resist the orders of my superiors?"

"Yes, since Christ invites you to do so. When the time comes, he will know how to change the disposition of their hearts. While waiting for the brief to arrive from Rome, place your foundation under the obedience of the bishop of Ávila. Besides, I shall write to him."

In a trembling hand, the saint wrote:

To my Lord Álvaro de Mendoza,
A nun of the Incarnation at Ávila, Doña Teresa de Ahumada—may God sanctify her!—wishes to found a small monastery of thirteen cloistered nuns, under the strict original Rule of Carmel. A request for authorization was sent to Rome on February 6, and I have good reason to think that it will be accepted. Madre Teresa wishes to place her foundation under the obedience of Your Highness. As to me, I declare to you, my Lord, that I am satisfied with the persons who are to be the stones of this edifice. They are selected friends whose virtue is well proven. And for the one who is to be at their head, I am convinced that the spirit of our Lord dwells in her.
May this same Spirit live in the soul of Your Paternity, Amen.[7]

TERESA WAS RECEIVING unqualified support from this saint, the uncontested arbiter of religious Spain. This was confirmed by Christ in person, "during a deep rapture with so many remarkable effects that I couldn't have any doubt the desire was from God."

She was overjoyed when she received a letter from Father Ibáñez. The theologian had changed his mind, and he approved! Teresa was exultant. "It seemed to me I possessed all the world's riches in resolving to live by the love of God."

SIX MONTHS HAD PASSED since her departure. The results of her stay in Toledo were striking. The shared friendship with Doña Luisa de la Cerda and the cordial support of Peter of Alcántara had given Teresa an opening at the national level that would take her out of her province. Her encounter with Father García de Toledo was no less important. He exhorted her to rewrite her first manuscript and encouraged her in this difficult work. He would have a great influence on her life and on that of the Discalced Carmelites. Meeting María de Yepes was also decisive for the Reform. It confirmed Teresa in the most perfect path, the one indicated by the visions of Christ and the one of St. Clare: for the person seeking perfection, there can be no compromise between spiritual life and money.

Doña Luisa de la Cerda, strengthened by Teresa's support and her radiant example, had found the spiritual equilibrium that allowed her to live again. In spite of her sadness at having to be separated from her, Teresa announced her departure. Father Provincial was authorizing her to return to Ávila without, however, obliging her to do so. How enigmatic their relationship seems to have been at the time, if they even had one while she was in Toledo. Teresa could have visited him, consulted with him, written to him to discuss her projects. Nothing. She was careful not to do so, and he likewise.

That is when the news reached her like a thunderbolt: the Incarnation was about to vote to re-elect its prioress or choose another.[8] A goodly number of the professed nuns planned to vote for Teresa the rebel, reviled only yesterday. She was horrified at this, seeing "that being superior would be very dangerous for my conscience." She wrote to her friends, asking them to refrain from voting for her, and decided to remain in Toledo for a few more days to allow the threat to pass.

She now understood the provincial's ambiguous attitude. After having sent her to Toledo to prevent the foundation of St. Joseph, he was bringing her back to Ávila, hoping that her election at the Incarnation would lock her into a new role in which anyone else would have reveled. Clearly, he did not know Teresa well.

What was she to do? Not to return immediately to Ávila was to refuse to face the difficulty. Within her, Christ's voice was ordering her to return, for "since I desired the cross, a good one was ready for me." She did not doubt that this cross would be the priorate of the Incarnation, an untenable situation since half of the community would not support her reforms.

She finally decided to go "place myself in a fire," once she "understood that it was something more perfect" to which Christ seemed to be inviting

her. Despite her fears, she felt at peace: "The more I saw I was losing consolation for the Lord's sake, the happier I became at losing it."

The torrid summer sun was beating down on the plateaus of Castile
when she set out. "I was happy in going; and since the Lord had desired me
to go, I was disturbed that I hadn't entered the battle immediately." She was
especially in a hurry to find once again her dear St. Joseph, for "this house
was a paradise of delight for Him." The construction work would be well
advanced, the postulants impatient—those elite souls whom, she had no
doubt, His Majesty had selected, "souls so austere, poor, and prayerful."

But, in the meantime, she had to face the storm at the Incarnation.
There, Teresa expected the priorate, but what was about to happen would be
even worse!

CHAPTER 16

The Storm:
Foundation of St. Joseph

(1562–1563)

Returning to Ávila, Teresa settled in again at the Incarnation, where she learned with great relief that Doña María Cimbrón, her cousin, had been elected prioress. Shortly thereafter, she was called to the parlor, where she found her old friend Don Francisco de Salcedo in a state of excitement.

"*Madre!* The brief from Rome authorizing the foundation has just arrived! It was signed by Cardinal Rainucio Farnèse, in the name of our Holy Father Pope Pius IV."

"God be praised! It was high time for me to return!"

She perused the precious document. As she had requested, her name was not on it. The titular foundress was Doña Guiomar de Ulloa.

"Father Peter of Alcántara is here, lodging with me," Don Francisco continued. "In spite of the deplorable state of his health, he has come to Ávila particularly to persuade our bishop to place you under his jurisdiction."

"And what has our Lord of Mendoza decided?"

"He is absolutely against doing so. 'To deliberately forego receiving revenues is characteristic of a woman who is said to have visions. This convent will have an income or will not be founded.' In fact, what he dreads is to have to support it. Having to withdraw a few ducats from the pensions of the canons of his cathedral would be intolerable to him. Knowing his opposition, Father Peter came. But exhausted by his trip on the back of a mule, he had to take to his bed. By force of this circumstance, he was limited to sending the bishop a letter in which he pleaded in favor of 'the complete perfection, in conformity with the original Rule, implemented by a foundress inhabited by the Holy Spirit.' Not at all convinced, our bishop did not even respond. Advised of your return, he thought it best to go to a cool place, El Tiemble, his summer residence in the mountains. Unyielding, Father Peter had his mule saddled up, covered forty-five miles of steep paths, and forced his way into the bishop's residence. But nothing good came of it. The bishop would not give in on the question of income. Near death, clinging to his mule, Father Peter has returned to Ávila, where he is attempting to recover."

"Is everything lost?" Teresa cried out.

"No. That very night, the holy bishop, struck by the Spirit of the Lord, had a message delivered to Peter of Alcántara. He is yielding to his reasons; he accepts a monastery that is in conformity with evangelical poverty. He is returning to Ávila. He wants to see you. Expect his visit."

Teresa could not contain her joy, but the holy gentleman curbed her enthusiasm. Lowering his voice, he added: "It is advisable to act discreetly, for there is a powerful party in the city that remains opposed to this foundation. Even here, at the Incarnation..."

"I know. The prioress, my cousin, is hostile to us. And what is happening at St. Joseph?"

"Your sister Juana has left with her son. Her husband Juan de Ovalle is keeping watch over the house, but he has fallen ill. Doña Guiomar thought it prudent to leave the city. As to the workmen, because they were not being paid, they stopped working. Everything is neglected, unfinished."

"Well then," said Teresa, "I shall take care of everything. And first, I shall see His Excellency."[1]

THE INTERVIEW TOOK PLACE in the parlor at the Incarnation. As could have been foreseen, Teresa won the bishop over. Nothing and no one resisted her. Marcelle Auclair writes, "He was completely won over, charmed, all resistance gone.... Whether he knew what he wanted or not, he would always know quite definitely what Teresa wanted."[2] But would this be enough to overcome the resistance of the provincial prior, the ultimate master of the monasteries?

The bishop, this great lord, reluctantly accepted what appalled him: a convent of poor nuns. "Everything was done in deep secrecy; if it hadn't been, nothing could have been accomplished since the people were opposed to the foundation," Teresa wrote.

She then bade farewell to the saint to whom she owed everything. Peter of Alcántara and Teresa de Ahumada knew that they would not see each other again in this world. Teresa obtained permission to have him come to dine at the Incarnation parlor. She herself lovingly prepared a delicious dish for him who only ate bread. Then, standing near him, she served him in silence. Through the half-open door, the sisters believed they saw Christ in person serving him.

Later, during a meeting in which Teresa greeted her new prioress, Teresa obtained authorization to leave the Incarnation to look after her sick brother-in-law, Juan de Ovalle, who was living in a state of abandonment in the unfinished future monastery. Mother María Cimbrón dreaded her relative so much that she did not mind seeing her go away again. She did not seem to be aware of the plot that was being hatched; as the papal brief authorized Doña Guiomar to found, the house was in the name of Ovalle.

> I had a lot of trouble with some persons at times—and with others at other times—that the monastery be accepted. I had trouble with my sick brother-in-law and with the workmen to get them to convert the house into a monastery and make it ready quickly, for there was still a lot to be done.

His final mission accomplished, Peter of Alcántara had immediately departed to take to his bed in a neighboring city, Las Arenas, where on October 18 he breathed his last, giving up his celestial soul to God. Thanks to him, Bishop de Mendoza had agreed to go along with what we are obliged to call a machination, since the foundation did not have the consent of the provincial, Prior Salazar, nor of the prioress of the Incarnation. In her memoirs, Teresa skillfully attempts to justify herself, but one senses that she did not feel at ease: "I was there with permission; and I hadn't done anything without getting advice from learned men so as not to go one iota against obedience." But which persons? Her confessor, a Jesuit; Father Ibáñez, a Dominican; Peter of Alcántara, a Franciscan; Gaspar Daza, a secular priest; and Francisco de Salcedo, a lay theologian. Of course, she was in possession of the brief from Rome, and the bishop, Álvaro de Mendoza, had finally accepted to take her under his jurisdiction. But, as to Carmelites, there were none!

Teresa paid no attention to this. Her main preoccupation remained the Holy Order of Carmel, purified and brought back to its original authenticity. In *The Life*, she wrote, "All things fail; You, Lord of all, never fail!"[3] "Since these learned men observed that for many reasons the monastery would be very beneficial for the whole Order, they told me that I could go ahead even though I did so secretly and was careful that my superiors not find out about it." In her mind, the will of Christ, with whom she carried on ineffable dialogues, dominated. He alone was acting in her:

> ...although I desired to withdraw more from everything and live my profession and vocation with greater perfection and enclosure, I desired this in such a way that if I had found out it would have been of greater service to the Lord to abandon the project, I would have done so with complete peace and calm...

FINALLY, THE GREAT DAY ARRIVED—August 24, 1562. The construction on the building had been completed. Teresa herself had made the homespun habits of the four elect, and she hemmed the white veils of the novices. Statues of St. Joseph and the Virgin Mother with Child had been placed in front of the two doors of the small chapel, thirty-three or so feet long, ornamented with flowers. Drawn there by the shrill sound of a humble three-pound bell—whose ringing would regulate religious services and work—the people of the St. Rock neighborhood rushed to see at last what was happening behind those walls. These decent people crowded into the tiny chapel that seemed to have shot up overnight and that the bishop had discreetly authorized. They saw in this monastery a source of heavenly blessings.

A priest came forth in a chasuble: Master Daza, representing Bishop de Mendoza. He went up to the altar. By his side was Teresa de Jesús, deeply moved and radiant with joy. Then the four novices came forward, "four poor orphans" to whom *la Madre* would give the veil, the first members of the Reformed Carmel:

> My first daughters were four orphans—for they didn't bring any dowry—and four great servants of God (for this is what I had in mind from the beginning, that persons would enter who by their example of prayer and a very perfect life would be a foundation upon which we could achieve our goal).

History has retained the names of these four women. Antonia de Henao (Antonia del Espíritu Santo), twenty-five, Teresa's cousin and the spiritual daughter of St. Peter of Alcántara, entrusted by him to the new Carmel as a sign of his confidence. Holy and candid, she often entered into ecstasy during mental prayer. Úrsula de Revilla y Álvarez (Úrsula de los Santos), converted by Father Gaspar Daza, forty years of age. A widow belonging to the nobility of Ávila, she had led a merry life before her conversion. María de la Paz (de la Cruz), the purest of Doña Guiomar's followers; Doña Guiomar was letting her go, but not without emotion. Finally, María de Ávila (de San José), thirty-five, the sister of Father Julian de Ávila, the first chaplain of the Reformed Carmel, an enthusiastic and simple man full of goodness and fervor.

Teresa had also received verbal promises from three other women: Isabel de Ortega, twenty-one, another disciple of Peter of Alcántara; María de Salazar from Toledo, who was intensely eager to rejoin Teresa, but whom Doña de la Cerda had not yet authorized to do so, as she thought her too young; and finally, María de Ocampo, also too young.

Teresa had done away with noble titles as well as family names in order to fully enter into the ideal of poverty in which one was reduced to oneself alone.

La Madre proceeded with the taking of the habit, "a new habit of such coarse fabric that it looked like the camel's hair that covers the hermits we see in pictures."[4] The nuns wore a brown, rough wool robe with a brown scapular and a white coif under a black veil, a white woolen choir mantle, and bare feet in sandals made of hemp (*alpargates*), the distinctive sign of the Discalced Carmelites. Then Father Gaspar Daza, assisted by Julian de Ávila, celebrated the first Mass in the Reformed Carmel. The four novices were hidden in the choir behind the double wooden grille of monastic enclosure, separated from the group of faithful: a few artisans from the area and some housewives with their children, their eyes still misted over from slumber.

In the first row, Teresa was surrounded by her most faithful friends: Don Francisco de Salcedo; Juan de Ovalle and his wife, Juana; Don Gonzalo de Aranda; Doña Guiomar de Ulloa; and two other sisters from the Incarnation who had been in on the original plot, Inés and Ana de Tapia, Teresa's cousins. To avoid any provocation, they continued to remain in the shadows. In any case, it was impossible for them, as it was for Teresa, to leave the Incarnation without the authorization of the provincial prior, and they had been careful not to solicit it. They would enter later, God willing. By their side was the faithful Juana Suárez, but she had no intention of leaving the Incarnation, to which she remained very much attached. Being fifty years of age, she also feared the austerities of the Reformed Carmel.

Unaware of the dark clouds amassing over her head, Teresa was jubilant: "I was so intensely happy that I was as though outside myself, in deep prayer."

But nothing in Teresa's life happened without drama. When she came out of her state of ecstasy, she was assailed by doubts; the night of the spirit darkened her soul. "After all was over and about three or four hours had passed, the devil stirred up within me a spiritual battle.... He brought doubts to my mind about whether what I had done was wrong...."

She was finally struck by the fact of her casualness with regard to her prioress and her provincial; she was belatedly questioning herself!

> And there were doubts as to whether those who lived here would be happy with so much austerity. What if they lacked food? Wasn't it all foolishness? ...The devil raised doubts in me also about how I wanted to shut myself up in so austere a house, and with my many illnesses. How would I be able to endure so much penance...? I had obligated myself to a great deal; perhaps I would despair. The devil by chance may have intended to take away my peace and quiet so that on account of such disturbance I wouldn't be able to pray and thus would lose my soul.

By a kind of perverse effect that she attributed to the devil,

> all that the Lord had commanded me, and the great deal of advice, and the prayers that for more than two years had gone on almost without cease, all was erased from my memory.... And all the virtues, and my faith, were then suspended within me without my having the strength to activate any of them or defend myself against so many blows.... It seems to me the anguish I experienced was like that of someone in the death agony.... Certainly, I think, it was one of the most difficult periods in my life.

For many hours she remained in the depths of this night. Then she slowly emerged from it. Desiring to love and serve God, she had wanted to suffer at the foot of the cross. Now she had to shoulder this ideal and go to the very end of Calvary. The reformed monastery had been constituted according to regulation, and now she and a few other nuns of the Incarnation had to obtain authorization to enter it themselves.

AT ABOUT FIVE O'CLOCK, the bishop himself came to greet the new community. Suddenly, two Carmelites burst into the room. Ignoring the bishop's presence, they delivered to Teresa and her cousins, as well as to Juana Suárez, an order from the prioress of the Incarnation to return there at once.

Taking leave of their sisters, they complied with docility. The "four poor little ones" became orphans once again. "I believed they would immediately throw me into the prison cell. But I thought this would make me very happy since I wouldn't have to speak to anyone and would be able to rest a little in solitude...."

On her return, Teresa found the monastery in an uproar. The news of the consecration of St. Joseph had been received as an insult. Mother prioress did not spare her. Flanked by her council, she ordered Teresa to appear before them.

"So you want to affront the holy Carmelite Order by pretending to found a more perfect convent? Constantly away from here, you have never been able to follow our Rule that you claim is relaxed. How will you observe the one that a pope has judged to be too strict?"

Kneeling before Mother María Cimbrón, Teresa remained silent. The prioress went on: "Through your pride, you have created turmoil in our community, sown discord, hatched intrigue with secular priests or religious who are foreign to our Order, brought discredit to Carmel, fomented scandal. Do you not hear the cries of the crowd in the street?"

It was only too true. Incited by certain influential citizens, the people were convinced that this convent without revenues or resources would eat the bread of the poor. Stones were being thrown, the Incarnation door was being shaken. What would happen at St. Joseph? Teresa did not tremble for herself but for her "four poor little orphans."

"By your irresponsible attitude, Teresa, in refusing to defer to the injunctions of your provincial prior, you have slandered our monastery and its prioress with this *gravissima culpa!*"

According to the Constitutions, this was "a grave fault against authority"! Teresa knew the penalties: a lengthy stay in prison, receiving only bread and water. Twice a day in Chapter she would be given the discipline—the whip—in front of the assembled professed nuns! Each day, she would make public penance in the refectory with red tongues sown on her habit "so that the great vice of her tongue might be punished."

"Speak! What have you to say in your defense?"

"Being very much at fault, Reverend Mother, I recognize my wrongs."

"But after all, why not be content to serve the Lord in peace in this house where twenty-five years ago you made profession and promised obedience? Such a pleasant house, where you have so many friends!"

"Just a short time ago, Reverend Mother, I would not have given up my happiness here for any bliss on earth! And yet..."

She discreetly opened her heart to Mother María. It had all come from interior prayer. In it, the Lord had filled her with his love. Then he had spoken and ordered the creation of a small nest of more fervent religious in strict enclosure. This could not be done in the noise and uproar of the Incarnation. Teresa had not acted without the accord of her confessors. She also showed the prioress the letters of Peter of Alcántara and the papal brief, and she referred to the bishop's consent.

Stunned, Mother María Cimbrón felt herself yielding. She no longer saw in Teresa the proud rebel who had defied her authority, but only a woman of absolute submission to the Spirit who had made his dwelling in her. However, as prioress she was responsible for the Incarnation, now threatened with being broken apart. What was she to do?

She helped Teresa up. Her tone had changed. "Go back to your cell, Teresa, and don't leave it again. Your meals will be brought to you. Remain there under lock and key until our Father Provincial has decided your fate."[5]

THE VERY REVEREND ÁNGEL DE SALAZAR arrived the next day. This whole matter troubled him. From Toledo, he managed the Carmels of the two Castiles, communities that were numerous and unstable, always threatened on the one hand by decadence and on the other by the spirit of Reform wished for by the Council of Trent and upheld by a few visionaries. As for Teresa, although inspired by the Holy Spirit, she kept both feet on the ground. Avoiding her legitimate superiors, from whom she expected nothing, she had enlisted the help of the pope, the bishop, and holy persons respected by the king and all of Spain. And, since her stay in Toledo, she had influential backing at court. The provincial would have to take all this into account.

An elaborate ceremony had been prepared at the Incarnation to judge the disruptive member. In the great Chapter Hall sat the provincial prior, Don Ángel de Salazar, beside the mother prioress and her council.

Teresa prostrated herself and waited. Father Ángel ordered her to explain herself. She spoke clearly in a calm voice, as though what she said concerned someone else:

"I am being wrongly condemned on certain points. I have not acted to draw esteem to myself. On the other hand, I am told with good reason that I am 'worse than others,' and that I was not able to conform to the holy practices of perfection in current use in this monastery, which does not authorize me to claim that 'I could keep it in another stricter one.' Also, I am told that 'I gave scandal to the people and was promoting novelties.' All of this causes me turmoil and sorrow. I humbly ask you to pardon me, Very Reverend *Padre*, to give me a heavy penance, and not to be angry with me any longer." Later, Teresa recalled the scene in her writing: "I begged to be pardoned and punished and that he not be vexed with me."[6]

Then Ángel de Salazar reprimanded her. Eyes lowered, she waited without attempting to exonerate herself from the core of the accusation.

I accused myself of the fault as one who was very much to blame, and this seemed true to anyone who didn't know all the reasons. After having received a serious reprimand, although not one as severe as the transgression deserved or in accordance with what many told the provincial, I did not want to excuse myself....

Father Ángel was, in fact, nonplussed by this woman who radiated the Lord. Everything in her pleaded in her favor. He had been summoned from Toledo to judge a proud rebel claiming to be a visionary. He had before him a mature Carmelite, humble, serious, anchored in her certainty, which was shared by the most eminent theologians, a saint, a bishop, a pope, God! He felt himself on the wrong side of the fence, like Pilate judging a rebel named Jesus.

He asked the council to leave the hall. Then Teresa gave him an account of what had transpired between Christ and herself and explained why she could not have acted any differently. Again, she humbly asked his pardon for the trouble she had caused. Then she looked him straight in the eye. "I implore you, Very Reverend *Padre*, not to break apart the small, fervent nucleus that has just been created at St. Joseph; to take it under your wing; and to authorize me, along with some of the nuns from the Incarnation, to join the novices."

Father Ángel de Salazar, like Bishop de Mendoza, was not a bad man. Nor was he equal to opposing such a strong personality who drew her energy and legitimacy from the Holy Spirit dwelling within her. But he had to appease the mitigated community that she had disrupted without intending to and especially the city that a handful of poor nuns could not threaten.

"Go in peace, Teresa. If your foundation manages to survive—nothing is certain, since you are refusing revenues—I authorize you to go there as soon as the upheaval here and in the city has calmed down."

BUT THINGS DID NOT SIMMER DOWN. "The clamor throughout the whole city was vehement...and they were all condemning me...." Nobles and bourgeois alike were stirring up the people. It was more than a simple matter of "four orphans." Everyone understood that this profound Reform risked calling into question an Order undermined by an insidious decadence. This Reform was worrisome because it was a solemn reminder of the Christian ideal expressed in the words "Happy are the poor." The primacy of voluntary poverty struck at the heart of a Spain in the fullness of its Golden Century—a century of conquistadors and caravels laden with riches wrested from ancient civilizations. Families dreaded the thought of their daughters succumbing to the fascination of this visionary and her ascetic ideal. They preferred the relative comfort, the parlors without restrictions, and the security of the mitigated Carmel. Turmoil was thus spreading throughout the city. "A sudden appearance of the Moors at the gates of Ávila would not have produced more rumbling," wrote Juan de Ávila.[7]

On August 25, 1562, the City Council met and ordered the destruction of the new monastery. This assembly of men found it intolerable that a woman who had been judged insubordinate was still free. The minutes of this historic session have been preserved:

> On this 25th day of August in the year 1562, in Ávila. At the sound of the bell, the City Council met around the illustrious and magnificent Lord García Suárez de Carvajal, chief magistrate of this city and its territory in the name of His Majesty, the king. Women who claim to be Carmelite cloistered nuns have occupied a house, set up altars, and had Mass said. There are so many poverty-stricken monasteries in this place that theologians of this city must be convened to find a remedy for this situation.

The next day, as if it had nothing better to do, the Council gathered once again. The problem of alms was raised, then Lazaro Dávila, who was in charge of the fountains, maintained that St. Joseph had been built too close to the city's public fountains and could possibly dry them up or pollute them. When no one was convinced of this, he exclaimed: "These women have erected a house that puts the water sources of the city in the shade. In the depth of winter, the water will freeze and not flow anymore!"

Julian de Ávila, who reported all this, adds: "They wanted to terrify the aforesaid nuns to compel them to leave."

Fortified by a unanimous vote, the chief magistrate, surrounded by constables, appeared at the door of St. Joseph, where the four novices had barricaded themselves in.

"Open in the name of the king! Or come out!"

"We will leave this monastery only on orders from the one who brought us here," replied Sister Úrsula, to whom Teresa had entrusted the community.

"If you do not open of your own accord, we will break down the door and expel you."

"Smash it in and much good may it do you! But you are acting against the brief of our Holy Father, the pope, and against our protector, His Illustrious Lordship, our bishop."

Then the novices withdrew to celebrate the Office.[8]

Impressed, the magistrate fell back to give an account to the governor and the councilors. These men could not endure the prospect of being defeated by four frail women. They decided to convene an enlarged assembly, "the most solemn junta which could be held in the world." They gathered together everyone that Ávila had in the way of spiritual authorities: jurists, theologians, university graduates, headmasters, pastors, canons, priors, abbots of various monasteries, "two educated religious from each Order," as well as a few *hidalgos* and other influential "magnificent lords" of the city. The bishop refused to attend. Because of the heat, he had returned to his mountain residence, but this was only a pretext to avoid the agitation. He was represented by his vicar general, Brizuela.

Coming to order at the sound of the bell on August 30, 1562, the junta deliberated passionately and invited the representative of the lord bishop

> to give all due consideration to the grave damage that the existence of this convent could cause the city and the monasteries of Orders quite confirmed in sanctity, religion, and good example, which could be infringed upon by the alms donated to the said convent.[9]

Brizuela protested. The lord bishop had placed the monastery under his jurisdiction, the Carmelite provincial prior did not oppose it, and, moreover, no Carmelite from the Incarnation had joined St. Joseph.

The tumult intensified. Brizuela felt very much alone. The magistrate took advantage of the situation.

"This foundation is a novelty and therefore suspect. The foundress is a woman who claims to be favored by celestial revelations, and this suffices to make us wary of her. One more monastery without revenues would be a burden for the city. Public charity would have to impose voluntary contributions upon itself. Religion, stronger than nature, will snatch bread from the mouths of the people of Ávila."

"But they are asking for nothing!" exclaimed Brizuela.

"When they come to tell us that these poor servants of God are dying of hunger, what will happen then?"

"All of this is pathetic. A handful of nuns making the vow of poverty cannot put a strain on the budget of such a large city."

"They are supposed to be twelve; tomorrow, they could be a hundred. I accuse Doña Teresa of having opened this convent without the city's consent. This offense renders its existence illegal. As a result, I demand that the Blessed Sacrament be taken out of the chapel, the religious expelled from the cloister, and the walls demolished immediately by virtue of a vote of the junta."[10]

At that moment, a Dominican, Father Domingo Báñez, stood up. Thirty-four years old, tall, lean, and with an ascetic face, Báñez towered above all those rich bourgeois and canons. Everyone grew silent. From Salamanca, where he had taught theology, he was respected for his knowledge and feared as a consultant of the Holy Office—the Inquisition. Having sat at the Council of Trent, he was favorable to the reformist tendency. He could not be suspected of having fallen under the charm of *la Madre*, since he had not yet met her. A professor at the Dominican college of Ávila, he had only known of her writings through his colleague, Father Ibáñez. He now proclaimed: "I am opposed to the annihilation of this monastery. Far from being a menace to our holy religion and the Order of Carmel, it is its best hope. What you consider to be novelty, I call renewal. This convent rebuilds what has fallen; it restores what has been weakened."

The assembly listened to the unexpected appeal from the newcomer, a man already respected and crowned with the prestige of having taught at the University of Salamanca, one of the most renowned in the Christian world. It was also a surprising plea, for nothing was further from his religious approach than the mysticism of contemplation dear to Teresa of Ávila. In her feminine approach to divinity, she proceeded by loving intuition, affectivity, and direct experience. Father Báñez, by contrast, took his teaching from his master, St. Thomas Aquinas, whose *Summa Theologica* developed a rigorous metaphysics, masculine in nature. This Thomistic scholasticism used human reason and logic to penetrate the mysteries of the faith. But it concurred with Teresa on what was essential.

> Would St. Joseph be a burden for the city? Is that what is troubling you? What fire devours the city? What plague ravages it? It seems to me unworthy of the city of knights to convene a junta for such a weak motive: four humble, peaceful nuns housed in the far reaches of a suburb! Certainly, I also regret their lack of revenues, for they are exposing themselves to very harsh privations. But it is up to the lord bishop and not to secular authority to examine this question. You have no right to take hurried measures which go against common law, Christian sentiment, and the honor of the city![11]

Surprised, the magistrate changed his tactics: "Regarding the approval of our bishop, the very powerful Lord Álvaro de Mendoza, which relies on the pontifical brief, I respectfully denounce a legal irregularity. This brief was not presented, as the law requires, to His Catholic and Royal Majesty King Philip, our lord, as well as to the lords of his Royal Council."

A profound silence fell over the assembly. At once Father Báñez acquiesced. "I consent to appearing before the Royal Council. While awaiting its verdict, the new monastery will remain under the protection of our lord, the bishop."

Because the matter was now taking a legal turn, passions were defused. Father Báñez, who knew that the king favored reform and that Teresa had some powerful support at court, had gained some time.

By reading *The Life*, it is possible to have a precise idea of Teresa's state of mind as she faced events that would determine the fate of her Reform:

> Some of the spokesmen were silent, others condemned the new founda-tion. Finally they concluded that it should be suppressed at once. Only one member, a *presentado* of the Order of St. Dominic...said it wasn't some-thing that had to be suppressed, that the matter had to be considered care-fully, that there was time for this, that such a decision pertained to the bishop.... What he said was very helpful for they were so furious that it was a wonder they didn't carry out their decision right away. What happened, finally, was that the foundation had to continue in existence, for the Lord was pleased with it.

Secure in this certainty, Teresa was ready to give her life. What an ordeal!

> The uproar among the people was such that they talked of nothing else, and they were all condemning me and appealing to the provincial and my monastery.... I was fearful the new house would be suppressed. This caused me great disturbance, as did also the realization that the persons who helped me were losing their credibility and suffering great trial; for what others said against me, I think, made me rejoice. If I had had a little faith, I wouldn't have experienced any disturbance. So, I was very afflicted for the two days in which these meetings...among the people took place.

Secluded in her tiny oratory at the Incarnation, she believed that all was lost. She plunged into the prayer of quiet: "Lord, this house is not mine; it was founded for You; now that there is no one to take care of its affairs, You, Your Majesty, must do so."

She then heard Christ's voice answer: "Don't you know that I am mighty? What do you fear? The new monastery will not be suppressed."

She then felt "as at ease and undisturbed as I would have if the whole world had been taking care of the business for me."

Two months later, on October 18, 1562, Peter of Alcántara died while on his knees, his eyes turned toward heaven, his face radiant, murmuring: "I am going to the house of the Lord!" At the instant of his death, he appeared in glory to Teresa and said to her: "I am going to my rest."[12] A few days later, Teresa received confirmation of his death and a note that he had written just before dying. In it he stated that

> he had known about the strong opposition and persecution we were undergoing—that he rejoiced the foundation was being so vehemently

opposed, that [it] was a sign the Lord would be very much served in this monastery in that the devil was interfering so much to prevent it, and that I should in no way decide to receive an income.

IN MADRID, THE TRIAL got underway. An ecclesiastic from Ávila, Gonzalo de Aranda, pleaded pro bono for St. Joseph. The bishop, fortified by the brief from Rome, confirmed his support. Teresa had alerted Doña Luisa de la Cerda, who enlisted her powerful relations at court. La Madre remained wisely secluded at the Incarnation. Impressed by her silence as much as by her resoluteness, her prioress and the provincial prior, Don Ángel de Salazar, hesitated from taking sides. Teresa is very clear on this subject:

> The Lord so provided that my provincial never ordered me to give up my involvement in the project. The provincial is so well disposed to everything virtuous that, even though he gave no actual help, he didn't want to oppose the foundation. He didn't give me permission to come here [to St. Joseph] until he saw what the outcome of the lawsuit would be.

No one could have been more prudent, opportunistic even. What mattered, however, was that Salazar was not openly opposed. He remained troubled by Teresa's visions. Was she a true visionary or a crazy eccentric with unrealistic plans? In the meantime, she was torturing herself, knowing that her "four poor orphans" were left to themselves. "The prioress gave me the order not to have anything more to do with the new monastery."

The orphans were not alone. Julian de Ávila said Mass for them. Master Daza gave them spiritual counsel. Francisco de Salcedo and Doña Guiomar brought them the material aid that helped them to survive.

The issue remained unsettled for nearly six months. In Madrid, the Royal Council seemed in no hurry to rule on a matter that could set a judicial precedent.

> Finally they came to agree that if [St. Joseph] had an income they would pass over the matter and let the foundation continue. I was already so wearied of seeing the hardships of all those who were helping me, more so than in seeing my own, that it didn't seem to be a bad idea to have an income until our adversaries quieted down, and then give it up afterward.... I was disposed to accept the compromise.

Teresa was about to sign the agreement when, during mental prayer, "the Lord told me not to agree, that if in the beginning we accepted an income, they wouldn't allow us afterward to renounce it." But she was so weary that she still hesitated.

That same night St. Peter of Alcántara appeared to her in a dream. "This time he looked severe and told me only that I should by no means accept income and asked why I didn't want to take his advice, and [he] disappeared immediately."

Was this merely a dream prompted by the warnings the saint had addressed to her a few days before his death, or was it a true apparition? Teresa had no doubt about its nature:

> That same night the holy Friar Peter of Alcántara appeared to me, for he was already dead.... I had already, two or three times since his death, seen him and the great glory he possessed; so I wasn't frightened. Rather I rejoiced greatly, for he always appeared in his glorified body, filled with great glory; it gave me a powerful feeling of glory to see him.

The following day, Teresa ordered Don Francisco de Salcedo to break off negotiations and henceforth to accept no compromise, a situation that made the holy gentleman "very happy."

The matter became even more bogged down. At St. Joseph, the "orphans" were lamenting their situation while their *Madre* remained confined at the Incarnation. Months passed. To answer the city's appeal to the king, Teresa asked Rome to confirm its brief, this time in her own name.

Finally, thanks to the energetic intervention of the Dominican, Father Ibáñez—who had left the desert in order to support her—the disruptive elements in the city calmed down. A second brief from the Holy See, signed December 5, 1562, authorized Teresa de Ahumada by name to found a monastery in strict poverty, without income.[13] Strengthened by this document, Teresa dared to write, in April 1563, to her Father Provincial, Don Ángel de Salazar: "May Your Paternity be on guard about resisting the Holy Spirit."

Salazar finally gave in. In a letter dated August 22, 1563, he granted Teresa permission to leave the Incarnation and go to St. Joseph to recite the Divine Office and to teach it to the sisters there. Two professed Carmelites of the Incarnation were authorized to follow her: Isabel de los Ángeles and Ana de Velada. Two novices—other cousins of Teresa, María de Ocampo and Isabel de San Pablo (Cepeda y Ocampo)—also went.

Teresa took very few items with her, and she promised in writing to return the following to the Incarnation: a straw mat, a hair shirt of small chains, a discipline (leather whip), and her old mended habit. She also allowed the Incarnation to benefit from her annuity. In passing by the Basilica of San Vicente, she went into the crypt to thank the Virgin. There, she took off her leather ankle boots and put on the *alpargates*—sandals made of hemp like those worn by the poor of Castile—that would become the distinctive sign of the "Discalced Carmelites."

Even before entering the cloister of St. Joseph, which she hoped never again to leave, Teresa prostrated herself at the foot of the altar in their little chapel. There, "being almost in rapture, I saw Christ who seemed to be receiving me with great love and placing a crown on my head."

She felt herself dying to the world. Then, raising her eyes to heaven while pointing out her dear novices, she cried out: "Here before you, O my God, are the living stones you have chosen to raise up your edifice. Make them worthy to be a part of its construction and grant them so much strength that time cannot weaken them. Far from the vanities of this world, may only your love reign in this house."[14]

In the city, opposition to the foundation had died down. The people came to the religious services and, of their own accord, brought those small alms that were more precious to the foundress than revenues. The provincial prior's agreement rendered the Madrid trial useless. The municipal opponents withdrew.

However, a covert threat remained: Roman authorization did not detach St. Joseph from the mitigated Carmel. Teresa was still dependent on the provincial prior and the prioress of the Incarnation, which continued to receive her annuity. Strictly speaking, St. Joseph was not legally independent but a priory linked to the motherhouse.

CHAPTER 17

Toward the Way of Perfection: The Prioress of St. Joseph

(1563-1567)

eresa emerged uplifted from this ordeal: "God has given me great courage; and the greater these trials were the greater was the courage." She learned from it that it was better to rely on God, "the true friend," than on human beings, who are "like little sticks of dry rosemary...for when some weight of contradiction or criticism comes along, these little sticks break."[1] Finally settled in a small community that observed silence and was fervent and poor, inspired by love and the ideal of perfection, she would now give the full measure of her ability.

Just as quickly as it had revolted, the city calmed down. "The Lord started to inspire our most vigorous persecutors to show us much favor; and they gave us alms. So they approved of what they had so greatly disapproved."[2]

To defuse the anger at the Incarnation, Teresa agreed to have Doña Ana Dávila named prioress of St. Joseph. She was a pretentious aristocrat whom Doña María Cimbrón imposed upon the community, for she meant to keep St. Joseph under her authority. But Doña Ana Dávila found the ascetic regime intolerable and returned to the Incarnation three months later. Teresa was then elected prioress. Out of humility, she at first refused this responsibility, but she finally accepted by order of the bishop.

She would spend the five happiest years of her life at St. Joseph, a place she considered heaven on earth. Twelve Carmelites now surrounded the foundress. They were immersed in poverty—and that winter would be a cold one!—but they were ablaze with love! The women meditated, worked, and slept in their small cells with brick-paved floors and no seats or tables. In the

174

corner of each cell, placed on four wooden planks almost at floor level, lay a straw mattress covered by a single woolen blanket. There were no mirrors. Everything was designed for total forgetfulness of self. On the whitewashed wall hung a bare wooden cross, recalling the one and only necessity, and a holy water font. A narrow window opened out upon Castile's blue sky, the only color to enliven the harmony of this white-and-brown universe. On a small shelf were ten or so books.

At St. Joseph, the nuns arose at five o'clock, "happy to serve...and if this humility is true, blessed be such a servant in the active life...."[3] They washed in a small washbowl filled with cold water drawn from the well. One hour of silent prayer was followed in succession by the short morning Offices: Prime, Terce, Sext, and None. The highlight of the day was the Mass celebrated by their chaplain, Julian de Ávila.

To the right of the chapel choir, the nuns, behind a grille, prayed kneeling on the floor. There were no seats, but they were allowed to sit on their heels, receiving Communion through the "communion window," a small shutter in the grille that opened.

SINCE THERE WERE NO LONGER any lay sisters, all of the Carmelites participated in the housework: cleaning the common areas, cooking, and gardening. When not occupied at a particular task, each one worked in her cell, sitting on a floor mat or on a sheet of cork. At the Incarnation, the common workrooms encouraged conversation. This relative isolation aimed at promoting personal meditation and self-knowledge. First, to truly see oneself in all humility. Then, to work on one's relationship with others, characterized by kind thoughtfulness and goodness. Finally, to enter into the prayer of quiet—a relationship of trust and love with the God who seeks each of us and to whom we speak as a friend. This prayer can lead to permanent union, to the spiritual marriage.

Teresa was thus restoring to Carmel its characteristic as a laboratory of spiritual culture. She wanted her daughters to be "solitary, mute, contemptuous of their body and its demands, but gay like children, humble, but conscious of the dignity of their souls, submissive, but to the Spirit, enamored, but of Christ, stripped of everything, but queens of the world."[4]

In her cell, each Carmelite prayed, spun wool, wove, sewed, or mended. Some of the nuns had at their disposal an hourglass to measure time and a small oil lamp. A few read. Peter of Alcántara's *Treatise on Prayer and Meditation*, introduced by Teresa, was much appreciated.

At eleven o'clock, an examination of conscience was made. "It marks the beginning of this methodical exploration which, from the surface of the soul, then penetrates into the depths as far as the obscure sanctuary where, by the benefit of grace, the light may shine."[5] As Teresa said, "I think I see the great care He takes of me.... I was a sea of sins and iniquities before receiving these favors...."[6]

At noon, the meal was eaten in common in the refectory, the silence broken only by the lector's voice. What did they find in their bowls? *La Madre* had recommended that they not worry about this: "Never seek sustenance through human schemes, for you will die of hunger.... Your eyes on your Spouse! He will sustain you."[7] Upon entering St. Joseph, they all knew what awaited them: perpetual abstinence from meat and sweet treats that bring happiness to people, frequent fasts (except on Sundays), the great fast of six to seven months prescribed by St. Albert starting on September 14 and lasting until Easter, and only water as a beverage.

Isabel, the postulant from Fontiveros, had spent the night in Ávila at the home of relatives who attempted to dissuade her. "You want to enter a convent where famine reigns? Fast and abstinence are making them go crazy!"

She entered there the following day. "On the menu, there was only a slice of bread, a piece of cheese, and a fig. At abundant meals, we had an egg or a sardine," she wrote. Crazy? Yes, but for God!

Poverty was certainly a hallmark of the beginning at St. Joseph. Water, for example, the most ordinary and necessary thing, was not available to the nuns because of the persisting resentment of the Fountain Master Dávila and the avarice of the City Council, although Ávila's principal water source gushed beneath the convent walls. The Carmelites were obliged to draw muddy water from their old, shallow well.

Against the advice of specialists who wanted to dig another well, Teresa asked the counsel of the young María de Ocampo, who had become Sister María Bautista. She had been the first person at the Incarnation to suggest to Teresa the foundation of a small, very poor monastery. As beautiful as she was intelligent, generous, and spontaneous, she had finally obtained her parents' permission—even though they had initially foreseen a rich and beautiful marriage for her—to leave the world and enter St. Joseph. Now regarding the well, María made an act of faith and said that they only had to dig deeper into the existing well. This was done, and crystal-clear water sprang forth at the heart of the monastery.

The nuns no longer tormented themselves on the subject of income. Teresa reassured her daughters with her joy and optimism: "Let's earn our living! With a pound of spun wool, we receive a *real*. For the rest, it is up to dear Providence!"

Actually, "His Majesty sent us what was necessary without our asking for it; and when we were in want, which was seldom, their joy was greater."[8] The essential thing was that there be enough candles on the chapel altar and joy in the hearts of the nuns. Joy was the essential component. And if there was only bread in the wooden bowl and water in the terra-cotta pitcher, they gave thanks to God! According to the season, fortunately they had at their disposal vegetables from their garden: cabbage, turnips, radishes, chick peas, and a handful of olives. Sometimes, they found deposited in the turn by an anonymous person some eggs, or, divine surprise, salted fish. For dessert, an apple or a fig. Never any meat except in the case of sickness. Each one in turn served in the kitchen for a week, including *la Madre*, who was an excellent cook. She liked to treat the nuns with her varied creations, which were prepared with the most humble ingredients and without leaving the company of her Beloved, for, as she is quoted as having said, "The Lord walks among the pots and pans."[9]

The day passed by quickly at the Reformed Carmel. After the noon meal, there was an hour of recreation in common. Teresa said:

> Amuse yourself with your sisters, for relaxation is a necessity of our nature. People say that for persons who profess penance, recreations are nothing but rubbish and manure. I agree. But the manure which fertilizes very poor soil makes it fertile, and our souls are very poor earth. What would become of our little house if each one applied herself to bury the little that she has of wit?[10]

She detested "scowling saints."

At recreation, they talked, sang, laughed, and sometimes danced to the rhythm of castanets! They played a little music; the humble flute and the lute were just as good as the harp and the viola da gamba, the rich instruments of the Incarnation. Some of the nuns embroidered.

In the afternoon after Vespers, each nun spun wool in her cell while praying. At that time, prayer was not practiced in common in the chapel, which was too cramped. Some of them found a quiet corner: a cellar (baptized St. Jerome's hermitage), under the stairs (St. Alexis's hermitage), or, later, the little huts built in the garden.

Night came without their realizing it. Starting at eight o'clock, strict silence was the rule. After a light snack came the Office of Compline and an hour of mental prayer. At eleven o'clock, after having chanted Matins and Lauds, the nuns went back to their cells. They stopped before the door and knelt on the threshold. The youngest novice gave three raps of her clapper and intoned with two notes a *saetilla* or little *saeta* (arrow), a sort of modulated song developing a short poem on the theme for meditation given by the mother prioress:

> When the Gentle hunter
> Wounded and subdued me,
> In love's arms,
> My soul fallen;
> New life receiving,
> Thus did I exchange
> *My Beloved is for me,*
> *And I am for my Beloved.*[11]

After mother prioress had blessed each one, they retired to their cells, small but open to celestial infinity. *La Madre*—who stated the following about her sisters in the *Foundations*: "...the Lord brought them to His house, endowing them with so much perfection that it was to my embarrassment"[12]—then went to her own cell and closed the door. The silence of the night spread over Carmel.

Only six hours of sleep; it was very little for these undernourished young sisters, but Teresa had told them: "Oh, my Sisters, do not feel secure or let yourselves go to sleep!"[13] How, in any case, would they find sleep, these women whose hearts had swelled with an incredible hope? With passion, they had engaged in the unending dialogue with "their beloved Jesus." It was enough for them to look at their Mother, herself engaged on the luminous path that leads to the seventh dwelling.

Only a small light shone in the room of *la Madre*, whose window opened upon the starlit firmament of Ávila. No one heard the scratching of her pen. Teresa would be seated on the floor, a stone window ledge serving as her table. The oil lamp would be smoky, its flame barely lighting the paper. But *la Madre* could have written soley by the light of the stars. She would never reread herself. For her, time was as though suspended.

FIVE YEARS OF HAPPINESS, even if she writes:

> Now then, the first thing we must strive for is to rid ourselves of our love for our bodies, for some of us are by nature such lovers of comfort that there is no small amount of work in this area.... Be determined, Sisters, that you came to die for Christ, not to live comfortably for Christ.[14]

But now Teresa's ecstasies and illuminations began again, even in public. Her legend was already growing. In the city people talked about how the

The signature of Teresa of Ávila appears below a seventeenth-century painting
(Mechlin Carmel) of the Carmelite mystic and reformer.

Portrait of Teresa of Ávila, prolific writer and master of the spiritual life.
Pope Paul VI declared St. Teresa a Doctor of the Church
on September 27, 1970.

Anonymous sixteenth-century painting of St. John of the Cross, mystic, poet, and close collaborator with St. Teresa in the foundation of the Discalced Carmelites.

The meeting between St. John of the Cross and St. Teresa of Ávila.
Engraving, French school, sixteenth century.

Gian Lorenzo Bernini's Ecstasy of St. Teresa of Ávila. The marble sculpture is part of the Cornaro Chapel of Santa Maria della Vittoria, Rome.

The cathedral of Ávila.

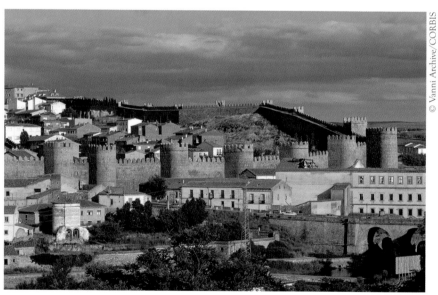

The city walls of Ávila.

tentaua nj dad y mentira me parece lo q
yo no beço ba gça do ael serbiçio de dios q no
lo sabria yo deçir como lo entiendo y las las
tima q me açen los q beo con las cuidad
q estan en esta verdad y con esto (otras gananç
çias q aquj dire y muchas no sabre deçir dijo
mea quj el señor vna particular palabra de
gran disimo fabor yo no se como esto fue por q no
bi nada mas q de se vna suerte q tan poco se de
çir con grandisima fortaleza y muy deveras
ya cumplir con todas mjs fuerças la mas peqña
parte de laescritura divina pareçeme q njn
guna cosa se me pornja delante q no pasase por
esto q dome vna verdad de esta divina verdad
y se me tepresento sin saber como nj q es culpido
q me a tener vn nuebo acatamjento adios por
q dando tiçia de su majestad y poder de vna manera
q no se pue de deçir se entender q es vna gran
cosa q dome muy gran gana de no ablar sino co
sas muy verdaderas q bayan adelante de lo q a
ca se trata en el mundo y anfi començe a tener
pena de bibir en el de lo me con gran ternura
y regalo y vmjldad pareçeme q sin entender
como me dio el señor aquj mucho no me q do njn
guna fus pecho de çeros y lusion no bi nada mas
entendi el gran bien q ay en no açer caso de co
sa q no sea ya lle gar nos mas adios y anfi enten
di q cosaes an dar vn alma en verdad delante de

A page from St. Teresa of Ávila's original handwritten manuscript of
The Life. *The first draft of this now famous work was begun in 1562,*
and the final draft was completed in 1568.

The Foundations of Teresa of Ávila.

noble sister of the bishop had to wait patiently in the parlor for the saint to come out of her ecstasy, her dialogue with Jesus. Teresa knew she did not merit this, describing herself as being "so useless, I sometimes become fearful in thinking that I may be deceived. So I see clearly that from these revelations and raptures—for I play no part in them, nor do I do anything more to receive them than be a blank tablet—there come to me these benefits." Then, filled with both wonder and confusion, recalling the words of St. Paul, she understood that "I neither live, nor speak, nor have any desire but that He who strengthens and governs me might live in me."[15]

Not only did the bishop's sister and the bishop himself witness her ecstasies, but so did her confessor. One day, Father Báñez was giving a lecture in the parlor. With the community gathered there, Teresa entered into ecstasy. The priest stopped speaking and then left on tiptoe.

She could not escape the ecstasies. She asked that she be shaken. She latched onto the most humble realities of tangible life, "but, in these raptures most often there is no remedy; rather, without any forethought or any help there frequently comes a force so swift and powerful that one sees and feels this cloud or mighty eagle raise it up and carry it aloft on its wings."[16]

Fortunately, she could practice the prayer of quiet in her cell and not in the choir. One nun, María de San Francisco, regretted this: "We deplored it. If we had stayed together, we would have known more."

They knew quite enough! Teresa ordered her daughters not to talk about her ecstasies. But "trying to resist them doesn't help, nor can they be disguised," she wrote to her brother Lorenzo. "I'm so terribly embarrassed that I want to hide I don't know where."[17]

Isabel de Santo Domingo (Isabel Ortega, the spiritual daughter of Peter of Alcántara), who was close to Teresa, confided some secrets to Father Báñez. Teresa had frightened her by admitting that she feared not awaking from a rapture and being brought to heaven never to return. This was a justifiable concern. According to Isabel:

> The Lord gave our Mother such impatience to see him and escape her bodily prison that she seemed in danger of losing her life. Even this impatience caused a sort of ecstasy, accompanied by an intensity of desires which tortured her to the point where she seemed close to breathing her last.

Isabel de Santo Domingo implored the Dominican: "*Padre!* Command our Mother not to withdraw or remain alone during her ecstasies! For, when she senses that she is about to enter into that state, she takes care to seek refuge in the most solitary places."

One day, according to Isabel, "I saw her leave the choir in the middle of the night. She did not even have a light. She withdrew to a hermitage. I listened."

Hearing her moans, Isabel understood. "I went in and approached her in the darkness. She told me to go away and leave her alone. I touched her hands: they were clasped and icy like those of a dead person. I experienced so much fear that I began to scold her.

"Be careful, *Madre!* You are in danger. You are killing yourself. And us along with you. Ah! The devil will laugh at seeing your days for serving God cut short. It's insane to go to such great lengths to see His Majesty before he wants or orders you to do so."

Teresa answered her in a gentle voice: "Be quiet, you innocent! Do you think that this is my doing?"

During her raptures, which Teresa described as "an arduous, delightful martyrdom" in Chapter 20 of *The Life,* witnesses noted that her pulse was hardly perceptible and her entire body stiff. When she awakened, she remained paralyzed for a considerable length of time, saying, "I feel pain in the pulse and in the body, as if the bones were disjointed." But she was radiant with joy; she had seen a resplendent dove and sometimes Christ in glory.

She never recommended that her daughters seek ecstasies. "They should work instead!" She wanted to protect herself and them from pride, their worst enemy:

> What each of you will understand, daughters, if you are advanced, will be that you are the most wretched of all. And this understanding will be manifested in deeds done for your own spiritual growth and for the good of others, and not in having more delights and raptures in prayer, or visions.... This attitude includes the great virtues of humility and mortification, careful obedience.... I have paused to give these counsels to those to whom He doesn't give contemplation. By practicing them, the contemplatives, also, may humble themselves.[18]

She wanted her daughters to be first and foremost "happy to serve in what they command you to do.... And if this humility is true, blessed be such a servant in the active life."[19] As to the delights of contemplation, raptures, and visions, "we have to wait [until] being in the other world to know what that is worth."[20]

St. Joseph's convent, "God's little corner," was enhanced by solitude and the limited number of the elect. All their time was given over to prayer, but also to pondering books of spirituality and the discoveries of the interior journey! For Teresa, however, as for those who had been entrusted to her, it was not a question of confusing dream with reality. Her role as prioress imposed discernment on her. Between her mystical "incidents," the humble religious could be found at her spinning wheel or in the kitchen surrounded by saucepans, for she was as much an expert at cooking as she was in mental prayer. Teresa was thus protecting herself from illuminism, so frequent in her time. She would always distrust her visions. What if they came from the devil? She dared to speak to the Grand Inquisitor Don Francisco de Soto about this question. Troubled by her revelations yet reassured by her humility, he answered that this matter did not concern him in his role as Inquisitor, guardian of the Doctrine. He sent her back to her regular confessor, Father Báñez. This remarkable theologian knew how to go beyond purist scholasticism by respecting Teresa's mystical transports and loving contemplations. While distrusting affective deviations, he knew that "theologians are as nothing without the mystical flashes which tear open the night of faith."[21]

Thanks to the peace and fervor of the tiny convent, postulants flocked to join it, sometimes in an unforeseen fashion. One September day in 1563, a rich retinue with ladies in a palanquin and gentlemen on horseback arrived at the door. At their head was a young woman of great beauty, stunning in "a great deal of silk and gold and all imaginable jewels."[22] This niece of Teresa, María Dávila, twenty-two and the sole heiress of the riches of the recently deceased Don Álvarez y Salazar, was followed by a retinue of marriage suitors. She cleverly concealed her plan: "I am going to greet my aunt Teresa," she said, bidding them to leave.

The monastery door opened, and la Madre came toward her, presenting a large crucifix that María kissed with humility. Then, without turning around, she entered the cloister. The door closed, and the men were left astounded. Inside, she removed her rich clothing and jewels, receiving from la Madre the brown, rough wool habit of Carmel and her name: Sister María de San Jerónimo.

They were now thirteen, the number set by la Madre—thirteen, like Jesus and his apostles. "Thirteen poor little women...[who] make no noise,"[23] she states. But the sound of their silence still resonates in the world centuries later.

LITTLE BY LITTLE, THE NEW CARMEL was taking shape. It was a small, fragile group and, for this reason, all the more precious for wanting to be totally dependent on the divine will. The wall of the cloister, at first a wicker mat on wooden pickets, was, above all, symbolic. The house could not have been poorer. In the cell rooms there were no wooden floors but rustic tiles, "inhabitable to fleas," they laughingly said. As was the case in all poor districts devoid of hygiene, they faced this problem of insect parasites with humor. One of the nuns had even written a couplet to the lice, "this evil livestock, this uncivil mob," that sometimes hid in the nuns' habits; Teresa and the nuns would alternate the verses:

> Now that you give us clothing new,
> Heavenly King,
> From all nasty creatures
> Free this cloth of wool.
> These nasty creatures
> The prayer disturbs
> Of the spirit
> In devotion weak;
> Yet strongly kept
> Is that heart in God.
> From all nasty creatures,
> Free this cloth of wool.[24]

TERESA ENDEAVORED TO ACQUIRE the abandoned hovels around the monastery. Lacking the money to build a real monastery, she converted these rickety and dilapidated buildings into living space. She liked this precariousness, for "it would not be right for the house of thirteen poor little women to make a loud crash when it falls...on the day of judgment."[25]

Thanks to María Bautista's dowry, Teresa had four small hermitages built in the sun-filled garden, little "corners for God" where mental prayer could be practiced; to this day, they retain her living memory. She liked to meditate in the hermitage dedicated to Our Lady of Nazareth. Leaning on a wooden chest, she read and meditated upon *Morals on the Book of Job* by St. Gregory, *The Life of Christ* by the Carthusian Ludolf of Saxony, and *Treatise on Prayer and Meditation* by Peter of Alcántara. Or, taking refuge in St. Augustine's hermitage, she reread his *Confessions,* which had guided her life.

What today is called the upper cloister was nothing but an attic. Wooden beams supported the tiled roof, darkened by the sun. A flourishing vine rose as high as the roof, a sign of divine generosity. And up there was also the cracked bell bought at little cost. Under the eaves nested the small infirmary, and beside it was a cell filled with light where Teresa would later reside to complete *The Interior Castle.* On the floor lay a straw mattress, and on a shelf sat ancient pottery from Peru given to her by her brother

Lorenzo. In St. Joseph's early years, Teresa, not wanting to disturb her sisters' sleep when she left before dawn, lived in a narrow cell near the door of the monastery and slept in an *artesa,* an old kneading trough.

Teresa de Jesús was very busy! In addition to religious services, prayer, and the numerous tasks of a prioress, she found herself obliged to write! She had just finished the second version of *The Life* at the request of Father García de Toledo. Now her daughters and her confessor, Father Báñez, were asking her to compose a collection of daily counsels for the spiritual formation of the novices and for training them in how to live in community. It was no small matter to direct and watch over fraternal relations among religious of very different ages, personalities, and characters! The work would be known as *el librillo,* the little book, later edited and published under the title *The Way of Perfection.*[26] "I write as the ideas come into my head," she admitted without irony.

Fifteen chapters were devoted to asceticism, which she treated with discretion, for she knew the fearsome effects of excess. Ten chapters on mental prayer, what she cared most about, followed. Whether a person is living in the world or in a monastery, these chapters can be read with great benefit. The book contains much of value because of its precision, richness, psychology, and especially because of Teresa's own experience, which informs the work and makes this way of perfection come alive. The text always takes into account each person's nature and personality. The style is so lively that one has the impression of hearing rather than reading the words, as though it were addressed to us personally; as if Teresa, alive and present, were speaking to us.

The book also contains a commentary on the Our Father, shedding light on the prayer and setting forth full weight of meaning on each petition. Teresa emphasizes the personal and universal dimension of the prayer of Jesus and the necessity of allowing the heart to be permeated by it rather than reciting it in a mechanical manner. She did not like prayers to be repeated with the mind elsewhere, as if anxious to get them over with.

TERESA DE JESÚS WAS A REMARKABLE prioress and an incomparable teacher of mental prayer, as her writings attest. She was also an astute psychologist, profound in her analyses and practical in her directions.

She was very attentive to the initial recruitment of postulants, recognizing the need to discern from the start a real vocation in a young woman's motivations in order to ensure that she would enter with a conscience that radiated faith and a well-balanced personality inclined to joy. Life in Carmel is of a contemplative and not apostolic nature, or, rather, the apostolate is pursued within the cloister, by the heart and the spirit, through prayer.

As a general rule, Teresa avoided giving orders, knowing that individual limitations make it difficult for everyone to carry them out. However, the aim was truly to follow the counsels as perfectly as possible.

Teresa knew she was responsible for the health of her nuns, though in a city where half the population went hungry, she did not concern herself with whether the food was sufficient and balanced. From her writings it is clear that she had a certain disdain for the body, which she saw as a millstone dragging down the elevation of the spirit. In her time, it was viewed as the source of urges and passions that were too often attributed to the devil. In her Constitutions, she devoted three lines to food, and they are meant to highlight the importance of fasting; by way of contrast, there are twelve pages on acknowledgment of sin and on penances!

Asceticism is meant to overcome the body, to subdue the passions and the senses. The aim is not to die, to kill the body, but to die to oneself in order to be reborn in God through Christ.

Teresa, who had experienced serious depressions, wanted to keep the body from weakening the soul. This is difficult since it implies acting contrary to the natural and human inclination to flee suffering and pursue pleasure. A person enters Carmel in obedience to an invitation from Christ to sacrifice oneself in order to "atone for the sins of the world." It's a question of "embracing the cross." Discipline also strengthens bodies and souls in preparation for life's battles and ordeals. So the novices had to arm themselves to face physical and moral suffering and, more frightening still, possible dryness and boredom. What if the time spent in prayer is like a house with windows wide open and battered by the four winds? Teresa knew that her novices would be good religious if they acquired self-mastery, which involves body, spirit, and soul. In addition, this "work" had to be oriented toward others so as to attain the most fraternal union.

She advised the novices to read the works of spiritual masters who had succeeded in conquering themselves and to follow the example of Christ in his humanity. She deemed the spiritual adventure similar to the adventures of the conquistadors or crusaders, but divested of their monetary or mercenary motivations. She did not fear her Carmelites experiencing the dryness inherent in the religious vocation or their difficulty concentrating; she knew that these are useful to the extent that in learning to overcome them, the soul is fortified and the person advances in his or her spiritual life. All of this resembles the arduous training of an athlete, as St. Paul emphasized.

If Teresa's writings are lacking in and, to be truthful, indifferent toward the body—except concerning hygiene, for she had a cult of cleanliness—she was considerably ahead of her time in matters of the spirit, the soul, and psychology. In times past Carmelite convents were sometimes reproached with practicing what today might be called the crushing of the ego, that effort to suppress the ego in order to "gain" heaven. Teresa practiced this type of asceticism and obtained remarkable results, but she refused to stifle an awakening personality, and she would never use the phrase of certain Jesuit masters: "Obey like a cadaver." She would, however, attach a great deal of importance to obedience; it was a sign of humility. To test María Bautista, her niece, Teresa one day ordered her to plant a half-rotten cucumber.

"Must I plant it upright or sideways, *Madre?*"

"Sideways!" answered Teresa, unruffled.[27]

Thanks to her ability to discern, the prioress would recognize the light wind of grace or the most powerful tradewind. Just as a good captain selects the sail to hoist, she would organize the spiritual life by proposing progressive exercises. She developed this approach in her *Interior Castle*, and it leads to a gratifying experience of the Absolute.

It goes without saying that at St. Joseph silence and solitude were respected. No more distracting parlor visits, useless chatter, or inordinate affection for lay persons, in the midst of which one could not "ripen the fruits of divine love which turn golden only under the fiery rays of a unique sun." It was a matter of "closing the breaches of the spiritual citadel to launch oneself in an assault upon the invisible."[28] But as we have already stated, Teresa did not encourage the novices to seek raptures, the suspect intoxications of that time of spiritual betrothal, and those ecstasies that can hamper the use of reason.

In the final analysis, she remained very balanced, a rational woman in an era ready to abandon itself to any and all types of vertiginous undertakings. Her watchword was to flee suspect pleasures and excitement that the senses and ego could retrieve and thereby extinguish the divine fire. In contrast, she warned against anything that risked slackening the springs of the spirit: sadness, apathy, indifference.

She also reminded her charges that personal efforts are useless if they are not borne of the will of God, since we cannot do anything by ourselves. True spiritual work consists in preparing to do the will of God, staying vigilant, and always having on one's lips this prayer: "Your will, Lord, be done in me in every way and manner that you, my Lord, want." She invited the Carmelites not to resist divine grace but to give the consent of their will despite difficulties, even if God's request seemed incomprehensible. When the will, understanding, and trust are refused, a person cannot possibly receive the graces corresponding to God's request.

It is in this equilibrium between the divine and the human, between passion and reason, action and contemplation, that all of Teresa's genius lay.

SHE WOULD NEED THIS BALANCE regarding that immemorial institution of monastic life: the parlors. She had used and misused the practice at the Incarnation and later denounced its abuse. Quite determined to limit the nuisances of this practice, she had had to compromise. But at St. Joseph there were very strict guidelines for visits with outsiders, which were reserved for close relatives, confessors, and spiritual advisers. Teresa accepted these visits because they allowed the little community to be known and to receive vocations. She also received prayer intentions for cures and conversions. The influence of St. Joseph grew in proportion to what it gave to the community of believers and nonbelievers.

Visitors were not only separated by a double wooden grille but also by a curtain (no longer seen today). Even *la Madre* kept the curtain drawn, allowing her to spin her wool without qualms while she listened to her visitor, though the sound of her spinning wheel gave her away! Don Francisco de Salcedo, accustomed to seeing Teresa through the grille, took offense at this.

"What's this, *Madre!* You are not listening to me. A person cannot listen while spinning with such vehemence."

"I am doing what I must to feed my daughters."

"In that case, I'll make a deal with you. When I come to see you, I will pay you the equivalent of one hour's work, without being obliged to hear your wheel spinning behind this black veil."

Laughing, she accepted.

For Teresa, the Carmel sheltered the Lord's chosen ones against the vanities of the world, allowing those called to give themselves entirely to their Spouse. This divine Lover eludes egotism to the extent that the prayer of the spouses affects the entire Church and all of humanity. The vocation of a Carmelite is not to take pleasure from the contemplation of God—although this is not forbidden—but to bring a silent contribution to the salvation of all souls, directly in line with the evangelical message.

A reading of the Constitutions demonstrates the concern of the foundress for the slightest details. The grille, like the Rule, is a symbol, a tangible sign of the Carmelite vocation: the accepted separation from the world. As a reaction against the laxity of the mitigated Rule, Teresa imposed norms that have been renounced today, although their spirit remains. The confessional had a shutter made of sheet metal pierced like a grater and covered with a linen cloth. Teresa must have remembered the perilous dialogues with her confessor in Becedas! At St. Joseph, the separation was complete. In case of contact with any man (visitor, cleric, doctor, confessor), the nuns had to remain entirely veiled, as a woman reserved for her spouse, pulling down over her face her black or white veil. Teresa allowed exceptions for a sister's father, mother, siblings, and some privileged confessors, but not the bishop. In her correspondence *la Madre* mentions Father García de Toledo, saying, "For him, no veil"; it was considered an exceptional favor for this holy priest to see the Carmelites face to face.

Naturally, there was no contact with the city. The windows of the cells opened out onto the interior patios, the cloister, and the garden. From the outside, the Carmel presented only blank walls and impassable grilles. This heightened the mysterious character of the place in the minds of the lay people and sometimes led to erroneous judgments—what was taking place behind those high walls?

How did the nuns communicate with the outside world? The convent had to be supplied with provisions, since the kitchen garden and the orchard did not suffice. A turn, an ingenious monastic invention consisting of a cylindrical wooden drum pivoting in a cavity of the surrounding wall, allowed for the passing of offerings without the nuns being seen. The massive windowless entrance door had, of course, a small spy-hole, but its function was limited to allowing the nun in attendance at the turn to identify authorized visitors and the nuns who had had to absent themselves from the convent. This door was double-bolted—one key was kept by the prioress and the other by the nun in attendance. It was impossible to unlock the door with just one of the keys.

Teresa remembered the windowed walls of the Incarnation through which gallants and other "devout" persons passed small notes and tiny gifts. The high cloister wall is indeed an old monastic tradition intended to prevent a suitor from jumping over to kidnap a nun locked in by her father against her wishes!

These restrictive measures were meant to protect the nuns from outside perils. As to the interior, made confining by all these enclosures, the nuns also had to be protected from each other. That is why they spent most of the time in their cells for, as Teresa stated, "Silence is better observed when each nun is by herself."[29]

There was indeed separation from the world, but there was also voluntary poverty. At one point Teresa wrote: "That day we didn't have so much as a stick of wood to make a fire to cook a sardine."[30] Later on, the Carmel would receive many gifts, but such donations would be used primarily to adorn the chapel, to help the poor, and to pay for the new foundations.

To summarize, the changes at St. Joseph with respect to the mitigated Rule were as follows: the nuns lived on a day-to-day basis from manual labor and alms and not from regular income; they devoted themselves to prayer; there were no lay sisters, so the housekeeping tasks were assumed, each in turn, by all the nuns, including the prioress: "The Mother prioress should be the first on the list for sweeping so that she might give good example to all."[31] No postulant was accepted without a vocation, and candidates had to be at least seventeen years of age. After a favorable vote by the community, a postulant would be accepted without a dowry and, on occasion, with no possessions at all.

At the monastery, the nuns did not own "any coffer or small chest, or box, or cupboard," everything being put in common. They lived in strict enclosure, not being allowed to go out unless an exception was made, and they took the vow of stability (meaning that a nun never transfers to another monastery). Silence (total silence from 8:00 PM until 5:00 AM) was strictly observed, with discretion in relationships among the sisters; it was forbidden for sisters to visit each others' cells. "Let no sister embrace another or touch the face or hands. The sisters should not have particular friendships, but should include all in their love for one another...." The number of members was reduced to thirteen nuns. Certain sisters, called monitors, were entrusted with the responsibility of denouncing serious misdeeds.

Later on, Teresa found herself compelled to modify her Rule on three points. She had to accept certain revenues, gifts, and dowries (but no pensions); otherwise, it would have been impossible to buy, restore, and maintain the buildings, or to extend the Reform with new foundations. The maximum number of nuns would be raised to twenty-one. Two or three lay nuns, who volunteered for certain tasks—in the kitchen, the garden, the orchard, or as portresses—requiring specific aptitudes, would be admitted. This also allowed the community to take in nuns so humble that they would have felt embarrassed in the choir, not being able to read or chant. But as for the rest of the stricter Rule, the spirit of the Reform would be respected.

In everything, sisterly charity remained of highest importance:

> The sick should be cared for with fullness of love, concern for their comfort, and compassion in accordance with the poverty we practice.... The

mother prioress should be very careful that the healthy nuns be deprived of something necessary rather than have the sick ones go without some deeds of kindness.

And *la Madre*, who had imposed going barefoot in sandals upon the "Discalced," cited the Spanish proverb: "One no longer speaks about God to someone whose feet are cold." The Constitutions do state, accordingly: "Let sandals made from hemp be worn and, for the sake of modesty, stockings of rough wool or of cloth made from rough tow."

The Constitutions also suppressed noble titles and even family names. And "never should the prioress or any of the sisters use the title *Doña* [Madam]."

"The house, with the exception of the church, should never be adorned.... Let the house be small and the rooms humble: something that fulfills rather than exceeds the need."

The mother prioress "should strive to be loved so that she may be obeyed." This was a considerable innovation. Where the mitigated were concerned, the prioress was often imposed on the community for financial reasons. Sometimes she was a rich widow of the aristocracy. At St. Joseph, the prioress, the subprioress, and the key-bearers were elected. "Documents and funds" were locked away in a coffer that had three keys, one kept by the prioress and the other two kept by "the oldest key-bearers."

The weekly Chapter meetings were important. Here the sisters were obliged to publicly denounce their misdemeanors and lapses in living the Rule. Among the grave faults punishable by the whip and food deprivation were quarrels, lies, gossiping, and breaking the fast. Some graver faults carried the possibility of excommunication, the whip, and solitary confinement in a cell. These were: disobeying the prioress and lacking in the respect due her, "conspiracy and malicious plotting," spiteful gossip that sowed discord, and unauthorized contact with persons outside the monastery. The gravest faults—incorrigibility, an unauthorized outing, the sin of sensuality, violence against the prioress, and revelation of monastery secrets—were punishable by prison along with excommunication. The prison sentence could be decreed as perpetual in the case of apostasy and sins of the flesh.

If the guilty person was the prioress, she would be deposed immediately by the priest-visitator and would be severely punished.

This lifestyle has a name: heroism. For Teresa, the way of perfection passes through poverty, abnegation, obedience, and mortifications sought in daily life, leading to a heroism all the more remarkable because it is not noticed. This constant effort, often contrary to nature, can only be sustained through mental prayer, a dialogue of love with Christ, which justifies it.

The miracle is that this lifestyle was successful. Postulants were arriving in large numbers so that the flock exceeded the number set by Teresa, and she had to consider expanding the foundation.

CHAPTER 18

The Mission

(1567)

In February 1567, Teresa was advised of the extraordinary visit to Ávila of Father Juan Bautista Rossi, known as Rubeo de Ravenna, the prior general of the Carmelites who resided in Rome. At the invitation of King Philip II, the highest-ranking member of the Order left Rome for Spain. This worried Teresa. De Ravenna might well reproach her for her foundation and for having placed it under the authority of the bishop. Worse still, he could order her to return to the Incarnation.

As was her habit, Teresa met the danger head-on by speaking to Bishop de Mendoza. She even requested that Father de Ravenna visit St. Joseph.

Father de Ravenna first visited the two mitigated Carmels in Ávila, then he spoke to the bishop. "My plan, Your Grace, is to reform the Carmelite Order according to the intentions of the Council of Trent. This is a mission that has been confirmed by King Philip and the Holy Father. His bull *Circa Pastoralis* imposes enclosure on all women's communities."

"May heaven assist you!"

"Yes, it is a difficult and sometimes impossible task. According to the word of our Lord, one does not put new wine in old wineskins. I have just experienced this in Andalusia, where nothing has come of my plans."

Father Rubeo had called together a Chapter in Seville with the aim of putting the primitive Rule into effect. But the mitigated Andalusian Carmelites, well connected at court, had sabotaged his plan for reform. Passing through Madrid, King Philip berated Father Rubeo, for his actions threatened the peace of the status quo. Without allowing himself to be discouraged, the prior general had then turned toward Castile, prudently avoiding Toledo. But he had been poorly received in Ávila at the mitigated Carmelite monastery of men and at the Incarnation. His entire mission having been compromised, he turned in desperation to Bishop de Mendoza. He suggested: "Why not rely upon new foundations such as the one that *Madre* Teresa de Jesús has just created in this very city? Go to see her. She is an exceptional woman who is at the same time a mystic and a woman of good sense. Moreover, she is requesting a visit from you."[1]

FACING HER PRIOR GENERAL, Teresa was frank in her approach. "I gave him an account of my soul and of almost my whole life.... He consoled me much and assured me that he wouldn't order me to leave St. Joseph's."

She then had him visit the monastery. Father de Ravenna marveled at the difference in the Carmelites at St. Joseph, who were "strangers to splendor and so humbly steeped in mortification." He questioned Teresa at length and read her Constitutions. He became enthusiastic, realizing that he had his reform at last!

"*Madre!* Your way of life delights me. I find in it the model of our holy Order at its origin when we were observing the primitive Rule in all its rigor. Would you consent to found other monasteries of strict observance?"

Teresa felt faint. She had believed she could rest now at St. Joseph. Soon she hoped to pass on the responsibility of prioress to the most capable of her daughters, María de San Jerónimo. She would then be able to devote herself entirely to mental prayer in her little cell and to pursue the interior journey culminating in the spiritual nuptials. Her hope was now receding.

Then she remembered a meeting the year before with a Franciscan missionary, Friar Alonso Maldonado de Buendia. On his return from America, "the Indies," he had come to preach at St. Joseph. "He began to tell me about the many millions of souls that were being lost there for want of Christian instruction."[2]

It is likely that this Franciscan, also the general commissioner of the West Indies, had informed Teresa of the atrocities inflicted upon the indigenous peoples for the past forty years by the Spaniards—colonists and soldiers alike. At least Marcelle Auclair suggests this when attributing these words to Friar Maldonado: "Millions of souls are being lost in these conquered lands *where the sword does not always clear the way for the cross.*"[3] Though nothing in Teresa's known writings confirms this, it was obviously a taboo subject.[4]

Today we know that Friar Maldonado had pronounced a scathing indictment before the king and the court, concluding with these words: "The

Council of the Indies in its entirety is in a state of damnation." Another
Franciscan, Marcos de Niza, spoke of "millions of dead" in a report to the
king. Obviously he spoke of the Native Americans, since the Spanish conquistadors numbered only several thousand. Everyone knew of the *Brief
Relation*, the vehement writings of the Dominican Bartolomé de Las Casas,
presented to Charles V in 1540 and published in 1553, as well as the 1550
controversy of Valladolid. It seems difficult to imagine that Teresa, with
three of her brothers having died in America, would not have been aware of
all of this in 1566.

On the other hand, like all Spaniards, she knew of the spread of Protes-
tantism in Europe, which also threatened the Catholic Church in Spain.

The visit of Friar Maldonado had deeply distressed her: "I was so grief-
stricken over the loss of so many souls that I couldn't contain myself. I went
to a hermitage with many tears."[5] The world was on fire, and there they
were, a few powerless, poor women, sheltered from everything!

Teresa, immersed in her century, retained the image of the Church of
her era. For her, the Spanish conquest of the New World was first and foremost a missionary endeavor destined to save pagan souls through their conversion. It was an extension of the apostolic work of the universal Church.
After her first vision of hell, she embarked upon a personal path of conversion. After her second vision, she prayed ardently for the return to Christian
unity by bringing the Protestants back to the Roman Church. Her third
vision of hell now impelled her to hope that the indigenous races could be
converted peacefully. She was, before all else, a "daughter of the Church,"
and would be so until her death.

Her conquistador brothers were propagators of the faith, and Rodrigo
was a martyr! To his counselors' suggestion that he abandon unprofitable
territories, King Philip II replied: "I would prefer to lose a kingdom rather
than risk compromising the eternal life of a single one of my subjects." Such
was the mindset of this era.

Yes, for Teresa the problem was clear. "God's little corner" had been
founded, a jewel in the land of Castile, but the world was vast—"millions of
souls...were being lost there"—and the thirteen poor women of St. Joseph
would not save themselves alone. Teresa then felt herself to have the soul of
a missionary. Her four years of mental prayer had armed her for action. But
given the status of women at that time, action seemed impossible. And as
she beseeched the Lord to give her the means to act, Christ appeared to her:
"He showed me much love, manifesting His desire to comfort me, and said:
'Wait a little, daughter, and you will see great things.'"[6]

Six months later, there in Ávila, the general of the Order was giving her this mission! At that instant, Teresa felt her destiny as a foundress being born in her. "He gave me very extensive patent letters so that more monasteries could be founded, along with censures to prevent any provincial from restraining me."

According to the testimony of Julian de Ávila, the chaplain at St. Joseph, Prior General Rubeo de Ravenna first reminded Teresa that she was under obedience to him. To this, she supposedly replied respectfully that she was under the obedience of the Ordinary and showed him the pope's brief placing her and her monastery of St. Joseph under the bishop of Ávila. The prior general, without becoming angry, said that as apostolic visitator he had the power to correct the irregularity contained in the brief. The pope had not been sufficiently informed. With her diplomatic skill, Teresa settled matters by respecting both parties. She pledged her obedience to Father Rubeo while remaining submissive to her bishop. In any case, both men were favorable to the creation of reformed monasteries dedicated to prayer in order to touch the heart of God and help save the world. As for the provincial prior of Castile residing in Toledo, they hoped that he would come around to Father Rubeo's point of view.

Teresa felt like she was dreaming. Not only to found monasteries, but "as many as I had hairs on my head!" "This seemed to me foolish because a useless little woman as helpless as I well understood that she couldn't do anything.... Faith and the love of pleasing God make possible what to natural reason is not possible."

She immediately set out. "It seemed to me that I saw them founded [already]."

PRIOR GENERAL RUBEO DE RAVENNA remained in Ávila for a few days and had many conversations with *la Madre*. "I had grown to love him very much," she wrote. He was already affectionately calling her *la mia figlia* (my daughter). They spoke about mental prayer as the necessary cement for the Reform. Such a strict Rule could not be imposed if it were not supported by love for God, for neighbor, and for people afar. One could not be separated from the other, and Teresa saw no contradiction between the contemplative and the apostolic life, one supporting the other.

Father Rubeo also saw the bishop again. At Teresa's suggestion, the bishop asked him to authorize the foundation of monasteries of the strict observance for men—the Discalced Carmelites—so that the nuns would not have to depend upon mitigated instructors, confessors, visitators, and celebrants. Having already consulted the Carmelite monks of the mitigated Rule and having faced their general outcry, Father Rubeo reached no decision for the time being: "And thus, so as not to disturb the province, he let the matter go for then."

The patent letters he left Teresa were clear: "We grant the right and powers to Mother Teresa de Jesús to found, in all localities of the two Castiles, monasteries of our holy Order where the nuns will live according to the original Rule. And we will give them vicars to govern them."

But what vicars? "Seeing how few friars there were in this province, [I] even wonder whether or not they were going to die out...." wrote Teresa.

That is why, after Father Rubeo's departure, she took up her pen and threw the ball back into his court. Could her nuns remain submissive to the visitators, confessors, and other "timorous semi-literates" of the mitigated Order from whom she had had to suffer at the Incarnation and who had made them walk "like fettered chickens"? "A great turmoil" might result.

From Valencia Father Rubeo hesitated for a long time. Finally, he authorized the foundation of *two* monasteries of Discalced Carmelites in Castile. Teresa's heart swelled with joy as she read through these new patent letters:

> We desire that all the religious sons of this Order be as clear mirrors, burning lamps, blazing torches, and resplendent stars to enlighten and aid those who stray in this world. And so we desire that they give themselves entirely to the continual and regular frequenting of God. Dedicated to mental prayer in holy meditation and contemplation, they must strive to unite themselves to him so closely that their spirits, although still hampered by the flesh, be already living in heaven. Forgetful of themselves, absorbed in these frequent and soaring flights that cannot be defined, for they are extraordinary, their light passes quickly by, whether because it is inherent in the soul and so merges with it, or that it walks, rises, descends, and challenges understanding to seize it. It brings tears to the eyes, but leaves the most soft and beneficial dew in the heart.

This mystical lyricism could only enchant Teresa. Father General continued:

> So, urged on by this desire for the growth of our Order, we assent to the petition that has been made to us to authorize the foundation of two houses of religious occupied with celebrating Mass, praying, and chanting. They will consecrate the suitable number of hours to mental prayer, meditation, and other spiritual exercises in such a way that they will be called monasteries of contemplative Carmelites. They will also help the others and live in conformity with the old Constitutions.[7]

Teresa's enthusiasm waned, however, when she read these last lines. The prior general was keeping St. Joseph and all the future reformed monasteries of Castile under the authority of the provincial prior, the mitigated Carmelite Ángel de Salazar, whose irresolute and opportunistic character meant that nothing good would come of it. Doubtless Father Rubeo was not asking himself whether or not these new foundations should be under the authority of the provincial prior, since there was only a single Order of Carmel. He set a veritable time bomb in motion. Teresa found herself with a mission to execute, menaced at its base and without financial means.

As to the reform-minded monks, "my concern grew in that there was no friar in the province that I knew of who could begin this work." Teresa was as demanding concerning men who would belong to the Reformed Carmel as she was with women. She dreamed of real monks enamored of perfection, experienced in contemplation, ablaze with love of Christ, and tested by asceticism. She expected that the future confessors of her daughters would teach them far more by their example than by their words. In addition to an irreproachable life, they had to attain an elevated state of spirituality to be qualified in directing souls.

Spain was not lacking in saints, but they were in hiding since the Council of Trent obligated them to be affiliated to an accepted monastic Order. And the mitigated Carmels did not attract them!

But "...since the Lord had given the one thing, He would give the other. Everything now seemed very possible, and so I set to work."

AUGUST 13, 1567. Everyone was sleeping at the St. Joseph Carmel. Outside, the chaplain, Julian de Ávila, controlling his excitement and his mules, was covering three carts with a canvas sheet. It was three o'clock in the morning. Soon the door opened and some veiled Carmelites emerged— Teresa and her companions. She had slept near the door so as not to awaken her daughters as she descended the time-worn stairway. Only the muffled sound of the small bells worn by the mules could be heard. Before dawn, they had passed the ramparts of Ávila. The beasts were struggling. Seated on the hard wooden benches, the Carmelites of the second foundation were praying fervently. The mission was on its way under the bright starlit sky.

Teresa wanted to establish her second foundation in Medina del Campo, an important city of Old Castile with thirty thousand inhabitants, sixty-two miles northwest of Ávila and famous for its markets. Why this city?

Teresa had valuable support there; Father Baltasar Álvarez, her former confessor, had just been named rector of the Jesuits and had also been elected provincial of the Jesuits of Castile.

In addition, the new prior of the mitigated Carmelites in Medina, Antonio de Heredia, had for many years been the prior at Ávila. Paradoxically, although he was a follower of the mitigated Rule, he was now prepared to support Teresa. This odd and captivating man seemed suddenly to have been touched by grace.

Born in 1517 into a noble Castilian family, his mother had consecrated Antonio to the Virgin when he was ten years old. Refined, loving life yet attracted to the religious experience, he had entered the Carmelite Order at the age of twenty. A handsome man concerned with his appearance, de Heredia wore a habit of fine, soft wool. He had preached at court and at the age of twenty-six had been named prior of the mitigated Carmelites of Ávila.

We do not know why Teresa never mentioned him as she recounted her life. The Carmelites of Ávila were the confessors of the Incarnation, but Teresa had only had Jesuits and Dominicans as spiritual counselors.

After having occupied various important positions, Father Antonio de Heredia, who discreetly agreed with the Council of Trent's reformist tendency, had, in 1567, just been named prior of the mitigated Carmelites of Medina del Campo. Teresa was only too happy to solicit his help. They were almost the same age. He welcomed her with kindness, for there were no women Carmelites of the mitigated Rule in Medina to take offense at this new foundation. Thanks to him and to Father Álvarez, *la Madre* had easily obtained authorization from both the bishop of Medina del Campo and the civil authorities to establish a foundation there.

This foundation was, at the very least, a hurried affair. "I didn't have a house or a penny to buy one with. Furthermore, how could a poor wanderer like myself get credit for a loan...?" The only money Teresa had to start the foundation was a few ducats from "a very virtuous young lady, who, because of lack of room, could not enter St. Joseph's.... She had some money, which was very little and not enough to buy a house but enough to rent one."[8]

With this one and only postulant, the first community at Medina was composed of seven religious, two from St. Joseph in Ávila (María Bautista and Ana de los Ángeles) and four from the Incarnation (Ana and Inés de Tapia, Teresa de Quezada, and Isabel Arias) who had received the unexpected permission of the prior general. Father Julian de Ávila, chaplain at St. Joseph, was to celebrate the first Mass with exposition of the Blessed Sacrament, an act meant to secure the foundation.

None of this happened easily. Ávila condemned this latest folly of *la Madre*, who, in their opinion, was decidedly incapable of standing still: "When our intention became known in the city, there was much criticism. Some were saying I was crazy; others were hoping for an end to that nonsense." Given the lack of material means, the bishop of Ávila was hostile to the idea of another foundation, but he did not prevent Teresa from leaving, "for he loved me much and didn't want to hurt me."

She was placing her trust in God, convinced that he would resolve the material problems: "...come what may, happen what may, whatever work is involved, whatever criticism arises, whether they arrive or whether they die on the road, or even if they don't have courage for the trials that are met,"[9] perseverance was all-important.

THE DIFFICULTIES INCREASED. Antonio de Heredia had, in fact, found in one of the suburbs an old house that could be restored. But a neighboring monastery of Augustinians suddenly opposed this new foundation, fearing it might reduce the alms that sustained them. While awaiting an uncertain arrangement, Father de Heredia proposed that Teresa settle in the city, as discreetly as possible, in rented lodging. Once the Blessed Sacrament was established there and the first Mass had been celebrated, the Discalced Carmelites could not be uprooted! To believe this, one must read the account of the chaplain, Julian de Ávila:

> We arrived at midnight. We had to leave the carts at the entrance to the city, for they made such a racket in the night that they would have awakened the population. There we were, in the streets, carrying vases and ornaments to outfit the chapel and say the first Mass. We looked like vagabonds who had burglarized a church.

Medina del Campo was preparing a great feast for August 15. A few drunken night owls were already lurking in the city. They took the religious to task, shouting obscenities at them. "We dismounted at the monastery of St. Anne's so as not to make noise and proceeded to the house on foot."

They awakened the guardian of the house. The religious had barely gotten inside for shelter when six bulls hurtled down the street, charging toward the arena for the August 15 bullfight. By dawn, the chapel was ready. The bell was rung to announce the Mass. The good people of the neighborhood, astonished to see that a convent had sprouted up during the night, invaded the improvised chapel. From what enclosure would the nuns worship? A stairway remained standing and they hid behind it, and "through some cracks in the door that was in front of us, we attended the Mass, for there was no place else for us to do so."

Once Mass had been celebrated and the bishop's provisor duly verified it with all the necessary authorizations, the convent was officially founded according to regulations. Day was breaking. The nuns realized only then how dilapidated the building was. While they awaited the completion of the reconstruction, a decent merchant offered the community lodging in his home. He gave them the entire upper floor of his house, which contained a "large gilded room" for services.

Two months later, the monastery was well equipped: alms and vocations arrived, "and the favors he gave them were so great that I was amazed," wrote Teresa. Among the new members were young aristocrats weighed down with dowries, but there were also young, fortuneless women whom Teresa was happy to receive for their personal qualities and "for love of God alone." She taught them the way of perfection, beginning with sacrifice and asceticism as well as mental prayer, which can lead to union with Christ all the way to the folly of love.

Teresa had grouped around her a handful of young women in love with Christ and burning with desire to know him. In a letter written in 1578, she denies having carried out a change. "It is said that this is a new Order and invented. Let them read our primitive Rule. We are only observing it without mitigations just as the pope gave it to us in its primitive rigor."

Teresa's personal contribution should, however, be highlighted; she gave importance to mental prayer to enliven the contemplative ideal of the founders, and she stressed the primacy of the observance of the Rule in its essence and not only its letter. To fast is useful, to love God is everything. And to engage women on the path of mental prayer constituted a revolution!

Teresa never ceased asserting that her little monasteries, contrary to common assumption, were not refuges against the temptations of the world. On the contrary, in them one had to face real battles, notably against oneself, to conquer one's natural egotism. And it was more difficult to live in a community of thirteen than in a larger one. In a small community, a person could not hide. That is why Teresa was attached to her smaller communities; they facilitated transparency, sisterly life, and silence. "They must all be friends, love and help one another," she used to say. This explains her haste in founding a convent at Medina del Campo. As the number of postulants was growing at St. Joseph, it was time to move some of the sisters so as to utilize this human and divine wealth of vocations as well as to remain poor when gifts were given to the community. In her *Way of Perfection*, she wrote that "prayer and comfortable living do not go together." She constantly referred to the first poor hermits at Mount Carmel, who did not concern themselves with the needs of the next day. The small, fervent group of Discalced was bound to succeed or to disappear, but not to vegetate!

Sixteenth-century Spain was rife with violence and war, and the influx of American gold was making it lose its soul. Teresa wanted to extend the Church's missionary work by supporting it with prayer and sacrifice; this desire propelled her to found more Carmels.

However, she was colliding with the Rule of the feminine branch, a contemplative Order hostile to action, which the Carmelite monks reserved for themselves, thereby forcing the women religious to remain in the background. Teresa knew that her travels were the object of harsh criticism.

That is why, at the bottom of the very large pocket of her habit, *la Madre fundadora* fingered Father General's letter authorizing her to found two convents of Discalced Carmelites for men. She was certain that her Reform would not succeed without a reservoir of confessors, visitators, and spiritual masters from their ranks. But where were they to be found?

On the other hand, this dual enterprise—foundations for men as well as women—risked culminating, sooner or later, in a heartrending separation between the mitigated and the Discalced, rupturing Carmel's unity in a way that very few were prepared to face.

CHAPTER 19

John of the Cross

(1567–1568)

One day when Teresa declared to Father Antonio de Heredia, the new prior of the mitigated Carmelites in Medina del Campo, that she also wished to found a monastery of Discalced Friars, he enthusiastically exclaimed: "Then I shall be the first one!"

Obviously, he too had fallen under the spell of the charm, strength of character, and spiritual radiance of *la Madre*. He confessed to Terea that he had been dreaming of leaving his monastery to enter the Carthusians—but now hearing of her plans, he wanted by all means to be included in them.

Teresa was hesitant in responding. She did not see in Father Antonio the man she was seeking to found the masculine branch of the Reformed Carmelites.

> For although he was always a good friar, recollected, very studious, and fond of his cell—in fact, he was a learned man—it didn't seem to me he was the one for a beginning like this. Neither would he have the courage or promote the austerity that was necessary, since he was fragile and not given to austerity.[1]

This great lord, already fifty-seven years of age, was used to a certain level of comfort and seemed to be too rooted in the mitigated Rule, unsuited to the asceticism that Teresa saw as the necessary path to perfection. She could not tell him so, however, without wounding him.

"Your health is too frail to endure the rigors of the primitive Rule."

Then, as he began to beg her with touching humility, she added: "Be patient. Your day will come. Between now and then, practice keeping what you will be committing yourself to."

He promised her that he would put the primitive Rule into practice each day. To Teresa's great surprise, he strove to do so in his own monastery, fasting with perseverance and submitting his tall body to excessive penances. He lost weight, and soon his mitigated community of Santa Ana, which had no intention of adopting such radical measures, came to hate him. When he announced to them that he planned to follow Teresa de Jesús, he lost their esteem entirely; then he had every occasion to put true humility into practice. The desire for perfection that Teresa and her daughters embodied prevailed over everything.

For months, Teresa, while pursuing the foundation of her own Carmelites at Medina del Campo, observed Father Antonio. She admired his intrepid faith and spirit of sacrifice, but she could not bring herself to launch him into the adventure of founding a monastery for men. What did he lack? Youth? The strength to break old habits? Perhaps he was not sufficiently inclined to love his fellow man, to embody the paternal tenderness that makes the most rigorous asceticism bearable to a community. She finally decided to accept him in the Reformed Order, but not as the founding prior. Who, then?

One day in October 1567, Teresa received a visit from a venerable Carmelite friar, Reverend Master Pedro de Orozco of the mitigated community in Medina. Father Antonio had sent him. The old man was fascinated by *la Madre's* projects, but declared himself too old to cooperate in them.

"However, I know a young monk of our Order, Juan de San Matías, who is enamored of perfection. He has returned from the University of Salamanca, where he is completing his studies. Like our Father Prior, he too is dreaming of becoming a Carthusian. You should meet him."

Teresa grew excited. Decidedly, this mitigated convent of Santa Ana had many surprises in store for her. She immediately questioned Antonio de Heredia about this monk.

De Heredia told her, "This young twenty-five-year-old Carmelite friar is burning with love for Christ and dreaming of austerities. He will certainly not stay with us. Like me, he feels called to the cenobitic life of the Carthusians. I have a great deal of esteem for him. He is a pure person, all ablaze!"

"Tell me about him!"

"First, I have to tell you about his father, a remarkable individual."

Gonzalo de Yepes was born of a noble Toledan family, but he was orphaned early in life and left without resources. His rich uncles, who were merchants, brought him up. When he came of age, they put him in charge of the fairs of Medina del Campo. During a stay in Fontiveros while visiting a weaving workshop, he fell in love with a poor working-class orphan girl, Catalina Álvarez, also from Toledo. She was as beautiful as she was virtuous. He married her in spite of the opposition of his uncles. Disowned by his family, he became a weaver by her side to earn his living.

Teresa interrupted him. "And Juan?"

"Born in 1542, he was their third child. Two years later, the father died, leaving the family in a very precarious financial situation."

Catalina and her children then settled in Medina del Campo, where they lived in poverty. Very talented, Juan was fortunately admitted as an orphan to the School of Doctrine for Children. Then, after a trying internship as a nurse at the hospital for victims of the plague, he entered the Carmelite monastery at the age of twenty-one.

"We sent this excellent Latinist to the University of Salamanca, where he stayed for three years, leading an austere existence of mortification. His professors have nothing but the greatest praise for him. I have also noticed his many good qualities here at Santa Ana, but I do not approve of his excessive penances. He has just been ordained as a priest and will be returning to Salamanca for a final year of theology."

Teresa's eyes had begun to shine. She already sensed that Juan was being sent to her to be a key component of her Reform. But could she ask him to renounce the desert and the blessed quiet in God in order to serve him in another way, as she herself was doing, knowing the weight of the sacrifice involved?

The following day, the person who would enter history under the name of St. John of the Cross presented himself at the parlor to meet Teresa.

Upon seeing him, Teresa gave a start. Very thin, with an emaciated face and a shaven head, he was under five feet tall. But his black eyes radiated passion, intelligence, and humility. "He projected an impression of mute suffering and superhuman strength."[2] Despite his youth, he expressed himself with the ease of a master, in total simplicity. Teresa confessed that she was enthralled.

"It's being said that you are castigating the relaxation of the Carmelite Order and that you want to leave it."

"Yes, *Madre.* I feel that I am called to the Carthusian monastery of Santa María de Paular in the deserted valley of Lozoya, where a person can lead the most rigorous cenobitic life."

"Is it at the Dominican University of Salamanca that you acquired a liking for such a life?"

He smiled. "There, I studied canon law, philosophy, grammar, astrology, rhetoric, a little medicine, Latin, Hebrew, and Chaldean. I also met there the greatest theologians of Spain, disciples of Domingo de Soto, who was the emperor's confessor. I mostly followed Luis de León."

"And what did he teach you?"

"This very holy Augustinian monk takes issue with the scholastic thinking of Dominican Thomists. He favors the mystical theology to which one accedes through the mental prayer of contemplation. Without falling into illuminism, he highlights the close links that exist between asceticism and mysticism. He is one of the first great theologians who dares to proclaim that the mysticism of contemplation is a work of love and not of knowledge. He risks being burned for that!"

Teresa remained thoughtful for a moment, then she cried out: "Love wants works!"

"What do you mean, *Madre?*"

"My brother, come to us!"

Friar Juan knew the reputation of *la Madre fundadora* and the requirement of perfection in her convents of strict observance. He was unaware, however, that the prior general of the Carmelites had authorized her to found two monasteries of men. That seemed unthinkable! Teresa understood his astonishment.

"You have decided to enter the Carthusians? Wait a bit."

"Why wait when the Lord is calling me?"

"It would be an increase of perfection for you to be able to serve him without leaving your habit as a son of Our Lady of Carmel. The Lord will soon be giving me a house to found a monastery of Carmelite Friars of the strict observance that will have no cause to be jealous of the cenobitic life of the Carthusians."

The young monk did not take his eyes off her. "When, *Madre,* when?"

"When the Lord wants it. Soon. In the meantime, go to Salamanca to complete your studies, for we will need learned men."

"I will go and await your foundation on the condition that it will not be too long in coming."

Returning to her daughters, Teresa joyously—but with a touch of mischievousness—exclaimed: "With Father Antonio and Friar Juan, I have a monk and a half to set up my reform!"[3]

HAVING COMPLETED HIS STUDIES, Juan returned to Medina in the summer of 1568. During the months that followed, he became a familiar visitor at

Teresa's convent parlor. She could not praise him enough, writing to Don Francisco de Salcedo:

> Although he is small, I know that he is great in the eyes of God. Certainly we will miss him very much here, for he is wise, and just right for our way of life. I believe our Lord has called him for this task. There's not a friar who does not speak well of him, for he has been living a life of great penance, even though he is young. It seems the Lord is watching over him carefully, for...we never saw an imperfection in him. He's courageous....[4]

She was not the only one to marvel at his qualities. "In this city of Medina del Campo, a marketplace where everything can be found, la Madre also found the cornerstone of her Discalced monasteries," wrote her chaplain, Julian of Ávila.

What remained was to start the foundation.

Teresa had received two offers of donations. One was from her Toledan protectress, Doña Luisa de la Cerda, who wanted the new foundation to be located on her lands in Malagon in New Castile. The other came from a young lord, Bernardino de Mendoza, a brother of the bishop of Ávila. He was offering property in Rio de Olmos, near Valladolid in Old Castile. In both cases, it was a question of Carmelite convents. What was she to do?

Teresa was also troubled by a call of distress from María de Jesús Yepes, whom she had met in 1562 at the palace of Doña Luisa de la Cerda. This woman devoted to poverty had succeeded in founding a Carmel of strict observance at Alcalá de Henares thanks to the donation of Leonor de Mascarenhas, the former governess of Philip, the prince royal. She begged Teresa to visit the convent, which was in a state of collapse.

Torn by all these pleas, Teresa headed for Alcalá without hesitation. But en route she ran into Bernardino de Mendoza himself. Anguished over a gloomy foreboding, this young lord, who led an agitated life, feared for his eternal salvation and dreaded hell. Using the donation of Rio de Olmos as a pretext, he lured Teresa to Madrid (where he lived as a courtier to the royal court), supposedly to settle the question of the land's transfer.

Poor Teresa! The arrival of the "saint of Ávila" at the residence of Doña Leonor de Mascarenhas caused somewhat of a sensation. She was in great demand, and the fine ladies of court could already picture entertaining themselves with her ecstasies and levitations as though they were at the theater! She disappointed them by speaking only of ordinary things.

To escape this importunate eagerness, she took refuge with the Franciscan Sisters of Madrid, a fervent convent founded by Princess Juana, King Philip's sister. Their prioress, Juana de la Crúz, was none other than the sister of Francis Borgia. Teresa stayed there for two weeks, edifying them all with her humility. After she left them, Juana de la Crúz exclaimed:

> God be thanked for having made it possible for us to know such a saint. Each one of us can imitate her. She eats, she sleeps, she speaks, she acts like everyone else; and yet she is a saint. Her spirit is truly that of the Savior: humble, simple, sincere. She lives among us as he himself lived among men, without frightening anyone and consoling all hearts.[5]

Teresa was in a hurry to leave this noisy and opulent capital to find once again the simplicity of the Castilian countryside. But she was haunted by the image of María de Yepes. What had happened at Alcalá? She saw María as her double; they shared the same austerity, the same ardor to restore the primitive Rule of the Carmel that María had found in Mantua. She had been the first to obtain the pontifical brief to authorize her to start a foundation in Spain.

Doña Leonor de Mascarenhas took Teresa to Alcalá. Unrecognizable, María de Jesús Yepes welcomed Teresa at the door of the convent, handing her the keys as a sign of humility. Then she brought her to her cell. In the corridors, where dead silence reigned, Teresa passed somber shadows. On their faces, Teresa detected only distress and anguish.

"María, what has happened here?"

"God only knows, Teresa! Yet for five years now, we have never stopped leading an austere life, alternating the strictest form of fasting with the most severe penances."

"But, you have understood nothing about the Carmelite spirit! This spirit is love! It is not suffering sought after for suffering's sake, it is joy!"

Teresa drew herself up to her full height. Her face was radiant. She felt deeply moved, carried along by the ineffable attraction of her God. Love! Love alone mattered. Her eye finally caught that of the pathetic, poor woman before her, and the strength of Teresa's God passed into María. Color returned to her face. Deep in her lackluster eyes a flame had been lit. She burst into tears. She had understood. Penances and the strictest observance serve for nothing if they are not infused with the sisterly charity that unites the members of the community like members of the same family.

Despite her eagerness to start foundations elsewhere and her fear that little Friar Juan would slip away from her, Teresa remained at Alcalá for seventy days. During that time, she patiently settled the life of the community, initiating the nuns in the mental prayer of love on the way to the perfection that leads to the seven dwellings.

Having resuscitated the life of the community, she left in April 1568, finally taking the road to Toledo, where Doña Luisa de la Cerda impatiently awaited her in order to found a convent of Discalced Carmelites on her lands. Doña Luisa was stubborn and tormented by a secret guilt. Her deceased husband, Marshal Arias Pardo, had bought these distant lands from Emperor Charles V, who had taken them from the Church. It was thus an ill-gotten gain, and Doña Luisa, fearing for the salvation of her husband's soul, wanted to make amends.

At first sight, Teresa judged the town too poor to ensure daily alms for the nuns. Generally speaking, she preferred to establish her convents in cities. So she had to accept the pension Doña Luisa offered her in order to resolve this dilemma.[6]

On April 11, 1568, Teresa settled four nuns from the Incarnation and two from St. Joseph of Ávila in the newly founded Carmel of St. Joseph in Malagon. A month later, she went north again toward Valladolid, the former prestigious capital of the Catholic kings where Philip II was born and his court had been established in former times. On August 15, Teresa founded at Rio de Olmos—situated less than two miles from Valladolid—her fourth monastery, Our Lady of the Conception, thanks to the donation of the young brother of the bishop of Ávila, Don Bernardino de Mendoza, who had just passed away. The faithful chaplain, Julian de Ávila, celebrated the first Mass. During it *la Madre* fell into an ecstasy and had a vision of Don Bernardino, who through her prayers had been released from purgatory, where he had been awaiting his deliverance.

The location of the foundation had been badly chosen because the area was rife with malaria. In 1569, Don Bernardino's sister, María de Mendoza, would offer the small community a more secure house in the city of Valladolid.

THE FOUNDRESS INVITED the young John of the Cross to Rio de Olmos so he could be initiated into the practices of the Reformed Carmel. She was already calling him her *Senequito* (little Seneca) and was unremitting in her praise: "He was so good that I had much more to learn from him than he could learn from me."

Despite her numerous foundations for women, Teresa remained preoccupied with this convent of Discalced Carmelites pledged to Friar Juan and to Prior Antonio de Heredia, who continued to hold fast to his promises of austerity.

The Lord had indeed exercised Father Fray Antonio de Jesús in trials during the year since I had spoken with him; and he suffered them with much
perfection. As for Father Fray John of the Cross, no trial was necessary.
Even though he had lived among the calced friars, those of the cloth, he
always lived a life of great perfection and religious observance. Since the
Lord had given me the chief requirement for a beginning, which was friars,
He was pleased to arrange the rest.[7]

On her way to Valladolid, Teresa had stopped in the very tiny village of
Duruelo, located twenty-four miles north of Ávila and containing twenty
homesteads. There, Don Rafaelo Mejia Velásquez, a nobleman from Ávila,
had offered her a small, modest, secluded farm that served as a lodging for
the steward of his farm lands and also housed the reapers during the summer harvest.

On the back of a mule under a blazing sun, Teresa, accompanied by
Julian de Ávila and Sister Antonia del Espíritu Santo, looked for the hamlet. They finally found it at nightfall at the very end of a hidden valley planted with holm oaks. The place was peaceful and silent, watered by a small
river. One could not hope to find a poorer village and a more modest
dwelling anywhere. The problem of alms was not a concern for the men
since, as priests, they could minister in the villages. Visiting the place, Teresa
exclaimed: "A vast entrance hall, a large room, an attic with a sloping ceiling, and a small kitchen; this would be an ideal place for a Discalced
Carmel! The vestibule will become the chapel, the monks' choir will be
under the stairs, the room will become a dormitory, and the kitchen a refectory."

For her nothing seemed too austere for her little Seneca. Dismayed by
the condition of the house, Sister Antonia said: "Oh no, Madre! Not here.
No one in the world could withstand such conditions! This casita looks like
a stable!"

Julian de Ávila felt the same way. Teresa was delighted, for it reminded
her of the manger in Bethlehem. Night had fallen.

"Let's go to sleep," she said, exhausted by the long mule ride.

Since the farm building was occupied by the harvesters, who were joyously celebrating the month of August, they took refuge in the small village
church. A few days later, Teresa returned to the convent of Medina del
Campo and met her two monks. Father Master Antonio and Fray Juan had
rushed to see her.

"I have your house! It is a poor farm in an isolated village, Duruelo,
between Medina and Ávila."

"God be praised!" exclaimed the priest.

"Finally!" added Fray Juan.

"Do not rejoice until you have visited it. If you are courageous enough to settle in there, God will surely come to your aid. The important thing is to begin. Are you ready?"

"Yes. We would willingly shut ourselves in a stable and even in a pigsty for the love of God!"

Teresa was overcome with joy at their enthusiasm. Recalling this poor dilapidated house, the birthplace of the masculine branch of the Reformed Carmel, she wrote in her *Foundations*:

> What little these buildings and exterior comforts do interiorly...never fail to be very moderate in this matter of large and magnificent houses.... Truly I have seen that there is more spirituality and even inner happiness when suitable accommodations for the body are seemingly lacking than afterward when the house is large and the accommodations good. What benefit is it to us that the house be large since it is only one small room that each one habitually uses? That it be well designed—what help is that to us? Indeed, if it isn't well designed, we won't then have to go around looking at the walls. By considering that the house will not be ours forever, but ours only for as short a time as this life lasts, even though that may be long, everything will be easy for us.... For it is all a matter of but a little effort, and that becomes delightful....[8]

By founding so discreetly, Teresa hoped not to arouse the ire of the new provincial of the mitigated Carmelites, Alonso González, on whom they had to depend. Prior General Rubeo de Ravenna had authorized Teresa to found two monasteries of men in Castile, but the foundations would obviously be subject to the agreement of Castile's provincial prior and, added Teresa, to that of his predecessor. She did not worry too much over this. "I pointed out that in that little place and house the foundation would not attract attention."[9] All the same, she feared the opposition of the outgoing provincial, Ángel de Salazar. Fortunately, the new provincial "was elderly, good-natured, and without malice.... The latter provincial had need of assistance from Doña María de Mendoza. This fact, I believe, helped a great deal."[10]

On September 30, 1568, Fray Juan, accompanied by a young mason, set out on foot for Duruelo, some twenty-seven miles away. He had just received from *la Madre* the habit of the Discalced that she had sewn for him with her own hands in the rough wool fabric offered by a novice at Medina. He carried with him straw sandals, liturgical objects, and paper images that she had given him to decorate the chapel. *La Madre* had also forced him to accept a handful of ducats, the dowry of a postulant, but she was quite sure that he would give them away as alms en route.

Juan de Yepes, who was taking the name John of the Cross, pledged to renounce the mitigated Rule. He was going even further, walking in his bare feet, spurning even the *alpargatas*, the sandals made of straw that Teresa had adopted for the sisters. He discovered with delight the lowly farm in the poor village. There, following *la Madre's* instructions, the two men undertook its transformation into a mini-monastery. The entry was converted into a chapel, above which the attic became the monks' choir. The large room, which had served as a dormitory for the harvesters, was divided to create small cells so narrow that they could only be used for sleeping on the straw mattresses put together by Juan. A stone or log served as a pillow. On the walls, he hung bare wooden crosses.

When night fell, the exhausted mason went to beg a small loaf of bread, which they shared as they drank the clear water from the nearby brook, giving thanks to God.

Father Antonio de Heredia joined them on November 27, taking the name of Antonio de Jesús. According to the order of the provincial, he became the first Discalced Carmelite prior. He governed three monks: John of the Cross (subprior and master of novices), José de Cristo, and Luis de Celis. About Father Antonio, Teresa recounts:

> It was only with clocks that he was well provided, for he had five of them; this greatly amused me. He told me they were meant as a help to follow the daily schedule, which he wanted well fixed; I don't think he even had any bed yet to sleep in.... He went to his little house with the greatest happiness in the world.[11]

Concealing his astonishment, and with a certain degree of reproach, the provincial prior, Alonso González, nonetheless celebrated their first Mass on November 28. Indefatigable, although always ill, Teresa had already set out for Toledo to establish a new foundation.

Three months later, *la Madre* returned unannounced to Duruelo to visit "her little stable of Bethlehem." A light dusting of snow covered the austere landscape. The first person she saw was Father Antonio. "With that joyful expression on his face," the former prior of the shoe-wearing Carmelites "was sweeping the doorway to the church," barefoot in the snow like the most humble of novices. She cried out to him: "What's this, *mi Padre*; what has become of your honor?"

"Ah, *Madre!* I curse the day I attached great importance to it."

Teresa was moved when she saw her "little Seneca" once again. John of the Cross had become even thinner, and he seemed to be lost in the celestial dwellings. Teresa visited the new monastery.

The choir was in the loft. In the middle of the loft the ceiling was high enough to allow for the recitation of the Hours, but one had to stoop low in order to enter and to hear Mass. There were, in the two corners facing the church, two little hermitages, where one could do no more than either lie down or sit. Both were filled with hay because the place was very cold, and the roof almost touched one's head. Each had a little window facing the altar.

At night, instead of sleeping, they "remained there in prayer, for their prayer was so deep that when it came time to say Prime their habits were covered with snow without their having become aware of the fact."[12]

Teresa was struck by the transformation of John of the Cross. For the first time in his life, he was experiencing solitude and extreme poverty, committing himself with delight to the road toward perfection that Teresa had taught him at Rio de Olmos.

The monks divided their time between prayer and the apostolate, for this poor and isolated area lacked priests. "For their preaching...they journeyed barefoot a league and a half, or two, [four and a half to six miles] for at that time they did not yet wear sandals (afterward they were ordered to wear them), and in much snow and cold." Seeing them so fervent in their return to the origins of Carmel, Teresa "experienced the greatest interior joy." Then, seeing the old prior shivering in his homespun wool habit, she pleaded with him: "Do not be so rigorous in your penitential practices, *Padre*. Do you at least eat your fill?"

"Yes, for the people in the neighboring towns provide us with more than we need. This has become a pilgrimage site."

Taking leave of them, Teresa repeated: "Moderation is necessary in the direction of souls."

The deplorable example of María de Yepes continued to haunt her.

I feared lest the devil would attempt to put an end to this beginning [and ruin their health through these austerities] before what I hoped for could be accomplished. As one who is imperfect and of little faith, I did not observe that this was God's work and that His Majesty would carry it forward. Since they engaged in practices in which I did not, they paid little attention to my words about giving them up. And thus I went away greatly consoled, although I did not give God the praise so great a favor deserved.

"Love wants perfection," Fray Juan had told her. And without the most complete deprivation, no union with the Absolute is possible.

Teresa would later write that Fray Juan was one of the purest souls on God's earth, richly bestowed with heavenly wisdom.

Then she smiled, remembering her recommendations and warning for greater moderation with regard to their brutal penances. He took no notice. In a letter, she reported his arguments: "It seems the Lord is watching over him carefully, for although in trying to get everything settled we met with a number of troubles—and I myself must have caused trouble at times by becoming annoyed with him—we never saw an imperfection in him."[13]

Fray Juan's contact with *la Madre* first at Rio de Olmos and then at Duruelo had nonetheless softened this austere ascetic. She now felt an immense tenderness for him. She would later call him "my son, my brother, my father." They had a one and only love in common, Christ, and henceforth they found themselves united in the great project of the Reform. Teresa had its pillars at long last.

The Reform did not take place without difficulty, nor without gnashing of teeth! The mitigated Carmelites felt themselves targeted by *la Madre's* foundations and her attempts to bring the Order back to its primitive ideal of perfection. But the grumblings were becoming harsher. After the women, the men of the Order! What was she doing meddling in their affairs? And they mocked this half-monk, John of the Cross, who had been formed by a woman and had received from her the new monastic habit of common, rough serge. "It was something new, assuredly, to see a priest, a religious, being trained for monastic life by a woman; it was something even newer and more bewildering to see this woman undertake, with the help of her disciple, the reform of an Order of men," wrote the anonymous Carmelite of Caen in her *History of St. Teresa.* And she justified this anomaly by pointing out "the supernatural character of her mission and the very virile strength of soul of the holy mother."

Opposition to *la Madre* was hardening. It was one thing to write a treatise on mental prayer, but quite another to call to task a multitude of good monks steeped in a cozy life with their annuities. That was intolerable!

Today, no historian questions the fact that while John of the Cross is "the first-born of the Carmelite Friars, the master and the model of this great family, St. Teresa laid the groundwork for the early beginnings of its spirit, entrusted to her by Heaven. Heaven is the source of everything at the Reformed Carmel."[14]

Fray Antonio and Fray Juan would make it possible for the Carmelites to consolidate and extend Teresa's reforms, something her being a woman would have prevented. Contrary to the humble nun enclosed behind her grille, the monk was permitted to "come out of his solitude in order to make the world hear the word, made more arresting by the examples of his life."[15]

Henceforth, supported by this small nucleus of Discalced Carmelites, "her status as a woman" no longer restricted Teresa. Deaf to the rising threats, she started out over and over again on the rocky roads and routes of Castile in order to establish new foundations.

CHAPTER 20

Mother Foundress

(1569–1571)

*T*eresa's foundations followed one upon another at an accelerated pace: 1569, Toledo and Pastrana; 1570, Salamanca; 1571, Alba de Tormes. And just as the exhausted Teresa longed to retreat to her small cell in Ávila, she heard Christ speak to her again: "He told me that now was not the time for rest, but that I should hurry to establish these houses; that He found His rest with the souls living in them.... Do you think, daughter, that merit lies in enjoyment? No, rather it lies in working and suffering and loving."[1] And so, despite her age and the ills from which she suffered, she set out once again.

Teresa was accompanied by nuns volunteering to go as foundresses and by a priest, usually Julian de Ávila. A few devoted and muscular servants assisted them in leading the mounts, repairing the carts, extricating them from mud, and defending them against highway bandits. After receiving the Eucharist, the nuns would take their places in two or three carts, which were completely covered, thus becoming small oratories. A tiny bell and an hourglass determined the monastic hours and spiritual exercises. They lacked nothing, neither an image of Christ nor holy water. As at the convent, times of common and silent personal prayer were interspersed with recreation periods, full of gaiety.

But this fine arrangement was often turned on its head in the chaos of rutted, sometimes muddy roads that shook the carts, each drawn by two mules, causing the axels to creak. Summers in Spain are torrid, winters glacial. In her *Foundations*, Teresa evoked "the great hardships endured in the traveling: the cold, the heat, the snow (once it didn't stop snowing the whole day); sometimes getting lost, and at other times being very sick and having a fever."[2]

The men on mules plodded ahead of or behind the covered carts. Sometimes a violent storm delayed their travel. The carts would get stuck in the mud. In one place, they remained in the middle of a ford in a river swollen by floods; in another, they were stranded because of broken axels, the canvas coverings torn away by a gust of wind—they had no other recourse but to implore heaven.

When all went well and the caravan moved along at the slow pace of the mules under the Castilian sun, Teresa filled the silence by giving short instructions. But we can imagine that more than one of the travelers, in spite of their faith, suffered from the anxiety of an uncertain future. Where would they spend the night? In what disreputable inn (for they were poor) if they did not find shelter in some monastery or parish church?

One can imagine the people's surprise on seeing these entirely veiled women disembarking from their carts. Their habit (similar to clothes worn by the poor) was not always respected. In sordid inns, jeers spewed forth from the mouths of intoxicated men. The tip of a naked foot, an ardent look under the veil, stirred up wicked desires. Teresa asked for rooms set apart. The most robust of the nuns stood guard in the hallway. If only one room was available, it was divided with blankets so that each nun could have a little "cell" to pursue mental prayer. Sometimes their lodging had neither light, nor fire, nor nourishment worthy of the name. The travelers, chilled to the bone, could neither dry their clothes nor warm themselves. But *la Madre* was there to raise their morale: "Take courage! Here are rich ordeals to earn heaven for us!"

Before daybreak, Teresa, the first one up, gave the signal for departure. The trips could last up to ten days. Finally, they would reach their destination, but other trials awaited them there. At the beginning of the foundations, the reception they received was rather hostile. Teresa had to use cunning, make the most of the collusion of nighttime, and resist the more or less open opposition that came from the local bishop (jealous of his prerogatives) and some religious communities (where this irruption of sanctity upset their habits).

Thus Teresa often had to proceed by using the element of surprise: Mass was said and the Blessed Sacrament was exposed—like the flag that is hoisted by an explorer over a newly discovered island—so that what was essential for establishing a foundation had taken place. Afterward, she would stoically suffer the anger of the prelate faced with "the boldness of a little woman." It was

up to Teresa to thwart the quibbling and other procedures, to ignore the
stunts of the bailiffs sent by the vicar general and other Church administra-
tors, and to resist the threats to remove the Blessed Sacrament as well as the
sacrilegious interruptions that occurred in the very midst of religious offices.

However much Teresa brandished the licenses for her actions—the
pontifical brief and the accord of the Carmelite prior general—every city and
every bishop held to their privileges. One could not found a convent just
anywhere, especially not in places where alms were fought over and work was
uncertain, and especially not a convent for women, who were expected to
bear children rather than say prayers.

Teresa drew her energy and unfailing optimism from her faith and
Christ's revelations. The opposition of men was of little consequence to her
since she had Christ the King on her side! However, she sometimes collapsed physically; she suffered from fevers, sore throats, vomiting, cardiac
disorders, asthma. A local doctor would be called in and his remedy, blood
letting, was worse than the malady! Then she was miraculously on her feet
again, giving the signal for departure before dawn.

No difficulty could dry up the deep spring that vivified her being,
despite so many obstacles from the crowds, the indifferent, the merchants,
the hierarchy, and those who conspired to ruin her. She had the certainty of
belonging to God and of achieving her plan! "Never has the tête-à-tête with
the Eternal One been more impassioned than on the grey rocky plateaus of
Castile where only broom bushes grow sparsely, or on those desolate roads
of Estremadura where the villages seem to be deserted."[3]

As Teresa's reputation grew, her reception turned from hostile to toler-
ant, then became warm and even enthusiastic. Clandestine consecrations
were now a thing of the past! Once they had recognized *la santa Madre*, people crowded around the nuns' carts and clusters of joyous children surrounded them. The poorer the area, the more fervent the people, for the
hope of the poor is in God alone. Nurslings were brought to her to be
blessed, sick people to be healed, and even flocks of animals! This handful
of poor little women wearing the garb of the Reformed Carmel aroused an
insane hope in the treasures of eternity promised to persons of good will,
offering a source of blessings for all. And the people of the two Castiles,
soon Andalusia and León, threw themselves upon this treasure since they
could not finger the famous American gold that everyone spoke about but
whose color few had seen.

When the nuns could not travel by cart because of snow-covered passes
in the mountainous regions or deep rivers, they traveled on the backs of

mules. These pathetic and unusual silhouettes in their long brown habits, their white capes flowing in the wind, their faces veiled in black, their bodies shaken by the jolts of an uncomfortable saddle, were sustained by *la Madre*, who trembled with fever but remained undaunted in her desire to obey the Beloved.

Sometimes Teresa traveled in a *tartana*, a small covered cart drawn by a mule and driven by the *arriero*, the muleteer. Starting in 1570, this was the type of transport she preferred, accompanied by a single assistant inured to that particular hardship. Her growing reputation meant that she could not always avoid the honor guard of *caballeros* who fervently surrounded her, knight-escorts of the wandering Lady of God; *hidalgos* on horseback attired in richly colored brocades; grave clerics in black, more modestly mounted on mules; hooded monks following on foot; anonymous beggars mixing in with the crowd and avidly seeking to receive, for lack of small coins, at least some blessings from *la santa Madre*. She lent herself to this graciously. Cheers or insults, it was all the same to her as long as God's will was being done.

Teresa would tread the soil of Spain from Burgos to Seville to found seventeen monasteries (not counting those for men) over a span of twenty years, thwarting in the process a thousand intrigues that would have shortened her life. She would fall, then get up again, brandishing her patent letters, murmuring her prayers, marveling at this God who gives "courage to an ant," convinced that in the end it was the "thousand fears" of human prudence that prevent the accomplishment of God's marvels.[4]

When she had hardly arrived and settled in either at the residence of a princess or in a rented hovel, she would reveal the plan for the new Carmel: two superimposed quadrangular cloisters with well-ventilated upper galleries, the cloister below retaining coolness during the summer and offering protection against storms in the winter. Next to the monastery would be the wash-house, the place to filter water, and a large garden to supply vegetables, fruit, and medicinal herbs. If the property was large enough, a few small hermitages for mental prayer, the dialogue of love, would be built in some out-of-the-way spots.

When *la Madre* inspected her construction sites, she often had to face the anger of neighbors whose peace and quiet was being disturbed, and sometimes that of the poorly paid workers—masons and carpenters. Only too happy to be perceived for what she thought herself to be—a weak woman, less than nothing—she allowed herself to be insulted by them, taking delight in humiliation. Then, with a well-chosen word accompanied by a smile and a promise, she would calm them down. Who could resist her?

And writing, she was always writing! Hers was a minister's correspondence—up to a thousand letters a year. She wrote at each stage of her journeys while her daughters slept; a courier would carry her letters to their destination the next day. And the books! After *The Life* and *The Way of Perfection* came *The Foundations*, an account full of humor and indefectible faith.

Serene and smiling, Teresa mastered the most difficult situations: visiting convents, uplifting people's shaken morale, finding necessary funds. Her genius burst forth; she was both a spiritual master and an organizer, a businesswoman capable of remonstrating with lawyers and merchants who could in the next breath use her charm, gentleness, and holy "wiles" to beguile a bishop or a humble postulant. Without that strength that she derived from her God and the love of her Spouse, would she have brought so many foundations to a successful conclusion?

Between two voyages, she would return to her little paradise, the St. Joseph Carmel, which she had entrusted to her niece, María Dávila (María de San Jerónimo), as prioress. But there was no rest for *la Madre fundadora!* Always veiled, she received her visitors in the parlor, where she went from heaven to earth—and sometimes to purgatory—comforting, counseling, and speaking of God. She could also be found appeasing quarrels; haggling over a contract, rental, loan, or purchase; discussing a new foundation and trying to thwart snares; or attempting to detect the unacknowledged intentions sometimes concealed in a donor's gift.

Her one desire was to give herself over completely to the love of God, embodied in the silence and solitude of the cloister. Yet in the parlor she had to come to grips with the hatred, admitted or hidden, of those whom the Reform condemned or upset. The visitors she dreaded most were "those clerics dressed in black, cunning and secretive, organizing an interrogatory, for the Inquisition was on the watch everywhere."[5] Her adversaries suspected her of being an ambitious schemer, a fake mystic, or—worse still—an *illuminada*, and a wandering one besides! She would even be accused of heresy, she who proclaimed herself "a daughter of the Church" and who did nothing without first referring it to her confessor. Like a ship among the reefs, Teresa de Jesús navigated her way, driven by the wind of the Holy Spirit.

Toledo Foundation: 1569

On March 24, 1569, Teresa arrived in Toledo with two young nuns from Ávila: Isabel de San Pablo and Isabel de Santo Domingo. This time it was not her dear benefactress, Doña Luisa de la Cerda, who drew her there, but the Jesuit Father Pablo Hernández. This holy man had persuaded a rich unmarried merchant, on his deathbed, to endow a Reformed Carmel. Toledo, capital of New Castile, had twenty-seven parishes, vibrant with many processions, religious services, and feast days. There were twenty-four monasteries of women and twelve of men, along with 147 religious confraternities. Did they really need Teresa? Oh, yes indeed! Underhanded quarrels and rivalries were dividing the clerics. Aristocrats and merchants were jealous of one another.

For Teresa, the city of Toledo meant more than Madrid, though the royal court had left it in 1560. The former imperial city, cradle of her paternal ancestors, remained the religious capital of Spain, the see of the all-powerful Archbishop Bartolomé Carranza de Miranda, primate of the kingdom, second only to the king. Yet his power had declined since the Inquisition, suspecting him of heresy, had thrown him in jail, alleging that his *Commentary on the Christian Catechism* bore a hint of illuminism.

A wretched population walked Toledo's streets, which wound around the walls of the palaces. The Jews and Arabs who had once lived in the city had been expelled by the intolerance of Philip II. However, all the merchants of Europe traded there, and American gold flowed like water.

As often happened, Teresa had been obliged to proceed secretly. This time, the deceased donor, Martín Ramírez, was not an aristocrat. Persons of distinction, among them Doña Luisa de la Cerda, at whose home Teresa and her daughters were temporarily residing, were scandalized that a merchant commoner and converted Jew could thereby have his name forever inscribed in the archives of a Carmel. Teresa, for her part, "esteemed virtue more than lineage."[6] To complicate matters, Ramírez's brother, executor of his will, was opposed to the promised donation of twelve thousand ducats. Actually, he was quite willing to hand over the money, but only on the condition of being as honored as his brother!

Donations were thus stirring up absurd obstacles. After a life of luxury, sometimes not in accord with Christian morality, a donor, convinced that he had escaped hell thanks to a sincere confession, hoped also to lessen the punishment of purgatory through the perpetual intercession of the contemplatives. At the same time, he had to be careful not to infringe upon the rights of his heirs too much, or they might assert them.

Unable to acquire the house in question immediately, Teresa installed her daughters elsewhere. She rented a place, using up the few gold ducats—as well as one hundred *reales* borrowed from Doña Luisa de la Cerda's steward's wife—intended for converting the house.

On May 14, the first Mass was celebrated. There was a general outcry! The delegate of the imprisoned archbishop declared himself hostile to the enterprise. The City Council, alerted by some jealous religious, expressed their reservations, their chief motivation being the late donor's social status as a commoner. Threatened with excommunication, the three Carmelites stood firm despite their destitution, but the situation was becoming critical. Even Doña Luisa continued to sulk. Teresa refused to solicit her aid, and she persisted obstinately throughout this ordeal when they "...didn't even have so much as a stick of wood to make a fire to cook a sardine." Yet in "this lack we experienced was the cause of a sweet contemplation"! "From then on my desire to be very poor increased. And I felt freedom in having so little esteem for temporal goods, for the lack of these goods brings an increase of interior good. Certainly, such a lack carries in its wake another kind of fullness and tranquility."[7]

Then public opinion swung to the other side, and as the alms of the poor began to pour in, Teresa's two assistants became upset: "It's as though they have stolen our poverty!"

At last, having been satisfied by a compromise in which he would gain a small, appropriate burial vault in the Carmel's chapel, Ramírez's brother released the twelve thousand ducats. Thus Teresa was able to acquire and convert the house for the creation of a real Carmel. The aristocrats of Toledo protested as a matter of form. The Carmelite provincial, whom Teresa had kept informed, remained silent. Postulants were arriving in large numbers. In the midst of a thousand worries, la Madre pursued her loving dialogue with Jesus. In her, action and contemplation remained united.

During Teresa's stay in Toledo, one of her religious was on her deathbed. As she entered the throes of her agony, Teresa left her bedside to go to the chapel and beg the Lord "to give her a good death."

> I went to her room to be with her.... And when I entered I saw His Majesty at the head of the bed. His arms were partly open as though He were protecting her, and He told me that I could be certain He would protect all the nuns that die in these monasteries and that they should not fear temptation at the hour of death.

Indeed, the dying nun passed away demonstrating that "her happiness and joy were so great that, as though she were going to another country, we were able to talk to her about how she should recommend us to God when in heaven and to the saints to whom we were devoted." And then, "after a little while I began to speak to her, and she said to me: 'O Mother, what great things I am going to see.' Thus she died, like an angel."[8]

Pastrana Foundation: 1569

At the end of May, Teresa was completing the consolidation of her Toledo foundation when she received a peremptory message from a grand lady, Doña Ana de Mendoza y la Cerda, princess of Éboli, Duchess of Pastrana. Teresa had first met the young noblewoman in Toledo in 1562 at her aunt Doña Luisa de la Cerda's palace.

This thirty-year-old princess was very beautiful despite being one-eyed (she hid her empty socket under an eyepatch of red silk inlaid with precious stones). However, she displayed a detestable character and bore within her simultaneously all the defects possible: she was proud, egotistical, quarrelsome, domineering, ambitious, and unscrupulous. Her anger and her intrigues were dreaded at the court where her husband, the powerful Prince Ruy Gómez da Silvá, held the posts of minister and counselor to the king and grand master of the palace.

Daughter of the viceroy of Peru, which sustained the royal treasury, the princess of Éboli was half viper, half cat. Pious when it suited her, atrociously superstitious, she had good reasons for fearing hell. The gossips said that she was the king's mistress—and she permitted them to spread such rumors. Now she had decided to edify the kingdom, the court, and heaven by founding *two* monasteries in her duchy of Pastrana, some thirty miles northeast of Madrid. She simply could not bear the idea that two of her relatives, Luisa de la Cerda and María de Mendoza, had founded monasteries on their lands before she had.

Instinctively distrustful because of the princess's psychotic personality, Teresa hesitated. To thwart the princess was tantamount to angering her father the viceroy and her husband the prince. Teresa would thereby run the risk of alienating the king, whom the foundress needed to counter the resistance of the "cats," as she called the mitigated Carmelites who were conspiring against her. Later, Teresa would maintain that she left Toledo for Pastrana only after receiving a precise injunction from Christ.

The princess sent a carriage for her. The adventure was beginning! Passing through Madrid, Teresa won to her cause two Italians who were exceptional men. Having grown sick and tired of the world and its intrigues, they had decided to become hermits. Unusual recruits for the future Carmel! Mariano de Azaro was a Neapolitan engineer who had built canals on the Tagus and the Guadalquivir Rivers and was a friend of King Philip II. The other Carmel postulant was a talented artist, Giovanni Narducci, who had taken the name of Fray Juan de la Miseria. It was he who, later in

Seville, would paint an immortal portrait of Teresa, the only one done during her lifetime and which still exists today.

Neither of the two men was any longer attempting to canalize the great Iberian rivers, but rather their own overflowing love for Christ. Abandoning their idea of a hermit's life, they accepted Teresa's spontaneous offer to become the founding stones of the male convent she wished to establish in Pastrana along with one for nuns. Here again, *la Madre's* personality, radiant faith, and charm were put to good use. Won over, the hermit engineer admitted that he did not understand how he had been able, so quickly, to "give in to the influence of a woman," especially when Prince Ruy Gómez had already fitted out a comfortable hermitage for him in the hills of Pastrana.

Bringing her two hermits and a future Carmelite, Beatriz Brancés, with her, Teresa finally left Madrid for Pastrana. We can imagine her badly lodged with her daughters at the ducal palace that dominated the village, haggling with the princess on the selection of postulants, who were already pouring in, and on the size of the income that Teresa had been obliged to accept, since the village was too poor to ensure regular alms.

The Carmelite convent that the Princess of Éboli had endowed was built in the village. Endowed by her husband the prince, the monastery for men was constructed on the hill facing the princess's convent. The consecrations and inaugurations took place in July 1569 in the presence of the Madrid court, and it included a pageant-like display of gold and silver, bells and relics. Only the king's presence was lacking. The princess was satisfied. She finally had her Carmel—two even!

The gentle Isabel de Ortega (Isabel de Santo Domingo), spiritual daughter of St. Peter of Alcántara, became the prioress of this new Carmel at age twenty-eight. Ah, if only Teresa had followed her original mistrust of the capricious princess of Éboli! But we are getting ahead of ourselves.

Complications would also multiply at the men's monastery in Pastrana. At first, vocations would pour in from the neighboring University of Alcalá. But under the influence of the two Italians, who were too enamored with perfection, this community of men would fall into an excessive asceticism like that of María de Yepes. Teresa would respond by sending them a master, John of the Cross, to rectify the situation. The monastery would thus become one of the pillars of the Reform from which the nuns would draw their spiritual counselors.

These two foundations having become a reality, an exhausted Teresa agreed to go back to Toledo in one of the princess's carriages. A priest, seeing her emerge from it, was scandalized: "So, you travel in a carriage? You, the saint, are deceiving your people!"

Teresa bowed her head before the angry man, acknowledging: "You are the only one who dares to point out my errors."

Salamanca Foundation: 1570

A friend of Teresa's, Father Martín Gutiérrez, rector of the Society of Jesus in the famous university city of Salamanca, had invited her there. Both a contemplative and a reputed professor at the great Catholic university, he dreamed of seeing a monastery of Reformed Carmelite nuns in that city. "Once I had permission from the ordinary," Teresa wrote, "the monastery was as much as founded.... Thus I immediately sought to rent a house."[9]

But the house Teresa chose was already inhabited by some students. One of them, Juan Moriz, who would later become a bishop, told how, upon seeing la Madre, "he was forever struck with admiration." Unfortunately, he was the only one. The other students had to be evicted. They vacated the premises while making a great fuss, but some of them, out of resentment or malice, hid themselves in the attic. By the time Teresa and her assistant, Sister María del Sacramento, arrived with only a bundle of hay for furniture, night had fallen. "My companion and I spent the night of All Saints alone.... The house was very large, was in a mess, and had many garrets."

One may well be a Carmelite but can still be fearful of ghosts, especially at that time of the year! The said companion, hearing suspicious sounds, grew petrified. "We locked ourselves in a room where there was some straw, which was the first thing I provided for the founding of the house, because in having straw we would have a bed. We slept there that night with two borrowed blankets," wrote Teresa. Trembling, her companion was constantly looking about from side to side, still fearful. Teresa said to her, "Why are you looking around? No one can get in here."

"Mother, I was wondering what would happen if I were to die now; what would you do here all alone?"

That thought flustered Teresa. "I began to think a little about it and even become afraid.... And since the tolling of the bells helped matters along, for, as I said, it was the vigil of All Souls, the devil had a good means of making us squander our thoughts on trifles." She pulled herself together at last.

"Sister, when this happens, I'll think about what to do; now, let me sleep."

La Madre claimed that "sleep came soon and took away our fears."[10]

The house was very large, humid, and cold. The small community (six nuns who had come from Ávila) quickly settled in under the direction of Ana de Tapia, and they soon faced further persecution—not by ghosts but by the proprietor. Having changed his mind, he no longer wanted to rent; he wished to sell the building to give dowries to his daughters. True to form as always, *la Madre*, who lacked money and had to insist on the right to rent, was not in the least dismayed.

> Whether or not [we] have a good house matters little. Rather, it gives us great pleasure to find we are in a house that we can be thrown out of, for we remember how the Lord of the world didn't have any. It has happened to us at times in these foundations that we were in a house that we didn't own, and the truth is that I never saw a nun distressed about that. May it please His Majesty that through His infinite goodness and mercy we will not be in want of the eternal dwelling places, amen, amen.[11]

Teresa now found herself physically and emotionally exhausted by her foundations and journeys. Later, in *The Interior Castle* (sixth dwelling), she would return to this time of depression, highlighting the fact that she had spent Easter Sunday in Salamanca in such spiritual aridity and dryness that she forgot the solemnity of this feast day.

At midday recreation, surrounded by her six daughters, she asked a young novice endowed with an angelic voice, Isabel de Jesús, to improvise the kind of spontaneous lament that she liked. The novice's inspired song moved Teresa to the very depths of her desolation, where an intense thirst for God—the desire to rejoin him—burned within her.

> O, that my eyes may see you
> Gentle, good Jesus;
> May my eyes see you
> And then, may I die!
> Let him who wishes see
> Roses and jasmine.
> If I saw you,
> I would see a thousand gardens.

Overcome, Teresa immediately went into ecstasy. She was transported, frozen and inert, to her cell, where she remained in the same state throughout the night, watched over by her worried daughters. When she awakened, "broken in body and soul," she wrote her most famous poem, in which, as if echoing the lament of Isabel de Jesús, she expresses her suffering at living in this vale of tears, separated from God:

I live without living in myself,

...

Since I die of love,

...

Ah, how weary this life!
These exiles so hard!
This jail and these shackles
By which the soul is fettered!

...

Ah, how bitter a life
When the Lord is not enjoyed!
While love is sweet,
Long awaiting is not.

...

I die because I do not die.[12]

In her *Meditations on the Song of Songs,*[13] Teresa also alluded to this fearsome trial:

I know a person who while in this kind of prayer heard someone, with a beautiful voice, singing; and she certifies that, in her opinion, if the singing had not stopped the soul would have gone out of itself on account of the great delight and sweetness the Lord gave it to enjoy. His Majesty provided that the singing stop, for the one who was in this suspension could easily have died. But because she was powerless to stir or make any exterior movement, she couldn't tell the one singing to stop. And she was clearly aware of the danger she was in, but her state resembled that of someone in a deep sleep who is unable to come out of it and speak even though he may want to. In this suspension the soul would not want to come out of this sleep, nor would death be painful to it but great happiness, for this is what it desires.

This text was meant to warn her sisters against the temptation of escaping the world through contemplation. Teresa tells us that God asks us to be present to the world in order to accomplish our task in it, no matter how hard it might be.

She made herself clear on this point in *The Interior Castle*:

Two experiences, it seems to me, which lie on this spiritual path, put a person in danger of death: the one is this pain [the night of the spirit], for it truly is a danger, and no small one; the other is overwhelming joy and delight, which reaches so extraordinary a peak that indeed the soul, I think, swoons to the point that it is hardly kept from leaving the body.[14]

Teresa returned very often to this unaccustomed ecstasy of Salamanca. In the twelfth of her *Spiritual Testimonies*, a work written at the request of her

Dominican confessor, Father Báñez, she wrote, in what is one of the most mysterious and most beautiful of these *Testimonies*:

> At night [Easter Sunday] when I was with all the sisters, a little song was sung about how hard it is to endure life without God. Since I was already afflicted, the effect upon me was so great that my hands began to grow numb. My efforts to resist weren't enough; but just as I am carried out of my senses through the joyous raptures, so in the same way through extreme affliction my soul is suspended, for it is left enraptured. And even to the present day, I haven't understood this.[15] ...Now, since the pain has increased, it has reached this extreme of transpiercing the soul. I have understood better what Our Lady experienced, for until today—as I say—I did not understand the nature of this transpiercing. The body remains so torn apart that even what I write today causes suffering, for my hands are as though disjoined and in pain.... Even this morning I felt the pain, for while in prayer I experienced a great rapture.[16]

Teresa had gone from extreme desolation to illumination, like Christ from agony to resurrection. It was an ecstasy of joy and fullness in which she felt herself united to her God at last: "And it seemed that our Lord brought my spirit next to His Father and said to Him, *'This soul you have given to Me, I give to You.'* And it seemed the Father took me to Himself."[17]

This recalls the words of Scripture, repeated by so many mystics, that one cannot see the face of God and live (cf. Ex 33:20). Teresa's visions of God the Father are very rare. For this reason they are all the more precious.

> This was not an imaginative vision, but it caused such great certitude and had a delicacy so spiritual that I don't know how to describe it at all. He spoke some words I do not recall; certain of them were about granting me a favor. It was for some time that He kept me near Him.[18]

Overcome, Teresa called for her confessor, but he had left Salamanca. So she took up her pen, giving us this moving testimony in which she unburdens herself of too heavy a weight: "Our Lord told me there is a difference between this one and the imaginative ones and that there couldn't be any fixed rule about the favors He grants us because sometimes it was fitting that they take place in one way and at other times in another way."

After the vision of the Father, she felt reassured by the Son.

> One day after receiving Communion, it seemed most clear to me that Our Lord sat beside me; and He began to console me with great favors, and he told me among other things: "See Me here, daughter, for it is I; give Me your hands." And it seemed He took them and placed them on His side and said: "Behold My wounds. You are not without Me. This short life is passing away."

Christ's words in Teresa's vision are an allusion to the doubt that had assailed St. Thomas when he saw the resurrected Christ.

> He told me that immediately after His resurrection He went to see our Lady because she then had great need and that the pain she experienced so absorbed and transpierced her soul that she did not return immediately to herself to rejoice in that joy. By this I understood how different was this other transpiercing, the one of my soul.

Thus did she relate what can be called her second transverberation. On that Easter night in 1571, in Salamanca, God the Father had preserved her from dying so that she could pursue her reforming missionary work. She still had many foundations to establish and books to write. Ten monasteries had already seen the light of day.[19] *La Madre* repeatedly visited them, sustaining them singlehandedly, settling the material problems that sprang up—the questions of income, rents, construction, and the admittance of postulants—nurturing the morale of her daughters, sometimes rectifying the government of the prioresses, and always writing: letters, books, and still more letters. Teresa always came out of her ecstasies stronger and more lucid than ever.

But in that year 1571, an unforeseen catastrophe was about to risk bringing her down for good.

CHAPTER 21

Teresa, Prioress
of the Incarnation

(1571-1574)

*J*n 1569, the papal nuncio had noted the inadequacy of the regulations enforced by Rubeo de Ravenna as prior general and the disloyalty of the Castilian mitigated Carmelites in observing them. In agreement with the king, he named Father Pedro Hernández y Orellana apostolic visitator to the Carmelites of Castile in an attempt to rectify the situation. This decision created a real quagmire, and it would be followed by failure.

In April 1571, a discouraged Father Hernández spent some time at the men's Carmel of Pastrana founded by Teresa and John of the Cross and was immediately edified by their reforms. He then visited the neighboring women's Carmel and became very eager to "know the little woman capable of such great things." He met her in Ávila. Teresa did not fail to win him over, for it was not a little woman but a grand lady whom he discovered, a strong soul and daughter of God, full of grace and gentleness. At Teresa's request, Father Hernández granted her permission to found other Carmels for men in Castile. This decision was tantamount to ignoring the instructions of Prior General Rubeo, who had wanted no more than two such Carmels. A conflict thus ensued between Teresa's reformed group and the Carmelites who followed the mitigated Rule.

In the meantime, Father Ángel de Salazar in Toledo had once again become the provincial prior of the Carmelites of Castile. After having at first appreciated Teresa's work, he had decided to do all that he could to prevent the extension of her Reform now that it also concerned the monks. The situation seemed intolerable to him. Who was governing the Carmelite Order?

In 1570, de Salazar had attempted to impose upon the Teresian Carmel of Medina del Campo a nun who was devoted to him, Teresa de Quezada, who had made profession at the Incarnation and who was, moreover, favorable to the Reform. Teresa required elections as the Constitutions prescribed, and the provincial's choice had not been ratified. In May 1571, he attempted to impose his protégée upon the Incarnation priorate in Ávila, but she wasn't accepted there either. The apostolic visitator Hernández intervened in this tense situation.

Provincial Prior de Salazar was asking himself how to "neutralize the little woman," referring to Teresa. He persuaded the apostolic visitator to assert his higher authority and oblige her to accept the priorate of the Incarnation, which was foundering under insurmountable difficulties. De Salazar argued that since Teresa possessed genuine holiness and well-placed relations, she alone would be capable of putting things in order. In reality, by imposing this new office on Teresa he counted upon rendering her ineffective, as he had tried to do once before in 1562. So this was a poisoned gift for Teresa, one that could wear her out both physically and morally.

In 1571, the Incarnation Carmel, which numbered 160 nuns, had not changed much since 1561, the year Teresa had left it to found St. Joseph. They were indeed mitigated, that is to say, relaxed in their Rule and satisfied to be that way. With Teresa as prioress, the nuns foresaw what they most dreaded sweeping down upon them: penance, silence, and solitude; rigorous fasting, an unbending discipline, a primitive Rule that they considered outdated, the end of chatting among themselves and of society visits—even gallant ones—at the visiting room, grilles everywhere, and a ban on going out.

These measures, which were certainly rigorous, could only make sense if they were done out of a deep love, a passion even, for Christ and as a generous gift of self for others—in short, qualities only found in an authentic contemplative religious vocation. The majority of mitigated religious were far from this ideal. Often poor daughters of the nobility, they had entered Carmel because they had not been able to find a husband or because they dreaded the crushing responsibility of motherhood. Their goal was to earn salvation easily while avoiding the perils of motherhood and society. Teresa herself was of the opinion that they had the right to make such a choice. "...Changing a habit is death, as they say," she wrote to her friend Doña Luisa de la Cerda.[1]

In fact, the situation at the Incarnation seemed desperate. Donations, dowries, and other income having become scarce, this overpopulated monastery did not have enough revenue to survive. The previous winter had been a cruel one. The impoverishment of the people, caused by devaluation, was as rampant in Ávila as it was in the rest of Spain. Through the convent's disjointed roof tiles "the north wind sent snowflakes down on the pages of the breviaries."[2] In the refectory, turnips cooked in water were being served with crusts of black bread. In the city, poverty was so grievous that starving marauders were jumping over the cloister wall trying to pilfer the nuns' loft, where they stored their meager reserve of food grains, cabbages, and chick peas. Armed with an arquebus, or antiquated type of musket, one sister had tried to shoo them off by firing into the air from the upper cloister!

The primitive Rule of Carmel adopted by Teresa was incompatible with a large community. It would have been necessary to send one-third of the nuns, those without a real vocation, back into the world and divide the rest into two or three monasteries. But the superiors did not have enough authority to impose such a radical solution. And Teresa herself was not prepared for this type of mission. As a former professed nun at the Incarnation, she had humiliated this convent by leaving it to found St. Joseph close by. A majority of the Carmelites, considering themselves to be as wellborn as she, detested her; her ecstasies, her visions, and her levitations frightened them. To proceed with an authoritarian nomination of the prioress was contrary to the practice at Carmel, where the prioress was supposed to be elected, allowing for exception. An exception would indicate some grave fault within the community, such as too much relaxation regarding the Rule. But a community cannot be reformed against its will. In one of her letters, Teresa would write that she dreaded one dissatisfied nun more than many devils, and that she would prefer to found four new convents rather than to reform a single one.

She was all the more in an awkward position here because she had drawn heavily from the Incarnation community to found her own monasteries. Father General had at first authorized two of these sisters to join the Reformed Carmel and then all those who asked to be volunteers. In all, thirty-four had joined the Reform. The Incarnation had thus been deprived of its best members.

Teresa tried at first to refuse the responsibility, putting forward good reasons for doing so: her age, the state of her health, and her still-needed presence at Medina del Campo, where the new foundation lacked stability.

But on July 10, 1571, a command from heaven distressed her deeply.

One day...while I was...praying to God for one of my brothers,[3] I said to the Lord..."Why is my brother in a place where his salvation is in danger?"... The Lord answered me: "Oh, daughter, daughter! These sisters in the Incarnation are My Sisters, and you delay? Well, take courage; behold I want it, and it isn't as difficult as it seems to you.... Do not resist, for My power is great."[4]

Teresa then informed the apostolic visitor that she would accept the position, on the condition that the lay boarders be made to leave and that the Incarnation community be obliged to adopt the strict primitive Rule progressively. To have acted otherwise would have betrayed her mission. The time bomb planted by the provincial had now been primed. Teresa borrowed two mules from a water carrier and set out for the Incarnation Carmel.

A FEW DAYS LATER, she entered Ávila, her heart pounding, but she dared not confront the Incarnation immediately. She wanted first to study the situation, so she stayed in her dear convent of St. Joseph. What she soon learned filled her with consternation. At the Incarnation at least fifty nuns without pensions were suffering from hunger, and the others were not doing anything about it. The famished sisters were leaving the monastery to beg in the streets or going home to be fed by their families. The situation was so dire that the prior general had suspended the admittance of novices.

Teresa's first act was to take care of temporal matters. She asked her old friend Don Francisco de Salcedo to send them fifty hens and her sister Juana to send a few turkeys. She wrote to her rich friends to solicit their financial assistance as a matter of the utmost urgency. Ironically, some months earlier, Teresa had written to her brother Lorenzo regarding St. Joseph:

> I was very relieved not to have to appeal to others. They would not fail to help me, but it pleases me to be free in dealing with these gentlemen so as to be able to tell them my opinion.... So, I will not keep for myself anything of what you sent, but I will keep my freedom.... There are people who will go so far as to lend me one or two thousand ducats. So, just at a time when I have come to abhor money and business affairs, the Lord desires that I deal with nothing else....[5]

It was not until October 6, 1571, that she ventured to approach her former monastery in order to assume her position. The provincial, Father Ángel de Salazar, assisted by two other Carmelite monks, was to enthrone her. The nuns, the majority of whom were very bitter, awaited them behind locked doors, determined not to budge. Their exasperation was even greater because Father de Salazar was himself a mitigated Carmelite, and they felt betrayed by their own hierarchy.

The small party came up against the closed door. A hostile crowd of family and friends, which had been incited by the Carmelite nuns, had gathered under the convent walls. The provincial called for the intervention of the constables, and the door was broken open to the boos of the crowd. The scandal was enormous. *La Madre* remained calm and determined, as though this tumult did not concern her.

Not entirely sure of himself, Father Provincial attempted to defend himself by reading the patent letter of the apostolic visitator naming Teresa prioress of the Incarnation. His voice was immediately drowned out by shouts and protests.

"We demand a straightforward vote!" cried the outgoing prioress, Mother Ana de Toledo.

Father Provincial finally managed to make himself heard: "So, you do not *want Madre* Teresa de Jesús?"

A unanimous shout of "No" arose from the nuns. Then suddenly, a firm voice, that of Mother Catalina de Castro, was heard above the outcry: "We want her and we love her!"

This remark was so unexpected that the most virulent rebels temporarily stopped shrieking. Regaining their courage, the sisters favorable to Teresa now dared to affirm their support. Forming a procession, they then attempted to reach the choir, according to the enthronement rite, with Teresa at their head and three Carmelite monks at her side. The uproar started up again and could be heard as far as the city's ramparts, with some persons even coming to blows! Teresa was jostled by the crowd of Carmelites. Once again, Father Provincial called upon the constables for support. The scandal was complete, and *la Madre* looked on in consternation. Her disillusioned comment was: "There is nothing surprising in this! No one can be compelled."[6]

From the shadows, the provincial was secretly rejoicing. There were two possible outcomes to the situation: *la Madre* would go away discredited or she would persist. And if she persisted, either she would attempt to impose her reforms, for which the mitigated nuns would make her pay, or she would compromise with mitigation and lose face.

Once the constables re-established order and the patent letters were read again, one might have thought that the question was finally settled. Evening came, and each nun returned to her cell to spend the night, which, it is said, brings with it good advice. However, it was in an ominous atmosphere of hatred and suspicion that the community met the next morning in Chapter, convened there by Teresa.

And, surprise! Instead of seating herself in the prioress' chair, Teresa, in all simplicity, went to the place she had occupied for twenty-four years in the stalls as an ordinary professed nun. A great burst of laughter erupted from the community, clearing the air. "What humility! Could she really be a saint?" the hesitant nuns were asking themselves.

During the night Teresa had given the matter much thought. The superiors' order had disregarded the most elementary principles of psychology. So she had decided not to impose herself as prioress. Caught between her duty of obedience to Christ and to her superiors and the demands of freedom, she would not attempt to reform these women against their will.

Closing her eyes, she invoked Our Lady of Carmel, and it immediately became obvious to her what she should do. Leaving the Chapter room, they went to the chapel, where Teresa took a statue of the Virgin dressed in silk and wearing a crown. Then, in a dramatic gesture, she set the statue in the stall of the prioress, placing the convent keys at her feet and calling out: "Ladies, here is your prioress. She is Our Lady of Clemency. As for me, I come to you in the name of obedience to serve you. I am a daughter of this house and your sister. Any one of you can teach me and correct me. If I must give my blood and my life, I will do so willingly."

Then, according to a witness, "the hardest hearts melted like wax in the sun."

Uplifted by fervor and emotion, Teresa then spoke to them with both her heart and her head.[7]

"Since prioresses have different talents and virtues, they seek to lead their nuns along their own way. The one who is very mortified thinks that anything she commands is easy to submit to, as it would be for her.... We must be careful about this.... Discretion is an important aspect of government, and very necessary in these houses. I would say much more necessary than in other houses, for the account one must render concerning one's subjects is greater."

As she spoke, the faces before her grew more and more relaxed. She went on: "Other prioresses, who are very spiritual, would like to reduce everything to prayer.... The Lord leads souls by different paths. But the prioresses must remember that they are not there for the purpose of choosing a path for others according to their own liking, but so as to lead subjects by the path of the Rule.... Thus it happens that if a prioress is absorbed in prayer, even though the hour is not one set apart for prayer, but after Matins, she keeps the whole community there even though it would be much better if the Sisters went to bed.... I...would want them to observe the

Rule, for with that there is plenty to do; and the rest should be done with gentleness."

Teresa stopped for a moment. There was total silence, her listeners' faces solemn and attentive. The Rule? But, which one? She continued: "This is especially important in what pertains to mortification. For love of our Lord, the prioresses should be attentive in this, for discretion and knowledge of each one's talents are very important in these matters.... They must reflect that this mortification is not a matter of obligation.... Although mortification is very necessary in order that the soul gain freedom and high perfection, it is not accomplished in a short time.... The prioress should help each one according to the spirituality and amount of intelligence God gives.... With some nuns, much time will pass before they come to understand perfection and even the spirit of our Rule (and perhaps they will afterward be the holiest), for they will not know when it is good to excuse oneself, and when not, or other trifling matters that if they understood they would perhaps carry out with ease. And such nuns do not completely understand, nor does it seem to them that these are matters pertaining to perfection, which is worse."

Once again, Teresa broke off. It seemed to her that Christ was carrying her along, encouraging her.

"The prioress must not then think that she understands a soul at once. Let her leave this to God, for it is He alone who can understand it. Rather, the prioress should strive to guide each nun along the way His Majesty is leading that one, provided that the nun is not failing in obedience or in the more essential matters of the Rule and constitutions."

To herself, Teresa was thinking: *The prioress should take heed not to try to make such a one perfect by force but should allow her to proceed gradually until the Lord does the work in her.*

"Therefore, some nuns will suffer great mortifications, and the greater the mortifications they are ordered to perform the more they will enjoy them because the Lord has given them the strength of soul to surrender their wills. Others will not suffer even little ones; and to impose mortifications on them would be comparable to loading a child down with two sacks of wheat. Not only will the child be unable to carry them, but he will bow under the weight and fall to the ground.... May it please His Majesty to continue to give this grace long into the future. Amen."

Teresa had finished. But everything remained to be done. In a movement of fervor and love, she entrusted the community to Christ, Mary, and Joseph.

THE HOLY GENTLEMAN Francisco de Salcedo, who had become a priest and had already endowed St. Joseph of Ávila, sent sixty-two hens to the Incarnation. In thanking him, Teresa described the situation there: "The indigence of this house is so great and there are so many sick nuns that we really needed it [the poultry sent]."[8] She now understood the fear that her arrival had aroused. No more nourishing visits to their families, no parlor visits where they nibbled as much as they chatted; their suffering could now only be increased. To send away the lay boarders would take away precious income. As for the nuns who were well-to-do, they trembled at having to share their meager pensions. Finally, earning their living through work was easier said than done. It was unthinkable, in any case, for the aristocrats. And what work? In Castile, unemployment and poverty were pandemic. Yet in spite of all this, one month after her arrival, Teresa wrote to Doña Luisa de la Cerda: "...glory to God, there is peace, which is no small thing. Gradually I am taking away the nuns' diversions and freedom.... It doesn't seem that my soul is disturbed in the midst of this whole Babylon, which I take to be a favor from the Lord."[9]

After taking care of temporal matters—thanks to the generosity of her brother Lorenzo, the Duchess of Alba, and Bishop de Mendoza—la Madre started the difficult task of spiritual reform. But how could she undertake the work of convincing the nuns to accept her ideal, which necessarily entailed rigorous discipline? With regard to the implacable sisters, Teresa first attempted to charm and then to persuade them.

Little by little, the anarchy fostered by the community's impoverishment was curbed. No more parlor visits during Lent—that was a real revolution! And no more romantic visitations there. One arrogant hidalgo, furious at being told by the turn sister that the little nun to whom he was devoted would no longer receive him, summoned la Madre to appear and disrespectfully berated her in the parlor. When he had finished his diatribe, Teresa answered him in a calm voice: "Your Grace will, from now on, leave this monastery in peace. If Your Grace persists, I shall appeal to the king."

The smug and conceited young man, who was aware of la Madre's well-placed relations at court, mounted his horse and was not seen again.[10]

Teresa put an end to deviations regarding parlor visits by taking control of the parlor's keys as well as those of the turn, something that had never been seen at the Incarnation. She only authorized the sick to go out. The first Lent was a hard ordeal for everyone. In a corner of her cell-office were piled up disparate objects that the sisters, of their own accord, had brought her as a sign of abnegation: mirrors, beauty creams, fans, jewelry, musical instruments, secular books. For certain religious, the most painful change was to give up the finery that they used to flaunt their social rank, decking themselves out on feast days or when they went out: skirts, trains, headdresses, leather boots inherited from their relatives. Teresa herself set the example of detachment from what was useless with her patched habit, her mended and worn veil, and her bare feet clad in frayed straw sandals.

By coming into contact with her and thanks to her teaching, which Teresa adapted to each one of the nuns, many were advancing on the road to wisdom. They were discovering mental prayer and the divine joys that it brings. Her example impressed everyone. For example, during Lent in 1572, she would rise in the middle of the night, despite her fatigue, to make the Way of the Cross in the chapel, following the Lamb wherever he went. Some of the sisters followed her; a fervent core of religious was being constituted, gradually bringing the others along with them. "The ones who were most forbidding are now the ones who are most satisfied.... Almost all the nuns are improving," wrote Teresa in a letter.[11]

THIS SEVERE TESTING—having to reform the Incarnation Carmel—did not distance her from Christ. She was still experiencing ecstasies. On Palm Sunday, Teresa received Communion as usual to give shelter to the Lord who would soon be abandoned after having been so celebrated on that day. To her great surprise, the host remained mysteriously on her tongue for an indefinite length of time, leaving a strange taste of blood in her mouth. She also heard these words: "Daughter, I want my blood to be beneficial to you... I shed it with many sufferings, and you enjoy it with the great delight you are aware of...."[12]

But the passion she particularly suffered was constant illness. She experienced vomiting, neuralgia, quartan fever, rheumatism—which she hid from the community, always smiling. She slept on a straw mattress on the floor and observed the obligatory fasts. To Sister Ana Gutiérrez, she confided: "Believe me, my child, our Lord has poured on my body the torments of purgatory."

She called these torments down upon herself, offering her sufferings for the conversion of the most obstinate nuns of that Carmel, which she knew was her responsibility before God. Divine strength carried her along. It was at the Incarnation that she would experience her greatest ecstasies and the spiritual marriage.

Order eventually returned to this great monastery that had been disorderly for so long. The provincial prior rejoiced at this transformation and believed he had succeeded in installing the foundress in one place, thus neutralizing her. The apostolic visitor could not hide his joy. In January 1573, he wrote to the Duchess of Alba:

> The one hundred and thirty nuns of the Incarnation are living all together with as much peace and sanctity as the twelve of your monastery. This has really surprised me and consoled me a great deal. The presence of *la Madre* is the sole cause of this. If she were absent for a single day, all that has been acquired here would be lost.

Were miracles taking place? The strangest rumors were circulating about the Incarnation. The Virgin in person had appeared in the stall of the prioress while the fervent community was singing the *Salve Regina* at Compline. The statue of St. Joseph that *la Madre* had placed next to the Virgin in the stall of the subprioress was secretly revealing even the smallest sin of the nuns, who nicknamed the statue *el parlero*, the chatterer! It was even said that he remained open-mouthed over it!

However, the Incarnation lacked good confessors. Those who visited it came from the small monastery of mitigated Carmelites built against the ramparts, where its dozen or so monks were not always available. Formerly, Teresa had rarely called upon them. Rather relaxed in their approach to the Rule, they undermined with a few words a week's worth of efforts.

That is why, in the summer of 1572, Teresa requested that the apostolic visitor, Pedro Hernández, authorize John of the Cross, the spearhead of her masculine Reform, to come to Ávila. Founded in 1568, John's monastery at Duruelo had received numerous postulants, expanding in 1569 to Pastrana, then in 1570 to Alcalá and Mancera. By 1572, Fray John, then rector of the Carmelite College of Alcalá de Henares, had been sent to Pastrana to bring order back to the community in crisis, characterized by "mortifications, penances, and scourges attaining a state of delirium."[13]

Father Hernández hesitated when he received Teresa's request. Sending John to Ávila risked angering the Calced Carmelites, those who wore shoes— "Fathers of the cloth," as Teresa called them. Then, after having consulted the nuncio, he agreed to do so. John of the Cross arrived in Ávila on September 15, 1572, but he had to reside with the mitigated Carmelites, who looked askance at him. If his ascetic practices did not convince them to embrace the Reform, he was, on the other hand, able to do excellent work at the Incarnation. Teresa had informed her daughters: "I am giving you a saint as a confessor."

This news had not failed to worry more than one of them! For John, however, it was a question of perfecting *la Madre's* work by making it lasting.

As has already been described, the man himself was very small and almost bald, although he was only thirty years old. In his face, emaciated by penances, burned two ardent black eyes that reflected a great gentleness, the presence of the invisible upon the visible. Although poorly attired and bare-footed, John impressed people by the radiance of his entire person and by his authority, which inspired in others both love and respect.

In her correspondence and her books, Teresa described at length her own method of spiritual direction, which was shared by John of the Cross. It implied real liberty: "Everything depends on what His Majesty desires and to whom He desires to give this food." "For a soul that is under duress cannot serve God well, and it is through this that the devil tempts it."[14]

John was well received at the Incarnation. "The more a confessor is a saint," he used to say, "the more gentle of heart is he and less scandalized by the faults of others, for he knows human weakness better." John's goodness, understanding, and patience moved the nuns. Even the most rebellious gave him their unqualified trust in the end.

Teresa and John relied upon a core of fervent religious who became the driving force of the Reform. For it to succeed, love was the only motivation possible, mental prayer the instrument. Through her example, la Madre could let the others glimpse its delights. All the peevish nuns who had dreaded the excesses of mortification that these two saints would bring—and the suffering that they feared would result from such mortifications—were very much surprised.

Nevertheless, the little monk did his utmost to minimize the search for spiritual pleasure while Teresa was singing the delights of the prayer of quiet and mystical union. John considered any and all searches for sentient experiences deviations from the religious experience. It was not a question of pleasure—a term that was foreign to him—but the attainment of supernatural knowledge thanks to illumination that was essential.

In his Spiritual Canticle,[15] John nevertheless recalled "the multitude of Your sweetness [gustos], O Lord, which You have hidden for them that fear You...a torrent of pleasure [that] You shall make them drink." But, just like Teresa, he knew the deviations that can be caused by a kind of ecstatic worship bordering on sensuality—especially where the Alumbrados were concerned—and he distrusted it. In the soul "united and transformed with an abundance of heavenly riches and gifts," "the passions are subjected and the natural appetites mortified."[16] This is an eternal problem that confronts Christian ascetics and that defines their specificity: finding one's delights in imitating a crucified Christ. Without hesitation, John relinquished such delights. Teresa would never have thought to deprive herself of them. She was more balanced, more human.

However, in her thoughts on the love of God—a commentary on the Song of Songs now known as *Meditations on the Song of Songs*—which she dared to write at that time for her daughters of the Incarnation, she heard this warning from the divine Spouse: "Do you think, daughter, that merit lies in enjoyment? No, rather, it lies in working and suffering and loving."[17] And she gave this very feminine answer, taken from the *Song*: "Sustain me with flowers."

In spite of these differences, Teresa and John both lived in the *company* of Jesus, following the Lord throughout his life, which had become their own life entirely. They experienced "company" in the profound meaning of the term, which St. Ignatius of Loyola had chosen to name his entire Order, and not only the group he was forming. Teresa and John knew what it was to be in Jesus' presence, in his company body and soul, linked by love to him who loved them and who could do everything in them, going little by little from fear to love, from worry to confidence, hope, joy, and the peace that fulfilled them beyond the night.

But each in one's own way, according to and with one's own character, sensibility, intelligence, particular gifts, and also according to the periods of each one's life and God's demand upon that person. They had undertaken to travel along a very personal, intense, and definitive path. It was the path of abandonment to the will of God, to everything that he wants. Mystery of divine love!

It is fascinating to follow the duo, the arguments and the complicities of these two exceptional human beings in the very cauldron of the Incarnation, that famous parlor where the young Teresa de Ahumada had received her devout suitors and shared with them delightful thrills! Although she could have been John's mother according to the flesh and the spirit, she submitted entirely to him, "her son, her brother, her father, her master." He directed her rigorously and with even more severity than he exacted from the other religious of the Incarnation. He allowed her no indulgence, even when he cloaked his criticism in a compliment.

"When you confess your sins, *Madre*, you exonerate yourself nicely."

"Good Lord, of what?"

"Of taking pleasure with Jesus-Love."

Christ had said to her: "While I was on earth, I took her [Mary Magdalene] for my friend; but now that I am in heaven, I have chosen you."[18]

She related with simplicity in her *Spiritual Testimonies* that on November 18, 1572

> ...when I was receiving Communion, Father John of the Cross who was giving me the Blessed Sacrament broke the host to provide for another sister. I thought there was no lack of hosts but that he wanted to mortify me because I had told him it pleased me very much when the hosts were large (not that I didn't understand that the size made no difference with regard to the Lord's being wholly present, even when the particle is very small). His Majesty then said to me: "Don't fear, daughter, for no one will be a party to separating you from Me...." Then He appeared to me in an imaginative vision, as at other times, very interiorly, and He gave me His right hand and said: "Behold this nail; it is a sign you will be My bride from today on. Until now you have not merited this; from now on not only will you look after My honor as being the honor of your Creator, King, and God, but you will look after it as My true bride. My honor is yours, and yours Mine." This favor produced such an effect in me I couldn't contain myself, and I remained as though entranced. I asked the Lord either to raise me from my lowliness or not grant me such a favor; for it didn't seem to me my nature could bear it. Throughout the whole day I remained thus very absorbed. Afterward I felt great gain, and greater confusion and affliction at seeing I don't render any service in exchange for such amazing favors.[19]

Thus was Teresa attaining the highest degree of mystical union in this spiritual marriage. The direction John of the Cross provided was bent upon purifying her of the somewhat sweet mysticism that she sometimes took pleasure in, upon orienting her toward a more perfect knowledge of God's nature. As an intellectual, a theologian, and a man of pure contemplation, John warned her against placing too much importance on action, which can be a deviation. They spoke about this at length, and these discussions highlighted the difference in their temperaments and their relation to Christ. For Teresa, to love was as much action as contemplation; for John, it was only and uniquely pure contemplation. Their differences enriched them both, but it was especially after Teresa's death that John of the Cross, finally in complete support of action born of contemplation, would faithfully pursue his work as a founder according to her example.

Her mission would not prevent Teresa from abandoning herself to the love of the spiritual marriage or from describing this in *The Interior Castle*, her master work (1577), and first in her *Meditations on the Song of Songs* (1572), written at Christ's own command. These hundred or so pages, which her daughters delighted in using, was a text so revolutionary that she would burn the original in 1574 upon a simple order from her confessor at the time, Father Diego de Yanguas, a Jesuit in Segovia. Fortunately, clandestine copies were saved. We quote here from the one at Alba de Tormes, approved by Father Domingo Báñez.

Given these celestial favors, Teresa wrote, the soul experiences

> a kind of divine intoxication so that it doesn't know what it wants or what it says.... But when this most wealthy Bridegroom desires to enrich and favor the soul more, He changes it into Himself to such a point that, just as a person is caused to swoon from great pleasure and happiness, it seems to the soul it is left suspended in those divine arms, leaning on that sacred side and those divine breasts. It doesn't know how to do anything more than rejoice, sustained by the divine milk with which its Spouse is nourishing it and making it better so that He might favor it, and it might merit more each day. When it awakens from that sleep and that heavenly inebriation, it remains as though stupefied and dazed and with a holy madness.[20]

Yes, John had much to do with making her turn away from her divine pleasure! Certain commentators have allowed themselves to gloss over St. Teresa's movement from eros to agape, from sensual love, which wants to take, to that love which gives of itself and shares. In her *Soliloquies*, Teresa, commenting upon the Song of Songs, that song of love of the chosen people of Israel and their God, quotes fifteen times the famous verse: *Let the Lord kiss me with the kiss of his mouth, for your breasts are better than wine.* For Christian exegetes, "the kiss of the Spouse" evokes a spiritual relationship. For Teresa, the union of the creature to the body of the resurrected Christ was no less total. She asserted herself to be the *spouse* of God, a word that endured through the centuries and continues to endure for all woman contemplatives.[21] Teresa was united, body and soul, to the One who had chosen her, and she wrote clearly that love often acts with such force that it takes possession of and masters all the forces of one's nature.

In the end, Teresa would not succumb to the excesses of the delights of mystical union. Her fulfilled heart fades into the background when faced with an apostolic project; it even becomes its springboard. From her union with God, children of light would come forth: her foundations and her books. Her union and her ecstasy would never be sterile.

It was a time when the Inquisition prohibited women from reading Scripture and the commentaries on it. Teresa herself was hesitant regarding this prudence. Fortunately, in Teresa, daring prevailed. She would soon be paying the price. The learned male theologians and other "cats," the "Fathers of the cloth," were plotting in the wings to reduce her to the status of a frail female: silent, cloistered, veiled, mortified—she and her buffoon of a mystic, the dwarf John of the Cross, that giant whom they perceived threatening to take them back to strict observance of the Rule!

Whatever the case might be, the superiors had to admit that Fray John, that radically poor, humble, detached witness, was succeeding where all the priest visitors had failed. Under the simultaneous influence of these two saints, the Incarnation, the most relaxed Carmel of Spain, was righting itself. So when Teresa asked the apostolic visitor for permission to build a small cabin named *la casa de la Torrecilla* for John of the Cross against the exterior wall of the Incarnation, he agreed to her request. Henceforth, Fray John became nearly a permanent resident in order to reform his daughters. And in answer to the question: "But, what can you possibly be doing to these nuns to bring them around to doing what you wish?" John responded, "God accomplishes everything, and for that reason, he orders them to love me."

One of the Carmelite nuns stated that he had "the grace to console those who confided in him." And Teresa said: "All the things that theologians tell me, I find combined in my little Seneca."

Very privileged relationships were established and lasted for those two years that John of the Cross spent in Ávila, and astonishing dialogues took place in the Incarnation parlor. On May 17, 1573, Sister Beatriz de Ocampo, looking for the prioress, went to the parlor, where she found Teresa in ecstasy and, on the other side of the grille, John of the Cross sent into levitation by ecstasy. Teresa excused herself, saying: "You cannot speak of God with Father John of the Cross without having him enter into ecstasy and leading you along with him."

She revealed to him in confession the favors that both fulfilled and overwhelmed her. To her words of transports, raptures, and ecstasies, he responded: nights of the spirit, tears of fire.

> Oh guiding night!
> O night more lovely than the dawn!
> O night that has united
> The Lover with His beloved,
> Transforming the beloved into her Lover.[22]

All of this evokes and makes necessary total nakedness "and the experience of an intense presence in the midst of absence," the pure act of faith.[23]

In agreement on essentials—the cross as the privileged site of encounter, divine revelation in the heart of the human being—they diverged on the manner of receiving this revelation. Teresa was lively and sensual, solar in

the astrological meaning of the term, "primary," having no university training. He, the scholastic logician, the learned theologian, was "solid but rigid,
not very capable of rendering an account of the life of the spirit."[24] And yet
he was cantor of the dark night, of renouncement, of shadow for the
purification of faith, "more categorically detached from all to find the All."[25]
She, closer to human realities, remained always smiling and joyous in spite
of her sufferings, loving and attentive to others. He extolled mortification of
the senses and total deprivation, abandonment of personal will, interior
nudity, and spiritual poverty, without which he thought there was no union
possible with the Absolute. He would explain all this himself in *The Ascent
of Mount Carmel*, his masterpiece, and in *The Dark Night*.

Thus did they differ in their method of quiet prayer: for him, it was a
matter of reaching God by disengaging from one's body; for her, the body
participated in this mystery of the incarnation. Teresa remained faithful to
the *Exercises of St. Ignatius*. John found them tied too much to the senses and
the imagination; he preferred the more intellectual Augustinian prayer of
quiet. Bound to her visions, Teresa fell in love with Christ in the carnal and
affective sense, as had Mary Magdalene, and no one would be able to take
that away from her.

What, then, did they have in common? They were both inhabited by the
same passion for this God, incarnate and resurrected, who possessed them
and would by turns break them and fulfill them, knead them and propel
them toward the heights from which they would fall, both amazed and broken, trying to understand the why and the how of this mystery.

Even in the midst of a monastery of contemplatives, states of ecstasy are
extremely rare. He or she who is thus fulfilled (or prostrated) feels very much
alone. John and Teresa found and recognized each other—a real happiness
for them—and their spirits engendered one another to join together what
they would be in eternity.

Consequently, in this domain, everything drew them together. They had
an immeasurably deep faith in God, a Platonic vision of the human being
in which the soul is a distinct and autonomous whole from the carnal body
that it animates. The resurrected Christ was for them not a symbol but a living model, a *visitor*: for her, an attentive Spouse; for him, a demanding
Master. They also had in common their approach to God through ascetic
renunciation; their thirst for perfection, for holiness, which necessitated the
gift of themselves; their humility before God; their love of nature and the
starlit sky as a reflection of divine beauty; their writing, another form of
asceticism, and especially their poetry, that divine means of release. Their

spirits met also in their refusal of mediocrity and routine and in the fraternity that must unite all the children of God.

But, it bears repeating, they differed on the subject of divine "favors." Of
course, John of the Cross, just like Teresa, received and experienced them,
though he was mistrustful of such phenomena: visions, voices, and especially physical manifestations, such as the stigmata and levitation. For him,
these manifestations were the dross of the mystical experience, the suspect
remainder of the shock between the body and the spirit, the unusual effect
of the mutation that the spirit calls forth and engenders. He would have
nothing to do with even the sweet pleasures of the mystical experience, that
"quietude" derived from mental prayer and sung by Teresa, for he feared a
compromise with sensuality. He stated his feelings rather paradoxically in a
phrase that he flung one day at a nun whom he was directing: "My daughter, do not seek anything else but the totally naked cross...an exquisite
thing."

In this way, he rejoined Teresa in the paradox of suffering-delight as she
had experienced it in the past. He sang:

> O Living flame of love
> That tenderly wounds my soul
> In its deepest center! Since
> Now You are not oppressive,
> Now Consummate! If it be Your will:
> Tear through the veil of this sweet encounter!
> O Sweet cautery,
> O delightful wound!
> O gentle hand! O delicate touch
> That tastes of eternal life
> And pays every debt!
> In killing you changed death to life.[26]

John's method was radical; it was that of the sculptor on wood or marble: "You have come to the cloister only to be hammered, cut, and polished
like a piece of marble." That is the meaning of the totally naked cross, "that
exquisite thing"! We can imagine the Carmelites' amazement at listening to
the blazing little monk of whom all they could make out through the grille
of the confessional were his black eyes, glowing from the passion for God
that inhabited and sustained him.

No one has recounted the torments of these nuns at the Incarnation,
their questions as they faced this torrent that uprooted them, this volcano
that consumed them. For, in the end, he epitomized everything that they
detested: suffering, purifying though it might be; a break with the world; for-

getting oneself; rejecting vanities and the "point of honor," that misplaced pride. He destabilized them by this affirmation, that of every mystic: life on earth is but a passing dream. Reality is elsewhere. This reality that he and Teresa were experiencing is the God who questions and invites us, and in whom and with whom we want to identify ourselves and perhaps even coalesce. This brings to mind the startling prayer that St. Elizabeth of the Trinity in her Carmel at Dijon would write three centuries later: "Oh, consuming fire, Spirit of Love, come upon me, and create in my soul a kind of incarnation of the Word: that I may be another humanity for Him in which He can renew His whole Mystery."

Teresa de Jesús, John of the Cross—a unique moment in the spiritual history of the world in which two exceptional beings taken hold of by the Absolute gave birth to one another.

THE TRUE MIRACLES TAKING PLACE at the Incarnation in those years from 1571–1574 were not the ecstasies and the levitations of John and Teresa, but the conversions of nuns who had been judged to be irretrievable. *La Madre's* greatest happiness was to see that virtue had returned to the Incarnation. She wrote to her friend, the Jesuit Gaspar de Salazar, on February 13, 1572: "I no longer have any more reason to be distressed over resistance to obedience and recollection here than at St. Joseph's." She added that one of the Discalced friars, "who is very saintly, has been the confessor here for some time,"[27] speaking of John of the Cross. But she nonetheless had no illusions about the fragility of this Reform.

Contrary to what Father Provincial had hoped, she never stopped looking after her other foundations. Beyond her priorate at the Incarnation, she retained the important role of spiritual counselor to the Reform. She was called upon everywhere, respected and venerated, although, as she laughingly wrote, "Even though we women are not good for giving counsel, we sometimes hit the mark."[28] After Compline, she answered her letters until very late into the night. She allowed herself only two to three hours of sleep, and at five in the morning she was up for the first Office on an empty stomach! Her health continued to deteriorate, but she took no notice, drawing strength from her union with Christ through mental prayer. Here we have a perfect example of contemplation fused with action.

Her main concern remained the nuns who had been entrusted to her. In writing "To my Most Reverend Señor and Padre Maestro Domingo Báñez, my lord," she highlighted what constituted the strength of her

Reform: the quality of the vocations—not money (the eventual dowry of the postulants), birth, or culture, but humility and sanctity. Regarding a young girl named Parda whom the Dominican had sent "without a cent" to be a lay sister, Teresa had decided from the first interview with her:

> I don't think I will have the heart to take her as a lay sister, knowing how you have helped her. So, I have decided that they teach her how to read and on the basis of her progress we will make our decision. My spirit has well understood hers even though I have not spoken to her. And there is a nun who cannot resist the deep prayer that this new sister stirs in her. Believe me, *mi padre,* it is a pleasure for me every time I accept someone who brings in nothing and is received for love of God alone.... I don't recall ever having refused anyone pleasing to me because she didn't have a dowry.[29]

The hardest thing for her was to refuse a postulant without a vocation— that is, lacking in fervor, love, and desire for perfection—who was recommended by a highly positioned and virtuous relation out of misplaced simple charity. Her conception of a Carmelite was exacting: a Carmelite should have "holiness...fortitude...much discretion...many talents—gifts that would be beneficial to the house.... There in your monastery, anyone who is accepted should be capable of being prioress or holding any other office that is given to her."[30]

Teresa's three-year term of office ended on October 8, 1574. One of the nuns, Catalina de Velasco, summarized her priorate as follows:

> She had exercised her position with heart and wisdom, placing herself at the level of each one. Every one of them quickly began to love her greatly. The very ones who only lately had opposed her came to be attached to her. She returned their affection, with the result that even before she completed her time in office, everyone thought of reelecting her as prioress.

But Teresa was already far away, her mind turned toward new foundations.

CHAPTER 22

An Angel Named Gracián

(1574–1576)

*E*ven before the end of her priorate, Teresa, obeying both her visions and Father Visitator Pedro Hernández, had again set out on the rutted roads of Castile. He had sent her to Alba de Tormes, and from there she had hastened to Salamanca to transfer her community to the interior of the city. There, in August of 1573, she had begun to write *The Book of Her Foundations*, ordered to do so by Father Jerónimo Ripalda, rector of the Jesuits in that city. Christ had already invited her to do the same in a vision of February 7, 1570.

In March of 1574 she had founded the Discalced Carmel of Segovia. "One day while I was there in prayer, our Lord told me to go to Segovia and make a foundation."[1] The project was an undertaking in which John of the Cross participated. The fourteen nuns from the Pastrana convent were later transferred there, for they had been betrayed by their donor, the unreasonable Ana de Mendoza, princess of Éboli. The king had personally banished her from the monastery for her aberrations, and she had taken revenge by cutting off the income that made it possible for the nuns to live, revenue that Teresa had accepted very reluctantly and only because the village was too poor to nourish the small community.

This scandalous affair, hardly believable, revealed *la Madre's* dependency on her benefactors. When the prince died in 1573, the princess of Éboli, inconsolable and unable to face the idea of leading the life of an ordinary widow, had decided, although she was pregnant, to take the habit of the Reformed Carmel under the name of Ana de la Madre de Dios. She had a patched habit of coarse wool made up in order to look poor, then she got into a covered wagon with her ladies-in-waiting, upon whom she also

247

imposed the veil. Abandoning her ten children, she set out toward the Carmel after having informed the prioress of her coming.

"The princess in the convent? This house is doomed!" Mother Isabel de Santo Domingo cried out.

She foresaw the worst and was not mistaken. Under the veil, the princess imposed the etiquette of the court upon the Carmel and blithely scorned the cloister enclosure. She received courtiers, treated the nuns badly, and defied the chaplains who attempted to reason with her. Faced with this continual disorder, the prioress respectfully asked her to leave.

"Your Ladyship does not belong here, in such a poor monastery. The court alone is worthy of Your Ladyship."

"Are you telling me that you are chasing me away from my own monastery? I shall appeal to the king!"

Which she did. The king, however, quickly put her in her place: "Your first duty is to take care of your children." Later, in front of his intimates, he used less polished language:

"God protect us from seeing this famous female at court ever again!"

In the meantime, informed of the affair, Teresa had ordered her fourteen daughters to abandon forever the convent at Pastrana and come to settle in Segovia.

Traveling night and day in open wagons, they had almost been submerged while crossing a river, then had been stoned by a crowd that believed them to be heretics being led to the Inquisition tribunal! This was to be a sinister portent for Teresa.

When the one-eyed princess discovered "her" monastery empty, she exploded in anger. But she held her revenge in her hand. Through trickery, she had extorted from Pastrana a copy of Teresa's autobiography, *The Book of Her Life*, which *la Madre* had imprudently brought with her and which the princess knew about from her aunt, Doña Luisa de la Cerda. The princess had especially marked out passages having to do with the ecstasies and levitations—anything that could link Teresa to the *Alumbrados*, whom the Inquisition was pursuing. Teresian spirituality, based upon the prayer of quiet and capable of leading to ecstasies, risked offending the theologians who were not gratified by them. The princess denounced the text to the Inquisition, accusing Teresa of reporting visions and revelations, and especially of "setting forth a dangerous doctrine."

Today these accusations might seem absurd, but we have to place them in the context of Teresa's times. The Church was following St. Paul's recommendation that women should *be silent* in the assemblies. As to writing!

Preaching and commentaries on Sacred Scripture were reserved for theologians who knew Latin. In its reaction against Lutheranism, the Council of
Trent had forbidden the translation of the holy books into the vernacular.
In her *Meditations on the Song of Songs*, Teresa had commented upon that canticle, a symbolic text of burning mysticism. That is why Father de Yanguas,
her Dominican confessor in Segovia, had prudently ordered her to burn it.
She had done so immediately out of obedience. Fortunately, the astute nuns
of the monasteries, the *urguillas* (the rummaging ones), had made copies.
But his prudence was justified. The famous mystical theologian Luis de
León, to whom Teresa had referred, had been thrown into prison for trans-
lating the Song of Songs into Castilian.[2]

Coming back to *The Book of Her Life*: Alerted by the vindictive princess
of Éboli, the Grand Inquisitor, Don Gaspar, Cardinal de Quiroga, had
placed the copy of the book under seal and was seeking the original. Sensing
danger, Domingo Báñez, Teresa's Dominican friend and confessor, who had
the original manuscript in his possession, took the initiative by bringing it
to his colleagues, saying to them: "You can readily see that her doctrine is
sound." Indeed! Thus this reference book, which has served all subsequent
biographers of Teresa, was spared.

For the time being, the danger menacing Teresa from the Inquisition
seemed to be contained. But another danger appeared on the horizon from
the mitigated Carmelites, the "Fathers clad in cloth," the "shod," who
definitely intended to remain that way!

IN OCTOBER OF 1574, having completed her priorate at the Incarnation,
Teresa, who had refused to accept a new three-year term, was relieved to
return to her convent of St. Joseph. But she would be able to enjoy there
only a few months of newly found peace. In January of 1575 she was once
again on the road. This time she headed south with nine nuns, Julian de
Ávila (the chaplain), and a few *caballeros* as guards. Their objective was a new
foundation on the border of New Castile in the small Andalusian city of
Beas, some 210 miles from Ávila, near Jaén in the province of Granada.

In Chapter 22 of her *Foundations*, Teresa belatedly reproaches herself for
undertaking this enterprise, given the distance and the need to cross high
mountains. When consulted, the apostolic commissary, Pedro Hernández,
had reacted rather unfavorably to the project, but he had agreed to it so long
as certain local obstacles to the foundation could be removed. Such arguments could not deter *la Madre*. She relied on the original recommendation

of the prior general, Rubeo de Ravenna, who had encouraged her never to refuse a foundation.

By February 24, 1575, the new convent had been founded at the request of a holy woman visionary, Doña Catalina Godínez, and her sister. They offered their house, six thousand ducats, and themselves also since they were taking the veil. That is how Teresa found herself engaged in an adventure that risked crushing her. What she had not realized when she began the foundation was that Beas was in Andalusia, not in Castile. The mandate she had received from the prior general authorized her to found convents in Castile only. By the time she became aware of her mistake, it was too late: "If when I went to Beas, I had known that it was in Andalusia, I would by no means have gone."[3]

Was it really a simple error that induced Teresa to extend the Reform beyond Castile? "Sometimes I think," she wrote with a half-smile, "...how that which our Lord wants, even though we may not want it, comes about in such a way that without our being aware we are the instruments of it."[4]

AT BEAS, A PERSON who would deeply affect her life awaited her: Father Jerónimo Gracián de la Madre de Dios. This Carmelite of the strict observance, having recently made profession in Pastrana, had been named visitator by the apostolic commissary, Francisco de Vargas. Gracián was entrusted by the king and Nicolás Ormaneto, the nuncio, with the impossible mission of reforming the Andalusian Carmelites! Passing through Beas, he could not avoid meeting Teresa, and, having done so, he fell under her charm.

Teresa described him, at the age of thirty, as being "tall, bald, and a bit too dark." The man himself was very attractive. Son of one of Charles V's secretaries, he knew that he was destined for a brilliant position at court. However, obsessed by a secret desire, he had obediently answered the call to a religious vocation. As a student at the Catholic University of Alcalá de Henares, he was preparing to solicit his admittance to the Jesuits when he opted finally for the Discalced Carmelites. Entering the Pastrana Carmel in 1571, he had found himself in the midst of the mystical mortification crisis that was then shaking up the young community. Disapproving of these excesses, he had very nearly renounced Carmel and only stayed thanks to the timely arrival of John of the Cross, who had come to put an end to this madness. In the hands of John, he had then made profession.

Erudite, eloquent, and learned, Gracián's austerity was never off-putting. He captivated *la Madre* at their first meeting with his moderate

approach to authority, his childlike joy, and his gentle and affectionate manner. She immediately took him as her confessor. In her thirty-sixth
Testimony, she recounted that a short time after this meeting, she went into
ecstasy in the middle of a meal and experienced a vision of Christ.

> It seemed to me our Lord Jesus Christ was next to me in the form in which
> He usually appears, and at His right side stood Master Gracián himself,
> and I at his left. The Lord took our right hands and joined them and told
> me He desired that I take this master to represent Him as long as I live, and
> that we both agree in everything because it was thus fitting.

Troubled by this vision, she asked herself if she was taking her wishes
for reality. But "I remained with very great assurance that the vision was
from God." The vision being repeated "twice more," she hesitated no
longer.

Was it a question of love at first sight? Reading her writings, one could
believe that to be so. "I will never have better days than those I had there
with my Paul,"[5] she wrote in a letter, the reference being to Paul the apostle. Father Gracián, she made clear, was either "on the mountain tops or
in the depths of the sea,"[6] going, like Paul, from enthusiasm to discourage-
ment.

In spite of this regrettable unevenness of character—cyclothymia—
"Gracián is like an angel," she wrote to Rubeo de Ravenna, the prior general.[7] Addressing a letter to the prioress of Medina del Campo, she went much
further: "He is without fault in my eyes, and for us better than what we
would have asked God for. What you must do now, and all the nuns, is to
beseech His Majesty to give him to us for our superior. In this way I could
rest from the government of these houses."[8]

She already saw him at the head of the Reformed Order, provincial prior
of the Discalced, a position that did not yet exist. John of the Cross did not
want it at any price, and Antonio de Jesús, who did want it, was not judged
qualified by *la Madre*, for "he lacks common sense, he is thin-skinned and a
trouble-maker."[9]

Despite the evident depth of feeling that this sixty-year-old woman had
for the thirty-year-old Father Gracián, Teresa did not lose sight of the interest of her Reform. But her feelings show through, nonetheless, in the end-
ing to one of her letters: "I have never seen perfection combined with so
much gentleness.... Julian de Ávila is all enthused about him and so is everyone else. He's a wonderful preacher,"[10] etc. With Gracián, she unwound
from all the tensions that weighed and would continue to weigh upon her
throughout the long march of foundations.

Gracián, the brilliant theologian of Alcalá, was human and warmhearted, spontaneous like she was, and all this attracted Teresa in the most natural meaning of the term. Between them, a bonfire of joy was immediately lit.
She was infinitely human because she was infinitely celestial, without any
mental reservation. And Gracián made her laugh! He was not a sour-faced
saint! "Oh! Father! Your Grace really made me laugh and amused me greatly," she wrote him.[11] And how he understood her! When la Madre opened
her heart, soul, and spirit to him in confession, what a relief it was for her!
Her visions, her ecstasies—were they a product of her imagination or her sensitivity going astray? Traps set by the devil? Not at all! He encouraged her to
continue along this path, the discovery of the soul's castle with its seven
dwellings.

With Gracián, she now had at her disposal a confessor whom she could
obey blindly and with pleasure! He had even authorized her to judge and to
think what she pleased. In addition to her authority and her spiritual influence, Gracián had recognized in Teresa an inspired woman. He loved her
like a sister—and like a mother. Writing to her, he one day signed his letter
"Your dear son," which deeply moved this childless woman.

Did she, who used the feminine arts in the most natural manner in the
world, love him otherwise? Later on, she would deny it. "I hold that it would
be impossible for me...to be so occupied with the thought of anyone that I
couldn't free myself from it by only a slight effort to remember this Lord."[12]
She admits, however:

> I experienced this freedom in the case of one of my confessors. Since I
> believe that my confessors stand so truly in the place of God, I think they
> are ones for whom I feel the most benevolence. Since I am always very fond
> of those who guide my soul and since I felt secure, I showed them that I
> liked them. They, as God-fearing servants of the Lord, were afraid lest in
> any way I would become attached and bound to this love, even though in
> a holy way, and they showed me their displeasure.... I laughed to myself to
> see how mistaken they were.... But, I reassured them....[13]

And this is how she answered María Bautista, her grandniece and the
prioress at Valladolid, who had dared to criticize Teresa's affection for
Gracián: "...in the former friendship the only bond is of the soul. Speaking
with him is like speaking with an angel, which he is and has always been."[14]

She did not experience an amorous feeling in the ordinary physical and
human sense of the term; hers was a spiritual affection tinged with profound
emotion, such as that experienced by so many saints. We can see this when
Teresa writes, using her exceptional capacity for introspection: "this...friend-
ship, as I say, rather gives freedom...."[15] But she would also dare to write, as

only a saint could: "...the affection I have for this other *padre* of ours causes me no embarrassment, as though he were no person."[16] Gracián, an angel?

Teresa's fervent hope was soon fulfilled when she experienced a dream that she described as "an imaginary vision," and which may have been no more than a dream of desire: Christ acting as the matchmaker (*casamentero*) uniting them to one another.

Unfortunately, Gracián was not her equal. His unstable and naïve character lacked levelheadedness and that mastery of self that makes men great. With a certain self-complacency, he boasted in public of *la Madre's* attachment, which flattered him. He even dared to read out loud the letters in which she opened her heart to him. Such behavior earned him this nuanced reproof: "I can express and have much love for you for many reasons.... I know whom I'm addressing and my age allows it." When these indiscretions later gave the mitigated monks the opportunity to cast a shadow over her honor, Teresa limited herself to writing: "I confess that I have striven to hide my imperfections from them [my daughters]—although there are so many that they must have seen a good number—as well as my love and concern for Paul."[17]

Beyond her personal feelings, *la Madre* saw far ahead. Thanks to Gracián's real qualities and relations at court, where two of his brothers were secretaries to King Philip, she projected making him the first provincial prior of the Discalced Carmelites, whom she planned to separate eventually from the common trunk, bogged down in mitigation. Such a proposal risked provoking catastrophes, because it dealt the final blow in setting the "Fathers of the cloth" against her. In Chapter 23 of *The Book of Her Foundations*, written during that time, she clearly admitted her worries regarding the Discalced monasteries of the friars. These foundations "were not going badly, but the basis was there for a very quick collapse. Since the Discalced didn't have their own province, they were governed by the Calced."

Henceforth, matters moved quickly. Paying no attention to legitimate susceptibilities, including those of her own Discalced, she went right to the top, writing to the king and asking him to appoint "a Discalced *padre*, named Gracián, whom I have recently come to know.... Although he is young, I was moved to praise our Lord greatly for what he has given to that soul.... And so I believe that the Lord has chosen this friar to bring many blessings to our Order."

Our Reformed Order! In this same letter to the king dated July 19, 1575, she wrote:

The grace of the Holy Spirit be always with Your Majesty. While much afflicted and praying to our Lord about the affairs of this holy order of our Lady and considering the great need there is that these initiatives God has taken in its regard not crumble, it occurred to me that the best safeguard for us would be that you realize what giving a solid foundation to this edifice entails; even the calced friars would benefit from the increase in numbers.[18]

Using logic and proceeding at full speed, *la Madre*, referring to her visions, swore obedience and submission to the one she now put in Christ's place, Father Jerónimo Gracián. He immediately took advantage of this. Without reflecting upon the consequences, he commanded her to found a convent in Seville. Seville was the turbulent capital of Andalusia, "the Babylon of the Great Sea," the richest and most licentious city in Spain. It was the great port to which entire convoys of caravels and galleons were bringing the gold, silver, and pearls of the New World! But this time, the Beas excuse of the uncertain border could not be used.

Was this order due to ignorance, rashness, or abuse of power on Gracián's part? The double authority, that of Rome and the king, had entrusted him with the Reform of the mitigated Andalusian Carmels. But not with creating new ones. The "cats," already humiliated by his nomination, saw in this decision a genuine provocation. Beas, that village on the contested border, was one thing. But Seville, where they were highly respected, was another matter entirely!

In the meantime, the nuncio in Madrid, paying no attention to the slander circulating at court—spread by the mitigated Carmelites regarding *la Madre's* attachment for her confessor—had extended Father Gracián's mission to Castile for the purpose of applying there, as in Andalusia, the reforms called for by the Council of Trent. To all intents and purposes, this action implicitly ratified Teresa's reforming mission and the choice she had made to designate Gracián by name as her deputy. But in Rome, the prior general of the Carmelites—of *all* the Carmelites—was fulminating. His Grace, Rubeo de Ravenna, had not been consulted either by Teresa or by the Vatican, by the nuncio of Spain or by the royal court.

In this dual nomination of Gracián, de Ravenna could see the outline of what he dreaded most: the division of the Carmelites into two provinces, one of observance (his own) and the other of strict observance. And he directed his anger against the person who supported this split—Teresa de Jesús—who, in addition, was now about to found a convent in Andalusia without his authorization!

On May 29, 1575, la Madre, surrounded by a handful of nuns "so courageous," said she, "that she could have risked going to the land of the Turks
with them," founded in Seville her thirteenth monastery. This foundation
was helped providentially by her brother Lorenzo, who had just disem-
barked there, laden with gold. María de San José, the most brilliant of her
daughters, instructed by Teresa in Toledo at Doña Luisa de la Cerda's and
then trained at the Carmel of Malagon, was named prioress. She has given
us this portrait of Teresa, in which she describes la Madre's face as her brother Lorenzo saw it when, for him alone, she lifted up her veil:

> She still retained her beauty at an advanced age. There was even something
> extraordinary about her face. The brow was wide, smooth, and handsome,
> the nostrils were curved and small, the nose somewhat prominent.
> Everything about her was marked by perfection. She was charming to see
> and hear. Her words and her gestures were full of gentleness and grace.

It was at that point that all heaven, or rather hell, broke loose. In
Chapter 28 of her *Foundations*, Teresa described the crisis as follows:

> The foundation in Seville, made more than four years ago, was the last
> one.[19] It was the last because of the great persecutions that broke out unex-
> pectedly against the Discalced friars and nuns. Although there had been
> many persecutions before, they were not so extreme. Now the whole under-
> taking was at the point of collapse.

What had happened? On the very day Teresa was founding a convent in
Seville, the General Chapter of the Carmelites, convened by Prior General
Rubeo de Ravenna on May 29, 1575, was taking place at Piacenza in Italy.
Did they discuss the irregular foundation at Beas, which had taken place on
February 24? It is likely that they did. Whatever the case may have been, a
large majority of mitigated Carmelites flew into a rage, especially against
Teresa's masculine foundations and at the untimely and humiliating inter-
ventions of Father Gracián, a Discalced named visitator by the nuncio,
Ormaneto, but not at all mandated by the hierarchy of the Carmelite Order.

La Madre's attempts to create a separate province of strict observance were
now being denounced. One can only be amazed that the crisis had not exploded earlier. The situation stemmed from the fact that Teresa did not want to
found a new Order. As St. Peter of Alcántara had done at first for the Franciscans, she wished to create small islands of strict observance attached to a
province, which could enjoy a certain autonomy within the existing Order.
Now, through their priors, who were General Chapter delegates, the mitigated Carmelites let it be known that they did not want these reforms.

To put an end to the confusion created by the priest visitators, the General Chapter and Father General Rubeo de Ravenna gave Jerónimo de Tostado, a mitigated Carmelite reputed for his authority, full power to act in Spain. The Chapter notified Teresa that she was to stop her foundations immediately; it obliged her to retire in a Castilian convent of her choice, under pain of being declared an apostate and excommunicated. Father Gracián was enjoined to return to his monastery at Pastrana under pain of being considered rebellious and in contempt of court. Lastly, all the monasteries founded without the authorization of Prior General Rubeo de Ravenna were ordered disbanded. These included Beas, Seville, and nine of the eleven monasteries of men!

Unfortunately for them, the mitigated Fathers had forgotten to consult the king and the pope, or at least his nuncio. It so happened that Philip II and Ormaneto, the nuncio, had remained in favor of Teresa's Reform, which followed the recommendations of the Council of Trent.

To add to the confusion, the Inquisition, warned by the vindictive princess of Éboli, began investigating the complaint of illuminism lodged against Teresa. They placed the *Book of Her Life* under suspicion and on February 15 sent three inquisitors flanked by police officers to inspect her new foundation in Seville. To these doctrinal charges were added other accusations from one of the novices there who, ill-suited to support the Rule of strict observance, had been refused profession by Teresa and nursed deep resentment over it. To avenge herself, she declared to the Inquisition that she had been the victim of ill treatment and that in this monastery the nuns acted like *Alumbrados*. Such accusations were, of course, little else but slander.

With the strength of the nuncio's mandate behind him, Father Gracián disregarded Prior General Rubeo de Ravenna's order. He rashly engaged in great activity in Andalusia. When he dared to appear at the mitigated Carmelite monastery of Seville, he was molested and interned. Teresa feared that he would be poisoned until a locution from the Lord reassured her as to her beloved son's fate. But Gracián's tactlessness had unleashed the protests of the mitigated Fathers of the province and the anger of Father Rubeo, an anger that inevitably extended to *la Madre*.

She attempted to placate the prior general, but her letter of humble submission reached him too late. The harm had been done.

Actually, things were going from bad to worse. Father Gracián, still supported by Nuncio Ormaneto, was refusing to submit to de Ravenna. For her part, Teresa would not disband the convent she had just founded in Seville amidst great material difficulties, and which had only been saved at the last minute by the arrival of her brother, Lorenzo de Cepeda.[20]

Fortunately, thanks to the support of Don Cristóbal de Rojas, archbishop of Seville, the new convent was solemnly inaugurated on June 3, 1576, with a large gathering of people on hand. Teresa wrote the following about the entire matter: "Here you see, daughters, the poor Discalced nuns honored by all. A little earlier it didn't seem that there would even be any water for them, although there is a great deal in the river."[21]

Deeply moved, la Madre knelt before the archbishop to receive his blessing. After giving it to her in front of the people, who were all rejoicing, he then knelt in turn before Teresa, asking her for the same favor.

Once the inauguration was over, Teresa took advantage of her brother's convoy returning to Ávila and left immediately to go into exile: Toledo. She carried in her pocket a letter from the bishop of Valladolid warning her that the Inquisition was searching for her writings, intent on causing her downfall. During an interrogation, visionary disciples of St. John of Ávila in Cordoba had referred to her. Her Dominican friend, Domingo Báñez, had also alerted her after receiving a note from the Inquisition in Seville.

La Madre was accused of "illuminism and practices foreign to Christian faith" and was suspected of being a heretic who professed "the superstitions and customs of the Illuminati of Estremadura." But she trembled only for Father Jerónimo Gracián, who was in hiding, fearful of the anger of the Fathers of the cloth and other "cats."

Had the winds turned against Teresa? The old nuncio Ormaneto was dying; in his place the Holy See was preparing to name Father Felipe Sega, a man openly hostile to la Madre's Reform, nuncio in Spain. Teresa summarized the state of affairs as follows:

> The discalced friars suffered...opposition on the part of almost all the Calced Fathers. These Fathers informed our Most Reverend Father General in such a way that even though he was a holy man and had given permission for all [sic] the monasteries...he was urged to oppose strongly any new foundations among the discalced friars. Toward the monasteries of the nuns, he was always well disposed. And so that I might not be helping the friars make foundations, he was induced into becoming displeased with me, which was the greatest trial I suffered in the work of these foundations, even though I have suffered many. On the one hand, very learned men who were my confessors would not agree that I should stop and counseled me to help toward the growth of the work, pointing out that I clearly rendered service to our Lord and helped toward the increase of our order; and on the other hand, going against the will of my superior [Rubeo de Ravenna] was like a death to me. For apart from the obligation I had

toward him because he was my superior, I loved him very tenderly and
there were many reasons for obeying him. It is true that even though I
wanted to please him by obeying this order, I could not because there were
apostolic visitors whom I was obliged to obey. A holy nuncio died
[Ormaneto] who greatly promoted virtue and, as a result, esteemed the
Discalced. Another nuncio arrived [Sega] who it seems had been sent by
God to test us in suffering.... He began to take seriously to favoring the
Calced and in conformity with the information they gave him about us he
was convinced that the right thing to do was to put a stop to these foundations. Thus, he began to act with the greatest severity, condemning those
he thought could oppose him by imprisoning them or sending them into
exile.[22]

Toledo: exile, blessed exile! The prospect of being shut in there in peace,
surrounded by a few chosen companions, calmed her. Imagine not having
to roam along the highways and byways, doing battle against one and all!
The menaces of the Inquisition did not affect Teresa. She wrote to Father
Gracián: "All the fear I previously had has left me, for I cannot feel it even
were this my desire."[23]

She remained haunted, however, by the prospect of failure, always alluding to "the basis..for a very quick collapse. Since the discalced didn't have
their own province, they were governed by the calced."[24]

CHAPTER 23

ℭempest over the ℭarmel

(1576–1578)

hy had Teresa chosen Toledo as the place of her exile and not Ávila, as her brother Lorenzo—who had organized the return to Castile and even rented a house—invited her to do? Because she liked Toledo, where her fifth foundation was located: "They have given me a cell set apart like a hermitage," she wrote in a letter. "[It is] very cheerful, and my health is good...."[1] In Toledo, the couriers functioned better than in Ávila. From there, she directed her foundations with a masterly hand as well as with the heart of a mother.

Never had she written so much. "I am laughing to myself to see how burdened I am with correspondence and yet spend time writing about trivia."[2] Everything can be found in these letters, from the selection of postulants and their dowries to the material from which the robes should be cut. On the manner of inflicting punishment: "By no means should you command or consent that any nun give another a slap (they also say pinches are given). Do not guide the nun with the rigor you saw at Malagon, for they are not slaves. Mortification should be used only for one's growth."[3]

She thanked María de San José for the gifts she had sent her from Seville: fresh tuna wrapped in bread, orange-flower water, candies of pink sugar, coarse woolen cloth for the nuns' habits. And she called to order that young sister of Seville who fasted too much and prayed instead of sleeping.

When her brother Lorenzo sought her advice, she told him to sleep for at least six hours, to avoid strong disciplines, to discontinue wearing a hairshirt during sleep, and above all to take care of his health. She directed him with vigilance in spiritual as well as temporal matters, entreating him also to

watch over the education of his two sons. "In everything, measure, moderation, a very pure form of love in which humility gives the cadence and har-
monizes the requirements."[4] One senses in this aging woman—sick and
exhausted in spite of her words to the contrary—a care for others that she did
not have for herself.

And always the search for perfection, which took precedence over material cares. Concerning the liturgical chant *recto tono:* "In no way do I think
they should sing anything until their number increases for this would bring
discredit on all."[5] "With regard to using linen and wool mixed together, I
would prefer that you wear linen when necessary. Otherwise you would be
opening the door to never observing the constitutions well."[6]

When she spoke of herself, her words were self-deprecating: "Now I am
beginning to be a nun."[7] And she was killing herself with writing and
answering letters: "...there were so many letters and business matters to
attend to that I kept writing letters until two in the morning."[8]

As though her correspondence were not enough, and in spite of her
headaches, she began, by order of Father Gracián, to write her chief work,
The Interior Castle.[9] Once when a visitor disturbed her, she simply said, "Sit
down and allow me to write what our Lord has just suggested to me."

She would say of this manuscript that it was far superior to her other
writings, because it was all about him.

Sometimes, without intending to, she slipped into her letters a
confidence about the dialogue she was having with Christ. To her brother
Lorenzo, whom she was teaching the prayer of quiet and who had already
received "favors" from on high, she wrote on January 17, 1577:

> I've begun to have raptures again, and this distresses me because they hap-
> pen in public sometimes. One came upon me at Matins. Trying to resist
> them doesn't help, nor can they be disguised. I'm so terribly embarrassed
> that I want to hide I don't know where. I plead with God not to let this
> happen to me in public. Beg this of God for me, because there are many
> disadvantages to experiencing them, and it doesn't seem to me that the
> prayer is better. I've been going around these days as though I were partial-
> ly drunk; at least I am well aware that the soul is in a good place. Since the
> faculties are not free, it is a difficult thing to have to attend to more than
> what the soul wishes.... I have said a great deal. The rest is not meant to be
> written or even spoken.[10]

For the moment a precarious calm still reigned over the Reformed
Carmelite monasteries. Father de Tostado, entrusted with the task of returning them to the ranks of the mitigated, had not yet arrived in Spain; he was
learning how to handle such matters in Portugal. However, this calm was

only on the surface, as is shown by a letter Teresa wrote to Father Mariano, dated March 15, 1577: "You must realize that all the devils are waging war against us, and that it is necessary to look for support only from God. This we do by obeying and suffering, and then he will take over."[11]

The stubborn will of Teresa and Gracián to maintain the foundations was encountering the anger of those men and women who felt threatened in their mitigated lifestyle. To Father Gracián, who took no account of slander against him, Teresa wrote: "Time will bring you to lose a little of your simplicity, which I certainly understand to be that of a saint."[12] In a letter of November 26, 1576, she mentioned to him the fate of the little monastery in Paterna, the first mitigated convent to which three Discalced nuns had been sent to apply the Reform. Threatened with death upon their arrival, they were soon crushed as the worst sort of calumnies were heaped upon them. Teresa had written in her letter to Gracián: "Let me know on what grounds the accusation was made against the nun who is a virgin and bearing a child. I think a charge like that is the greatest stupidity."[13]

In Seville, too, Teresa had felt the breeze of the bullet whiz by her Reform: "I am told they don't have enough food to eat.... It's a harsh trial to be so alone."[14] She now knew that she would be unable to impose her Reform from within the old Carmelite Order. She would have to build something new. "I will dedicate my life to our [being] made a separate province, because all the harm comes from our not being separate...."[15] She exhorted Father Gracián to visit all the convents of the Reform each year to ensure that the Rule of the Order was being followed, for "the women we want to govern must understand that there is a commander who will not allow himself to be swayed."

But was Gracián capable of filling such a role? He was not the best, as was John of the Cross, but he was the only one in a position to attempt doing it. And whatever Teresa may have thought of their relationship, she remained humbly submissive to him: "Ask God to make me a genuine Carmelite nun, for better late than never."[16]

However, her anguish can be detected in her correspondence of November 1576 with Father Gracián in Seville: "I don't think Paul is suffering anything in comparison with the fear he suffered on account of the angels."[17] Teresa believed that she had to use coded names in case her correspondence was intercepted. Paul, as we have seen, is Father Gracián, and by the *angels* she means the inquisitors. In other correspondence, she used the *Great Angel* for Gaspar de Quiroga, the Grand Inquisitor. The *cicadas* stand for the mitigated Carmelites, so named because of their chatter. The *butterflies* are the Discalced nuns; the *eagles,* the Discalced monks. The *cats* and the *night owls* designate the Calced, the Fathers of the cloth. *Methuselah* is the old nuncio Ormaneto, and Teresa is *poor Laurencia* or *Angela.*

And yet, despite the threats surrounding her Reform, she was reassured: "It's strange the way I feel, for nothing that happens can trouble me, so deeply rooted is the feeling of certitude about a succesful outcome."[18] In another letter, she added:

> I think the desire is being accomplished for which these monasteries were founded, which was to pray to God to help those who struggle for his honor and service, since we women count for nothing. When I consider the perfection of these nuns [of Pastrana], I am not suprised by what they obtain from God.[19]

IN JULY 1577, COMMANDED to do so by Father Gracián, Teresa overrode her relegation and left Toledo for Ávila in order to place her monastery of St. Joseph under Gracián's authority. Nicolás Ormaneto, the nuncio who supported her, had just died. How would his successor react?

Taking advantage of the fact that Father Gracián's authority was contested by some Discalced monks, the mitigated Carmelites mounted a plot that Teresa immediately denounced: "For this purpose they have made use of two discalced friars," she wrote to the king, hoping to put a stop to this offensive. One of the two monks was, of all people, the famous Baltasar de Jesús (the engineer, Nieto), one of the founders of the male Carmel of Pastrana. "Turbulent, ambitious, and harsh, he could not stand Father Gracián,"[20] writes Marcelle Auclair. Speaking cryptically, the two monks were accusing Gracián of inappropriate intimacy with the nuns under his responsibility. This was a false accusation. But we can imagine the sadistic joy taken by the other mediocre monks of the cloth, who gleefully swallowed this so-called fault on the part of the one who intended to reform them.

Teresa, who had imposed a strict enclosure, grilles, and veil, remained hypersensitive to this problem of the relationships between Carmelite monks and nuns. She wrote to Father Gracián, making clear how a visitator should act:

> ...If some friar should have to stay there, your paternity ought to advise him strongly not to spend much time talking to the nuns. Look, *mi padre,* this is very necessary. And I wouldn't even want the licentiate to do so, for even though he is so good, such goodness can give rise to bad judgements in people with malicious minds, especially in small towns, and everywhere else as well.

> Believe me, the more you see that your daughters are cut off from such very special relationships, even though they are very holy ones, the better it is, even for the peace of the house.[21]

The ideal situation would have been for the nuns to have elderly priests full of wisdom at their disposal. But there was only one of these, the good Father Julian de Ávila, Teresa's traveling companion. On the other hand, speaking of him, she once stated: "God preserve us from confessors who are too old."[22] As a further measure of prudence, Teresa reminded her nuns about the necessity of the veil. "There is no reason to receive a religious without being veiled. Matters of the soul can be discussed without raising the veil." And "the nuns should in no way offer anyone something to eat in the parlor, for this becomes a great disturbance for them...and except for you [Father Gracián] (for you are not to be included in such considerations, when there is a need), they should do so only reluctantly."[23] Teresa feared that the *cats* would poison him during one of his canonical visits, since he was still invested by the nuncio with a reforming mission concerning the mitigated Carmelites! On November 19, 1576, she had even written to the prioress of Seville: "I don't think it even entered my mind to say that he not eat there at the monastery [of the mitigated], for I see that the need is great. I only say that outside meal times he not go there often, lest this be noticed and he be prevented from ever going there.... For the love of God tell him to be careful."[24] When he went there, he only ate "boiled eggs served in their shells."[25]

Naturally, she had to react in the face of the calumnies circulated by the *cats*. On September 18, 1577, she wrote to the king from Ávila:

> For love of God I beg Your Majesty not to allow such infamous testimony to be presented to tribunals.... For more than seventeen years I suffered alone from these fathers of the cloth, and I no longer knew how to bear it; my own weak efforts were insufficient.... I reflect that since the Lord puts up with my indiscreet complaints, you will also.[26]

The two false witnesses later retracted their testimony, admitting that they had been forced into giving it. But the harm had been done.

THE NEW NUNCIO REPLACING Father Ormaneto—whose death had occurred on June 18, 1577—finally arrived in Madrid. Why was Father Felipe Sega so hostile to *la Madre*, whom he would denigrate as "a restless gadabout, disobedient and contumacious"? It seems that he had been brainwashed in Rome by Cardinal Filippo Buoncompagni, a nephew of the pope, who was an influential prelate and the traditional protector of the Calced monks.

El Tostado, as Teresa called the vicar general of the Calced Carmelites, had also arrived in Spain, and the "Fathers of the cloth" could now deploy their offensive, which sought to put an end to the Teresian Reform.

In Ávila, a new election of the prioress of the Incarnation had explosive consequences. The Council of Trent had required a regular vote of the professed nuns, any other compelled nomination imposed by superiors or founders being illegal.

But the Council had not prescribed a secret ballot. A majority of the nuns wanted Teresa as prioress again, although she had declared that she would not accept the position after having referred the matter to Gracián: "I have asked Your Paternity if he has the authority to give me the order and I have not received an answer. You should know that I will do anything to refuse the position. Please be charitable enough to write me *peremptorily* to tell me what I must do; you cannot write these things so vaguely."

La Madre was losing her sense of moderation with her superior. It is true that she was, as she said, "old and tired,"[27] and they wanted to place her once again at the head of the Incarnation, that overcrowded, ungovernable monastery that, after her departure, had gone back to its bad habits, reducing to powerlessness the small, fervent nucleus that she had formed.

Father de Tostado intervened to sabotage the elections. He sent Father Gutiérrez de la Magdalena, then provincial prior of Castile, "with threats of great censures and excommunications"[28] intended for those who would dare vote for Teresa. The Incarnation being the largest Carmel of Spain, its rallying to the Reform risked influencing other mitigated communities. The provincial assembled the choir nuns.

"Sisters, it is forbidden to elect anyone who is a stranger to this monastery."

A voice arose: "*La Madre* Teresa is not a stranger. She made her profession in this convent where she lived for twenty-five years. She left her dowry here, an annual pension."

On October 7, the voting took place, presided over by Father Gutiérrez—resulting in fifty-five votes for Teresa and forty-four for Ana de Toledo, the candidate of the Calced. But the provincial ignored the count. "As each vote for me was given to him, he excommunicated the nun, and he cursed," wrote Teresa to María de San José, the prioress at Seville, "and pounded and beat the ballots with his fist and burned them. He has left the nuns excommunicated for fifteen days now without their being allowed to hear Mass or enter the choir, even when the Divine Office is being said. And they cannot speak to anyone, not even their own confessors or parents."[29]

Father Gutiérrez annulled the vote and convened the community the next day for another round of voting, which turned out to be similar to the first. Called in for reinforcement, Father de Tostado decreed that the minority candidate had been elected, to which the rebels declared that they would only obey her as a subprioress. "All are stunned to see something like this which offends everyone," wrote Teresa to the Seville prioress. "I would gladly pardon the nuns if they would leave me in peace, for I have no desire to find myself in that Babylon."[30] Tongues were wagging briskly with malicious gossip. As previously mentioned, one of the confessors at the Incarnation was none other than John of the Cross, restricted, with Father Germán de San Matías, to the small house built for them against the monastery wall by Teresa's order. Poor John and poor Teresa, who aspired only to "taste the delicious fruit of forgetting oneself and all things!" The *cats* of the mitigated Carmel at Ávila, who had been the established confessors of the Incarnation, accused the two Discalced chaplains of having bribed the professed nuns to be favorable to Teresa. In this way, the *cats* were plotting to eliminate these two reforming monks and retrieve their once exclusive position. But a crowd of friends and relatives stood guard in front of the Discalced monks' cabin.

After some time calm seemed to return, leaving the two Discalced to their solitude. Teresa, who had received an order forbidding her to leave her monastery of St. Joseph, intervened in vain to have the excommunications pronounced against the rebel nuns lifted.

Father Hernando Maldonado, prior of the Calced Carmelites of Toledo, then announced his visit to Ávila. He claimed that he had been entrusted with the function of arbitrating the conflict. This was a trap.

Suddenly, during the night of the third to the fourth of December, a troop of *alguazils*, armed policemen, surrounded the hut, led by Father Maldonado and several mitigated Carmelites. He called out: "By virtue of the decree of the Piacenza Chapter, and acting under the orders of His Greatness Don Jerónimo de Tostado, vicar general of the Carmelites of Spain, I have requisitioned the secular arm to place you under arrest. Father John of the Cross will be imprisoned in Toledo, Father Germán at San Pablo de la Moraleja with our Carmelites of the observance. There, you will be judged according to the rules of our Constitutions."

Imprisoned by the *alguazils* with the mitigated Carmelites of Ávila while awaiting his transfer to Toledo, John of the Cross managed to escape before dawn. He went back to his cabin, where he locked himself in and began to methodically tear up the letters and documents concerning the Reform, burning some papers and swallowing others! He then gave himself up to Father Maldonado, who brought him to Toledo bound like a robber on the back of a mule.

An indignant Teresa wrote to the king: "[John of the Cross] is so great a servant of our Lord that the nuns are truly edified, and this city is amazed by the remarkable amount of good he has done there, and so they consider him a saint, and in my opinion he is one and has been one all his life."

She then went on to complain bitterly about Father Maldonado:

> ...he is more capable than the others of making martyrs.... The whole city is truly scandalized.... I feel very sad to see these confessors in the hands of those [calced] friars.... I would consider the confessors better off if they were held by the Moors, who perhaps would show more compassion.... I beg Your Majesty for the love of our Lord to issue orders for them to set him free at once.... Otherwise, I don't know where things will end up, because we have no other help on earth.[31]

Three days later, she wrote to her Jesuit friend, Gaspar de Salazar: "...for more than three months, it seems, hosts of demons have joined against the discalced friars and nuns. They have stirred up so many persecutions and calumnies...that all we can do is take refuge in God."[32]

She did not know at the time that even this holy Jesuit, harassed by the mitigated monks, had repudiated her.

Judged "rebellious and recalcitrant," John of the Cross had been transferred to Toledo. During the voyage, a young muleteer had offered him the chance to escape, but he had refused, "preferring this opportunity to suffer for the Lord to liberty."

In Toledo he was thrown into a dungeon where he could barely move, small though he was. He was also deprived of food, with blows and insults repeatedly heaped upon him. Flogged three times a week in front of the community in the refectory, John remained impassive and unshakable, awaiting death, always remaining true to himself: "I sank so low that I finally found what I was seeking." Perfect detachment in solitude, silence, suffering, and that great adventure that is the interior life.

In his adversity, John of the Cross had the good fortune to be assigned a new guard, Juan de Santa María. Touched by John's humility, this lay brother took care of him and even gave him something to write with, which resulted in perhaps the most beautiful poems ever written on the love of God: *The Spiritual Canticle* and *The Dark Night of the Soul.*

Placed in an awkward position by this whole affair, the king was not reacting. His silence had become deafening. In frustration Teresa turned toward heaven, but heaven also remained silent. Then a new mishap occurred: *la Madre* fractured her left arm, falling on the stairs of St. Joseph, an accident from which she never fully recovered. She was now a crippled old woman, suffering atrociously, who could not move about or even dress herself without the assistance of her faithful Ana.[33]

FIRST DAYS, THEN WEEKS and months passed. Sega, the nuncio, had ratified the election of the minority prioress while lifting the excommunication of the rebels, who persisted in their choice nonetheless. They received no news of John of the Cross. It was said that his coarse wool habit had been torn from him so he could be dressed in the cloth robe of the Calced.

Gracián had been ordered by Tostado to retire to his monastery of origin in Pastrana. In reality, he was living in hiding in a grotto, like a hermit. After what had happened to John of the Cross, he feared for his life. He was not even giving news of himself, which irritated *la Madre*: "Your fears...are like the fears of a man."[34] She then gently complained about him whom she still considered to be an angel: "Love, wherever it is, does not sleep in this way," she wrote him.

In August of 1578, she was almost relieved to see that Nuncio Sega had taken away his powers of apostolic visitator, which were visibly above his capacities. Teresa being banned from office, he remained, nonetheless, in spite of the nuncio's decisions, the unofficial superior of the men and women Discalced Carmelites.

Then events started to move forward. The Royal Council abandoned Father Gracián and ordered him to submit. On August 18, John of the Cross, indomitable and aided by his compassionate jailer, escaped from the convent of Toledo after nine months of incarceration, during which the Calced had tortured and humiliated him. He was "so wasted and disfigured that he seemed an image of death." He took refuge with the Discalced Carmelites of Toledo, who when they first saw him believed they were seeing a ghost. They immediately alerted Teresa; by this time she had believed him to be dead.

On September 4, death struck elsewhere, taking the prior general of the Carmelites, Rubeo de Ravenna, who died still convinced of his daughter's disobedience. With his death, all hope of reconciliation with the Fathers of the cloth disappeared.

Should they break away? Not worrying about the persecutions, the nine masculine convents of the Teresian Reform gathered in Chapter at Almodovar and unilaterally decided to establish themselves as an independent province, thus provoking the anger of Sega, the nuncio. He ordered that Gracián be imprisoned. Granting himself the government of the Discalced monasteries, Sega decreed their complete submission to the Calced superiors.

On December 24, at the convent of St. Joseph of Ávila, the envoys of the nuncio delivered his terrible decree to Teresa. He was submitting the Calced and the Discalced to the provincial and the superior of the mitigated Rule in Castile and Andalusia. Teresa was to be confined for life in a monastery that would be indicated to her.

"It was," she wrote, "a very trying morning. Our friends were terrified and I myself very distressed."[35] According to witnesses, she remained in a state of collapse for the entire day, faced with the ruins of her work, sustained only by Ana, her assistant. As night approached, sensing that Teresa was about to faint, Ana begged her to eat a little food before facing the great nocturnal Office of Christmas. *La Madre* agreed to follow her to the refectory, but she remained unmoving before her plate.

Suddenly, the faithful lay nun, who later gave testimony regarding this, saw Christ standing next to the table, wearing a linen robe. He broke the bread on Teresa's plate, then fed her as one feeds a child. As he fed her the pieces, he said to her, "Take courage, daughter; this is nothing."

Teresa came to life again. Afterwards she chanted the Christmas Office with her sisters, and from that day on, serenity never left her. "We will never know more beautiful days than those during which we suffer without being guilty," she once wrote,[36] for "God wants his elect to feel all their misery."[37]

Unfortunately, the situation of the Reformed was becoming more and more precarious. Teresa herself expected to be excommunicated and soon locked up in a convent of mitigated nuns, a fate that Fathers Gracián, Mariano, and Antonio de Jesús had been subjected to, being confined with the Calced of Madrid. Reduced to powerlessness, Father Gracián was then relegated to the Calced of Alcalá. In January 1579, Sega even deposed María de San José, the indomitable prioress of Seville who had refused to hand over Teresa's correspondence.

How had it come to this? "It was an enormous misunderstanding born of a conflict of duties," writes Father Jean Abiven charitably. But other factors contributed as well, such as the contradictory interventions of the Church through its successive nuncios, Ormaneto and Sega, as well as hesitations on the part of the king, who was favorable to the Reform but jealous of his right over the nominations. Matters were further exacerbated by the imprudence or recklessness of the Reformed Carmelites (especially Gracián), which turned the poorly informed prior general, Rubeo de Ravenna, against them. Then, too, there were the slander and intrigues of the mitigated Carmelites: the petty opposition of mediocre persons who were attached to their privileges and were religious in name only, who had little concern for perfection and were furious at seeing a "frail female" attempt to reform them. Finally, the hidden personal rivalries among the Discalced superiors themselves played some part in causing the situation to degenerate as it had.

Teresa expected to be imprisoned at any moment, unless she went back on everything she had done, which—God forbid—she would never do! This temptation had crossed Father Gracián's mind, and to it she had replied: "It would not be right to abandon the Virgin in these difficult times. We would not be fleeing from trials but sinking into them, for they will end, with the grace of the Lord, while those of another order might last an entire lifetime."[38]

Teresa's hope of seeing the two Carmelite branches separated seemed to be destroyed, and yet she retained an unswerving confidence. One day, in the middle of a conversation with Father Diego de Yepes, she entered into ecstasy. When she came out of it, she told him in a firm voice: "We still have a great deal more to suffer, but the Order will not be diminished."

He saw this clearly as a prophecy.

CHAPTER 24

"Happy the Enamored Heart"

(1579–1582)

eresa wrote: "Happy the enamored heart, / Thought centered on God alone, / Renouncing every creature for Him / finding in Him glory and contentment. / Living forgetful of self, / In God is all its intention, / Happy and so joyfully it journeys / Through waves of this stormy sea."[1]

The storm eventually abated. "Test everything," St. Paul had said, "retain what is good" (1 Thes 5:21).

Faced with the papacy's procrastination, the king finally decided to intervene. Teresa's letters had moved him, as had also the appeals of the great friends of the Reform: the Jesuit, Pablo Hernández; the Count de Tendilla, governor of Granada; the Dorias, influential friends of Doña Luisa de la Cerda; and Jerónimo Gracián's two brothers, who were court secretaries.

"We are outraged, Sire, by so many abuses and injustices done to *la Madre*, Teresa de Jesús, and to the Fathers of the Reformed Carmel."

The king summoned Sega, the nuncio, and berated him: "I have been informed of the war that the Calced are waging on the Discalced of the Carmel, who have, nevertheless, always demonstrated austerity, perfection, and fidelity to the crown."

"Perhaps, Sire..."

"Father de Tostado has never been able to furnish me with testimonies from the Discalced repudiating *la Madre* Teresa."

"No doubt, Sire..."

"I am told that Your Paternity dislikes the Discalced. I want peace in my kingdom. Show yourself to be favorable to virtue. That is the only criterion you should retain from now on."

270

"Your Majesty's wishes are commands."[2]

In her correspondence, Teresa confirmed that she owed the end of the persecutions to the king: "When the king learned what was going on, he took our side and did not want the nuncio to be the sole judge of our cause. He named four assessors to examine our rights." Teresa had already dealt with one of these men as apostolic visitator, the Dominican Pedro Hernández.

On April 1, 1579, the nuncio bowed to authority. Changing his policy, he liberated the Reformed Carmel from obedience to the mitigated prelates. The excommunications were lifted and the persecutions ceased. But they were still a great distance from being recognized as a separate province, which the king had not required as the foundress had hoped he would. Instead, the Reformed Carmels were placed under the jurisdiction of a mitigated Carmelite. Father Ángel de Salazar, the former provincial prior of Castile, had supported Teresa and even imposed her as prioress of the Incarnation.

Through this diplomatic compromise, the unity of the Carmel seemed to be preserved. Relieved to see the noose that was strangling her loosened, *la Madre* was exultant. Philip II was becoming for her *mi amigo el rey* (my friend, the king). To her close friends, she declared: "Whoever does not know all that I suffered during that time cannot imagine the jubilation that flooded my heart."

Father de Salazar was now the vicar general of the Discalced. Father Gracián, who did not breathe a word, had only limited powers. He had not shown any courage during his detention in Madrid, even contemplating renouncing the Carmel by going over to the Augustinians, which he did not do because of a stern admonition from his own mother...and a threat of death from the Count de Tendilla!

Fortunately, the Discalced friars now came out of their prisons or hiding places. John of the Cross, having survived his Toledo ordeal thanks to the protection of a canon at the cathedral, who hid him, took over as director of Baeza College, located near the Discalced community of Carmelites in Beas. "Thank God who wanted you to have him close by," wrote Teresa to her prioress Ana de Jesús. "He is a celestial and divine man. You have a great treasure in this saint."

WITH PEACE NOW REIGNING ANEW over the Carmel—each group in its own monastery—*la Madre* took up her pilgrim's staff once again. "I would go to the end of the world if obedience demanded it,"[3] she once said. She went forward with new foundations: Villanueva de la Jara, Palencia, Soria, and Burgos! Looking at a map, one sees how these cities are spread throughout the two Castiles!

Teresa had to hasten in order to consolidate and extend her work before her death, the date of which she was said to have known. Whether she actually knew or not, she only had to listen to her body to know that it was soon going to fail her. According to some of her biographers,[4] she was suffering from an advanced stage of uterine cancer. And so she was meeting death head-on!

At the end of June 1579, when taking leave of her daughters in Ávila, her niece Teresita, and her most faithful friends, Francisco de Salcedo and Doña Guiomar, she cut through the emotional atmosphere by laughing: "Look at her, the poor little old woman! En route for Medina, Valladolid, Malagon, Alba de Tormes, Salamanca. I tell you, it makes me laugh—for I feel that I have the courage to do a whole lot more."

She took to the road again, heading toward Malagon in New Castile. In February 1580, while crossing a market town in Mancha and waiting to attend Mass there, she was called to task by a crowd stirred up by some mitigated Carmelites who had not yet accepted the reconciliation effectuated by the king.

"Get out, sorceress!"

In Malagon, she found peace again in her dovecote—God's own. The saint was cheered, the sorceress forgotten! There she completed and opened the new convent, whose site she had found and whose modifications she had decided upon down to the slightest detail. She would have liked to prolong her stay, but an order from above sent her back on the road once again. She headed east on the Valencia road toward Villanueva de la Jara. There, on the Mancha border, nine *beata*, as fervent as they were ignorant, enamored of perfection, were impatiently awaiting the habit of the Discalced along with supervision and instruction. Teresa had never been so close to the mythic Mediterranean, which she would never actually see.

This foundation having been made, she set out again on February 21, 1580, crossing Spain from east to west en route to Palencia in order to found a convent in that city. On her way there at the end of March, she stopped in Toledo, where she spent a few days with Father Gracián. She took advantage of her stay to meet the cardinal archbishop, Don Gaspar de Quiroga, and ask him for the authorization to found a monastery in Madrid. As previously mentioned, Cardinal de Quiroga was also the Grand Inquisitor General of Spain. He had in his possession Teresa's most contested work, *The Book of Her Life*, which the princess of Éboli had sent to the Inquisition in hopes of having Teresa condemned. *La Madre* trembled when the cardinal alluded to it: "This book has been presented to the Inquisition and its doctrine examined with the utmost rigor. As for me, I have read it in its entirety, and I maintain that its doctrine is very sound, very true, and beneficial."

And then a miracle took place. This fearsome prelate, whose long nose, bitter mouth, and severe, disillusioned look had been painted by El Greco, actually smiled, saying, "I am delighted to know you, *Madre*, and have wanted very much to do so. See in me your chaplain. I will help you as much as will be necessary, and I beg you to recommend me always to God."[5] And he blessed her, promising to do all that she asked regarding the foundation in Madrid. But could she manage to do it? Her health continued to deteriorate. She wrote on April 2, 1580:

> Since Holy Thursday I have had one of the worst attacks ever of paralysis and heart pains. I've had a fever up until now—which still hasn't left—and I am in such a state of weakness that I accomplished a great deal in managing to stay at the grille with Padre [Nicolás], who has been here two days now and whose presence made me happy.[6]

Was she going to die in Toledo? She wrote on May 5:

> Blessed be God that you are in good health, for my illness no longer amounts to anything, as I have written to you. Only weakness remains, for I went through a terrible month, which I spent mostly on my feet. Since I am used to dealing with chronic pain, I thought that in spite of feeling quite sick, it was possible to put up with it. Certainly, I thought I was dying, although I didn't completely believe this, nor did whether I die or live matter to me. God grants me this favor, which I consider a great one, for I remember the fear I used to have at other times.[7]

Death struck elsewhere. In a vision of July 4, 1580, she learned that her favorite brother, Lorenzo de Cepeda, who lived in retirement near Ávila, had passed away. She murmured: "I am three years older than he and yet I'm still living."[8] Of this beloved brother, who had been a brilliant conquistador before becoming a skilled politician and whom she had converted, Teresa had written: "His prayer was continual because he always walked in the presence of God and His Majesty granted him so many favors that sometimes I was amazed. He was very inclined toward penance and so he did more than I would have desired him to do."[9]

Teresa was tempted to let herself go. Once again, her old heart, which bore the mark of stigmata, seemed to be giving out. Sometimes, given her paralyzed tongue, she could not speak, nor hear because of the buzzing in her ears. The vital energy that had carried her along for so many years seemed to be withdrawing from her exhausted body. Was she not, at long last, entitled to rest?

And yet by the end of 1580 she was again on her way toward Palencia, north of Old Castile. She stayed in passing at her convent of Valladolid, where an influenza epidemic was raging and nearly carried her off. All of Spain was being ravaged by this epidemic, which killed many of her friends: her former confessor, Baltasar Álvarez; the holy gentleman, Francisco de Salcedo; Father Pablo Hernández.

All this was too much for her to bear. Deeply shaken by the loss of those to whom she was most attached, sick unto death, and still more distressed at being deprived of action, she felt herself losing courage and confidence.

Suddenly, a voice arose. It was he, Jesus, the Beloved! Was he coming to take her at last? No. The voice was gentle, persuasive: "What are you afraid of? When have I failed you? I am the same; do not fail to make those two foundations."[10]

Palencia and Burgos. And there she was, setting out once more, this time on the back of a mule on the roads of Spain, which were alternately waterlogged and frozen. She finally arrived in Palencia on December 28, 1580. The bishop there, Álvaro de Mendoza, who had been her prelate in Ávila, affectionately welcomed her. The *corregidor*, or chief magistrate, was opposed to the foundation despite Father Gracián's urgent interventions. But faced with such a woman, he capitulated: "*La Madre* Teresa carries within herself the breath of the Royal Council of God. Even against our wish, we must comply with all that she wants."

Father Gracián had left to take part in an important General Chapter of the Discalced at Alcalá de Henares. They would be adopting the definitive Constitutions to which *la Madre* attached so much importance, for Christ had told her that the convents would flourish if they respected the Constitutions. Working day and night, she had put the finishing touches on the text, which was enriched by the wealth of her long experience with the Carmels and all that it entailed: precisions concerning the slightest details as well as the essential, a "very resolute strength" to live in God, from him, and by him in joy as in sadness.

Teresa would be able to enjoy the crowning of her work when she finally received Pope Gregory XIII's brief in Palencia. Our Lady of Carmel of the strict observance, detached from obedience to the mitigated, was now constituted as a separate province. It already included twenty-three monasteries. The priors were invited to assemble a Chapter in order to elect their provincial.

La Madre retired to her cell to write about the great news to María de San José, her prioress in Seville. She ended her letter with these words: "At last, I can speak like St. Simeon,[11] for I have seen the Order of the Virgin exactly as I desired it. Do not ask God any longer to let me live, but that he grant me to go to my rest for I am no longer useful."[12]

Discreetly, Ana, her faithful assistant, opened the door to the cell. Teresa had put down her pen. Eyes lifted toward heaven, she was moaning softly, not from suffering but from joy. From her face emanated rays of light.

But she was worn out, constantly sick. If she died, who would replace her as a unifying element of the reformed monasteries? They were now scattered throughout Spain, but, as she knew, they would spread to other countries in Europe. Should it be a man or a woman to take her place? A woman was unthinkable. Teresa constituted a striking exception.

Yet one of the nuns had the makings of a foundress: Ana de Lobera (Ana de Jesús), who had been referred to as "the queen of women" before her entrance in the Carmel. Teresa herself once declared: "Ana does the work and I get the credit."[13] She would found, with John of the Cross, the Carmel of Granada and later those of Madrid, Paris, and Brussels. There was also María de Salazar (María de San José), the most cultured of the nuns, who was prioress of Seville. She was one of Teresa's closest friends and someone with whom *la Madre* sometimes quarreled. "I have written her some terrible letters, but it is as though one were striking steel."[14] She even accused María de San José of a certain craftiness regarding some questionable accounts she had sent. However, Teresa had written to her: "After my death, and even in my lifetime, I would like you to be chosen as foundress, for you know more than I do and you are better [than I am]."[15]

Among the men, Teresa saw *no one* capable of taking the helm. John of the Cross was the greatest at the spiritual level. "Consider him as my other self," she wrote to the prioress of Caravaca, announcing his coming to visit her. "He will console you for his is a soul to which God communicates his spirit." But John soared so high that he would have been incapable of undertaking the procedures necessary to establish a foundation. It would be difficult for him to come down to the level of human and material management, which at times calls for moderation. Without moderation, a foundation is but a bonfire that blazes in the night and then sputters out.

Jerónimo Gracián? "He is fat and healthy," Teresa had written in all seriousness in 1579 at the end of the terrible trial. This sounds like a reproach.

Gracián had evidently disappointed her deeply. In spite of this, he retained her tenderness and trust: "Know how to be master of yourself and avoid excesses; benefit from the experience of others." She revealed her anguish to him in what seems like an appeal: "I am physically isolated with no one to sustain me."

There was also Father Antonio de Heredia (Antonio de Jesús), who called himself the first of the Reformed Carmelites and who was, in any case, the "patriarch" at the age of seventy-two. But Teresa had no confidence in him, seeing him as nothing more than Gracián's assistant. This made him angry, as he was higher born, the oldest, and the best in his own estimation. Thin-skinned and vindictive, he diverged from Teresa on how to govern the Order. Learned but authoritarian, he lacked an understanding of psychology and had no practical sense. And, what was more serious, he was wanting in true spirituality. Additionally, Teresa had judged him to be both pusillanimous and too authoritarian in his position as prior at Los Remedios.

Finally, there was Nicolás Doria. His name appears in 1581 in the *Foundations* with regard to the one in Soria. He would soon become prior of Pastrana. When Gracián was imprisoned, Doria discreetly assumed his responsibilities. Teresa gave Doria lengthy reports on the administration of convents, the choice of the prioress, and the role of the confessor, as though she wanted to prepare him to replace Gracián definitively in the event that it became necessary to do so.

The career path of this extraordinary monk was rather unusual. Born of the noble Doria family of Genoa, which had given a famous admiral to Francis I of France and then to Charles V, what would he do with the talents that the Creator had showered upon him? A remarkable businessman, he had made a fortune in Seville in foreign exchange operations by the time he was thirty. In that city, he also formed a friendship with Archbishop Cristóbal de Rojas, the great lord who had knelt before Teresa.

De Rojas had jeopardized the finances of his archdiocese through risky speculations. He entrusted the management of finances to Doria, who worked wonders. Informed of this, King Philip called him to his court. Later, to thank him for his good advice, the king offered him...a bishopric. Doria's career seemed to be all mapped out for him.

Fascinated by the Teresian Reform, however, he refused the bishopric, and at the age of thirty-seven he took the habit of the Discalced Carmelites from the very hand of Father Gracián and made profession at Pastrana under the name of Fray Nicolás de Jesús María. "...It seems clear our Lord chose him so that he might help that Order during these very troublesome times of persecution," wrote Teresa in the *Foundations*, recognizing in him the man for secret transactions.

Sure enough, in 1579, at the very height of the difficulties, utilizing his powerful relationships, he discreetly intervened in Rome and at the court of Madrid to plead in favor of the Reform. "I brought with me...a man of great perfection and discretion," wrote Teresa. "...We corresponded frequently ...and we dealt with suitable courses of action. It was during this time that I had experience of his perfection and discretion. Thus he is among those in this order whom I love much in the Lord and esteem highly."[16]

"This good Nicolás," as she would always call him, acted with the cunning of a Doria. While all the Discalced friars had been interned or exiled, Doria acted with impunity at the heart of Spain. The better to deceive adversaries of the Reform, he resided at the mitigated Carmel in Madrid, where the monks believed he was a renegade! "He is so discreet," added Teresa, "that while he was staying in the monastery of the Calced Carmelites in Madrid, as though for other business reasons, he dealt with the affairs of the discalced friars in such a disguised manner that the Calced friars never knew about it, and so they didn't bother him."[17]

But the man who would one day take over the Discalced Carmelites for now remained in the background. At the General Chapter, held in Alcalá de Henares, it was Jerónimo Gracián who was elected provincial prior on March 3, 1581, with a one-vote majority over Antonio de Heredia. This was thanks to Teresa's influence; upon hearing the announcement of this election she exclaimed: "And this for me was one of the great joys and satisfactions of my life."[18]

WOULD SHE NOW BE ABLE to rest at last? No! In June 1581, we find her in Soria, in the north of Old Castile, where she had been called to found a convent by Doña Beatriz de Beamonte y Navarra with the enthusiastic support of the bishop.

Upon her return to Ávila, she learned of her election as prioress of St. Joseph. Teresa tried to recuse herself, but Father Gracián ordered her to accept the position.

This monastery was in decline due to lack of revenues. Famine was rife, as in many other Spanish convents, because alms had become scarce. The accounts show that the work of the nuns (spinning and sewing) only brought in eleven *reales* per day, while food alone required eighty; alms accounted for only thirty *reales*, while the price of an egg could reach two *reales*.

Teresa, who had asked for voluntary poverty and even precariousness ("we must always live from alms and possess no annuity"), had already tried to meet these problems head-on by obtaining the pledge of an important donation from her brother Lorenzo. But after his death, the family contested the gift. And Father Gracián was reserving the Order's meager liquidities for the printing of the Constitutions.

That is when she saw John of the Cross arrive in Ávila with a caravan of carts and mules. He was coming to get her to go and found a convent of the Discalced in Granada! But it seemed to Teresa that it was more urgent for her to establish a foundation in Burgos, where Doña Catalina de Tolosa, a rich donor who had already entrusted her with four of her own daughters, was calling her. For the Granada foundation, Teresa sent Ana de Jesús, whom she had chosen as her delegate, and another experienced nun.

Before separating, never to see each other again, Teresa going north and John south, they lingered together for one last time. Did she give him advice on moderation? The terrible ordeal of Toledo had matured him. "There emanated from him a greater majesty than in any man on earth," one of his Carmelites said of him. John may have read to her one of his poems written while in prison. These inspired texts, which were beginning to nourish the spiritual life of the Reformed Carmelites, sang the joy of being poor and powerless before God but fulfilled by him beyond all desire. "O guiding night! / O night more lovely than the dawn! / O night that has united / The Lover with His beloved / Transforming the beloved in her Lover."[19] He had not changed. For him, the only thing that counted was union with God, *endiosamiento;* only total deprivation and detachment from things, beings, and finally from oneself could allow one the hope of attaining such union. But this time the detachment Teresa demanded of him was too harsh. He left her, deeply saddened that she was refusing to accompany him to Granada when he had prepared everything and was looking forward to the joy of founding a convent with her.

Teresa watched him go away in the raw light of dawn. Although exhausted, her thoughts were already in Burgos, where the Spirit was propelling her, caught between the pincers of necessity and action, striving not to separate herself from contemplation, which was always the driving force.

TERESA LEFT ÁVILA ON JANUARY 2, 1582, in the company of Father Gracián and six nuns. To reach Burgos, the former capital of Old Castile, they had to cover some 150 miles of roads full of potholes via Medina del

Campo, Valladolid, and Palencia. And the foundress's health was not improving. In addition to her usual ailments, she was suffering from an abscess in her throat, which prevented her from eating. Through torrential rain and swirling wind, the pitiful column of wagons dragged itself along the flooded lanes. A sudden rise of the Arlanzon River ahead stopped them. Through the downpour, the guide looked for the lightweight wooden bridges that had replaced the stone bridges earlier carried away by the flood. The water's expanse made it difficult to determine where the bridges ended and the water began.

"I'll go first," cried Teresa. "If I drown, turn back!"

Sheer folly! She jumped down from the wagon and waded through the water to test the ground under her feet and try to spot the bridge. She stumbled and injured herself. Soaked and discouraged, she turned her face toward the lowering sky, heavy with thick clouds:

"Lord! After so much suffering this one really is well-timed!"

A voice answered her: Teresa, this is how I treat my friends.

"O! God of my soul! That's why you have so few!"[20]

She finally found the bridge, hauling the wagons behind her.

After twenty-four days on the road—"a world of water without a road or a boat," she would later say—she reached Burgos half dead and soaked to the skin. She immediately took to her bed at the home of the donor, Catalina de Tolosa. Fever, dizziness, vomiting—Teresa was spared nothing.

And the foundation was starting badly. The archbishop, Don Cristóbal de Vela, to whom Teresa was even related, had changed his mind. This grand lord, the son of the former viceroy of Peru, claimed that he had never told her to come and found a convent, but only to "negotiate." A slight difference!

The archbishop was now demanding that the community be provided with an income in a fully owned house. And he suddenly became aware of the fact that there were already too many nuns living in Burgos! Had he been put on guard against Teresa? What had not been said about her! Saint or sorceress? De Vela refused to accept the foundation. The secret reason for his reversal was that the future donor of the Burgos foundation, Catalina de Tolosa, had already bequeathed part of her fortune to the Jesuits of that city. Whatever would go to the Carmel would thus diminish that inheritance.

"The Jesuits are afraid that Doña Catalina will catch our prayer...!"[21] said Teresa, laughing. As if it were a question of the plague!

She remained obstinate. The wait would last three months. "Don Cristóbal is a saint; he must have good reasons,"[22] Teresa admitted without rancor. For his part, the archbishop, assailed with remorse, admitted to someone close to him: "Listening to Mother Teresa, I believe I'm hearing St. Paul himself speaking!"

After a long stay in makeshift lodgings, Father Gracián, who was saying Mass for the nuns, was obliged to leave. He needed to inspect Granada and Seville, the Andalusian foundations. Teresa was relieved; she could no longer stand his faintheartedness when faced with difficulties. But his departure posed a problem for the tiny Burgos community, now deprived of a priest. This forced the Carmelites to leave their enclosure in order to attend Mass on the outside. Furthermore, Catalina de Tolosa's Jesuit confessors were threatening to refuse her absolution if she continued to give shelter to the Carmelites. So la Madre and her seven sisters were compelled to move to Conception Hospice, where they lodged in an attic above the common room. From a nearby gallery, they could discreetly follow the Mass of the sick celebrated in the chapel below. The groans of the sick and the moans of the dying; the stench of the gangrenous; the nightly noises of rats and bats; freezing cold, wind, and rain—nothing was lacking in this miserable tableau, which could have inspired the Dutch painter Hieronymus Bosch.

In spite of the ills from which she was suffering and her paralyzed arm, Teresa devoted herself to helping out at the hospital. Insensible to vermin or contagion, she comforted the sick and assisted the dying. And always, with humble persistence, she hounded the episcopal See.

Finally, to be rid of her, Archbishop de Vela granted his authorization, although he haggled fiercely over the terms. Since he was requiring that the community, besides the gift of a house, accept a regular revenue—income that la Madre did not want—she pretended to resign herself to this, with Doña Catalina providing the funds. But in a document that remained secret, la Madre relinquished these annuities, preferring to rely on God alone. Here as elsewhere, Teresa would have the last word, that of the destitute God living within her. Thanks to these subterfuges, everyone was satisfied: the archbishop, the Jesuits, and the Carmelites, who would be content in having the house without any additional income.

The residence they obtained was surrounded by a lovely garden watered by springs, and the Carmel was solemnly founded on April 18, 1582, in the presence of the archbishop.

As if the devil were interfering in all this, a new flood deluged the city on the following day, "sweeping away houses, disinterring the dead." It was a nightmare. As the river rose, the community took refuge on the upper floor behind Teresa, who remained calm as always. From the windows, the nuns could see cadavers being carried along by the raging waters. Tree trunks smashed the last bridges and nearby houses. For twenty hours, the Carmelites prayed while awaiting death.

"Why so much calamity, *Madre?*" asked Tomasina Bautista, the young prioress, a woman nevertheless inured to any ordeal.

"Well, daughter, could you want anything better than dying as a martyr for the Lord?"

The authorities sent a boat to evacuate the house, which seemed in danger of collapsing, but Teresa refused to leave this place where the Blessed Sacrament was exposed. In the city, someone went to beseech the archbishop to order the nuns to leave. He answered: "Let Teresa de Jesús make the decision. She has a safe conduct from heaven. She will leave when it suits her."[23]

At last, in the middle of the night, the waters stopped rising and then began to recede. And all of Burgos, with the archbishop in the lead, proclaimed that *la santa Madre* "had not only saved her convent but Burgos itself."[24]

THE BURGOS FOUNDATION having been established, Teresa, accompanied by her niece Teresita and Ana de San Bartolomé, started out again on July 26, 1582, en route to Ávila, where she expected to die—on this point she had no doubt. When she left Burgos, she had said to her confessor, Canon Manso: "*Adios, Padre!* I am going off to die."

She also wanted, without any further delay, to give the veil to her dear Teresita, Lorenzo's daughter, who had been following her devotedly for the preceding eight years. Would she be able to last this long? To María de San José, she had written: "You must no longer take any account of me. You would be frightened at seeing me so old and good for so little."

She thought only of her daughters. On August 27, she wrote her last instructions to Tomasina Bautista, prioress of Burgos: "Do not overburden the novices with too many occupations before having had the time to discern how far their spiritual strength can go. There must be a great deal of gentleness in your words. You believe that they must all have the same fervor that you have; you are mistaken."

She signed her last letter, addressed to Father Gracián, on September 1. It contained an enigmatic warning: "Do not trust the Andalusian nuns. If they want one thing, they will make you believe a thousand." Forgetting how much he had disappointed her in Burgos, she would have liked to have seen "her beloved son" again. He was being sulky with her by lingering in

Andalusia. "I felt your absence so keenly that I have lost the desire to write to Your Paternity."

Returning south and passing through Valladolid, she quarreled with the prioress, her grandniece María de Ocampo (Mother María Bautista), about her brother Lorenzo's inheritance. Lorenzo had designated Teresa as executrix of his estate, but it was a poisoned gift that was tearing the family apart! He had bequeathed his Spanish possessions—a mortgaged house—to his oldest son, Francisco. Lorenzo had also owned property and income-producing titles in America at Lima, which he had ceded to his younger son. But they had to be sold and the gold brought back to Spain. Francisco was contesting everything because, being recently married, he needed the money. Lorenzo had also endowed his daughter Teresita so that she could enter the Carmel. He had extended a large loan for the foundation of Seville, which the Carmelites were still unable to reimburse. With this money, which Francisco had his eye on, his father Lorenzo had ordered that a votive chapel be built in Ávila. Mother María Bautista took Francisco's side in the matter against Teresa, hence the family argument. María's resentment was such that, in taking leave of la Madre, she murmured: "Go away! And don't ever come back here!"

Teresa also clashed with the prioress at Medina del Campo, Mother Alberta Bautista, who did not like her. Teresa reproached her for her excessive zeal and useless mortifications. As a result, this prioress gave her an icy welcome. Instead of offering her some refreshment and rest, she sent Teresa to the parlor, where a Carmelite priest was waiting for her. Alas, it was not her dear Gracián, but his assistant, Father Antonio de Jesús, still steeped in resentment toward la Madre because of his eviction as head of the Order of which he was, nonetheless, the provincial vicar. Now ignoring la Madre's exhaustion, he ordered: "A carriage of the Duchess of Alba is awaiting you at the door. Prepare yourself to leave."

She cried out: "But what can possibly be happening in Alba de Tormes?"

"An heir is expected at the ducal palace—an affair of State! The duchess's daughter-in-law is about to give birth, and you are being called for. We shall leave tomorrow morning."

Teresa closed her eyes. Alba de Tormes—almost fifty miles from Medina and Ávila!

Marcelle Auclair sees in this extremely serious matter—for Teresa was an exhausted woman whom the Carmelite was sending to her death—an old settling of scores. Admittedly, Father Antonio, faithful courtier of the Duchess of Alba, could refuse her nothing. Was that reason to justify sacrificing la

Madre to her? No, the fact was that he had not forgiven the foundress for using her influence to have Father Gracián, whom he despised, elected provincial of the Discalced Carmelites.

Teresa obeyed "like a child." "The road of obedience is the one which leads most quickly to perfection."[25] But Ana de Bartolomé later acknowledged that she had never seen Teresa suffer more from an order given by a superior.

Who would have pity on her? En route, she fainted, and this time it was not due to an ecstasy. The travelers stopped at an inn so that she could catch her breath. Would this Calvary have no end?

They started out again on September 19. The road was very difficult, the wagon had a bad suspension, and they could not find food. In her autobiography, the faithful Ana tells of passing through a village and trying in vain to buy some eggs. She only found four figs, which she gave to *la Madre*, apologizing for not having found anything more:

> When I saw that all the money in the world could not have obtained a bit
> of nourishment to revive her, when I saw that lifeless face, and realized, in
> touching her hands, that she was burning with fever, my heart broke and I
> began to cry. *La santa Madre* was dying in my hands and I could not bring
> her any help. Gentle as an angel, she said to me: "Do not cry, daughter,
> since God wants it to be so. Do not fret. These figs are too good. Many
> poor people would consider them a feast. Believe me, I am very happy."[26]

As they were approaching their destination, a horseman met them to announce the happy birth of the heir to the Duke of Alba. All of this travel for nothing! Exhausted, Teresa murmured: "God be praised! Now they will no longer need the saint!"[27]

Should they cut out the stop in Alba and start back immediately for Ávila, so that she could die at home, as she wished? It was too late.

THERE SHE WAS, FINALLY, in that convent of Alba de Tormes, which she had founded in 1571 beneath the walls of the palace of the Dukes of Alba, not far from her sister Juana de Ovalle's home. The prioress, Juana del Espíritu Santo, who had been looking forward to giving Teresa a warm welcome, was dismayed to see her in such a poor state. This prioress was one of the pearls of the Reform, so humble that when she reprimanded one of her sisters, she would end up throwing herself at the feet of the one being scolded.

Compelled to take to her bed, Teresa excused herself: "It has been more than twenty years since I went to bed so early!"[28]

But the next day, she got up, attended Mass, and received Communion. Leaning on Ana's arm, she inspected the monastery. Would she ever know how to rest? That word meant nothing to her! Besides, people were rushing in to see her: the Duchess of Alba, Doña María Enriquez, surrounded by her ladies-in-waiting; the prior of Salamanca, who came to discuss with her the inopportune purchase of a new house for the nuns; and finally, the powerful and tyrannical donor, Doña Teresa de Layz, whom *la Madre* rebuked because she was persecuting the sisters.

"Ah, Madam! How different things are where Love really reigns!"[29]

That night, feeling very tired, she said to Ana:

"Daughter, as soon as you see me less sick, look for an ordinary cart and we'll leave for Ávila with Teresita."

She could not rest until her niece Teresita had taken the habit, which would tear her away from the legal procedures of the family eyeing Lorenzo's estate.

September was coming to an end in Estremadura in an apotheosis of golden light. The Tormes River was freshening the heavy atmosphere of summer. Above the old village with its pink and white houses rose the tall towers of the fortress-palace of the Dukes of Alba.

Suddenly, the window of the cell where Teresa had just been placed began to shine brightly in a supernatural way. All the nuns in the cloister understood that the end had come for *la Madre fundadora* on that twenty-ninth day of September, 1582, feast of the Archangel Michael. That morning she had suffered a hemorrhage, which had left her exhausted, and the doctors gave her only a few hours to live. She would actually hold on for another six days, as though she did not want to leave this world where she had suffered so much, she who now aspired only to the light beyond.

Her daughters, whom she loved, succeeded one another at her bedside: Teresita, her beloved niece; María de San Francisco, who, in Salamanca, had witnessed her ecstasies; Teresa de San Andrés, so beautiful and austere, whom *la Madre* had one day called "the honor of penance."[30] Teresa said to her: "I will come to get you when your turn comes."

And the young postulant Mariana Gaytán was also present. She was thirteen years old and so fidgety that Teresa called her "my little pest." Teresa guessed that the anxious postulant doubted she would be accepted for profession since she had no dowry. La Madre now reassured her, "Do not be distressed, little angel. You will make profession here."

Other phenomena occurred, which some called "miracles" and others "signs": supernatural lights in the choir and strange moaning sounds like those of an agonizing doe. One nun, Catalina de la Concepción, had a vision in which she saw arriving at *la Madre's* bedside a vast throng of holy martyrs accompanied by ladies and noblemen in resplendent clothing.

On October 2, Teresa asked for Father Antonio. He heard her confession, kneeling beside her bed.

Suffering and anguish, as well as humility, finally showed on the face of this monk who had too often been stubborn and preoccupied with worldly concerns and precedence.

"*Madre!* Ask the Lord not to take you. Not yet!"

"*Padre*, be quiet! I am no longer useful in this world."

She received a doctor, Francisco Ramírez. Surprised by her radiant face, he prescribed a licorice stick and cupping glasses. The following day, October 3, another doctor, Jerónimo Hernández, came to bleed her.

At five in the afternoon, she asked for the Viaticum, the final Communion reserved for sick persons in danger of dying. Father Antonio brought it to her. *La Madre*, surrounded by her community, summoned up what was left of her strength to make final recommendations to them:

"For the love of God, keep the Rule perfectly. If you do, you won't need a miracle to be canonized."

After a long silence: "Forgive me for the bad example I have given you!"

She then cried out: "I am a daughter of the Church!"

When Father Antonio presented her the host, she sat up in bed with unexpected vivacity and a radiant face.

"My Spouse and Lord! The hour so much desired has come. It is time to see you, my Beloved, my Lord!"

Night had fallen. At nine o'clock she called for Extreme Unction, which Father Antonio administered. He then asked her: "*Madre*, do you wish your body to be buried here or to be returned to Ávila?"

"Do I have anything here below which belongs to me exclusively? Will they not give me a bit of earth here?"[31]

When she found herself alone again with Ana, Teresa said to her: "Daughter, the hour has come."

The humble lay sister of Ávila, whom the Church beatified in 1917, has related everything: "I changed her completely. Happy at seeing herself so clean, she smiled at me and showed her gratitude with a sign." Teresa de Jesús could no longer speak.

Teresita and Ana, who never left her side, watched over her. She spent one night during which suffering alternated with ecstatic beatitude. At this point, it is impossible not to paraphrase John of the Cross, who would write, evoking the last moments of the one who called him "my son, my brother, my father": "The friends of God die in sublime transports and in the midst of delicious onslaughts that Love delivers, like the swan, which sings with more gentleness when it is about to die."

Ana, bending toward the dying woman, heard her murmur a verse of the *Miserere* psalm: "My sacrifice, God, is a contrite spirit; a broken, humbled heart, O God, you will not spurn."

After a difficult night, Teresa saw the break of dawn on October 4, the feast of her dear Francis of Assisi. She lay on her side clasping a crucifix, remaining silent in this position for the entire day. When night came, peace suffused her. She fell into an ecstasy, and her sisters were able to contemplate her transfigured face, "so calm and so luminous that it looked like a full moon," according to María de San Francisco. All of the wrinkles that had marked Teresa's face had disappeared.

Taking advantage of this respite, Father Antonio ordered Ana to take some rest and nourishment, which she had not done for the past two days.

Towards nine in the evening, *la Madre* opened her eyes and looked for her. Teresita ran to get Ana, and when she entered, *la Madre* smiled at her, took her hands, and laid her head on Ana's arms.

Teresa passed away in this manner, peaceful and trusting in the arms of the most humble of lay sisters, enraptured in God, and this time there was no return. "...The little butterfly...dies, and with the greatest joy because its life is now Christ."[32] A wonderful perfume spread throughout the cell. Teresa of Ávila's face was resplendent, "like a blazing sun," asserted the witnesses.

When she learned of Teresa's death, the Duchess of Alba, overtaken with remorse, rushed to the convent and had her body covered with a cloth of gold. Thus, without realizing it, she carried out Teresa's prophecy of 1538, made when she was only twenty-three years old: "Do not believe me to be dead until my body has been covered with a cloth of gold."

In various Carmels of Spain, *la Madre's* death was marked by strange phenomena. One nun saw her in heaven beside St. Francis. In the Alba convent's cloister garden, which Teresa could see from her window, was an almond tree that, on the morning following her death, had burst with blossoms during the night, although these trees only bloom during the winter.

In *The Book of Her Life*, Teresa had written: "Cost what it may, Lord, do not desire that I come into Your presence with hands so empty, since the reward must be given in conformity with one's deeds."[33] She had founded seventeen monasteries, not counting the eleven Carmels for men that had been established during her lifetime. The religious living in these monasteries numbered more than five hundred brothers and sisters. She had traveled over four thousand miles on the terrible roads of the two Castiles, Estremadura, and Andalusia, and had written ten books and twelve thousand letters. She had reformed the Carmel, giving it the possibility to start again upon its original foundation, the one still present in our day in all of its sanctity.

PART TWO

Her Achievements

"The Lord is less concerned with the grandeur of the works than with the love with which we do them."

"I have only written what I have done."

— TERESA OF ÁVILA

1

Portrait of Teresa of Ávila

Teresa's first biographer, Francisco de Ribera, who was a contemporary of hers, described her as follows:

> She was remarkably beautiful in her youth and still looked lovely at an advanced age. Plump, her skin was very white. Her face was round, full, and of a fine shape, well proportioned. Her hair was black and curly; her forehead broad, smooth, and very handsome; her chestnut-colored eyebrows were somewhat thick and slightly arched. She had round, black, prominent, admirably set eyes, lively and pleasing. Her nose was small, slightly raised in the middle, with a rounded end turned downwards a little; she had tiny, arched nostrils. Her mouth was neither large nor small; her upper lip was straight and thin, while the lower one was thicker and drooped a bit. She had good teeth and a chin that was well made and shapely. Her ears were of medium size; her neck wide and rather short; her hands were small and beautiful. On the right side of her face were three small distinctive moles, which gave her a great deal of grace. All of these particularities have come to me from persons who saw her very often and close up and had more opportunities than I did to gaze upon her at leisure. In fact, everything about her seemed to be perfect. Her bearing was majestic, her gait full of dignity and grace.

Let's dig a bit more deeply.

Obedient, unselfish, humble, lacking money but neither energy nor determination, Teresa kept her place: the last one. And yet, her powerful personality, sustained by God's revelations, continued to unfold. In spite of the extraordinary phenomena that illumined her life, she avoided aggrandizement and asked for counsel and direction from experienced theologians, soliciting the authority conferred by learning as well as the opinion of erudite men. Rational, she was constantly questioning herself. In Teresa we find a rare harmony between the marvels of her mystical life and her simplicity. This brings her close to anyone and everyone, even though she far surpassed ordinary persons by the strictness of her moral and ascetic life, based upon Carmel's primitive Rule.

Her burning faith, sustained by great fidelity to mental prayer and fortified by her visions, locutions, and ecstasies, never destroyed in her the most rational humanity. Sometimes suspended between heaven and earth and thrown, in spite of herself, as though outside her body, she knew how to find it again in the most natural manner in the world. She mastered the most complicated matters and the most wily persons, preparing her foundations in synergy with Christ and leaving nothing to chance. If a foundation or work became problematic, she humbly left the matter up to the Lord, trusting in him, knowing that he would help her when he wanted to. As she moved along in life and in her writings, she became an incomparable master of mental prayer. Her amorous passion for Christ recalls the words of St. Bernard: "The measure of loving God is to love him without measure." That is why her relationship to Jesus is so dazzling; it has the strength of things seen and lived by a witness.

Knowing how to accept supernatural marvels with humility, she recognized that she was but "a little nothing" thanks to her profound knowledge of human nature, which she could compare from experience to the greatness of divine nature revealing itself to her.

This did not prevent her from dialoguing, as one equal to another, with bishops and nuncios, writing directly to the king to express herself in the name of him who dwelled in her. Yet her strong and independent personality would always remain docile to her confessors and to the Magisterium of the Church. In her manner of reforming, she never attempted to compel her opponents to think like her. She loved them and prayed to God for their change of heart.

An expert in psychology, this director of souls was able to perceive from the very first conversation a true vocation in a postulant or real giftedness in a confessor. The profound influence that she exerted over those who approached her, from the humble lay sister to the papal nuncio, was derived from her sanctity, the radiance of God in her, as well as from her powerful and warmhearted personality, charm, and lengthy experience of the Carmels. According to the testimony of an anonymous Carmelite of Caen, these traits "were enfolded in a ravishing simplicity." One could not do otherwise but love her. Teresa de Jesús then led the person along in her vertiginous ascensions. "She burned you with the love that consoled her," and "no one left her without loving the God who filled her heart even more."

A model of patience, courage, reason, and faith, she reconciles us with a religion that at the time was dogmatic and uncompromising and in which fear and superstition often eclipsed love and reason. Cheerful and joyous, she rejected a narrow and glum piety for herself as well as in her monasteries. This devoted, tender heart remained focused through an intrepid and resolute will rooted in what is essential. A bishop said of her, "Her life is wisdom teaching love and disciplining heroism." In everything, she was by turns "gracious, kind, and superhuman through her courage and her passion for giving herself."

Her strength was an ardent faith, impassioned and enthusiastic. Her genius came from a fine intelligence of an intuitive nature joined to a great deal of common sense: she possessed "the perfection of common sense." Although experiencing strange phenomena, she always attempted to hide them and remained hostile to any indiscreet singularity just as to an excess of mortification. "Greatness of soul within a childlike simplicity, strength within gentleness"[1] can be found in her.

Does this mean she had no faults? In her youth, she imprudently indulged in sensuality; unpredictable, she displayed audacity and a redoubtable independence, regardless of legitimate authority. After her conversion, she constantly changed confessors to choose the one who corresponded to her wishes. This was an obedience "which was not without a bit of ingenuousness akin to artfulness."[2] After becoming a foundress, she sometimes showed herself to be authoritarian to the point of irritating her prioresses. At the sentimental level of human attachment, she also remained very dependent, notably upon Father Jerónimo Gracián, who, not always being equal to the responsibilities she entrusted him with, would provoke a major crisis in the Order, a crisis that she had not foreseen.

These faults make her all the more human to us, and we forgive her everything when we read what she wrote at the beginning of her St. Joseph foundation.

> I realized I was a woman and wretched and incapable of doing any of the useful things I desired to do in the service of the Lord.... As a result I resolved to do the little that was in my power; that is, to follow the evangelical counsels as perfectly as I could and strive that these persons who live here do the same.[3]

Let us try to study in depth certain character traits that made of her a contemplative, a woman of action, and simply a woman, and see how she assumed her physical and psychic ailments and the sufferings they gave rise to.

Contemplation or the search for the source of the real

Pragmatic and rational, Teresa—facing the Mystery that challenged and sometimes submerged her—walked between the night and the light, fearing to burn her wings in the process and fall into pride. She avoided this through cruel nights of the spirit during which she called herself into question. These were an obsessive reminder of the weakness and precariousness of the human condition.

Some persons advised her to think less and return to her spinning wheel and rosary beads. They were of the opinion that there are grave questions that a woman should never ask herself. But, spurred on by the Spirit, Teresa persisted. Like her brothers, she felt that she had the soul of a conquistador. Through the night and the fog, she divined that *terra incognita* where the source of the real resides. She wanted to arrive in this unknown land, fount of all riches, early—during her time here below. The three sails of her caravel were concentration, prayer, and meditation. The wind pushing her along was love. When she landed on the shore and tread upon the prayer of quiet's golden sand, she drank at a brook whose trickle of clear water lost itself in the sand. Her thirst was only half-quenched. She proceeded up the small stream toward the source, hidden in the woods. "Walk along to reach the source itself," she wrote in *The Way of Perfection.*

Just as the Samaritan woman met Christ at Jacob's well, Teresa finally met her God. She was almost forty years old. "The much wounded Christ" opened his arms to her and with him she crossed the invisible barrier that separated her from her God. "I saw that He was man, even though He was God."[4]

However, her visions were contested by timorous counselors. She would be reassured by the unrestricted approval of two saints, Francis Borgia and Peter of Alcántara. She finally gave herself over without reservation to supernatural reality: God is love.

By the time she believed she had arrived, everything was only just beginning. For God is not only love, he is also light and knowledge. He is energy. Intoxicated with him, full of new insight and energy, she became aware of her task here below. Far from egotistically isolating herself to enjoy her Love, she would throw herself into the world to make him known, and she would do this without betraying her contemplative vocation, the Carmel—but a Carmel returned to its primitive purity and demand for perfection.

The woman of action, the foundress

Teresa was forty-six when she embraced the adventure of the foundations in order to be faithful to the light that now pushed her forward and in order to share her treasure.

We can ponder the seeming contradiction existing between contemplation and action. Was Teresa not torn between the desire to be united in silence to Christ and the crushing obligations resulting from service to him after having recognized God's desire for her: the Reform of Carmel? During one of her ecstasies, however, she heard God saying to her: "It is time for you to take care of my affairs, I will take care of yours."[5] From then on, contemplation and apostolic action cohabitated in her, the one sustaining the other. Indeed, she does not seem to have questioned the situation. "It isn't a matter of thinking a lot, but of loving a lot," she said, that is, what was essential was sharing this love that she could not keep for herself without betraying it. This contemplative Carmelite would become a woman of action!

Having become *la Madre fundadora*, she confronted the material realities specific to her new office, sometimes with heroic courage. She developed no complex about using her feminine charm and utilizing saintly guile. These were the tactics of a "frail female" who knew no Latin and who was maneuvering in a world of learned men full of self-importance regarding their positions! It was her mission that she was defending, well beyond "the point of honor," which she had long before renounced after having been overwhelmed by the divine Majesty.

All the same! In Teresa's choice to have her sister buy the St. Joseph house in the name of her husband "can be recognized the Teresian art of doing only what she pleased, without, however, disobeying."[6] In the conflict over her two Andalusian foundations, she obeyed the superior who agreed with what she wished, praying for heaven to change the minds of those who were heading in the opposite direction. Faced with threats, she seemed to submit, all the while pursuing her plans, deriving strength from divine support. This would elicit the admiration of her disciple, Jerónimo Gracián: "*La Madre* shunned lying and used holy tricks. I have never seen a person more ingenious in the art of bedazzling truth without lying."

Teresa de Jesús was human—all too human! But so level-headed! Although she was a mystic who sought sanctity, she did not like excesses, especially with regard to penance and asceticism: "God desires your health more than your penance,"[7] she wrote to her brother Lorenzo. She was joyous, warmhearted, and had a great sense of humor! Teresa was exactly the

opposite of a scowling saint. "God deliver me from gloomy saints," she used
to say.

St. Teresa and her relationship with men

Emotional and hypersensitive as a child and youth, Teresa learned to control herself. As the sister of nine brothers, she knew the masculine condition.
Her sensuality was awakened at age fifteen when she kept company with her
cousins. Out of this arose a brief romance, more or less mastered, to which
her father brutally put an end by shutting her away in a boarding school run
by Augustinian sisters. Her radical choice of religious life at the age of twenty, thus in favor of chastity, allowed for the successful transfer toward a mystical marriage. She would be fully the spouse of Christ, and this would be the
great joy of her life. But this would take place belatedly, since she would not
immediately give up those too human relationships at the Incarnation parlor—verbal only, no doubt, but not devoid of sensuality and vanity.

Later depriving herself of a lay parlor, she did not lose, for all that, her
feminine sensitivity. Between two great impulses toward Christ, she took an
innocent pleasure with the men she authorized herself to frequent: her confessors. Two men thus marked her life, and we can say that she loved them
with the best and most honorable of intentions. Father Gracián was her
closest friend. She found his childlike purity, his *joie de vivre*, his naïve enthusiasm, and even his weaknesses, infinitely touching. She felt happy to be near
him. Father Emmanuel Renault speaks of "an outpouring of tenderness and
familiarity, of a warm and lively friendship" between them.

Very different is the feeling linking her to John of the Cross, who did
not have the naïveté and human weaknesses of Gracián. "My father Fray
John is a celestial, divine man; I have found no one like him in all of
Castile," she wrote to Ana de Jesús. Teresa did nothing of importance without consulting him, but there would never be between them the human
involvement that bound her to Gracián. Unlike Gracián, John of the Cross
surmounted the worst ordeals. As we have seen, he soared at inaccessible
heights, even for her. Father Renault speaks of "the discordance which
derived from their personal manner of feeling and living." Teresa was sometimes annoyed at this, and at one point she wrote, "God deliver me from
people so spiritual that they want to turn everything into perfect contemplation, no matter what."[8]

But, it was in her overflowing love of Christ, "true man and true God,"
that Teresa's personality would blossom and fulfill her desire for affection,
her daughters gratifying her maternal need.

Could she have been somewhat hysterical?

The psychosomatic illnesses of her youth can be explained by a conflict between the flesh and the spirit. The minor liberties that she indulged in at her father's house and then at the Incarnation parlor only stirred up her inner turmoil without fulfilling her desire, which only the spiritual marriage would succeed in doing.

Many of the physical disorders from which she suffered were no doubt linked to psychological wounds. More serious was her attack at age twenty-four when she found herself in danger of death. Her doctors were at a loss as to the source of her illness. At the end of her life, however, Master Antonio Aguiar, who examined her in Burgos in 1581, declared: "It is impossible to discover the seat of her pain, because this body is a whole arsenal of ailments and their principal origin is of a moral order."

Physically fragile through her maternal heredity, she remained hypersensitive, and every event had repercussions on her body. Her unexplainable and fleeting paralyses could point to a hysterical condition. However, none of the general symptoms of ordinary hysteria can be found in her.

However, she no doubt suffered from hysterical symptoms linked to the painful events of her life. This is known as neurosis. It is the result of a repressed conflict in a hypersensitive person with a passionate disposition. In Teresa, there existed a permanent conflict between being and having. She longed for human happiness, the pleasure of the senses, but she was diverted from this by an aspiration toward God alone. Later, while measuring herself against the incommensurable mystery of the divinity, it would become evident to her that here below "all is nothing," even in the Spanish Golden Age. She asked herself, "Where does the illusion lie?" In earthly realities or in the supernatural ideal? This privileged aristocrat had to make a radical choice, and she did so. It is not astonishing, therefore, that the physical, human side of her would then protest.

This reserve vis-à-vis the world affected her at the psychological level. Was it *the devil* who manifested himself to turn her away from her divine aspirations? Or was it "human nature"—invited, sometimes pushed, toward a crucifying transformation—that rebelled?

Faced with these conflicts, Teresa made a decision: "The instinctive thrust that drew her to earthly things had to be not only controlled but severed, if she did not want to lose herself," writes Father Renault.[9]

All of this did not prevent Teresa from showing what she was capable of. Her faith, her intuition, and her submission to divine love dictated the right medication: wanting to be nothing, taking a back seat to allow the All to act in her. The little ego had better behave! That is when Teresa's creative genius became liberated, and in all fields: mental prayer, foundations, writing.

Suffering transcended

It is impossible to paint a portrait of Teresa of Ávila without evoking her physical suffering. In *The Life*, written when she was forty-seven, she was already admitting that she almost never spent a moment without pain. Yet Teresa was out and about and still traveling up and down the country's roads even just a few days before her death at the age of sixty-seven.

In the absence of a reliable diagnosis, it is difficult to come to a conclusion regarding her ailments. Such a diagnosis was inconceivable in the sixteenth century, when the notion of a microbial infection or that of psychosomatic illness did not exist. Were her cardiac pains the consequence of transverberation? What caused her daily vomiting, her headaches? Were her frequent fevers due to malaria, widespread in her day? Her diet can be incriminated, for it was lacking in milk products and fruit (mineral salts and vitamins), something that the poorer classes of Spain suffered, and it was not offset by meat and wine, forbidden by the Carmelite Rule. Lack of sleep can also be mentioned. It is a fact that Teresa did not take care of herself, although she was greatly concerned about the health of her daughters: "If you are sick, eat meat, see the doctor, sleep for eight hours."

And yet she was always cheerful, welcoming, and joyous. She did not sacrifice the religious Offices to her myriad activities; she even wrote when she should have been sleeping. Taking into account her fasts, her exhausting activity, her responsibilities, her lack of sleep and care, the cold or the heat, the dust on the pot-holed routes, and the often impassable mountain roads, we should be astonished instead that she lived for so long.

Suffering transcended, utilized as a lever, is at the heart of her life. "Lord, either to suffer or to die," she wrote. Teresa, like many mystics, had access to the highest form of supernatural life thanks to the manner in which she accepted suffering without looking for it or letting it provoke a revolt in her.

I have been struck by a phrase of Simone Weil: "Evil being the root of mystery, pain is the root of knowledge."[10] Teresa de Ahumada, a young woman whom life had gratified, would experience at the age of seventeen, and then again at twenty-three, the most extreme physical suffering. All of these illnesses schooled her in poverty and humility. At first she drew the conclusion that "life is like a night spent in a terrible inn." Whether in the world or in her first convent, she sought out "the consolations of religion." Then something opened up within her, and Someone answered her prayer: Christ, who invited her to follow him, to love him. Mental prayer, which she would later bring to perfection, would at first be the way. And so would writing.

Teresa, the writer

Teresa's celebrity derives as much from her genius as a writer as from her sanctity. Her writings have come down to us through the centuries because they are accessible to everyone, are pleasant to read, and correspond to a spiritual necessity that transcends eras. Her literary genius included also being a letter writer.

However, she was not a "woman of letters." She did not study at a university, nor did she have a tutor; all she had received was a basic education proper for young girls of her class. She did not know Latin or any language other than Castilian. Her spontaneous vocabulary was that of a wellborn woman of her time. She never used scholarly words. Her writings have an unfinished aspect, for she never corrected herself and often for lack of time did not even reread what she had written. Father Gracián stated that she wrote "with the speed of a notary." Her precise style is fresh, alive, and without literary effects. She wrote in an unaffected manner, just as she spoke, and without concealing her thinking. That is why her style still touches us today.

Teresa's great texts are full of digressions; she clearly took pleasure in them. Her aim was to inform, but also to teach her readers, generally her daughters. Carried along by her role as a foundress, she then became a moralizer because she could not stand mediocrity. "The more I love someone, the less I can bear even a tiny fault."

Almost all her texts are written in her hand, and most of the originals have been preserved. Only at the end of her life did she dictate, and very little even then. Thanks to this, her thought is never betrayed.

What was the secret of this literary genius who brought the beautiful language of Castile to its height? Castilian would become the language of Spain, the fourth most spoken language in the world, "a simple language with words of love, trust, and faith," emphasizes Father Denis Vasse. "[It expresses] the simplicity of a woman who leaves silence behind through obedience and communicates love with tender discretion and precision in her account," who transcribes her personal experience "of the Word made flesh, of knowledge revealed, welcomed through trial and error and devoid of ornamentation thanks to her lack of learning, and [who] opens [it] out to humanity in suffering, joy, and love."[11]

Teresa of Ávila established herself as one of the greatest witnesses of the interior journey. "She has nothing to say to us except what happened to her," writes Father Jean Abiven. "She does so with an incomparable subtlety of analysis and felicity of expression, testimony to what divine grace can effect in a human being. With her, the mystical fact imposes itself as one of the inescapable dimensions of the human adventure."[12]

This Doctor of the Church was nothing like the classic spiritual master, doctrinal in the manner of St. Augustine or St. Thomas Aquinas. And yet, she is "the mother of spiritual persons," as the pedestal of her statue in St. Peter's Basilica in Rome reads today. As a mother, she gives spiritual life. She seizes her readers in the very depths of their beings, for in spiritual matters she has lived it all. Her experiences included discovery filled with wonder at the touch of the Divine and went as far as denial, ranged from conversion to mystical union, and were colored by a life filled with suffering but also with joys.

Finally, next to a mystical Teresa, instrument of divine grace, a Teresa as philosopher shows through, a witness to human liberty and the adventure that brings it forth.

The genius of Teresa of Ávila is, at one and the same time, extraordinary (in her ecstasies, levitations, and sanctity) and "ordinary" (in her existence as a loving and suffering woman, humbly submissive to the human condition). She shows a confused humanity the meaning of evolution: an ascension toward more wisdom, sharing, spirituality, and love.

Although often on the cutting edge, playing dangerously with the Inquisition, she made her way toward truth through the search for perfection, conforming her life to the Gospel of Christ—Christ, her only love, of whom she is one of the greatest witnesses.

Through its richness, Teresa of Ávila's oeuvre interests theologians of all religions and even atheists, philosophers, psychologists, psychiatrists, and medical doctors. Through her profound knowledge of the human heart, she addresses herself to all persons of good will in search of truth, be they religious or lay. Her influence thus extends down through the centuries. Her entire life is found in her writings. Let us examine them in a detailed fashion.

2

The Written Works

In 1588, with the approval of the king, the Augustinian monk Luis de León, a famous professor of theology in Salamanca who was fascinated by mysticism, began to publish in that city the complete works of Teresa of Ávila. They were to be immensely successful: 13 new editions in the sixteenth century, 243 in the seventeenth, 125 in the eighteenth, 269 in the nineteenth, and 530 in the twentieth, translated into all the major languages. Gregory XV, who canonized her, recommended that they be read. Pius IX and Leo XIII described them as containing "celestial wisdom." Pius X compared Teresa to the Doctors of the Church. All of the twentieth-century popes also recommended her, and in 1970, Paul VI officially declared her to be a Doctor of the Church.

MAJOR WRITINGS[1]

1562–1565:	*The Book of Her Life (The Life or Life)*
1562–1567:	*The Way of Perfection (Way)*
1574–1582:	*The Book of Her Foundations (Foundations)*
1577:	*The Interior Castle (Castle)*

MINOR WORKS

1560–1576:	*Spiritual Testimonies*
1563–1567:	*The Constitutions*
1569:	*Soliloquies*
1572:	*Meditations on the Song of Songs*
1572:	*Thoughts and Maxims*

	Response to a Spiritual Challenge
1576:	*A Satirical Critique*
	Sayings of Light and Love
1580:	*On Making the Visitation*

LETTERS

| 1560–1582: | Approximately 450 letters |

Major Works

The Book of Her Life
(Libro de la vida)

In 1561, in Ávila, Teresa wrote a first version of this autobiography at the request of her Dominican confessor, Pedro Ibáñez, and especially as a result of divine injunction. She completed it in 1562 during her stay with her friend Doña Luisa de la Cerda in Toledo. At the end of 1562, she submitted the text to the Dominican García de Toledo, who asked her to revise and complete it; she did so between 1563 and 1565. Only the second draft has been preserved. (A facsimile of page 2, Chapter 40 is reproduced in the photo section of this book). This personal text, which Teresa called *mi alma* (my soul), is a kind of general confession enriched with anecdotes and was not intended to be published. Having come to the realization that the manuscript might escape her, Teresa, not very sure of herself, submitted it to the Inquisitor, Francisco de Soto, "so that it be approved or burned." He approved it as a whole while suggesting some corrections and telling her to submit the text to St. John of Ávila, the apostle of Andalusia and the uncontested master in matters of mystical theology. "He has so much experience and authority that if he approves you will always be able to remain in peace."

After the corrections were made, Teresa entrusted the manuscript to Luisa de la Cerda, who, because she was about to go to Andalusia, was to personally hand it to the saint. But she kept it to read it, which irritated Teresa:

> I cannot understand why you have not yet sent *Maestro* Ávila what I entrusted to you! Do not delay any longer, for love of the Lord, but send it right away.... I would not want the holy man to die before reading it. While waiting, hide it. It is my very soul that I have placed in your hands.[2]

Like her advisers, Teresa feared the Inquisition's wrath, for women were cautioned against practicing mental prayer and especially against teaching it.

It was only in September 1568 that John of Ávila received the book and approved it without reservation, to Teresa's great relief: "Master Ávila wrote to me at length, and he is satisfied with everything." The saint passed away the following year. In the meantime, many copies of the manuscript had been circulated. The book was read and appreciated by various specialists who soon became Teresa's disciples.

It also reached María de Mendoza, the sister of Ávila's bishop, but, alas, her cousin, Duchess Ana de Mendoza, the princess of Éboli, had also seen it. Having quarreled with Teresa, she took revenge in 1575 by sending a copy to the Grand Inquisitor of Toledo, Gaspar de Quiroga. This stern theologian enjoyed the text. However, less indulgent than his colleague Soto, he confiscated the copies and the original. A very favorable report by Father Báñez ultimately saved the book. This Dominican confessor of Teresa suggested that it not be burned or published during Teresa's lifetime, something she had never even considered.

After her death in 1582, the manuscript was recovered thanks to Ana de Jesús, prioress of Granada, who had highly placed relations. It was published in 1588 in Salamanca by Fray Luis de León and then deposited in the Royal Library of the Escorial Palace, where it exists today.

In Chapters 1–9 of *The Life*, Teresa tells the story of her life and conversion. Chapters 10–22 are a veritable treatise on the degrees of prayer. Then the tone escalates and she relates the life of God in her and her ecstasies in Chapters 23–31. Chapters 32–36 recount the tumultuous foundation of St. Joseph in Ávila. Then Teresa returns to her ecstatic states.

The Life, which is the most famous of St. Teresa's writings, derives its originality from the freshness of its style, the deeply moving sincerity of Teresa's testimony, and the amazing account of the divine encounter.

The Way of Perfection
(Camino de perfección)

In 1559, the Grand Inquisitor Valdès had placed translations of the Bible and scriptural commentaries on the Index. This amounted to forbidding women—and notably nuns, who did not know either Greek or Latin—from having access to the Bible. In 1563, the Carmelites of St. Joseph, of whom Teresa was then the prioress "as wretched as I am...in the midst of angelic souls," asked her to remedy the situation by putting her teaching in writing.

After completing it, she submitted the text to her confessors. Father Báñez approved it, but Father García de Toledo expressed reservations, scandalized that this call to the prayer of quiet could be extended to anyone and everyone, especially women! In fact, *la Madre* was only "defending the right of every baptized person to mental prayer and contemplation, the complete development of baptismal grace."[3]

However, as a true precursor of feminism, Teresa had pushed her criticism a little too far:

> Nor did You, Lord, when You walked in the world, despise women; rather, You always, with great compassion, helped them. And You found as much love and more faith in them than You did in men.... Yes, indeed, the day will come, my King, when everyone will be known for what he is...these are times in which it would be wrong to undervalue virtuous and strong souls, even though they are women.[4]

Scandalized and especially terrified at the thought that these passages could fall into the hands of the Inquisition, Father García de Toledo returned her text to her after having crossed out one-third of it. Teresa took it up again and rewrote her copy. This is the second manuscript, known as Valladolid, for it was preserved in the Carmel of that city; it would be her only writing published during her lifetime. "The doctrine is substantially the same, but it has somewhat lost its edge."[5]

The primitive text, known as the Escorial Manuscript (deposited in the Royal Library of the palace), was barely saved at the last minute. Father García had crossed out sections in such a manner as to render illegible what he had deleted, and for centuries no one knew anything about it. Modern techniques of manuscript deciphering have remedied the situation. Actually, *La Madre's* ink, prepared by the Carmelites with their meager means, was better preserved than that of the learned censor!

In the *Way of Perfection*, Chapters 1–25 deal with the goals of the Reform and give advice on how to prepare for the prayer of recollection. Chapters 26–33 cover the different levels of the prayer of recollection or quiet, and Chapters 34–43 contain a commentary on the Our Father.

The text offers an education in the prayer of quiet, a synopsis of divine love. Teresa asserts that the Church of Christ will not resist against the forces of evil undermining the world if theologians are not supported by the humble prayer constantly rising up in cloisters from consecrated hearts enamored of perfection. This is a fundamental thought later taken up by Thérèse of Lisieux: "At the heart of the Church, my mother, I will be Love; thus will I be everything."

In this remarkable manual that teaches one how to live in God, Teresa insists also on the ascetic atmosphere needed for the life of prayer.

The Book of Her Foundations
(Fundaciones)

On February 9, 1570, in Malagon, Teresa heard Christ telling her to "write about the foundation of these houses."[6] In 1573, her Jesuit confessor in Salamanca, Father Ripalda, also exhorted her to undertake such a work; then her superior, Jerónimo Gracián, did so as well. She actually set about complying in 1574.

She would make this text, destined for her daughters, as lively as an adventure novel, a genuine epic! Completed at Alba de Tormes a few days before her death, the manuscript was deposited at St. Joseph in Ávila, obtained from there in 1586 by Ana de Jesús, and then entrusted to Father Luis de León for publication. In 1592, by order of Philip II, it was placed in the Royal Library of the Escorial, where it remains to this day.

St. Teresa's literary genius here is on full display, captured in the boldness of the book's intention, its realistic scenes, and the accuracy and humor of Teresa's gibes. A spiritual guide can also be found in Chapters 4-8, in which she discusses the necessity of discerning between real and false mystical graces.

The Interior Castle
(Las Moradas del Castillo Interior)

In 1577, fifteen years had passed since Teresa wrote *The Life*, whose manuscript and its copies, confiscated by the Inquisition, risked disappearance. *La Madre*, confined to Toledo, then received the order from her superior, Jerónimo Gracián, to write a great book of mystical theology. This work was to be a treatise on prayer that would be more complete than *The Way of Perfection* and divested of the personal considerations present in the three preceding works, which made them suspect for public reading. Teresa, who at that time was threatened with excommunication, caught in the turmoil that could destroy her foundations, refused: "Why do people always want me to write, I who am ignorant? Let them leave me be to spin wool and chant the Office with my sisters." Yet, further encouraged by her confessor in Toledo, Father Velásquez, she finally gave in and took up her pen on June 2.

This book, in which shines both Teresa's literary genius and her vocation as a Doctor of the Church, has a plan that seems to have been inspired by a vision. She began the manuscript in Toledo and finished it in Ávila. She wrote the entire book in ninety days, often at night and without any erasures, and she did not reread it. It has gained widespread acceptance in matters of spirituality. Comparing it to *The Life,* Teresa stated: "The gems are less apparent, but the quality of the gold is finer." Her personal experience is omnipresent in this work in which "she marks out the routes of the spiritual life."[7]

According to Teresa, the soul is a medieval castle made up of six dwellings surrounding the central keep or stronghold where the Lord resides. The spiritual itinerary consists of traveling to and fro in these dwellings before having access to the keep where, if God invites the soul to come in, union with Christ is consummated. In the first dwelling, a person learns how to relinquish one's own will to achieve God's welcome in him or herself. The second dwelling teaches perseverance; the third, humility. As early as the fourth dwelling, a person enters into the prayer of quiet. Love appears at last! God expands his ascendancy over the soul's faculties, but the person's mental powers are still active. In the fifth dwelling, a person is already experiencing the prayer of union and familiarizes him- or herself with Love. Thus fulfilled, the betrothal is celebrated in the sixth dwelling; and marriage, with its consummation in ecstasy and mystical union, in the seventh.

The soul is an unknown castle that the conscience discovers when, ceasing to externalize itself, it looks within, as it does in psychoanalysis. But while modern analysis is interested only in the self, the ego, the Teresian prayer of quiet postulates the presence of an Other at the heart of the spirit. It is a matter of discovering the Other. Teresa's originality lies here. In searching for God (a religious process), persons find themselves (a humanistic process), and vice versa. Having opened the door of the central dwelling place at the heart of the mystical experience, a person can be seized by God and then discover his or her own finiteness vis-à-vis divine perfection. This acquired humility promotes divine graces that are more and more lofty.

Such work is the step-by-step description of a spirit that is active and passive, loving and self-effacing, at the same time. It strives toward the God who calls to it in the very depths of its being. This teaching is not in the least dogmatic. It is first and foremost the testimony of a Christian life driven all the way to perfection, the account of an incomparable mystical experience. Teresa has a lived experience of Christ's humanity; she invites the reader to pray to him, that is, to love him by keeping him company, since Christ, who is first known through the Gospels, offers the surest access to God the Father. Teresa aspires to become a saint according to the Gospels by imitating Christ, who will, through grace, lift her up, when and how he wants, to the highest summits of mysticism.

Teresa's inspired work, which is kept in its original form at the Carmel of Seville, was to enjoy immense success worldwide. It remains the basic book of the Carmels and many other monasteries, as well as of lay people attracted by the interior journey.

Minor Works

Spiritual Testimonies
(*Cuentas y Mercedes*)

These short reports, some of which predate *The Life*, were written for Teresa's confessors to describe her states of conscience.

Apprehensive regarding her ecstasies, Teresa also submitted the texts to the Inquisitor, Francisco de Soto, who was passing through Ávila. Not only did he reassure her, seeing in them nothing diabolical, but he advised her to write the complete account of the divine favors she was experiencing. This would become the chronicle *The Life*, which we have already described.

The later *Relations (Cuentas)* and *Favors of God (Mercedes)* were written between 1569 and 1576 and are a complement to *The Life*.[8] They are short pieces in which Teresa practices writing down her thoughts with precision in view of her major writings.

Constitutions
(*Constituciones, 1563*)

Making use of the indult of 1562, by which Pius IV approved the first reformed foundation and gave authorization to draft the Constitutions, *la Madre* wrote them in 1563 at St. Joseph's in Ávila. They were approved by Msgr. de Mendoza, bishop of Ávila, who submitted them to the Holy See, which confirmed them in 1565. The General Chapter of the Discalced Carmelites at Alcalá adopted a variant drawn up by Father Gracián and put it into practice in 1581.

This text draws its inspiration from the primitive Rule of St. Albert and is enriched by the personal experience of the foundress. It addresses Offices, prayer, spiritual reading ("a nourishment as necessary to the soul as food is to the body"), income, alms, fasts, enclosure, the admittance of postulants, work, confession of sins, clothing, and relations among the sisters.

Soliloquies
(Exclamaciones, 1569)

After Communion one day, Teresa scribbled on bits of paper the love overflowing from her heart. These words are sometimes a cry of wounded love.

Meditations on the Song of Songs
(Conceptos del amor de Dios, 1572)

In 1572, Teresa, who was at that time the prioress of the Incarnation monastery in Ávila, heard these words of Christ: "Don't fail to write down the counsels I give you, so that you don't forget them. Since you want the counsels of men in writing, why do you think you're losing time by writing down those I give you? The time will come when you will need them all."9

Shortly afterward, Teresa was uplifted by a text from the Song of Songs. She immediately put pen to paper: "I will consider the time well spent that I occupy in writing and reflecting upon material so divine that I haven't deserved to hear it."10 She comments on the dialogue of love between the Sulamite and the king, a symbolic text that expresses the loving desire of the creature vis-à-vis God, then joy in the encounter, followed by suffering over the separation between the beloved and her Lover, who offers himself and then hides himself.

Frightened by Teresa's audacity and by the threat of the Inquisition, Father Diego de Yanguas, her confessor, to whom she had submitted her text, cried out: "Do not waste your time at this task. Indeed, it is not fitting for a woman to write on the *Song!* Burn it." She did so immediately. Fortunately, unknown to her, one of her daughters had made a copy!

In this song of love, Teresa represents the spouse of Christ. It is her freest and most feminine text. "She masters and teaches the mysterious art of the amorous exchange between God and the soul as spouse."11 Ecstasy is not reserved only to mystics. "It is at the heart of the eternal nostalgia of humanity."12

The copy of this manuscript is preserved in the Carmel of Alba de Tormes.

On Making the Visitation
(Modo visitar los conventos, 1580)

Written at the request of Father Jerónimo Gracián, this work deals with the canonical visits of superiors and the means of deriving spiritual benefit from them. The text is a complement to the Constitutions. An autographed manuscript is kept in the library of the Escorial.

Poems
(Poesias)

Teresa composed many poems to mark certain religious ceremonies: feast days, foundations, professions, burials. They are, for the most part, *coplas* (couplets) with short meters in the tradition of Spanish popular poetry. Prayer and poetry are mixed together in these hymns of jubilation where Franciscan joy is found. We can imagine *la Madre* in the midst of her daughters, accompanying on her tambourine the very pure chant of a novice declaiming her poems.

Others, composed under the immediate influence of a mystical grace such as an ecstasy, are as beautiful as those of John of the Cross—notably the famous "I die because I do not die." In this poem, Teresa sings of the despair of the night of the spirit, "the most terrible agony that I have ever seen." The text speaks of suffering having finally been accepted: "O! Cross, delicious repose of my life!" It affirms happiness in God, who "alone suffices." Translations, unfortunately, do not express all the fine details of these works.

No original manuscript of the poems has survived, only copies, and these are few in number—forty or so.

Sundry Writings

Thoughts and Maxims
Three thoughts, some prayers, and sixty-nine short maxims (or precepts).

Response to a Spiritual Challenge
Inspired by the Spanish custom, the Carmelites of Pastrana sent a friendly spiritual challenge to the Carmel of the Incarnation, where Teresa was prioress at the time. In this short text, the Pastrana Carmelites have chosen mortification as their theme. Teresa takes up the challenge. The combat, of course, is spiritual in nature.

A Satirical Critique
During a locution, Teresa heard the words, "Seek yourself in Me."

Sayings of Light and Love

Spiritual meditations.

Letters

It has been estimated that St. Teresa wrote between ten and fifteen thousand letters. Only about 460 have been preserved. Those addressed to St. John of the Cross are unfortunately not included in this number. He burned Teresa's letters to him to mortify himself or to avoid their being seized by the Inquisition.

Teresa wrote her letters mostly at night, stealing time from sleep. The muleteer waited in order to leave with them before dawn. At that time, the royal courier was used only in large cities; elsewhere, a private messenger had to be paid, which was very costly.

For the most part, the letters that have been preserved (1560-1582) were addressed to confessors (ninety-four were written to Father Jerónimo Gracián) or to prioresses (sixty-two were to María de San José). A few dozen were written to her family; others were to donors, superiors, prelates, lords, and three to the king.

In her letters to confessors, Teresa simultaneously utilized submission and firmness—even stubbornness. One is reminded of the correspondence between Father Charles de Foucauld and *Abbé* Huvelin. A reading of the *Letters* complements *The Life* and *The Foundations,* in which she reveals all the facets of her personality. According to Father Abiven, these letters are "a masterpiece of feminine sensibility as well as vivacity; we admire the fact that a heart which no longer beats but for God can love each one with such liberty and such appropriateness."[13]

3

Carmel after Teresa

Canonized

Teresa of Ávila was beatified in 1614 by Paul V and canonized in 1622 by Gregory XV. In 1626, she was proclaimed the patron of the kingdoms of Spain, but since the title was already held by St. James of Compostela, the decree of the Cortes was revoked.

Doctor of the Church

Her most prestigious title is the one bestowed upon her by Paul VI in 1970: Doctor of the Church, the first woman (with Catherine of Siena) to be so named. She is a Doctor "in the sense that she dispenses instruction on spiritual life with originality and depth, like a mother is the teacher of life with regard to her children."[1] Four centuries after her death, she remains "the mother of spiritual persons," the "seraphic virgin" of the Church, the most eminent figure of Carmel.

The Carmel after Teresa

Her work of renewal of Carmel would be lasting; her stamp persists even in our day. At her death in 1582, Teresa left behind seventeen convents of women and nine monasteries of men. Moreover, thanks to Prior General Rubeo de Ravenna, this spirit of Reform inspired by the Council of Trent, was also affecting the Calced Carmelites.

After Teresa, the Reform was led by Ana de Jesús and John of the Cross. The provincial prior, Jerónimo Gracián, gave up his post in 1585 to Nicolás

Doria de Jesús María, founding prior of the Carmel in Genoa. As a matter of fact, they tore each other apart; having won the election, Father Doria expelled Father Gracián from the Order in 1592. Rehabilitated by the pope, Father Gracián ended his days in 1614 at the monastery of the Calced Carmelites in Brussels. In 1999, the Order of the Discalced restored his good name.

Although of Italian origin and the founder of the Genoa monastery, Father Doria was opposed to foundations outside Spain and Mexico, claiming that he wanted to protect the purity of the Discalced's origins. This resulted in a certain amount of confusion among the reformed. For its part, the Cremona Chapter decided in 1593 upon the total separation between the Calced and the Discalced. Henceforth, the Discalced would not be considered a separate province, but an independent congregation with Teresa as its foundress.

In 1597, Pope Clement VIII authorized a foundation for men in Rome. To avoid a conflict with Father Doria, the pope then created two congregations of Discalced Carmelites: a Spanish one that respected the nationalist intentions of Father Doria and an Italian one that he authorized to found monasteries throughout the world. There was nothing now to limit the expansion of the Discalced Carmelites. This division was to last until the beginning of the nineteenth century.

Chronology

1492	Christopher Columbus, in the service of Queen Isabella of Castile, discovers America.
1494	Division of the world: Spain has the Americas with the exception of Brazil. Portugal has Asia except for the Philippines.
1515	*March 28*: Birth of Teresa in Ávila.
	April 4: She is baptized. On the same day, the Carmelite convent of the Incarnation is inaugurated.
	Spain annexes Navarre and the Basque country.
1516	Death of King Ferdinand. Charles is elected King of Spain.
1517	Luther, the German theologian, publishes his Theses against indulgences and rejects the Mass. He is condemned by the Church.
1519	Birth of Teresa's brother Lorenzo de Cepeda.
	Charles of Spain is elected German Emperor (Charles V).
1519–1521	Conquest of Mexico by the Spaniard Cortez.
1519–1522	Magellan, a Portuguese navigator in the service of Spain, circumnavigates the globe.
1520	Birth of Teresa's brother Antonio. The pope excommunicates Luther.
1521	Birth of Teresa's brother Pedro.
	Discovery of the Philippines by Magellan, colonized in 1525 by the Spaniards, who name it in honor of Philip, the *Infante*.
1521–1522	War of Francis I of France against Charles V.
1522	Teresa runs away from home with her brother Rodrigo.
	Birth of their brother Jerónimo.
	Luther translates the Bible into German. His reform spreads in Germany and France. The Catholic Counter-Reformation is organized.

313

1524	Massacre of the Incas of Peru by the Spaniard Pizarro.
1525	St. Ignatius writes his *Spiritual Exercises*. Francis I, king of France, is beaten at Pavia and taken prisoner by Charles V.
1527	Birth of Agostino, Teresa's brother.
1528	Birth of Teresa's sister Juana. Death of their mother, Beatriz.
1529	The Turkish Sultan Sulayman besieges Vienna and threatens the Christian West.
1530	Copernicus asserts that the earth turns around the sun, shattering the idea that man is at the center of the universe.
1531	Teresa is a boarder at the Augustinian convent of Ávila.
1531	King Henry VIII of England breaks with the Church of Rome.
1531–1541	Conquest of Peru and Chile by Pizarro and Almagro. Creation of the Spanish Empire, placed under the direction of a Royal Council of the West Indies and a Chamber of Commerce in Seville that receives gold from America. Genocide of the Indians and extension of the slavery of Black Africans despite edicts from the king and the Church.
1532	Teresa, who has fallen ill, returns to her father's house. Departure of her brother Hernando for Peru.
1533	Teresa visits her uncle at Hortigosa. First call of Christ. She announces her religious vocation. Her father's refusal of permission.
1534	Jacques Cartier lands in Canada. Ignatius of Loyola founds the Company of Jesus in Paris (which will be recognized in 1540).
1535	Rodrigo, Teresa's brother, leaves for Rio de la Plata. *November 2:* Teresa flees her home for the convent of the Incarnation, where she is received as a postulant.
1536	*November 2:* she takes the novice's habit. First conversion. The French theologian Calvin publishes his *Institutes of the Christian Religion* in which he preaches predestination. Rome condemns it.
1537	*November 3:* Teresa makes profession at the Incarnation.
1538	*January:* Teresa is authorized to leave the cloister due to illness. She discovers Osuna's *Third Spiritual Alphabet* at her uncle's house. First ecstasies. *April:* The pastor of Becedas attempts to seduce her. August: Return to her father's house; battle between life and death. *October:* She returns to the Incarnation.
1540	Departure for Peru of her brothers Lorenzo, Jerónimo, and Pedro.
1541	Philip II is invested with the government of Spain. Ignatius of Loyola is made superior general of the Jesuits.
1541–1554	Teresa falls into dissipation at the Incarnation.
1543	Copernicus's heliocentric theory of the universe is published.

December 26: Death of Alonso de Cepeda, Teresa's father.

A decisive encounter with the Dominican Barrón.

1545   First vision of Christ.

1545–1563   The Council of Trent renews the Catholic Church and puts an end to its decadence but is unable to stop the heresies.

1546   Teresa's brother Antonio is killed at the Battle of Iñaquito.

1552   Las Casas denounces the atrocities of colonization.

1554   The sight of the "much wounded Christ" causes Teresa to go from fear to love. The Jesuit Cetina, then the Franciscan St. Francis Borgia, put an end to her doubts.

            Philip II marries Marie Tudor. Abdication of Charles V.

1555   Teresa meets Doña Guiomar de Ulloa.

            First great ecstasy, first locution of Christ: "I don't want you to converse with men any longer."

1556   Philip II becomes king of Spain.

            Death of Ignatius of Loyola.

            April: Mystical betrothal; new locution of Christ: "Don't be afraid, I will not abandon you."

1557   Death of her brother Rodrigo in Chile.

            Spain goes to war against France.

1558   Cruelty of the Inquisition against the Protestants, the *Alumbrados*, the archbishop of Toledo, primate of Spain.

            Teresa is suspected of having diabolical illusions.

            Death of Charles V.

1559   The Inquisitor, Valdès, places religious books written in the venacular on the *Index of Forbidden Books*.

            June 29: Teresa receives an intellectual vision of Christ.

1560   *January 25*: Intellectual vision of the resurrected Christ.

            April: Transverberation. First levitation.

            August: First encounter with Peter of Alcántara.

            Philip II marries Elisabeth of France. Madrid becomes the capital of Spain.

            September: Teresa has a terrifying vision of hell.

            She makes a vow of perfection to save souls through prayer and penance.

            First plan of a reformed monastery. General opposition around her.

            October: First *Spiritual Testimony*.

1561   Clandestine preparation of the monastery of St. Joseph of Ávila.

            Summer: First miracle, healing a child.

            At the request of Father Ibáñez, she begins to write *The Book of Her Life in Ávila*. Then, after a vision of St. Clare (August 12), she drafts a first Rule.

August 15: Vision of the Virgin and St. Joseph, who comfort her in her mission to reform the Carmel.

1562   In Toledo, from January to June, Teresa resides in the home of Luisa de la Cerda, where she completes the first draft of *The Life.* Meets Father García de Toledo, who asks her to rewrite it. Encounters María de Yepes, who gives her the primitive Rule of the Carmel. Peter of Alcántara's approval.

February 6: Pius IV authorizes the foundation of St. Joseph at Ávila.

In France, start of the Wars of Religion.

August 24: **First foundation of St. Joseph at Ávila.** Violent opposition to it arises.

October 18: Death of Peter of Alcántara.

December: First draft of *The Way of Perfection.*

1563   New version of *The Life.*

John of the Cross takes the habit at Medina del Campo.

The Council of Trent comes to an end.

August 22: Teresa is authorized to leave the Incarnation for St. Joseph.

Philip II begins construction of the Royal Palace of Escorial.

1564   Rubeo de Ravenna becomes prior general of the Carmel.

1565   Hernando, Teresa's brother, dies in Columbia. She completes the last version of *The Life.*

1566   The missionary Maldonado upsets her vision of the world. Christ tells her: "You will see great things."

1567   *February:* Rubeo de Ravenna, the prior general, meets Teresa and asks her to found convents in Castile.

April: She writes the Constitutions.

August 15: **Second foundation at Medina del Campo.**

October: First encounter with John of the Cross.

Second writing of *The Way of Perfection.*

1568   **Third foundation at Malagon.**

August 15: Fourth foundation at Valladolid.

November 28: John of the Cross and Antonio de Heredia found the first monastery for men of Discalced Carmelites at Duruelo.

1569   **Fifth foundation at Toledo.**

Christ appears to her and promises a good death to all Reformed Carmelite women.

July 9: **Sixth foundation at Pastrana.**

July 13: Second foundation for men, also in Pastrana.

Teresa writes the *Soliloquies.*

1570   *November 1:* **Seventh foundation at Salamanca.**

Third foundation of men at Alcalá de Henares.

European war against the Turks.

1571   *January 25*: **Eighth foundation at Alba de Tormes** in the presence of John of the Cross.

April: Second transverberation. Vision of God the Father.

July: Teresa is imposed and then elected (on October 6) prioress of the Incarnation at Ávila.

The last Muslims of Spain are crushed.

The naval victory of Lepanto stops the Turkish expansion.

1572   *April*: Strange phenomenon of the host: "I want my blood to benefit you."

September 17: John of the Cross becomes chaplain at the Incarnation, under Teresa's priorate.

Meditations on the Song of Songs (Escorial manuscript).

November 18: Vision of Christ, spiritual marriage: "From this day forward, you will be my spouse."

Persecutions of the Protestants in France.

1573   She begins to write *The Foundations*—finished in 1582. Jerónimo Gracián makes profession at the Carmelite monastery at Pastrana. The princess of Éboli sows disorder among the Carmelites. Fourth and fifth foundations of men in Granada and La Peñuela.

1574   *March 19*: **Ninth foundation at Segovia.**

Second version of *Meditations on the Song of Songs* (Valladolid manuscript).

1575   *February 24*: **Tenth foundation at Beas.**

The Inquisition orders the seizure of *The Book of Her Life*.

April: Teresa meets Jerónimo Gracián for the first time.

Conflict erupts between the Discalced and the mitigated Carmelites.

General Chapter of the mitigated Carmelites in Piacenza.

May 29: **Eleventh foundation at Seville** (not authorized) provokes the General Chapter to order Teresa to stop her foundations and retire to a monastery of her choice.

Sixth foundation for men in Almodovar.

1576   *January 1*: **Twelfth foundation at Caravaca** by Ana de San Alberto.

June 4: Teresa leaves Seville and shuts herself away in the convent of Toledo while the persecutions against the Reform intensify ("the great storm").

Continuation of her *Foundations*.

She writes *On Making the Visitation*.

1577   Writes *The Interior Castle* from June 2 in Toledo to November 29 in Ávila.

June 17: Death of Nuncio Ormaneto, who had been rather favorable toward Teresa. He is succeeded by Nuncio Sega, who is openly hostile.

July: Return to St. Joseph at Ávila. Bishop Mendoza, who supported her, is transferred to Palencia.

October 7: Teresa is elected prioress of the Incarnation; the election is annulled.

December 4: Removal of John of the Cross, who is imprisoned at the monastery of the mitigated Carmelites in Toledo. Redoubling of persecutions.

December 24: Teresa breaks her arm in the St. Joseph Convent. Endures great suffering.

1578   *March:* Jerónimo Gracián hides away in Pastrana and lives as a hermit in a grotto there.

July: Sega, the nuncio, removes Gracián's powers and excommunicates him.

September 4: The death of the prior general, Rubeo, heightens the persecutions against the Discalced, whom Nuncio Sega makes subject to the mitigated Order.

October: The Chapter of the nine convents of Discalced friars sets itself up as an independent province. Sega opposes this and orders Gracián and other priors to be imprisoned.

December 24: The nuncio orders Teresa to place all her monasteries under the direction of the Calced Order and to retire to a mitigated convent. Trial of Gracián, who is interned with the Calced at Alcalá.

1579   *January:* María de San José, prioress of Seville, is removed from office by the nuncio.

April 1: Under pressure from the king, the nuncio reverses course; the persecutions come to an end.

June: Teresa leaves Ávila to visit her monasteries of Castile.

July: The nuncio asks the king to separate the two provinces. The king agrees. John of the Cross pleads in Rome to this effect.

1580   *February 21:* **Thirteenth foundation at Villanueva de la Jara.**

April–May: Teresa, seriously ill, is living in Toledo.

The Grand Inquisitor declares that he approves *The Life.*

June 26: Death, near Ávila, of Lorenzo, Teresa's favorite brother.

December 29: **Fourteenth foundation at Palencia.**

Gregory XIII approves the separate province for the men and women who are Discalced Carmelites (O.C.D.).

Philip II annexes Portugal and declares himself to be its king, but he will lose Holland.

1581   *March 3:* The General Chapter of Alcalá de Henares approves the new Constitutions established by Teresa. Jerónimo Gracián is elected provincial prior.

June 3: **Fifteenth foundation at Soria.**

August 16: Teresa is elected prioress against her will at St. Joseph in Ávila.

November 28: Last meeting of Teresa and John of the Cross (in Ávila).

1582   **Sixteenth foundation at Granada by Ana de Jesús.**

April 19: **Seventeenth foundation at Burgos.**

September 21: Arrival of Teresa at Alba de Tormes.

October 4: Teresa of Ávila dies in Alba (a reform of the calendar will place her feast day on October 15).

1602   Jean de Brétigny translates Teresa's writings into French. They had already been published in Castilian by Luis de León since 1588.

1604   *Madame* Acarie and *Abbé* de Bérulle found the first French Carmel.

1614   Teresa is beatified by Paul V.

1622   Teresa is canonized by Gregory XV.

1626   Teresa of Ávila becomes the second patron saint of Spain.

1925   Canonization of Thérèse Martin, spiritual daughter of Teresa of Ávila. (Thérèse was declared a Doctor of the Church in 1997.)

1926   Foundation in Rome of the *Teresianum*, an international college of theology and spirituality.

1970   Paul VI proclaims Teresa of Ávila a Doctor of the Church.

1982   Celebration of the four-hundredth anniversary of her death.

2004   Fourth centennial of the foundation of Teresian Carmels in France, which occurred after the first translations of her writings into French.

$\mathcal{N}$otes

Foreword

1. *Thérèse d'Ávila, qui es-tu?* *(Teresa of Ávila, Who Are You?)* (Carmel Editions, 1999), pp. 18–19.

2. All of the dialogues in this biography are based upon authentic documents (correspondence, testimonies, books) whose bibliographical reference is indicated.

PART ONE
Teresa's Life

Chapter 1

1. Ávila is located between Valladolid (to the north), capital of Old Castile, and Toledo (to the south), capital of New Castile. These two states merged in the fifteenth century, and the kings of Spain resided in one or the other before establishing themselves in Madrid.

2. See Index of Persons for references to him as well as the other principal persons referred to in the text.

Chapter 2

1. The Jewish roots of St. Teresa were revealed only in 1946, thanks to the research of the erudite Spaniard, Narciso Cortez, and in France by Marcelle Auclair in her *Vie de sainte Thérèse* (Editions du Seuil, 1950).

2. The present convent of Santa Teresa is built on the site of this residence with a museum preserving its vestiges.

3. See Index of Persons and the abbreviations for St. Teresa's works (Pt. 2, ch. 2).

4. *The Book of Her Life*, ch. 1.

Chapter 3

1. Marcelle, Auclair, *Saint Teresa of Ávila*, trans. Kathleen Pond (Petersham, MA: St. Bede's Publications, 1988), p. 15.

2. *The Book of Her Life*, ch. 2, as well as all the other quotations of Teresa in this section.

3. *The Book of Her Life*, ch. 37.

Chapter 4

1. *The Book of Her Life*, ch. 2. The rest of Teresa's quotations in this chapter are taken from *The Book of Her Life*, ch. 3, unless otherwise indicated.

2. Marthe Robin (†1981) often experienced this same phenomenon, as have numerous well-known saints.

3. *The Book of Her Life*, ch. 2.

4. *The Book of Her Life*, ch. 1.

5. D. Vasse, *L'Autre du désir et le Dieu de la foi* (Editions du Seuil, 1991), p. 108.

6. *The Book of Her Foundations*, ch. 31.

7. This is a reference to Matthew 10:37: "Whoever loves father or mother more than me is not worthy of me...."

8. *The Book of Her Life*, ch. 4.

9. A *fanega* is a Spanish measure of weight, the equivalent of almost 1.6 bushels. Twenty-five *fanegas* would amount to some 40 bushels per year.

10. By comparison, a worker or agricultural day laborer earned 50 ducats a year. Don Alonso's annual income must not have exceeded 2,000 ducats. The bishop of Ávila had 10,000 ducats at his disposal, and the great lords, between 50,000 and 100,000 ducats.

11. Minutes of the canonization trial, Burgos, 1610.

12. *The Book of Her Life*, ch. 4.

Chapter 5

1. It can still be seen today, a jewel of golden-toned stones with its square tower, its steeple, and its campanile amidst the foliage of the orchards and the gardens.

2. *The Book of Her Life*, ch. 9.

3. *The Book of Her Life*, ch. 4, as well as all of Teresa's quotations in this chapter.

4. Francisco de Ribera, *Vie de Thérèse de Jésus, 1590,* trans. by M. Bouix, (Lecoffe, 1887).

5. Pierre Lafue, *Thérèse d'Ávila et la vocation de l'Espagne* (Nouvelle France, 1946), p. 75.

Chapter 6

1. *The Book of Her Life*, ch. 4. Note the similarity between *Abecedario* and Becedas, the place of the treatment. Her problem lay there. This copy of the book, annotated in her handwriting, is kept at the monastery of St. Joseph of Ávila.

2. *The Book of Her Life*, ch. 4.

3. Christian Murciaux, *Thérèse de Jésus* (France-Empire, 1968), p. 31.

4. *The Book of Her Life*, ch. 4.

5. Emmanuel Renault, O.C.D., *Thérèse d'Ávila et l'expérience mystique* (Éditions du Seuil, 1970), p. 22.

6. *The Book of Her Life*, ch. 4.

7. Ibid.

8. *The Book of Her Life*, ch. 5, as well as the quotations which follow.

9. *The Book of Her Life*, ch. 6.

10. *The Book of Her Foundations*, ch. 27.

11. *The Book of Her Life*, ch. 6.

12. Cf. *The Book of Her Life*, ch. 6.

13. *The Book of Her Life*, ch. 6.

14. Elisabeth Reynaud, *Thérèse d'Ávila ou le divin plaisir,* (Fayard, 1997), p. 101.

Chapter 7

1. Murciaux, *op. cit.,* p. 35.

2. Marcelle Auclair, Editions du Seuil, p. 83.

3. Unless otherwise mentioned, all of Teresa's quotations in this chapter are taken from *The Book of Her Life*, ch. 7.

4. *Spiritual Testimonies*, 3.

5. Auclair, Editions du Seuil.

6. J. Abiven, O.C.D., *Thérèse d'Ávila, qui es-tu?* (Editions du Carmel, 1999), p. 53.

7. Auclair, Editions du Seuil, p. 83.

8. Anonymous Carmelite of Caen, *Histoire de la sainte Thérèse* (Lethielleux, 1882). I am granting myself permission to reveal the name of the author, while paying homage to her forgotten book: Marie Lecornu (Marie du Sacré-Coeur).

9. *The Book of Her Life*, ch. 8.

10. Ibid.

11. Denis Vasse, *op. cit.*, p. 75.

12. Ibid., p. 82.

13. Both quotes from *The Book of Her Life*, ch. 8.

14. Contrary to her hagiographer, the excellent anonymous Carmelite of Caen, who cleverly covered Teresa's idyll with Francisco by stating: "Her entrancing talent for conversation, which attracted so many visitors to her, was, in her innocent hands, but a net cast forth for the glory of the Lord."

15. *The Book of Her Life*, ch. 19.

16. The Spanish colonists, who could not manage without a workforce, had not only pillaged the Indian kingdoms of America, but also reduced the population to slavery. The pope and Spain's Catholic kings had tried in vain to curb their exactions. In 1532, the royal Spanish troops, led by Francisco Pizarro, the oldest brother of Gonzalo Pizarro, had occupied Peru and then Chile. Alerted by the protests of the Dominican Las Casas, Charles V had reminded his soldiers of their duties, always in vain. Francisco Pizarro having been assassinated, his brothers revolted against the Crown. Massacres among Spaniards resulted from this. Teresa's brothers were combating loyally for the emperor.

Chapter 8

1. D. Vasse, *op. cit.*, p. 154.

2. *The Book of Her Life*, ch. 8.

3. *The Book of Her Life*, ch. 9.

4. Ibid.

5. Ibid.

6. *The Book of Her Life*, ch. 10.

7. J. Abiven, *Prier quinze jours avec Thérèse d'Ávila* (Nouvelle Cité, 1993), p. 46.

8. *The Book of Her Life*, ch. 9.

9. A child's voice told him to open the Epistles of St. Paul at random, and he read (Romans 13:13): "Let us conduct ourselves properly as in the day, not in orgies and drunkenness, not in promiscuity and licentiousness, not in rivalry and jealousy. But put on the Lord Jesus Christ, and make no provision for the desires of the flesh."

10. *The Book of Her Life*, ch. 9.

11. *The Book of Her Life*, ch. 23.

12. J. Abiven, *Thérèse d'Ávila, qui es-tu?, op. cit.*, p. 146.

13. *The Book of Her Life*, ch. 37.

14. *The Book of Her Life*, ch. 8.

15. *The Interior Castle*, IV, ch. 1.

16. *The Interior Castle*, IV, ch. 1.

17. *The Book of Her Life*, ch. 9.

18. *The Book of Her Life*, ch. 8.

19. *The Way of Perfection*, ch. 5.

20. Ibid., ch. 13.

21. Ibid., ch. 9.

22. *The Book of Her Life*, ch. 12.

23. *The Book of Her Life*, ch. 16.

24. *The Book of Her Life*, ch. 23.

25. *The Way of Perfection* ch. 21.

26. *The Book of Her Life*, ch. 19.

27 *The Book of Her Life*, ch. 23.

28. Ibid.

29. Ibid. The dialogues that follow are inspired by this chapter.

30. *Letters*, Letter 24, par. 8.

31. *The Book of Her Life*, ch. 23.

32. Ibid.

33. *The Book of Her Life*, ch. 12.

34. Ibid.

35. Ibid.

36. *The Book of Her Life*, ch. 27.

37. *The Book of Her Life*, ch. 23.

38. Ibid.

39. Ibid.

40. *The Book of Her Life*, ch. 37.

41. J. Abiven, *Prier quinze jours avec Thérèse d'Ávila. op. cit.*, p. 45.

42. *The Book of Her Life*, ch. 22.

43. *The Book of Her Life*, ch. 24.

44. *The Book of Her Life*, ch. 11.

45. *The Book of Her Life*, ch. 22.

46. *The Book of Her Life*, ch. 27.

47. *The Book of Her Life*, ch. 24.

48. In 1671, Pope Clement X canonized Francisco Borgia, who had attended Joan the Mad and Charles V at their deaths, and had been elected, in 1565, the third general of the Society of Jesus.

Chapter 9

1. *The Book of Her Life*, ch. 14.

2. D. Vasse, *op. cit.*, p. 161.

3. This is what Pascal (1623–1662) would express a century later in his famous *wager* on faith in the existence of God: "If you win, you win everything; if you lose, you lose nothing. Bet therefore that he is, without hesitation" (*Thoughts: An Apology for Christianity.* 233).

4. *The Interior Castle*, II.

5. *The Book of Her Life*, ch. 24.

6. Ibid.

7. Ibid.

8. Ibid.

9. Ibid, ch. 7.

10. Ibid., ch. 20.

11. Ibid.

12. J. Abiven, O.C.D., *Thérèse d'Ávila, qui es-tu?, op. cit.*, p. 60. Unless otherwise indicated, all the quotations of this great specialist of St. Teresa are taken from this book.

13. *The Book of Her Life*, ch. 20.

14. *The Book of Her Life*, ch. 31.

15. This quotation and the previous quotation are from *The Book of Her Life*, ch. 25.

16. *Spiritual Testimonies*, ch. 1.

17. *The Book of Her Life*, ch. 18.

18. *The Book of Her Life*, ch. 16.

19. *The Book of Her Life*, ch. 20.

20. *The Book of Her Life*, ch. 13, ch. 40.

21. *The Book of Her Life*, ch. 30.

22. *The Book of Her Life*, ch. 21.

23. J. Abiven, *Thérèse d'Ávila, qui es-tu?*, op. cit., p. 57.

24. Auclair, Editions du Seuil, p. 105.

25. *The Book of Her Life*, ch. 26.

26. Unless otherwise indicated, Teresa's quotations in this chapter are taken from *The Book of Her Life*, chapters 25 and 26.

27. *The Book of Her Life*, ch. 14.

28. *The Book of Her Life*, ch. 13.

29. *The Book of Her Life*, ch. 30.

30. Ibid.

31. Ibid., ch. 26.

Chapter 10

1. If one makes an exception of the mystical phenomenon of 1554 that has been described previously: "With great severity, Christ appeared before me, making me understand what He regretted about the friendship. I saw Him with the eyes of my soul more clearly than I could have with the eyes of my body," (*The Book of Her Life*, ch. 7).

2. *The Book of Her Life*, ch. 27.

3. She would be more specific in the Sixth Dwelling of *The Interior Castle*. "Without seeing anything with the eyes of the body, one *knows* in an admirable way."

4. This dialogue recounts practically word for word the written confession that Teresa made in 1562 to Fr. García de Toledo. *The Book of Her Life*, ch. 27.

5. Teresa does not recount this second dialogue in *The Book of Her Life*. It is found in the *Relation* of Isabel de Jesus, 1690, quoted by Fr. Pierre Lauzeral in *Thérèse d'Ávila, une femme qui sut aimer* (Téqui, 1987), p. 77.

6. *The Book of Her Life*, ch. 26.

7. H. Bergson.

8. Jean Guitton and J.-J. Antier, *Les Pouvoirs mystérieux de la foi* (Perrin, 1993), p. 330.

9. I prefer this term to the one ordinarily used: *imaginary vision*, which can suggest that the vision could be the result of our imagination. All of the quotations from Teresa which follow in this chapter are taken from *The The Book of Her Life*, ch. 28.

10. J. Abiven. *Thérèse d'Ávila, qui es-tu?*, op. cit., p. 54.

11. Ibid., p. 112.

12. *Je veux voir Dieu* (Ed. du Carmel, 1949), II, p. 232.

13. J. Abiven, *Thérèse d'Ávila, qui es-tu?*, op.cit., p. 61.

14. *The Interior Castle*, VI, ch. 5.

15. *The Interior Castle*, VI, ch. 9.

16. Ch. 17.

17. *The Interior Castle*, IV, ch. 2.

18. *The Book of Her Life*, ch. 28.

19. Spiritual Testimonies, ch. 1.

20. P. Lauzeral, *op. cit.*, p. 68.

21. *The Book of Her Life*, ch. 28.

22. *The Book of Her Life*, ch. 28.

23. Ibid.

24. Ibid.

Chapter 11

1. Quotations from Teresa's writings in this chapter are, unless otherwise mentioned, taken from *The Book of Her Life*, ch. 29. The dialogues also refer to them as faithfully as possible.

2. Testimony of Isabel de Santo Domingo at the inquiry for beatification, Ávila, August 26, 1610. Published by the Carmel of Burgos.

3. *The Book of Her Life*, ch. 9.

4. Ibid

5. Ibid.

6. E. Reynaud, *op. cit.* p. 194.

7. Ps 42:1.

8. Still today, the heart of St. Teresa can be seen in the reliquary of the Carmelite monastery of Alba de Tormes; between the ventricle and the auricle is the scar of the wound that should have killed her. This is an exceptional figure of an internal stigma. Closer to us, Sister Marie de Jésus Crucifié of the Carmel at Pau in France would undergo, at age twenty, in 1868, the transverberation (meaning to strike through), a wound of the heart that is not pathological, but certified through autopsy. Seeing St. Teresa in a vision, the young Carmelite cried out: "Mother Teresa! Jesus has pierced my heart!"

9. *The Book of Her Life*. ch. 29.

10. Ibid.

11. To be compared with Marie de Jésus Crucifié: "O Jesus! All the water in the world would not be sufficient to refresh my heart! I can stand it no longer! Love is burning me, consuming me, I am being grilled! O Love! I cannot live without you!" (From the Minutes of the Beatification Proceedings, 1983).

12. J.-N. Vuarnet, *Extases féminines*, ch. 4 (Artaud, 1980).

13. Ibid.

14. *Soliloquies*, 17.

15. *Letters*.

Chapter 12

1. Quotations from Teresa in this section are from ch. 20 of *The Book of Her Life* unless otherwise noted.

2. H. Thurston, *Les Phénomènes physiques du mysticisme* (Gallimard, 1961; Rocher, 1990).

3. See J. Guitton and J.-J. Antier, *Les Pouvoirs mystérieux de la foi* (Perrin, 1993).

4. F. de Ribera, *op. cit.*

5. Canonized in 1669, Peter of Alcantara remains one of the three great Spanish mystics, along with Teresa of Ávila and John of the Cross. In 1558, he obtained permission to create a separate Franciscan province of strict observance with the support of St. Francis Borgia.

6. *The Book of Her Life*, ch. 30.

7. *Op. cit.*, pt. II, p. 244.

8. The preceding dialogue is faithfully reconstituted from *The Book of Her Life* (ch. 30), *Spiritual Testimonies I*, and texts published by Fr. Silverio in his critical edition of *The Book of Her Life*.

9. Auclair, Editions du Seuil, p. 121.

10. This dialogue refers to the first of the *Spiritual Testimonies*, the work which preceded *The Book of Her Life*, written in 1562.

11. C. Murciaux, *op. cit.*, p. 51.

Chapter 13

1. J. Abiven. *Thérèse d'Ávila, qui es-tu?*, *op. cit.*, p. 69.

2. *Ibid.*, p. 70.

3. *The Dark Night*, ch. 5.

4. "That the intellect reach union with the divine light and become divine in the state of perfection, this dark contemplation must first purge and annihilate it of its natural light and bring it actually into obscurity." *The Dark Night*, bk. 2, ch. 9.

5. *Ibid.*, ch. 5.

6. *Spiritual Testimonies*, ch. 3.

7. *The Book of Her Life*, ch. 20.

8. *Ibid.*

9. *The Book of Her Life*, ch. 32, and F. de Ribera, *op. cit.*

Chapter 14

1. All of the quotations that follow are taken from *The Book of Her Life*, ch. 32.

2. *The Book of Her Life*, ch. 7.

3. *The Book of Her Life*, ch. 33.

4. "Efficacy of Patience," from *The Collected Works of Teresa of Ávila*, Vol. 3, p. 386.

5. She says so herself : "He who was confessing me had a superior, and members of the Society [of Jesus] have this virtue to the extreme that they will not stir unless what they do is in conformity with their superior's will" (*The Book of Her Life*, ch. 33. The quotations that follow are also taken from this chapter).

6. E. Reynaud, *op. cit.*

7. See "Efficacy of Patience."

8. *Letters*, Letter 2, paras. 1–3.

9. Auclair, Editions du Seuil, Part 2, ch. 2, p. 137.

10. F. de Ribera and Msgr. de Yepes (Bollandists, *op.cit.*, p. 310).

11. *Ibid.* Teresa's hagiographers consider this healing as her first public miracle. Actually, people began to regard her as a saint.

12. Silverio, *Vida de santa Teresa* (Burgos, 1950).

13. Not to be confused with Gaspar de Salazar, rector of the Jesuit college of Ávila.

Chapter 15

1. *The Book of Her Life*, ch. 34.

2. *The Book of Her Life.* This and the following quotations are taken from ch. 34.

3. *Spiritual Testimonies*, ch. 2.

4. F. de Ribera, *op. cit.*

5. Father Silverio, *op. cit.*, and Teresa of Ávila, *The Book of Her Life*, ch. 35, as well as the quotations that follow.

6. Direct quotation from *The Book of Her Life*, ch. 35.

7. Diego de Yepes, *History of the Carmelites*; correspondence of St. Peter of Alcantara, April 14, 1562.

8. The Carmelite Constitutions require an election every three years. The outgoing prior or prioress is eligible for re-election once, but can be a candidate again after three years have passed.

Chapter 16

1. *The Book of Her Life*, ch. 36, as well as the quotations that follow.

2. Auclair, St. Bede's Publications, p. 137.

3. *The Book of Her Life*, ch. 25.

4. Auclair, Editions du Seuil, p. 156.

5. Silverio, *op. cit.*; F. de Ribera, *op. cit.*; Juan de Ávila, *General History of the Carmelites* and *The Book of Her Life*, ch. 36.

6. *The Book of Her Life*, ch. 36.

7. *Vida de santa Teresa*.

8. Account by Julian de Ávila, *op. cit.*

9. Bollandists, *op. cit.*, p. 277.

10. Juan de Ávila, *op. cit.*, II, p. 12.

11. Bollandists, *op. cit.*, p. 279.

12. *The Book of Her Life*, ch. 27.

13. For his part, the general of the Order had authorized the *Beata* Maria de Yepes to found a monastery in Alcala. Teresa rejoiced at the news.

14. Juan de Ávila, *op. cit.*, ch. 15.

Chapter 17

1. The three quotations above are taken from *Spiritual Testimonies*, ch. 3.

2. *The Book of Her Life*, ch. 36.

3. *The Way of Perfection*, ch. 18.

4. Auclair, Editions du Seuil, p. 170.

5. P. Lafue, *op. cit.*, p. 205.

6. *Spiritual Testimonies*, 3.

7. *The Way of Perfection*, ch. 2.

8. *The Book of Her Foundations*, ch. 1.

9. *The Book of Her Foundations*, ch. 5.

10. *Letters*.

11. *The Collected Works of Teresa of Ávila*, vol. 3, poem 3.

12. *The Book of Her Foundations*, ch. 1.

13. *The Way of Perfection*, ch. 10.

14. Ibid.

15. *Spiritual Testimonies*, 3.

16. *The Book of Her Life*, ch. 20.

17. *Letters*, Letter 177, par. 3.

18. *The Way of Perfection*, ch. 18.

19. Ibid.

20. *The Book of Her Foundations*, chs. 1–6.

21. E. Reynaud, *op. cit.*, p. 270.

22. F. de Ribera, *op. cit.*

23. *The Way of Perfection*, ch. 2.

24. *Poetry*, 31. trans., A. J. Cooney, O.C.D., in Kieran Kavanaugh, vol. 3 of *Collected Works of St. Teresa of Ávila*.

25. *The Way of Perfection*, ch. 2.

26. See pt. II, ch. 2.

27. This story is taken from *The Book of Her Foundations*, ch. 1.

28. P. Lafue, *op. cit.*, p. 146.

29. *The Way of Perfection*, ch. 4.

30. *The Book of Her Foundations*, ch. 15.

31. This and the following quotations are from the Constitutions.

Chapter 18

1. *The Book of Her Foundations*, ch. 2, as well as the other non-referenced quotations of Teresa's writings.

2. *The Book of Her Foundations*, trans. Marcelle Auclair. Father Gregory of St. Joseph translates it as "for lack of religious instruction." The latest translation, by Kieran Kavanaugh, O.C.D., reads "for want of Christian instruction."

3. *Op. cit.*, p. 185.

4. She may have broached the subject in her *Letters*, of which only 450 have been preserved when she must have written between twelve and fifteen thousand.

5. *The Book of Her Foundations*, ch. 1.

6. Ibid.

7. Silverio, *op. cit.*

8. *The Book of Her Foundations*, ch. 3, as well as the quotations that follow.

9. *The Way of Perfection*, ch. 21.

Chapter 19

1. *The Book of Her Foundations*, ch. 3.

2. E. Reynaud, *op. cit.*, p. 304.

3. Preceding dialogue constructed from *The Book of Her Foundations*, ch. 3, and Fr. Silverio, *op. cit.*

4. *Letters*, Letter 13, par. 2.

5. *General History of the Carmelites*.

6. "The absence of revenues was quite appropriate in principle; just as having them was, in the end," wrote, not without humor, F. de Ribera, Teresa's contemporary and her biographer. A few years later, the community would move outside the town to a more silent area offered by the marshal's wife, near her castle.

7. *The Book of Her Foundations*, ch. 13.

8. *The Book of Her Foundations*, ch. 14.

9. Ibid., ch. 13.

10. Ibid.

11. *The Book of Her Foundations*, ch. 14.

12. *Ibid*, as are the following uncited quotations.

13. *Letters*, Letter 13, par. 2.

14. *The Life of St. John of the Cross* by an anonymous Carmelite, quoted in *Histoire de Sainte Thérèse*, *op. cit.*, p. 398.

15. Ibid.

Chapter 20

1. *Spiritual Testimonies*, 32, 1572.

2. *The Book of Her Foundations*, ch. 18.

3. Murciaux, *op. cit.*, p. 94.

4. *The Book of Her Foundations*, ch. 2.

5. P. Lauzeral, *op. cit.*, p. 170.

6. *The Book of Her Foundations*, ch. 15.

7. Ibid.

8. *The Book of Her Foundations*, ch. 16.

9. *The Book of Her Foundations*, ch. 18.

10. The above quotations and dialogue are from *The Book of Her Foundations*, ch. 19.

11. Ibid.

12. "Aspirations Toward Eternal," *The Book of Her Life*, *The Collected Works of St. Teresa of Ávila*, Vol. 3, Poem 1.

13. *Meditations on the Song of Songs*, ch. 7.

14. *The Interior Castle*, VI, ch. 11.

15. Regarding the conflicts between the flesh and the spirit, see chs. 9 and 11 of this book.

16. *Spiritual Testimonies*, 12.

17. Ibid.

18. Ibid., as are the following uncited quotations.

19. In January 1571, Teresa, helped by her sister Juana and her husband Juan de Ovalle, had founded a monastery at Alba de Tormes where the couple resided, twelve miles from Salamanca. John of the Cross was to be its chaplain. The founders were Francisco Velásquez, chief steward of the Duke of Alba, and his wife, Teresa de Layz. It is there that Teresa passed away and where her stigmatized heart can be seen.

Chapter 21

1. *Letters*, Letter 38, par. 4.

2. P. Lauzeral, *op. cit.*, p. 210.

3. Agostino, a conquistador in Chile and among the most violent.

4. *Spiritual Testimonies*, 16.

5. *Letters*, Letter 24, pars. 11–12.

6. According to F. de Ribera, *op. cit.*, the rest of the account is also based upon the testimony he heard from Teresa herself.

7. *The Book of Her Foundations*, ch. 18. The following dialogue is also derived from this chapter.

8. *Letters*, Letter 47, par. 2.

9. *Letters*, Letter 38, par. 4.

10. F. de Ribera, *op. cit.*

11. *Letters*, Letter 41, par. 3.

12. *Spiritual Testimonies*, 22.

13. Auclair, Editions du Seuil, p. 253.

14. *The Book of Her Life*, ch. 22; loose translation from original Antier manuscript, as these letters are not yet published in English. (Letter 351 in the critical Spanish edition of Teresa's complete works.)

15. Ch. 38.

16. *Canticle*, ch. 40.

17. *Spiritual Testimonies*, 32.

18. Kieran Kavanaugh, O.C.D., notes to the *Spiritual Testimonies*, 28, 1572.

19. *Spiritual Testimonies*, 31, 1572.

20. *Meditations on the Song of Songs*, ch. 4.

21. See Jean-Jacques Antier, *Le mysticisme féminin, les épouses du Christ* (Perrin, 2001).

22. "Stanzas of the Soul," stanza 5, *The Collected Works of St. John of the Cross*, trans. Kieran Kavanaugh. O.C.D., and Otilio Rodiguez, O.C.D. (Washington, DC: ICS Publications, 1991).

23. Jean-Pierre Jossua, *L'Aventure mystique* (Découvertes-Gallimard, 1996), p. 87.

24. Ibid., p. 84.

25. Bernard Sesé, *Petite Vie de Thérèse d'Ávila* (DDB, 1991), p. 90.

26. "The Living Flame of Love," *op. cit.*

27. *Letters,* Letter 48, par. 2.

28. *Letters,* Letter 102, par. 8.

29. *Letters,* Letter 61, pars. 2–3.

30. *Letters,* Letter 41, par. 5.

Chapter 22

1. *The Book of Her Foundations,* ch. 21.

2. As an example of the reversal of history and mentalities, it would be Luis de León (at the request of King Philip II) who directed the publication of the works of Teresa of Ávila starting in 1588.

3. *The Book of Her Foundations,* ch. 24.

4. *The Book of Her Foundations,* ch. 22.

5. *Letters,* Letter 162, par. 11.

6. From Letter 351 in the critical Spanish edition of Teresa's complete works. Translated in Kathleen Pond's English translation of M. Auclair's *Saint Teresa of Ávila.*

7. *Letters,* Letter 83, par. 2.

8. *Letters,* Letter 81, par. 2.

9. Auclair, Editions du Seuil, p. 282.

10. *Letters,* Letter 81, pars. 2–3.

11. Loose translation from original Antier manuscript, as these letters are not yet published in English. (Letter 228 in the Critical Spanish edition of Teresa's complete works.)

12. *The Book of Her Life.* ch. 37.

13. Ibid.

14. *Letters,* Letter 88, par. 9.

15. Ibid, par. 10.

16. *Letters,* Letter 98, par. 2.

17. *Letters,* Letter 141, par. 1–2.

18. *Letters,* Letter 86, par. 3, par. 1.

19. With the exception of Caravaca by Ana de San Alberto, on January 1, 1576, a monastery that was placed under the personal protection of the king.

20. He brought her gold and jam. In exchange, she gave him...a hair shirt with instructions on how to use it. As she had already done for their father, she converted him to mental prayer in an astonishing manner, proof of her charismatic genius.

21. *The Book of Her Foundations,* ch. 25.

22. *The Book of Her Foundations,* ch. 28.

23. *Letters,* Letter 92, par. 6.

24. Ibid., ch. 23.

Chapter 23

1. *Letters,* Letter 128, par. 3.

2. *Letters,* Letter 175, par. 5.

3. *Letters,* Letter 148, par. 11.

4. P. Lauzeral, *op. cit.,* p. 284.

5. *Letters,* Letter 152, par. 2.

6. *Letters,* Letter 151, par. 9.

7. Ibid., par. 4.

8. *Letters*, Letter 182, par. 1.

9. See pt. II, ch. 2.

10. *Letters*, Letter 177, pars. 3-4.

11. *Letters*, Letter 189, par. 3.

12. *Letters*, Letter 141, par. 1.

13. *Letters*, Letter 162, par. 4.

14. *Letters*, Letter 152, par. 2.

15. *Letters*, Letter 162, par. 8.

16. *Letters*, Letter 138, par. 5.

17. *Letters*, Letter 154, par. 3.

18. *Letters*, Letter 154, par. 4.

19. *Letters*, Letter 162, par. 5.

20. Auclair, St. Bede's Publications, p. 314.

21. *Letters*, Letter 204, pars. 1-2.

22. From Letter 382 in the critical Spanish edition of Teresa's complete works. Translated in Kathleen Pond's English translation of M. Auclair's *Saint Teresa of Ávila*.

23. *Letters*, Letter 108, par. 11.

24. *Letters*, Letter 151, par. 5.

25. The French author writes "raw eggs." Kieran Kavanaugh, in a note to Letter 151, writes "boiled eggs served in their shells lest he be poisoned."

26. *Letters*, Letter 208, pars. 2, 4-5.

27. *Letters*, Letter 70, par. 3.

28. *Letters*, Letter 211, par. 3.

29. *Letters*, Letter 211, par. 3.

30. Ibid, par. 5.

31. *Letters*, Letter 218, pars. 5-7.

32. *Letters*, Letter 219, par. 1.

33. Teresa had found Ana de San Bartolomé (Ana García) at St. Joseph of Ávila in 1572. This young, illiterate peasant had just entered there, one of the first lay sisters of the Reformed Carmel. Insightful, intelligent, gentle, and sensitive, she would become the faithful assistant of *la Madre* until her death.

34. Loose translation from original Antier manuscript, as these letters are not yet published in English. (Letter 216 in the critical Spanish edition of Teresa's complete works.)

35. Loose translation from original Antier manuscript, as these letters are not yet published in English. (Letter 257 in the critical Spanish edition of Teresa's complete works.)

36. *Letters*.

37. *The Interior Castle*, ch. 3.

38. Loose translation from original Antier manuscript, as these letters are not yet published in English. (Letter 255 in the critical Spanish edition of Teresa's complete works.)

Chapter 24

1. "Happy the Enamored Heart," *Poetry*, 5, trans. A. J. Cooney, O.C.D.

2. Silverio, *op. cit.*

3. Loose translation from original Antier manuscript, as these letters are not yet published in English. (Letter 278 in the critical Spanish edition of Teresa's complete works.)

4. P. Lauzeral, *op. cit.*, p. 333.

5. Cf. Jeronimo Gracián, *Obras Completas*.

6. *Letters*, vol. 2, as yet unpublished. Translation by Kieran Kavanaugh. Used with permission.

7. Ibid.

8. Loose translation from original Antier manuscript, as these letters are not yet published in English. (Letter 326 in the critical Spanish edition of Teresa's complete works.)

9. Ibid.

10. *The Book of Her Foundations*, ch. 31.

11. Having recognized the child Jesus, he said: "Now, Master, you may let your servant go in peace, according to your word.... (Lk 2:29).

12. Auclair, Editions du Seuil.

13. Ibid.

14. Loose translation from original Antier manuscript, as these letters are not yet published in English. (Letter 290 in the critical Spanish edition of Teresa's complete works.)

15. Loose translation from original Antier manuscript, as these letters are not yet published in English. (Letter 410 in the critical Spanish edition of Teresa's complete works.)

16. *The Book of Her Foundations*, ch. 30.

17. Ibid.

18. *The Book of Her Foundations*, ch. 29.

19. "The Dark Night," stanza 5, *The Collected Works of St. John of the Cross*, trans. Kieran Kavanaugh, O.C.D, and Otilio Rodiguez, O.C.D.

20. Quoted by Fr. Leon Van Hove, *La Joie chez sainte Thérèse*.

21. Loose translation from original Antier manuscript, as these letters are not yet published in English. (Letter 420 in the critical Spanish edition of Teresa's complete works.)

22. Silverio, *op. cit.*, vol. II, p. 236.

23. Auclair, Editions du Seuil, p. 400.

24. Ibid.

25. *The Book of Her Foundations*.

26. From *Vie de la vénérable Mère Anne de Saint-Barthélémy*.

27. From Letter 380 in the critical Spanish edition of Teresa's complete works. Translated in Kathleen Pond's English translation of M. Auclair's *Saint Teresa of Ávila*.

28. Auclair, Editions du Seuil.

29. From Letter 429 in the critical Spanish edition of Teresa's complete works. Translated in Kathleen Pond's English translation of M. Auclair's *Saint Teresa of Ávila*.

30. Auclair, St. Bede's Publications, p. 427.

31. Testimony of Maria de San Francisco. The other quotations and dialogues were taken from the autobiographies of Ana de San Bartolomé and Father Gracián.

32. *The Interior Castle*, Seventh Dwelling, 2.

33. Ch. 21.

Part Two
Teresa's Achievements

Portrait of Teresa of Ávila

1. Quotations from bishops are taken from the preface to the *Histoire de sainte Thérèse* by an anonymous Carmelite nun of Caen in France.

2. J. Abiven, *Thérèse d'Ávila, qui es-tu?*, op. cit., p. 180.

3. *The Way of Perfection*, ch. 1.

4. *The Book of Her Life*, ch. 37.

5. *The Interior Castle*, ch. 7.

6. E. Reynaud, *op. cit.*

7. *Letters*, Letter 185, par. 6.

8. *A Satirical Critique*, 7.

9. J. Abiven, O.C.D., in *Médecine de l'homme*, no. 229.

10. Sixth Notebook, 1942.

11. D. Vasse, *op. cit.*, p. 23.

12. J. Abiven. *Thérèse d'Ávila qui es-tu?*, op. cit., pp. 18–19.

The Written Works

1. The dates given here do not always correspond exactly with those given by Kieran Kavanaugh, O.C.D., in the latest edition of Teresa of Ávila's works in English.

2. *Letters*, Letter 7, par. 3.

3. J. Abiven. *Thérèse de Jésus, qui es-tu? op. cit.*, p. 84.

4. *Way of Perfection*, ch. 3.

5. Ibid., p. 85.

6. *Spiritual Testimonies*, 6.

7. J. Abiven, *Thérèse d'Ávila, qui es-tu? op cit.*, p. 88.

8. In his Introduction to *Spiritual Testimonies*, Kieran Kavanaugh, O.C.D., explains that "in this new translation we have opted for keeping these writings [*Relations* and *Favors of God*] together under the general title of *Spiritual Testimonies*."

9. *Spiritual Testimonies*, 24.

10. *Meditations on the Song of Songs*, ch. 1.

11. E. Reynaud, *op. cit.*, p. 345.

12. Ibid.

13. J. Abiven, *op. cit.*, p. 91.

The Carmel after Teresa

1. J. Abiven. *Thérèse d'Ávila, qui es-tu?*, op. cit., p. 98.

Index of Persons